DIRK BRAECKMAN

DIRK BRAECKMAN

ECHTZEIT

HOPPER
&FUCHS

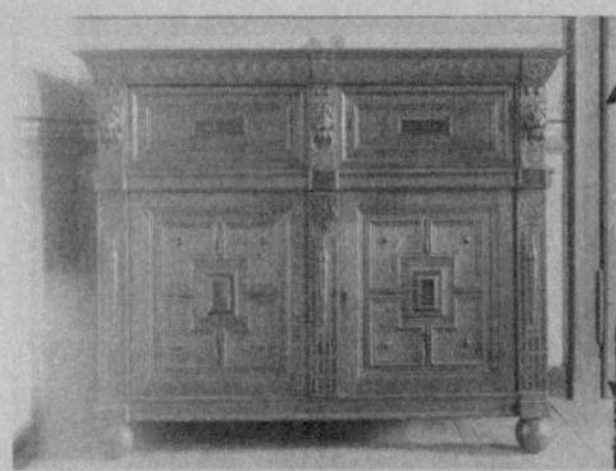

Fritz Wentzel (DE, 1877-1962), Cabinet, 1916-18, glass plate negative, 10 x 15 cm, Collection FOMU 2022/6/6/34

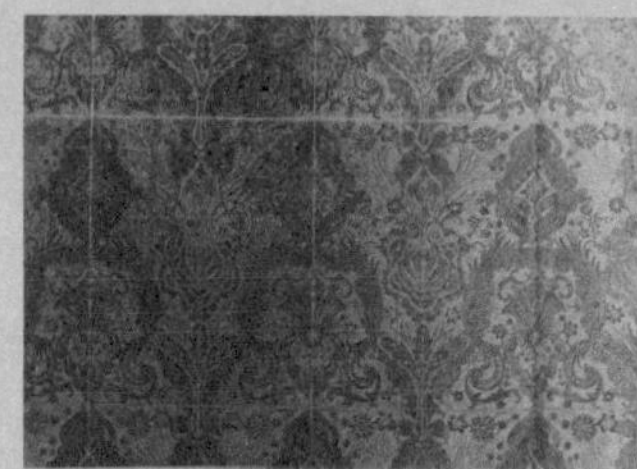

Fritz Wentzel (DE, 1877-1962), Leather wallpaper, 1916-18, glass plate negative, 10 x 15 cm, Collection FOMU 2022/6/7/7

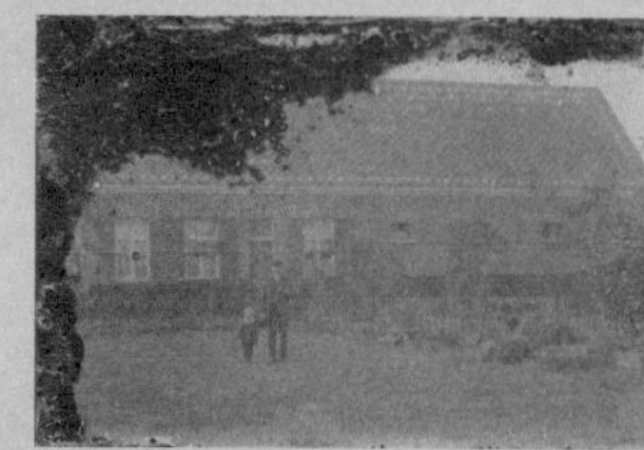

Anonymous, Man and child in front of a house, n.d., glass plate negative, 10 x 15 cm, Collection FOMU 2022/15/1/10

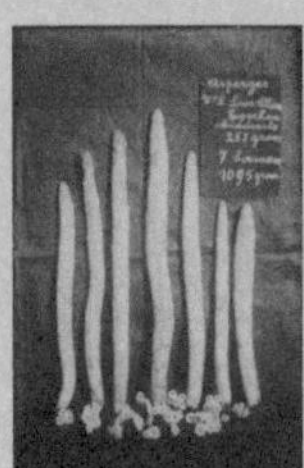

Anonymous, Asparagus, n.d., glass plate negative, 15 x 10 cm, Collection FOMU 2022/15/11/46

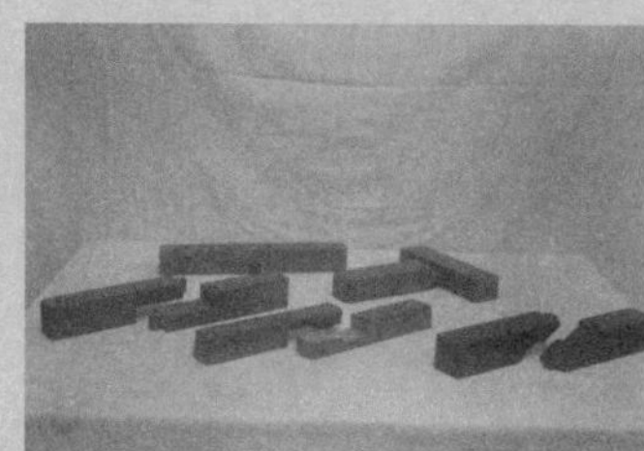

Anonymous, Wooden beams, n.d., glass plate negative, 10 x 15 cm, Collection FOMU 2022/15/17/19

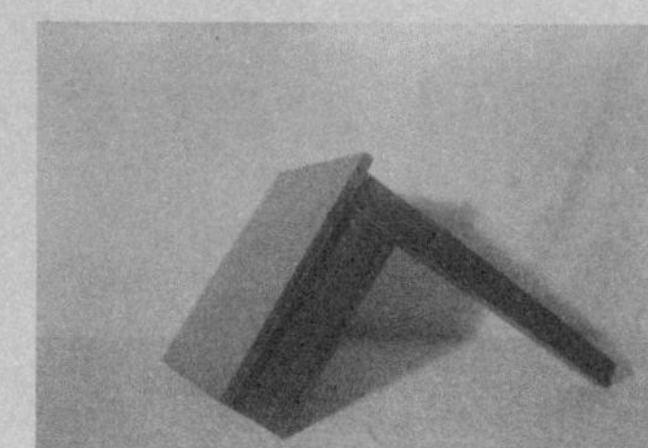

Anonymous, Fragment of a table, n.d., glass plate negative, 10 x 15 cm, Collection FOMU 2022/15/17/22

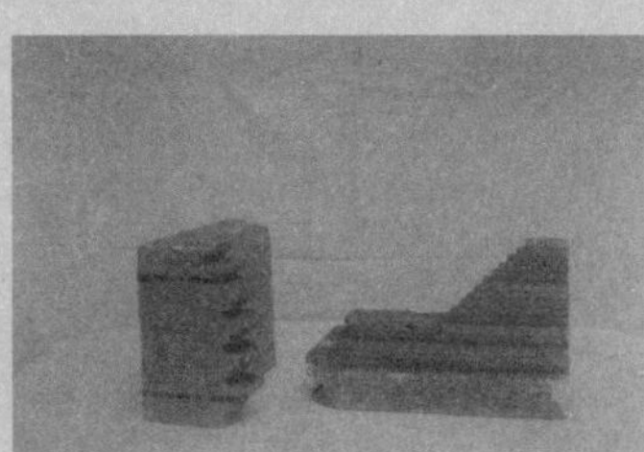

Anonymous, Fragment of a facade, n.d., glass plate negative, 10 x 15 cm, Collection FOMU 2022/15/17/26

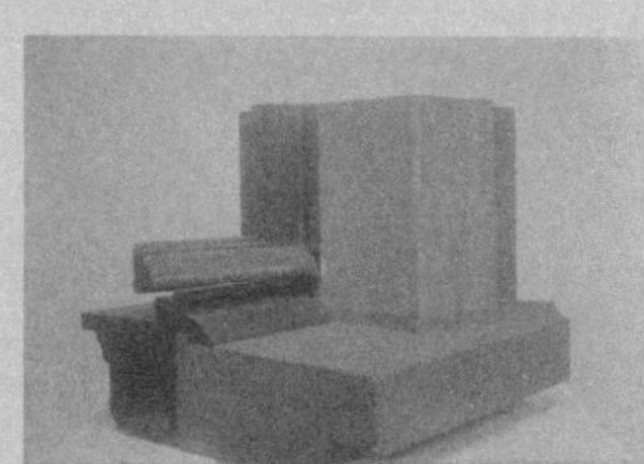

Anonymous, Fragment of a window, n.d., glass plate negative, 10 x 15 cm, Collection FOMU 2022/15/17/25

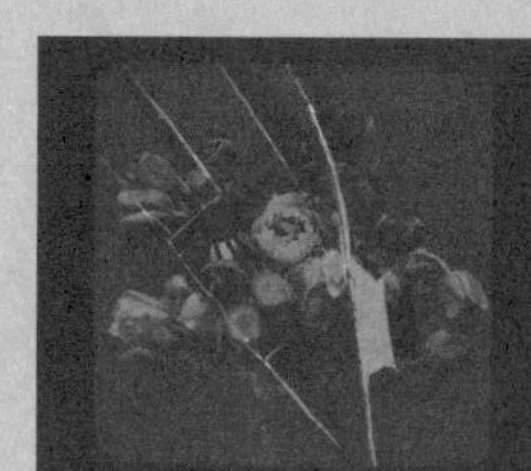

Anonymous, Vase with tulips, 1907-35, autochrome, 8.5 x 10 cm, Collection FOMU

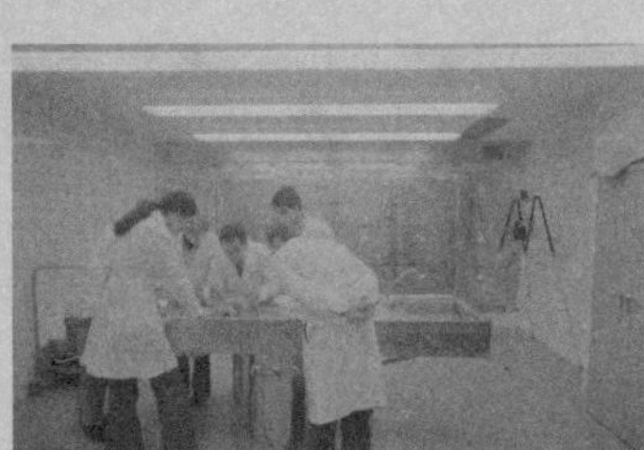

Filip Tas (BE, 1918-1997), Students at an autopsy, KULAK Kortrijk, 1974-75, plastic film negative, 2.4 x 3.6 cm, Collection FOMU B/2007/3906/448/29

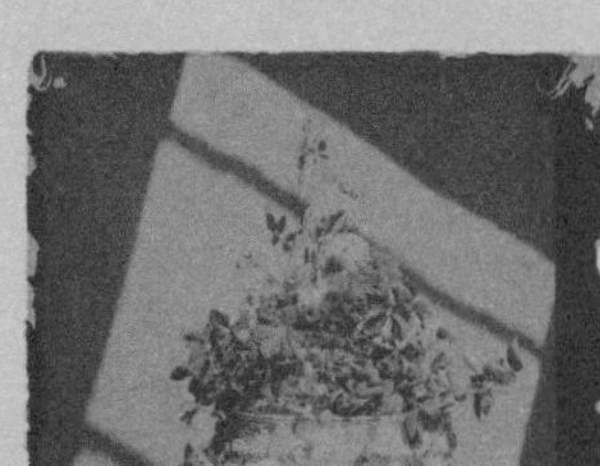

Anonymous, Flowers, 1907-35, autochrome, 13 x 18 cm, Collection FOMU DA5241

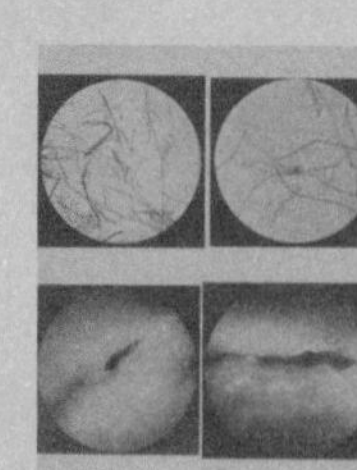

Anonymous, Photomicrographs, 1911, gelatin silver prints, 32.3 x 24.7 cm, Collection FOMU P/1964/42

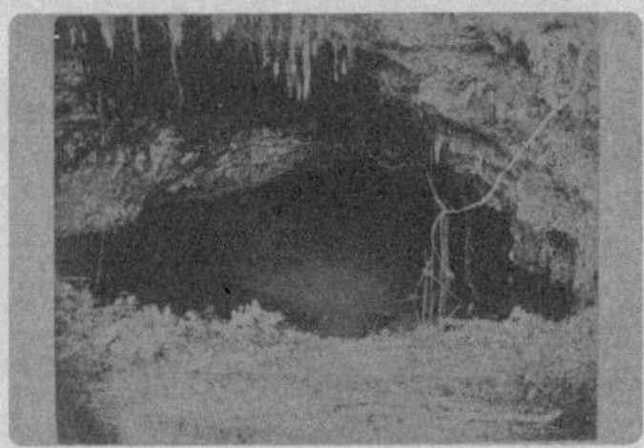

Sophia Hoare (GB, n.d.), Mara'a caves, 1879-1904, albumen print, 10.7 x 16.5 cm, Collection FOMU P/1965/496/5

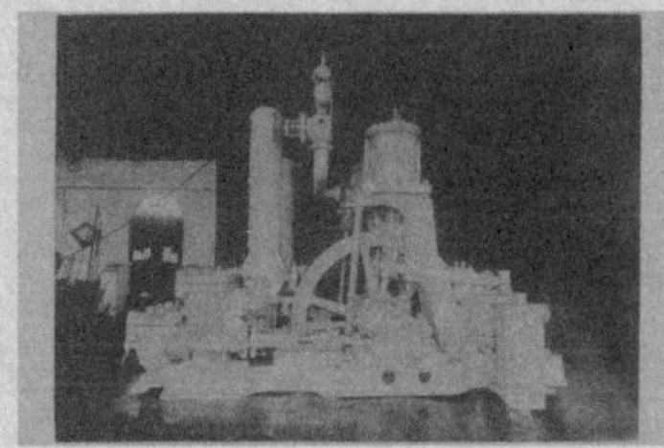

Anonymous, Industrial machine, S.A.M.C., ca. 1880, albumen print, 10.6 x 16.3 cm, Collection FOMU P/1965/499/5

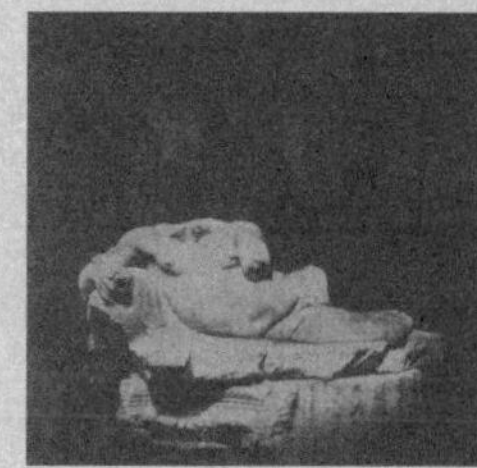

Charles Nègre (FR, 1820-1880), Arles, sculpture found in the Roman theatre, ca. 1852, salted paper print, 15.9 x 16.8 cm, Collection FOMU P/1966/28/1

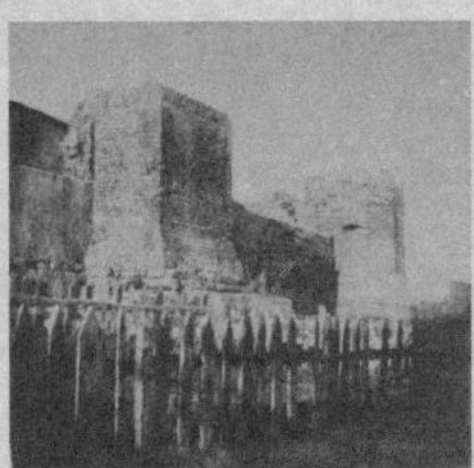

Charles Nègre (FR, 1820-1880), Arles, the Roman rampart, 1852, salted paper print, 15.9 x 16.8 cm, Collection FOMU P/1966/28/2

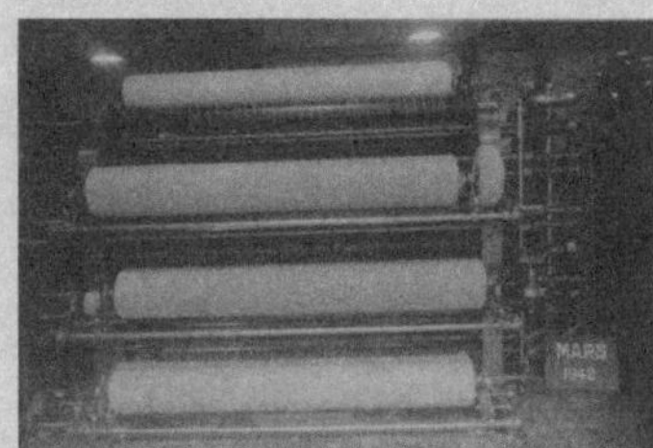

Félicien E. Wettstein (BE, 1894 -1962), Industrial machine, 1942, gelatin silver print, 12 x 17.7 cm, Collection FOMU P/1966/181/205

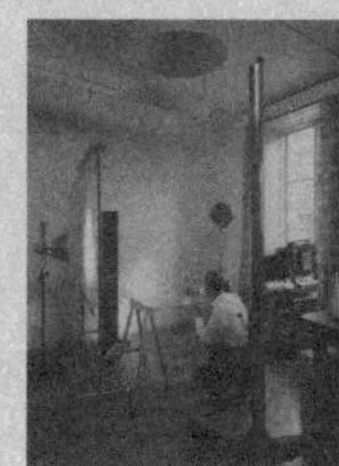

Sven Svenson (SE, n.d.), Workplace, ca. 1955, gelatin silver print, 30.5 x 24.1 cm, Collection FOMU P/1966/426

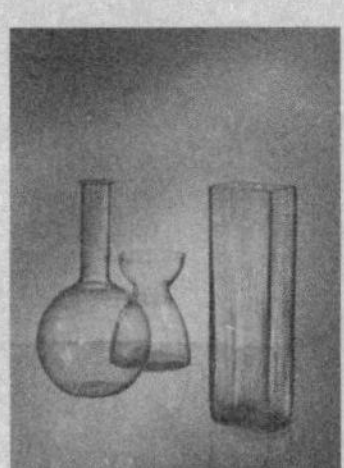

Sven Svenson (SE, n.d.), Glass vases, ca. 1955, gelatin silver print, 30.5 x 24 cm, Collection FOMU P/1966/427

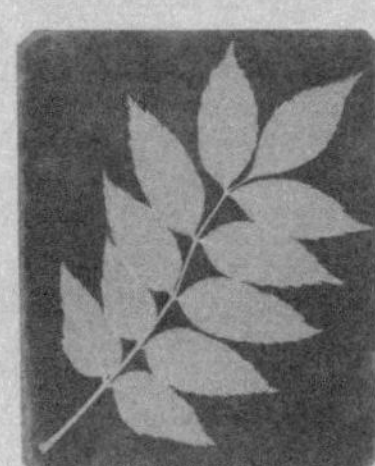

William Henry Fox Talbot (GB, 1800-1877), Leaves, 1840, calotype, 23 x 19 cm, Collection FOMU P/1971/4/2

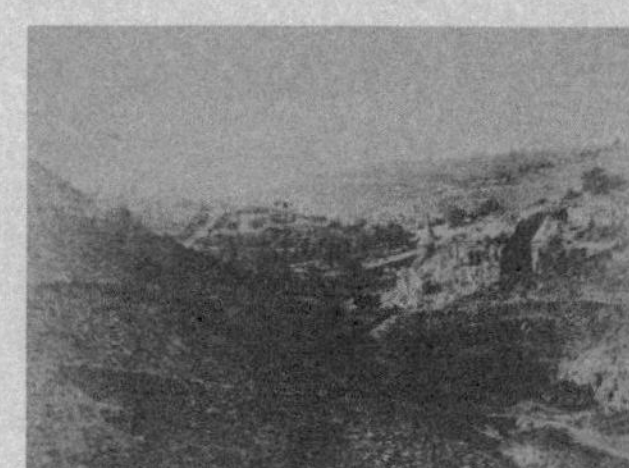

Auguste Salzmann (FR, 1824-1872), Jerusalem. Valley of Josaphat, 1854, salted paper print, 14.7 x 20.9 cm, Collection FOMU P/1973/161

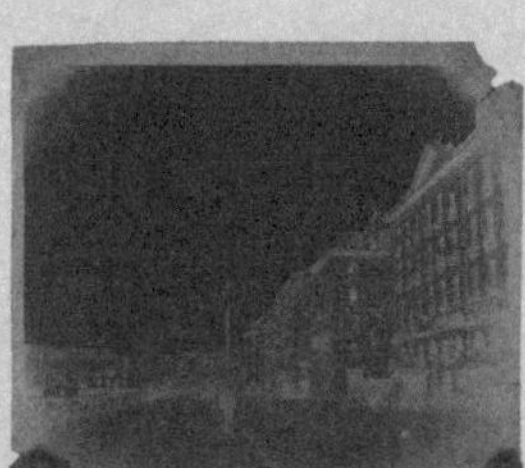

Jean Walther (CH, 1806-1866), View of 'Quai de Rive' in Geneva, ca. 1850, calotype, 15.4 x 18.3 cm, Collection FOMU P/1973/264

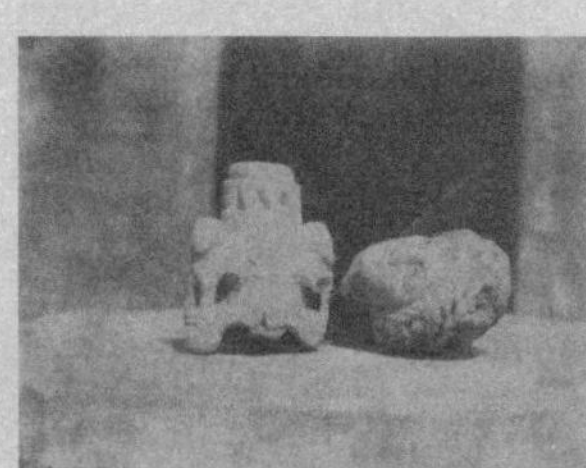

Auguste Salzmann (FR, 1824 1872), Jerusalem. Judaic and Roman fragments, 1854, salted paper print, 23.4 x 30.6 cm, Collection FOMU P/1973/286

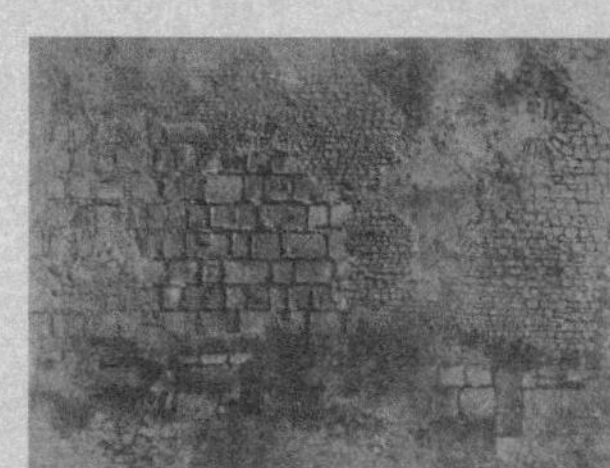

Auguste Salzmann (FR, 1824-1872), Jerusalem, temple enclosure, details of the probatic pool, ca. 1954, salted paper print, 22.3 x 31.9 cm, Collection FOMU P/1973/287

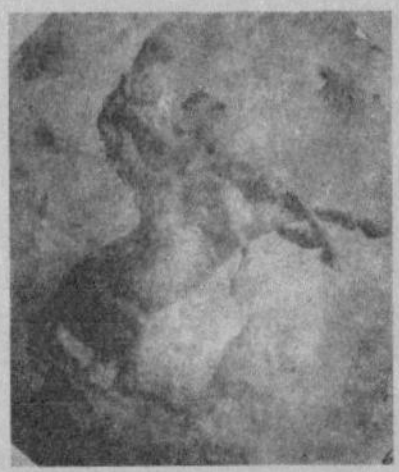

Joseph-Ernest Buschmann (BE, 1814-1853), Prancing horse, 1845-50, salted paper print, 11.6 x 10 cm, Collection FOMU P/1977/34/6

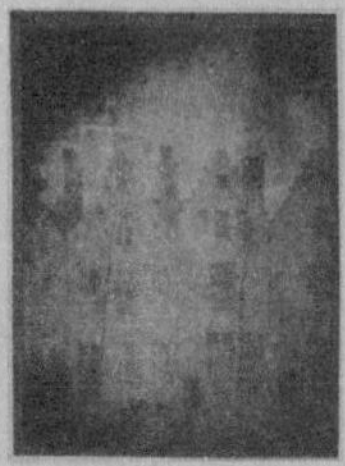

Joseph-Ernest Buschmann (BE, 1814-1853), Ossenmarkt, Antwerp, 1845-50, salted paper print, 11.2 x 8.5 cm, Collection FOMU P/1977/34/9

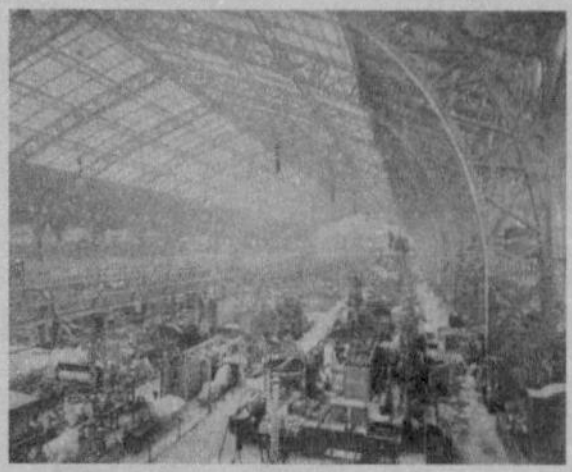

Neurdein Frères (FR), Paris Exposition, Gallery of Machines, 1889, albumen print, 21.7 x 27.2 cm, Collection FOMU P/1979/13/1

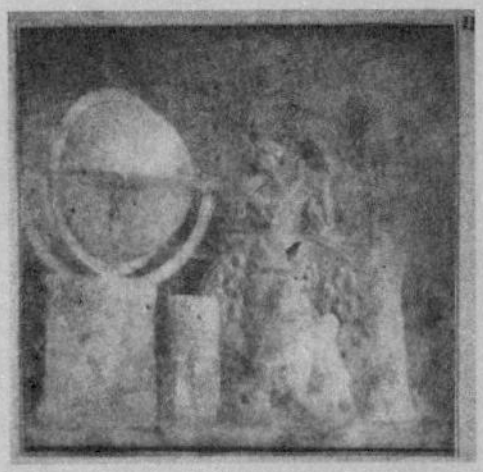

Joseph-Ernest Buschmann (BE, 1814-1853), Still life, 1845-50, salted paper print, 8.4 x 8.9 cm, Collection FOMU P/1977/34/14

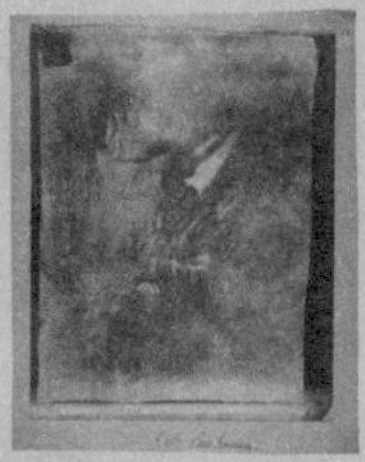

Joseph-Ernest Buschmann (BE, 1814-1853), Self-portrait, 1845-50, salted paper print, 28.2 x 23.9 cm, Collection FOMU P/1977/34/21

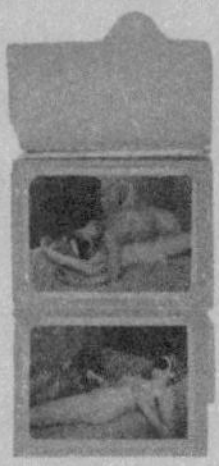

Anonymous, Pornographic souvenir from Paris, n.d., gelatin silver prints, 7.9 x 10.7 cm, Collection FOMU P/1980/218

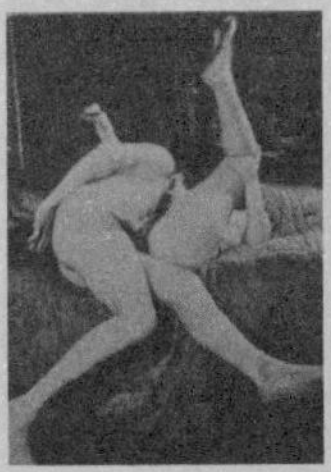

Anonymous, Pornography, n.d., gelatin silver print, 12 x 9 cm, Collection FOMU P/1980/220/21

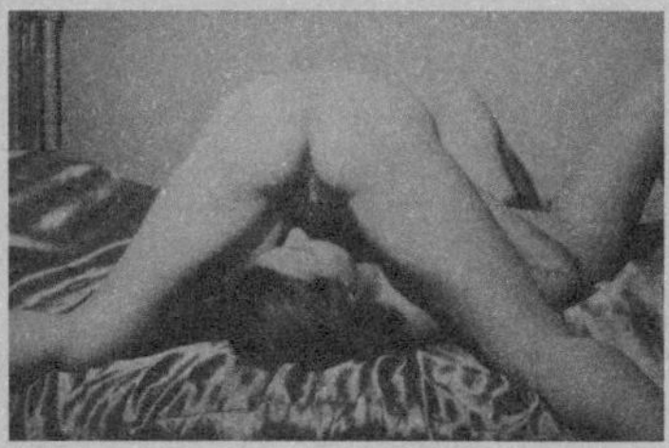

Anonymous, Pornography, n.d., gelatin silver print, 7.5 x 10.6 cm, Collection FOMU P/1980/222/22

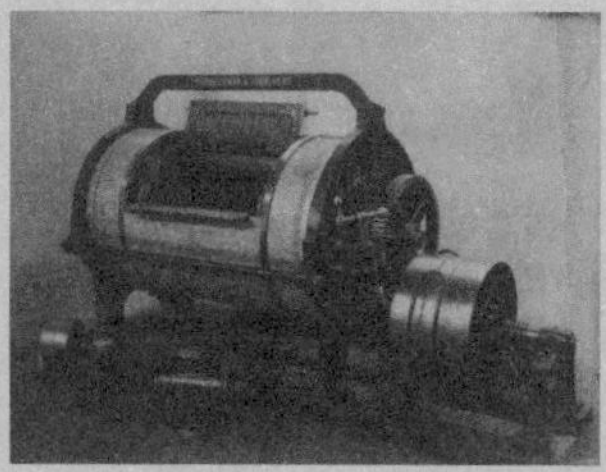

Joseph Buyens (BE, 1883-1971), Machine S. Braeckman & Zoon, Ghent, n.d., gelatin silver print, 16.9 x 22.8 cm, Collection FOMU P/1994/31

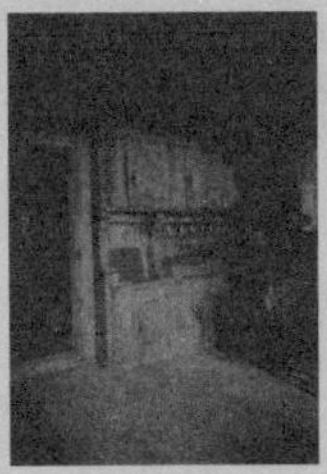

Anonymous, Farmhouse interior, n.d., platinum print, 17.3 x 12.1 cm, Collection FOMU P/1994/573/10

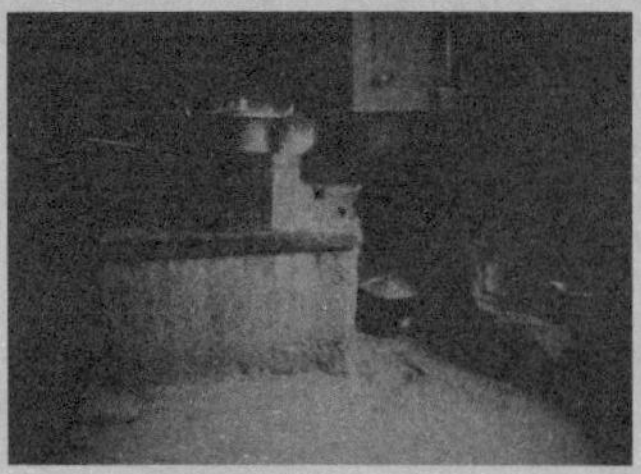

Anonymous, Farmhouse interior, n.d., platinum print, 12 x 17 cm, Collection FOMU P/1994/573/3

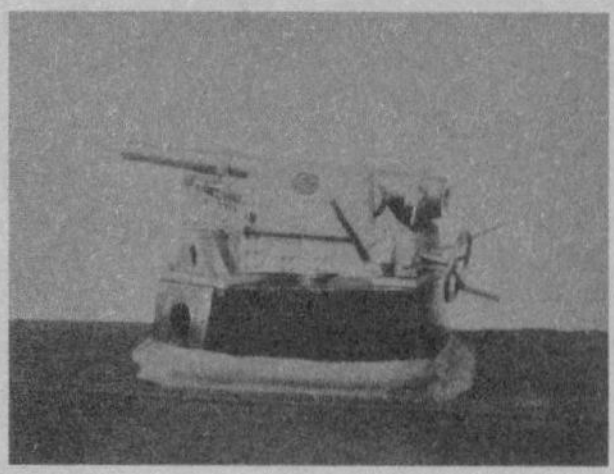

Photographisches Atelier des Grusonwerk (DE), Cannon, ca. 1870, albumen print, 28.5 x 38.3 cm, Collection FOMU P/1994/611/3

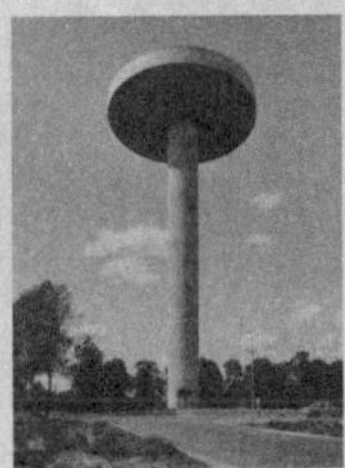

Georges Filleul (BE, 1908-1989), Water tower, 1950-70, gelatin silver print, 23.9 x 18.2 cm, Collection FOMU P/1981/69/226

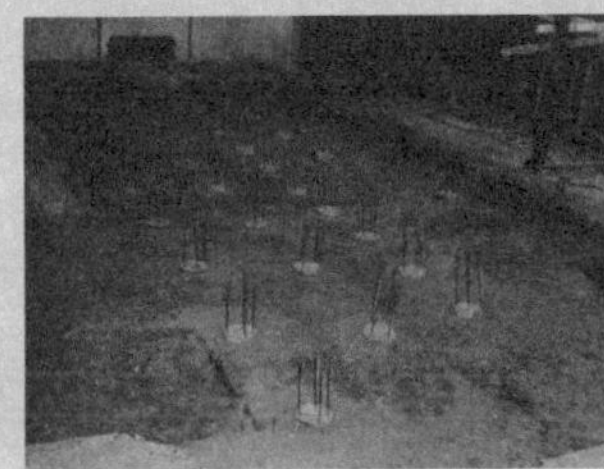

Georges Filleul (BE, 1908-1989), Construction site, 1950-70, gelatin silver print, 18.1 x 23.9 cm, Collection FOMU P/1981/69/290

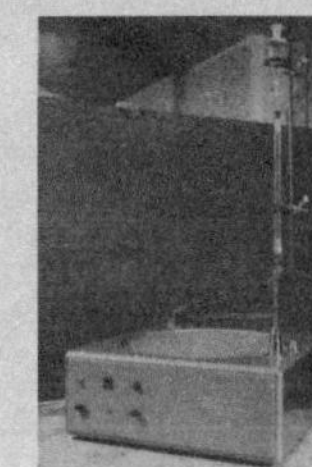

Georges Filleul (BE, 1908-1989), Fraction collector, Pleuger, 1950-70, gelatin silver print, 24 x 18.3 cm, Collection FOMU P/1981/69/395/2

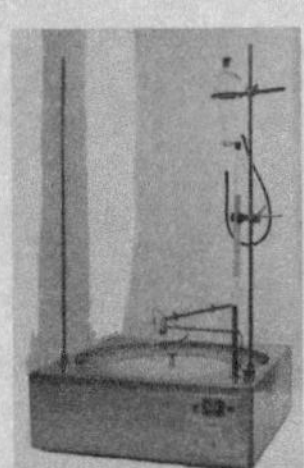

Georges Filleul (BE, 1908-1989), Fraction collector, Pleuger, 1950-70, gelatin silver print, 24 x 18.2 cm, Collection FOMU P/1981/69/397/2

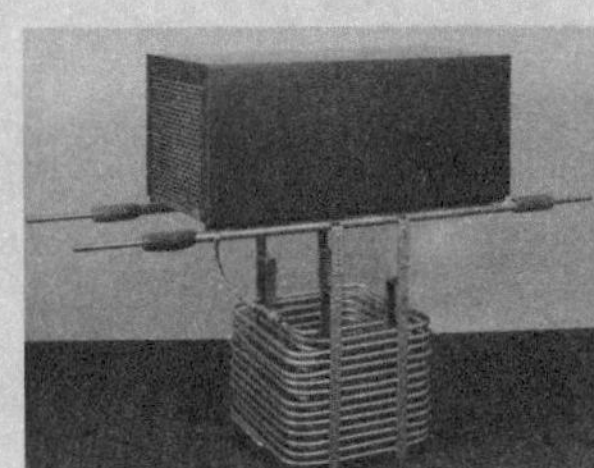

Georges Filleul (BE, 1908-1989), Cooling system, 1950-70, gelatin silver print, 18 x 24 cm, Collection FOMU P/1981/69/528/1

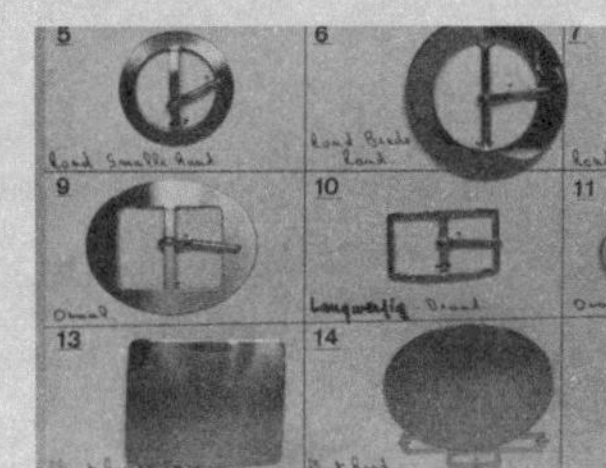

Georges Filleul (BE, 1908-1989), Buckles, 1950-70, gelatin silver print, 18.1 x 24 cm, Collection FOMU P/1981/69/883

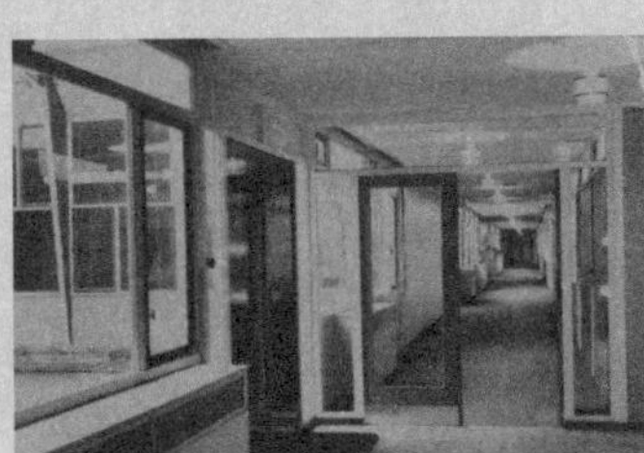

Georges Filleul (BE, 1908-1989), Architecture, 1950-70, chromogenic print, 13 x 18.2 cm, Collection FOMU P/1981/70/3/2

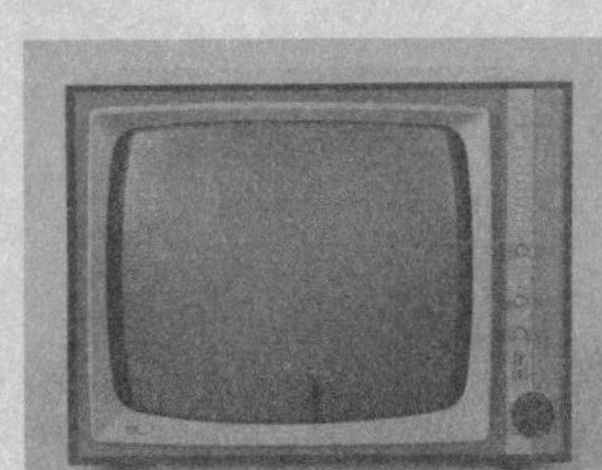

Georges Filleul (BE, 1908-1989), Television, Bel ITT, 1950-70, chromogenic print, 18.2 x 23.8 cm, Collection FOMU P/1981/70/14

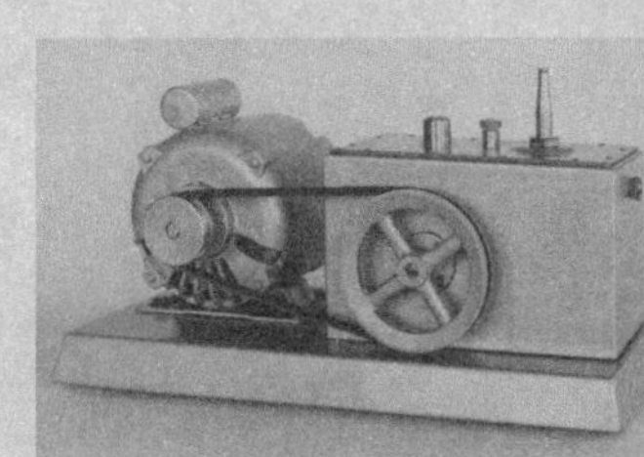

Georges Filleul (BE, 1908-1989), Engine, 1950-70, gelatin silver print, 13.1 x 17.9 cm, Collection FOMU P/1981/71/29/1

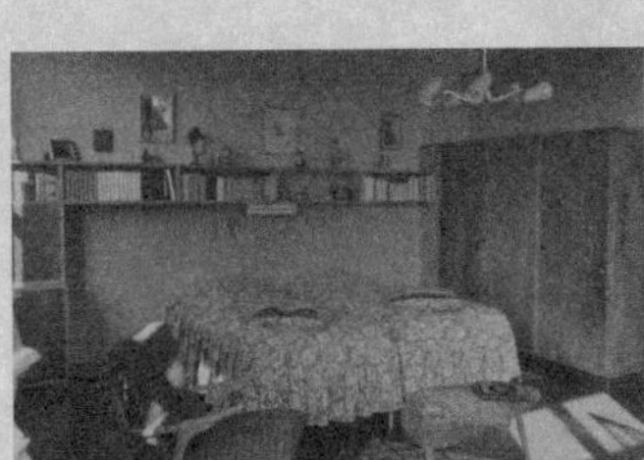

Georges Filleul (BE, 1908-1989), Bedroom, 1950-70, gelatin silver print, 12.9 x 18.1 cm, Collection FOMU P/1981/71/50

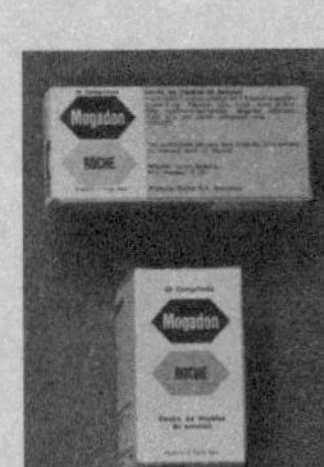

Georges Filleul (BE, 1908-1989), Pharmaceutical packaging, 1950-70, gelatin silver print, 17.7 x 12.7 cm, Collection FOMU P/1981/71/70/1

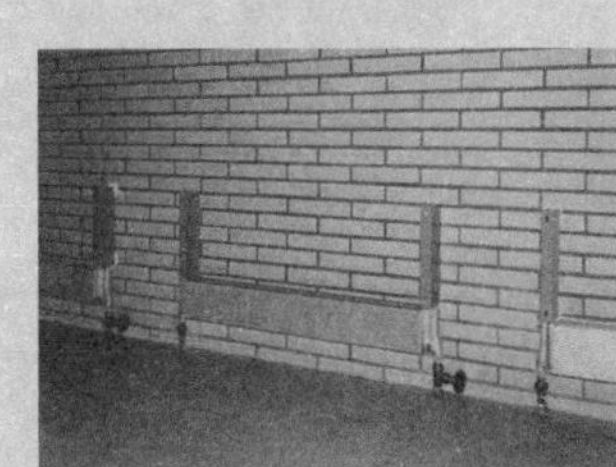

Georges Filleul (BE, 1908-1989), Heating, 1950-70, gelatin silver print, 12.8 x 17.7 cm, Collection FOMU P/1981/71/83

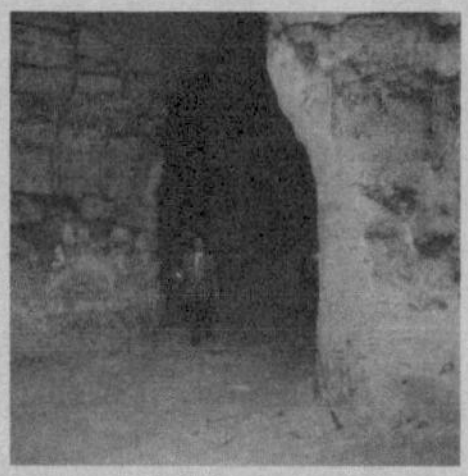

Georges Filleul (BE, 1908-1989), Two people in a cave, 1954, gelatin silver print, 11.9 x 12.2 cm, Collection FOMU P/1981/71/249

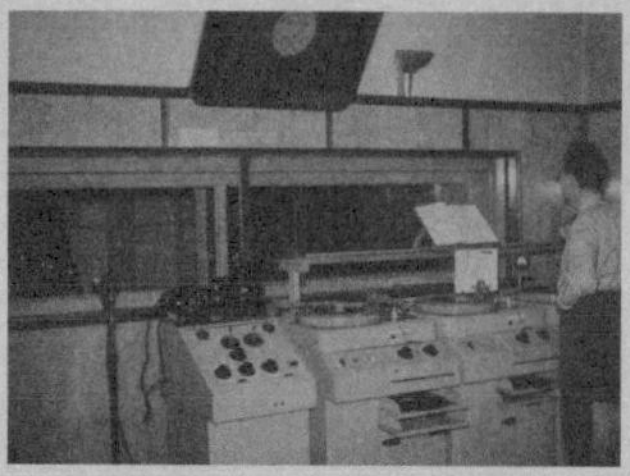

Georges Filleul (BE, 1908-1989), Interior recording studio, 1950-70, gelatin silver print, 13.1 x 18 cm, Collection FOMU P/1981/71/281

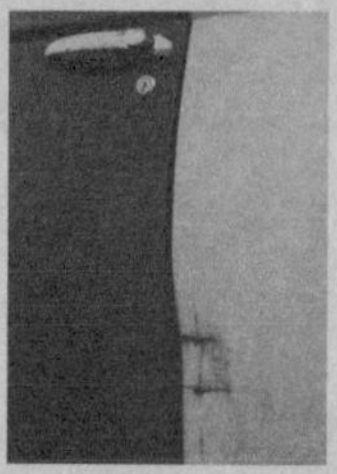

Georges Filleul (BE, 1908-1989), Car door, 1950-70, gelatin silver print, 18 x 13.2 cm, Collection FOMU P/1981/71/345

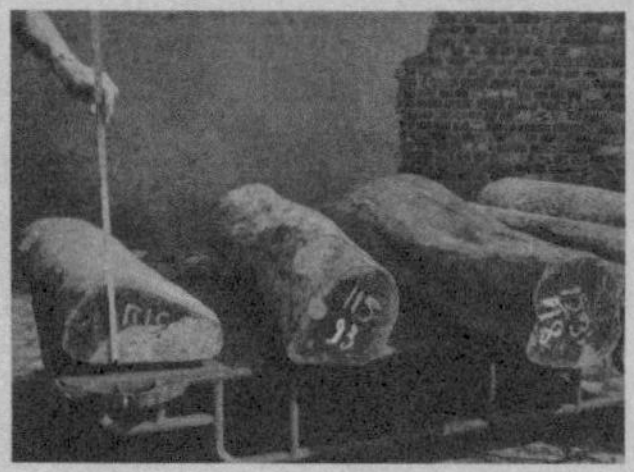

Georges Filleul (BE, 1908-1989), Tree trunks, 1950-70, gelatin silver print, 13.1 x 17.9 cm, Collection FOMU P/1981/71/346

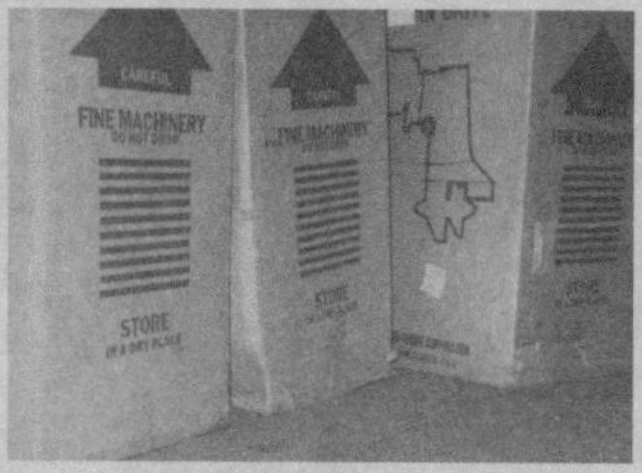

Georges Filleul (BE, 1908-1989), Cardboard boxes, 1950-70, gelatin silver print, 13.2 x 18 cm, Collection FOMU P/1981/71/351

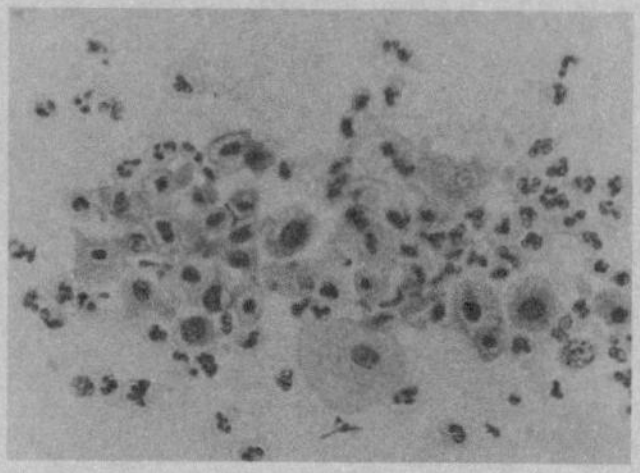

Georges Filleul (BE, 1908-1989), Photomicrography, 1950-70, gelatin silver print, 13.2 x 18 cm, Collection FOMU P/1981/71/372/1

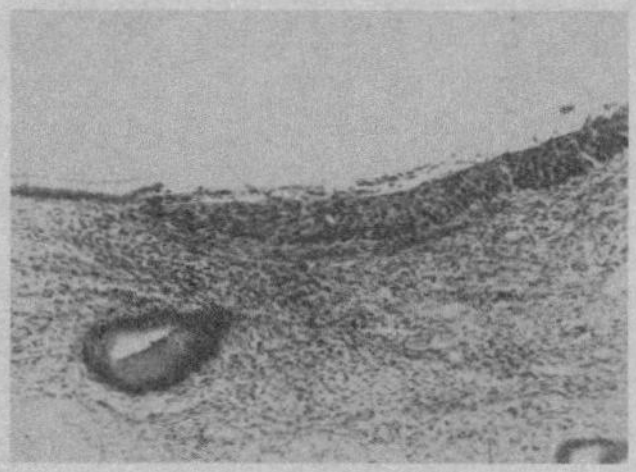

Georges Filleul (BE, 1908-1989), Photomicrography, 1950-70, gelatin silver print, 13 x 18 cm, Collection FOMU P/1981/71/373/2

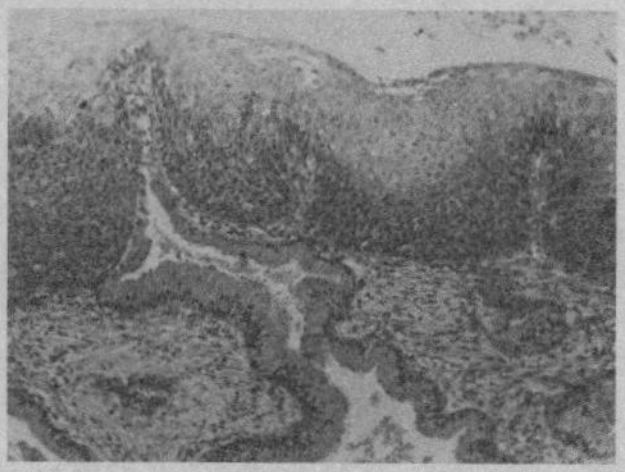

Georges Filleul (BE, 1908-1989), Photomicrography, 1950-70, gelatin silver print, 13.2 x 18 cm, Collection FOMU P/1981/71/374

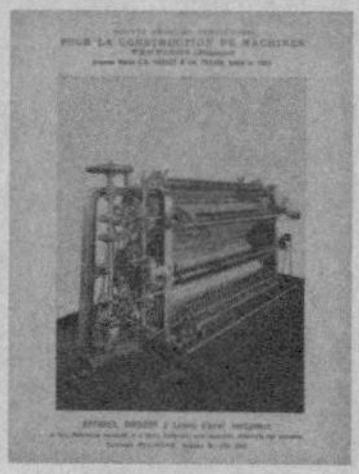

Edouard Wettstein (BE, 1868-1940), Industrial machine, 1900-30, collodion printing-out paper, 30.9 x 24 cm, Collection FOMU P/1991/44

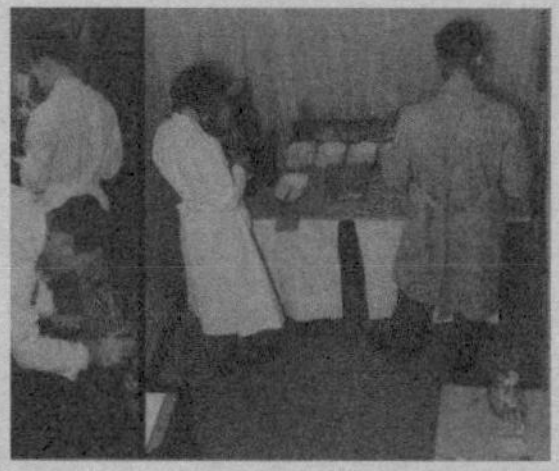

Anonymous, Microscopic examination, 1947, gelatin silver print, 32 x 39.3 cm, Collection FOMU P/1991/179/6

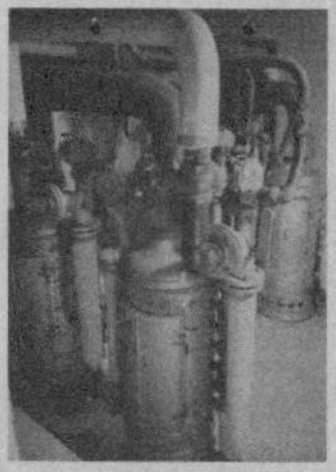

Willy Kessels (BE, 1898-1974), Industrial machine, G.M.C., n.d., gelatin silver print, 22.8 x 16.9 cm, Collection FOMU P/1992/15/43

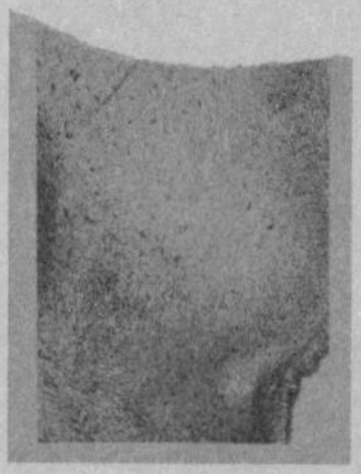

Louis Cools (BE, 1887-1986), Photomicrography, n.d., gelatin silver print, 16.5 x 12.9 cm, Collection FOMU P/1997/41/1

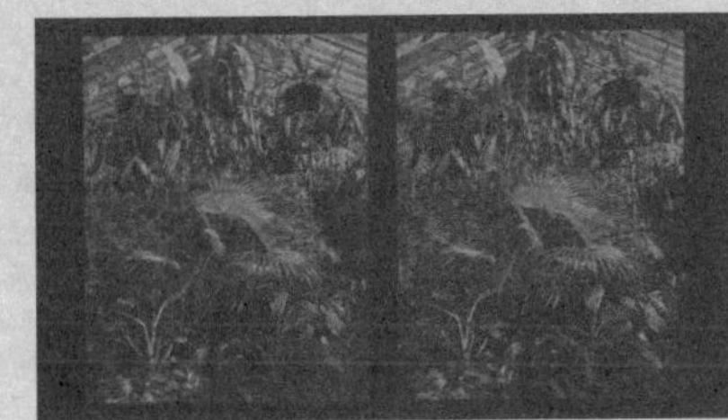

Hans Hildenbrand (DE, 1870-1957), Greenhouse with pitcher plants, 1910-11, colour relief halftone print, 9 x 17.9 cm, Collection FOMU P/1998/67/130

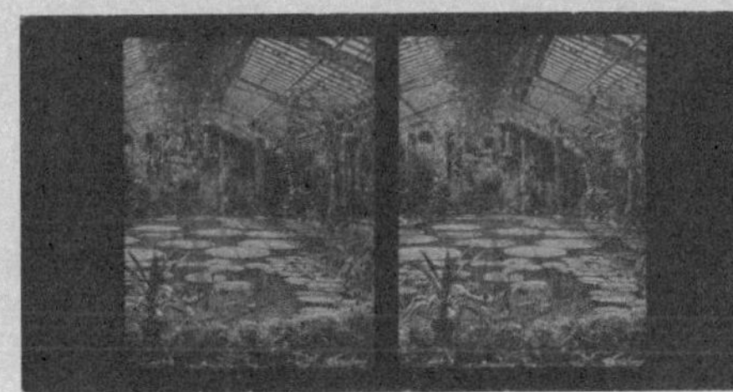

Hans Hildenbrand (DE, 1870-1957), Greenhouse with large water lilies, Victoria Regia-Haus, 1910-11, colour relief halftone print, 9 x 17.9 cm, Collection FOMU P/1998/67/131

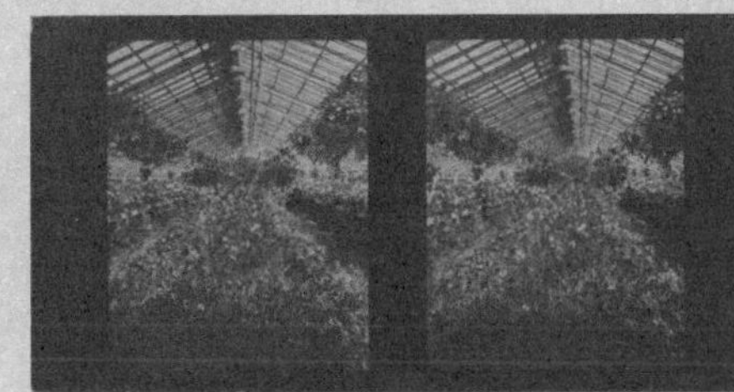

Hans Hildenbrand (DE, 1870-1957), Greenhouse with red carnations, Nelkenhaus, 1910-11, colour relief halftone print, 9.1 x 17.9 cm, Collection FOMU P/1998/67/132

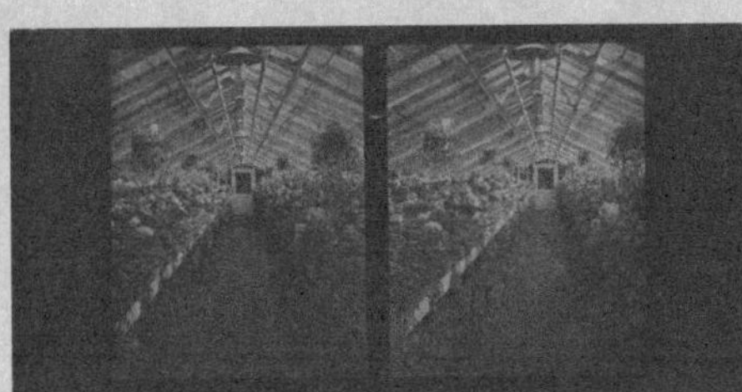

Hans Hildenbrand (DE, 1870-1957), Greenhouse with geraniums, 1910-11, colour relief halftone print, 9 x 17.9 cm, Collection FOMU P/1998/67/133

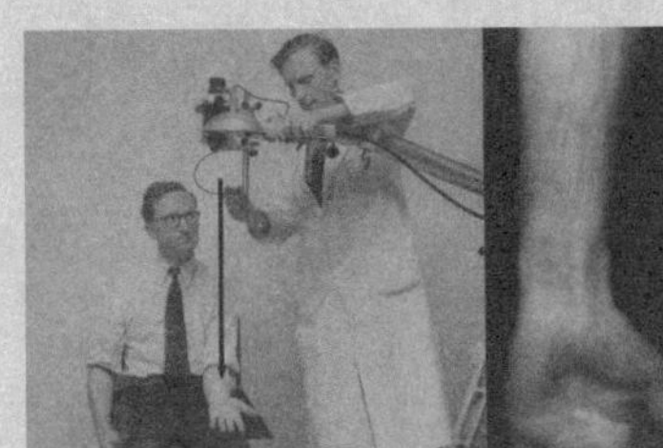

Laurence Hill (GB, n.d.), Infrared photography with one electronic flash close to the lens, ca. 1957, gelatin silver print, 16.8 x 26 cm, Collection FOMU P/2003/637/1

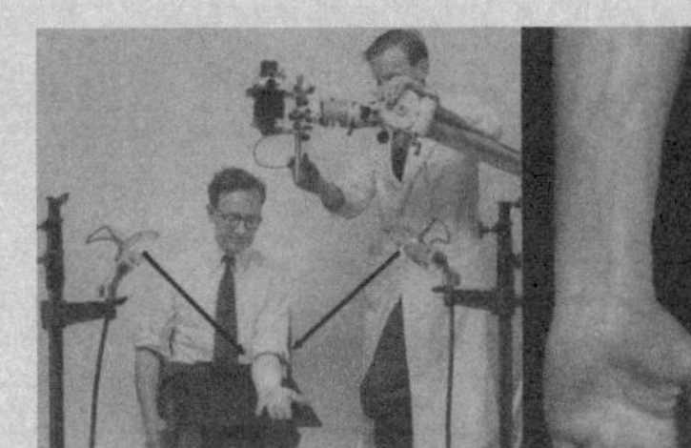

Laurence Hill (GB, n.d.), Infrared photography with two electronic flash lamps close to the lens, ca. 1957, gelatin silver print, 16.5 x 26 cm, Collection FOMU P/2003/637/2

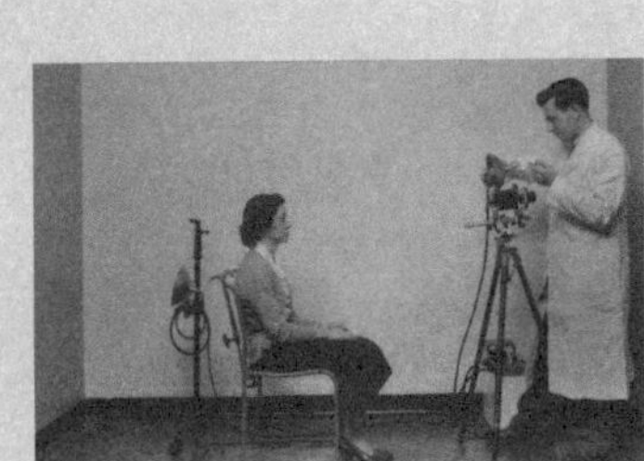

Laurence Hill (GB, n.d.), Medical application of infrared photography, ca. 1957, gelatin silver print, 16.5 x 26 cm, Collection FOMU P/2003/637/3

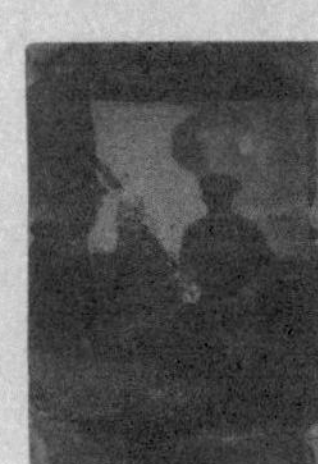

Anonymous, Portrait of a woman and a man, 1880-1930, ferrotype, 6.4 x 4.5 cm, Collection FOMU P/1998/63

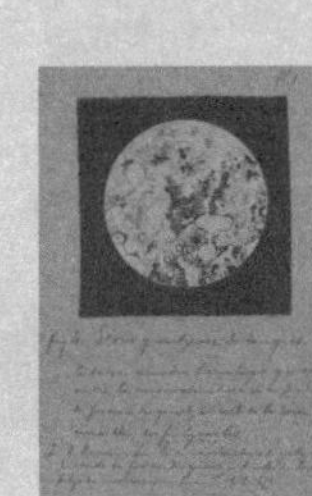

Anonymous, Photomicrography, 1878-79, gelatin silver print, 17 x 11,5 cm, Collection FOMU P/2001/12/5

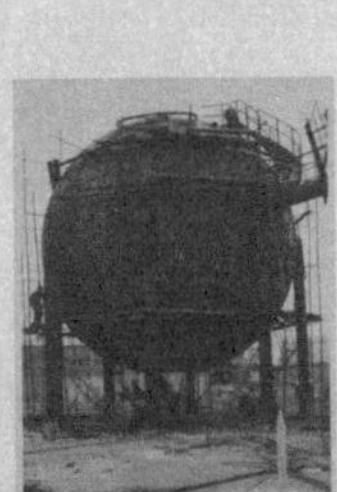

Anonymous, Factory halls Fulton Marine Engineering, 1960-61, gelatin silver print, 18 x 13.2 cm, Collection FOMU P/2005/20/15

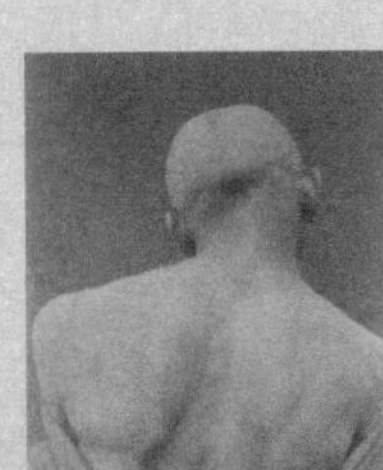

Arthur de Montméja (FR, 1841-1910), Congenital torticollis, 1872, from "Revue photographique des hôpitaux de Paris", albumen print, 11.5 x 9.6 cm, Collection FOMU P/1963/572/8

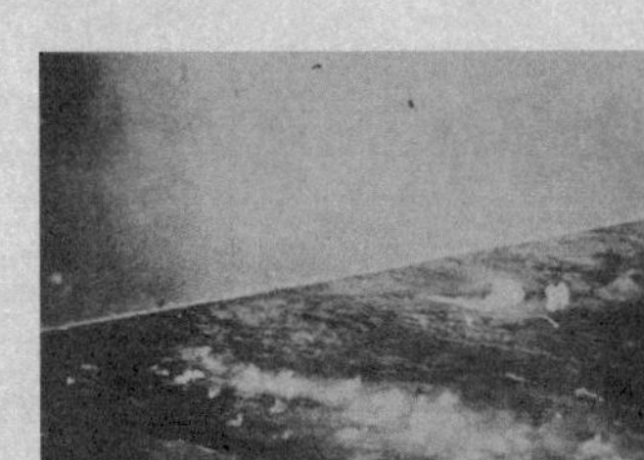

Service photographique de l'armée belge (BE), Aerial photograph of Nieuwpoort during the First World War, 1917, gelatin silver print, 5.2 x 7.6 cm, Collection FOMU P/2012/435

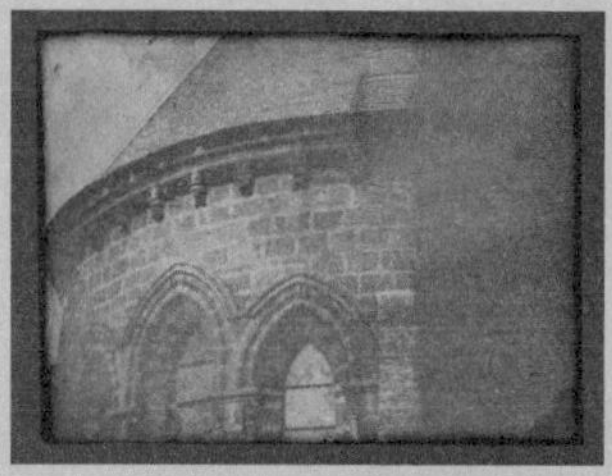

Anonymous, Architecture, 1839-60, daguerreotype, 18 x 24 cm, Collection FOMU P/1966/112

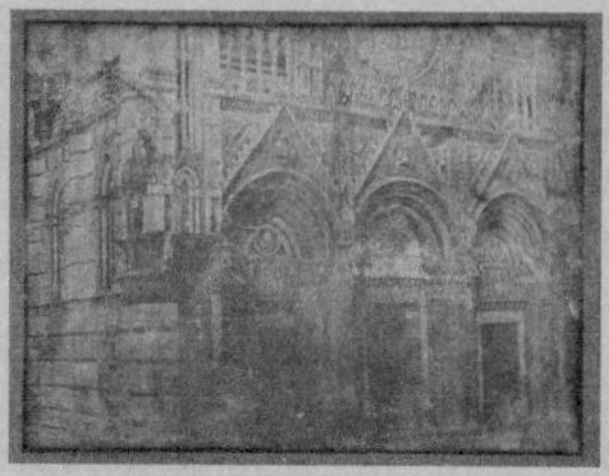

Anonymous, Siena cathedral, ca. 1845, daguerreotype, 18 x 24 cm, Collection FOMU P/1966/113

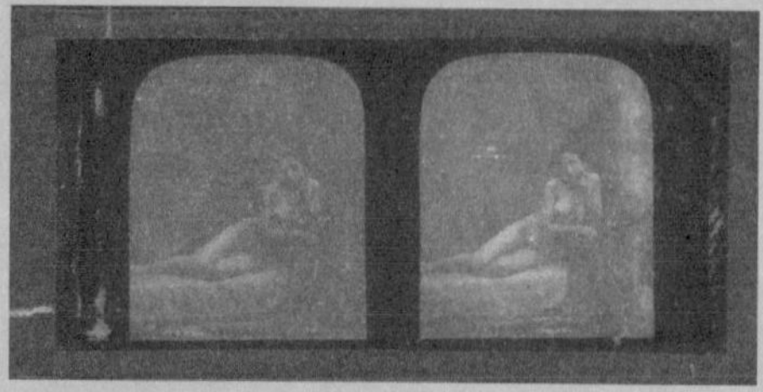

Pierre-Ambroise Richebourg FR, 1810-1875), Stereo portrait of a nude woman, 1850, daguerreotype, 8.5 x 17 cm, Collection FOMU P/1967/12

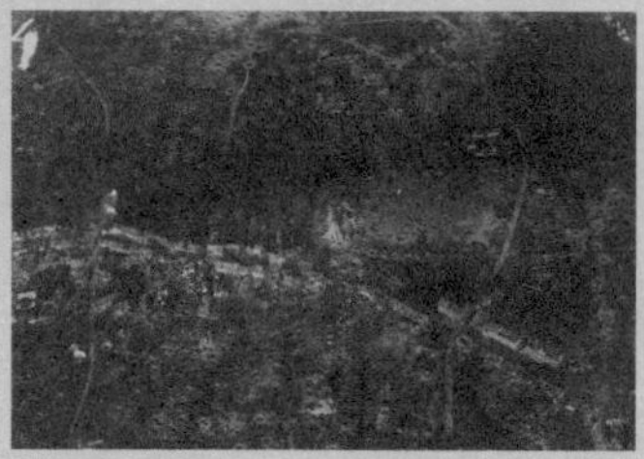

C. Hermann (n.d.), Aerial photograph of Beselare after bombing during the First World War, 1914-18, gelatin silver print, 27.7 x 39.3 cm, Collection FOMU P/1970/420

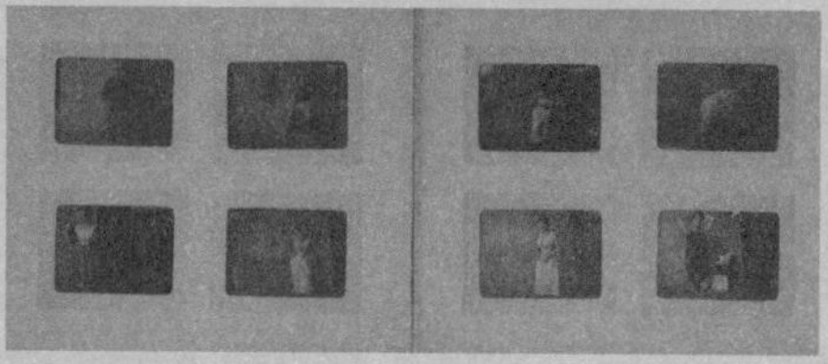

Anonymous, Photo album with snapshots, ca. 1905, collodion printing-out papers, 14 x 17.4 x 2 cm, Collection FOMU P/1971/95

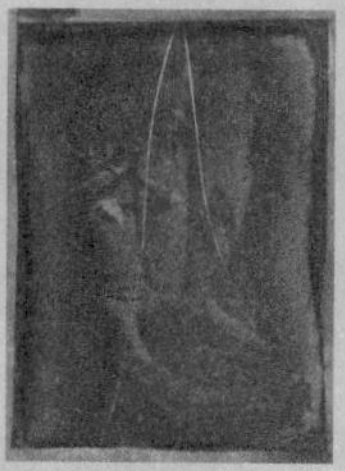

Anonymous, The drinker, 1840-65, daguerreotype, 13 x 10 cm, Collection FOMU P/1977/32/10

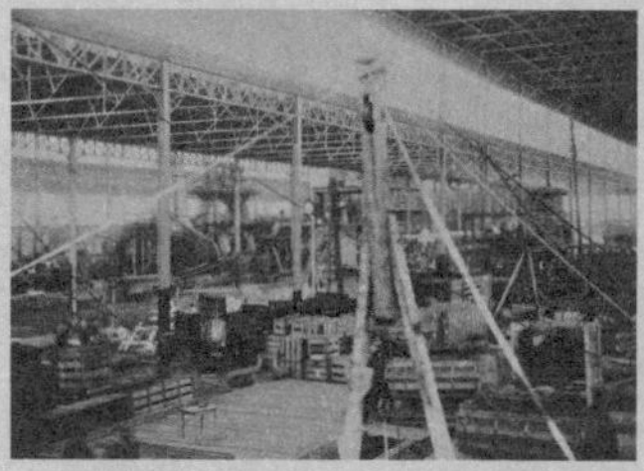

Theophiel Sanders (BE, 1858-1908), Machine Hall, Antwerp International Exposition, 1885, albumen print, 14.8 x 21 cm, Collection FOMU P/1981/295/2

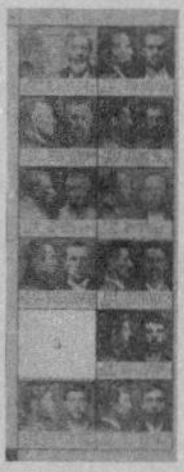

Paris Forensic Identification Department (FR), Identification photographs, 1903, gelatin silver print, 27.7 x 11.2 cm, Collection FOMU P/1984/215/3

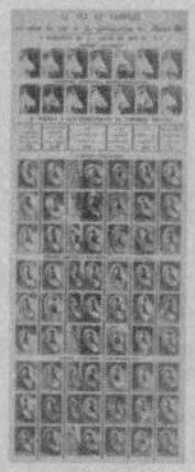

Paris Forensic Identification Department (FR), Classification of the nose and ear, ca. 1903, albumen print, 27.2 x 10.5 cm, Collection FOMU P/1984/215/4

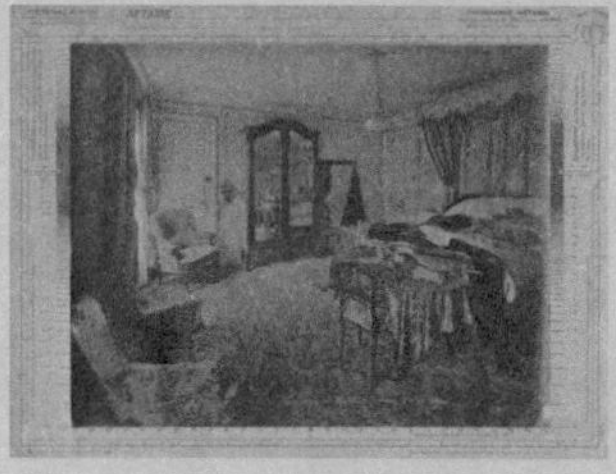

Paris Forensic Identification Department (FR), The Mielvacque case, Hôtel d'Orsay, 1904, gelatin silver print, 22.3 x 28.9 cm, Collection FOMU P/1984/215/5

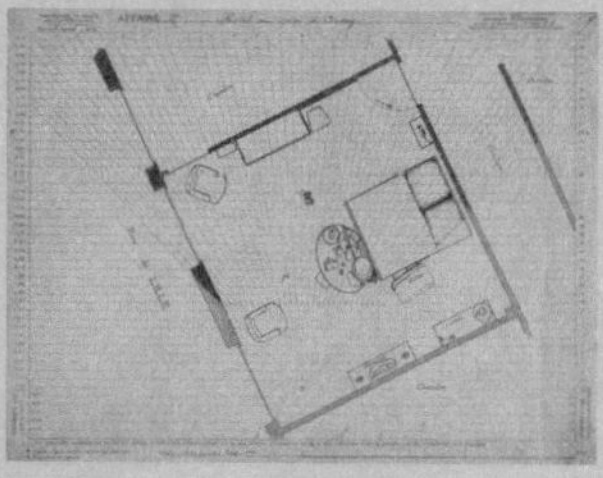

Paris Forensic Identification Department (FR), The Mielvacque case, Hôtel d'Orsay, 1904, gelatin silver print, 26.5 x 35.9 cm, Collection FOMU P/1984/215/6

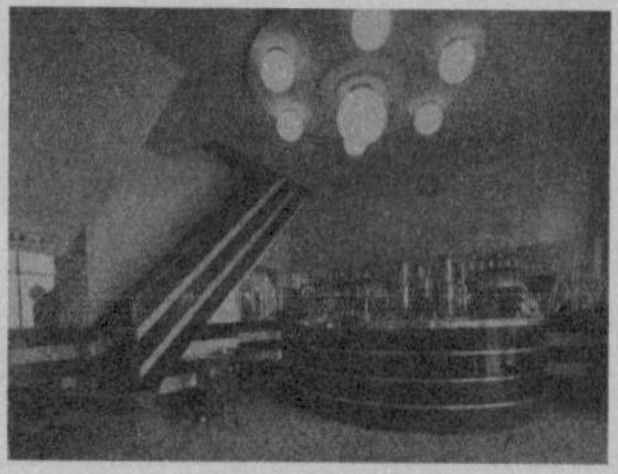

Georges Blanc (FR, n.d.), Café interior, ca. 1930, gelatin silver print, 16.6 x 22 cm, Collection FOMU P/1993/517

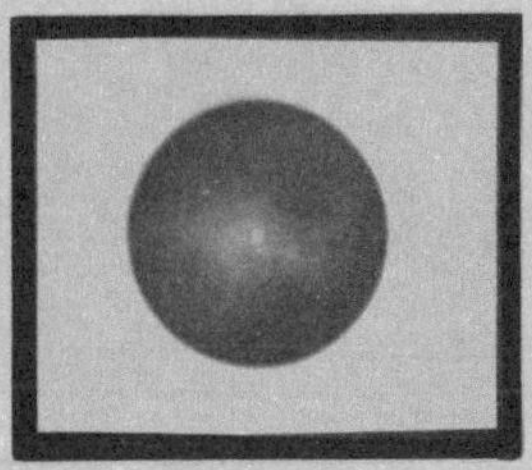

Paul Sano (BE, 1874-1960), Lunar eclipse, 1908-35, glass plate positive, 8.5 x 10 cm, Collection FOMU

Paul Sano (BE, 1874-1960), Garden, 1908-35, additive colour screen plate, 9 x 12 cm, Collection FOMU

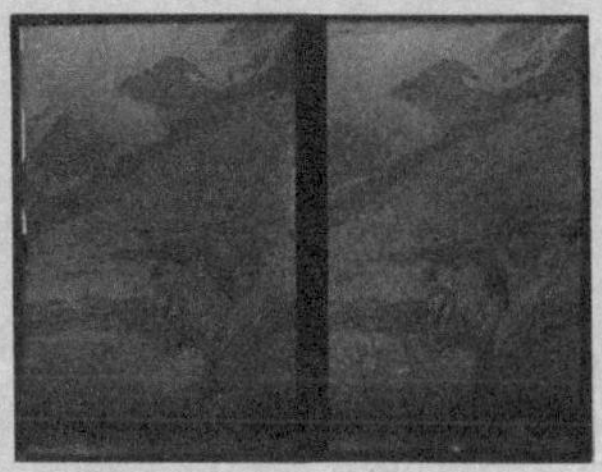

Paul Sano (BE, 1874-1960), Glacier, 1907-35, autochrome, 9 x 12 cm, Collection FOMU

Paul Sano (BE, 1874-1960), Photomicrography, 1944, additive colour screen plate, 12 x 9 cm, Collection FOMU

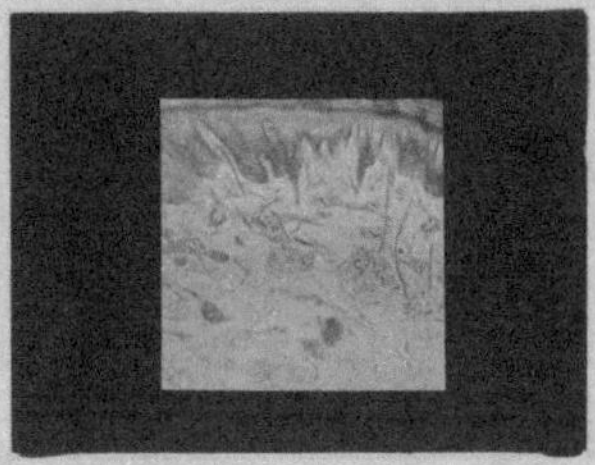

Paul Sano (BE, 1874-1960), Photomicrography, 1908-35, glass plate positive, 9 x 12 cm, Collection FOMU

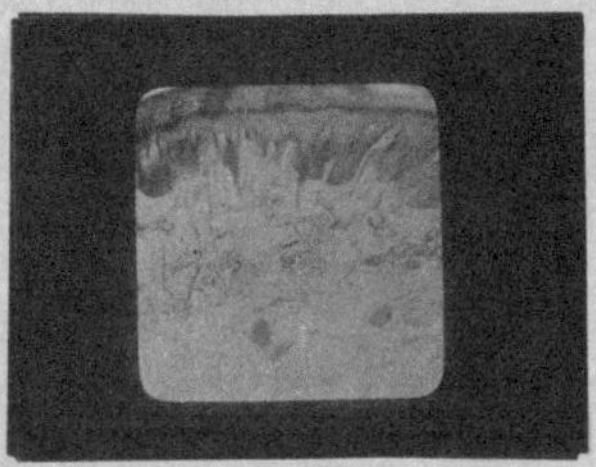

Paul Sano (BE, 1874-1960), Photomicrography, 1908-35, additive colour screen plate, 9 x 12 cm, Collection FOMU

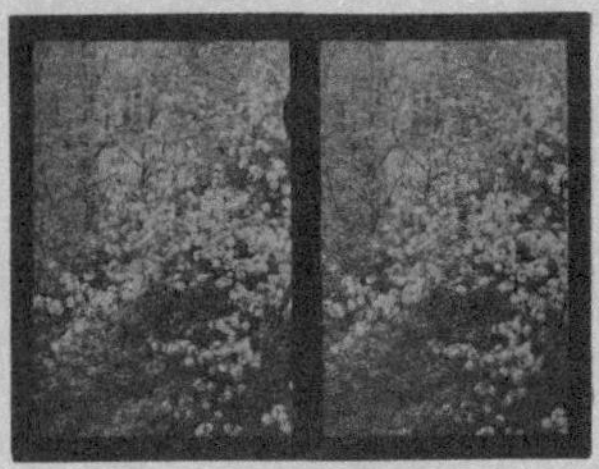

Paul Sano (BE, 1874-1960), Blossom, 1917, additive colour screen plate, 9 x 12 cm, Collection FOMU

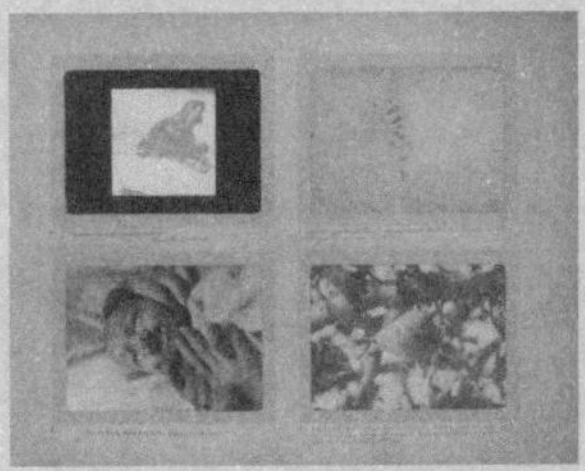

Paul Sano (BE, 1874-1960), Album with experimental and documentary photography, 1903-10, various techniques, 26 x 33 x 4 cm, Collection FOMU P/2002/905

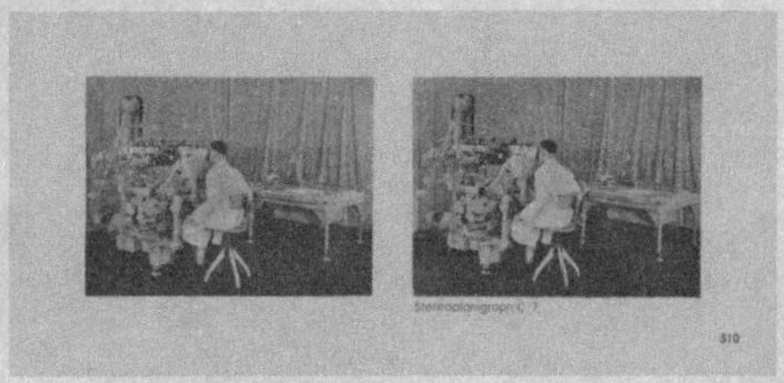

Anonymous, Stereoplanigraph, ca. 1950, gelatin silver print, 6 x 13 cm, Collection FOMU P/1998/65/93

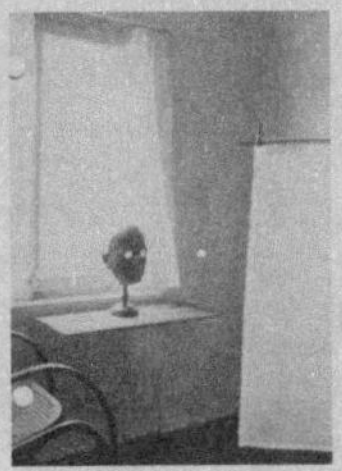

Suzy Embo (BE, °1936), Mask, ca. 1965, gelatin silver print, 11.6 x 9 cm, Collection FOMU P/1996/642/19

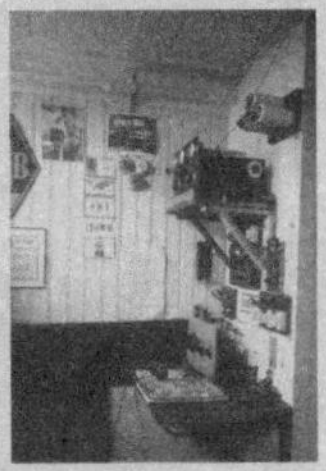

Anonymous, Radio station on a ship, n.d., gelatin silver print, 16.5 x 11.6 cm, Collection FOMU P/1997/19/1

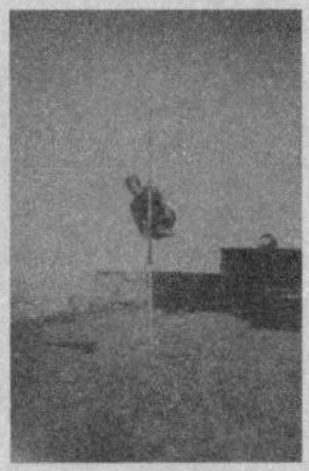

Anonymous, Pole vaulter, ca. 1900, albumen print, 17 x 11.7 cm, Collection FOMU P/1997/76

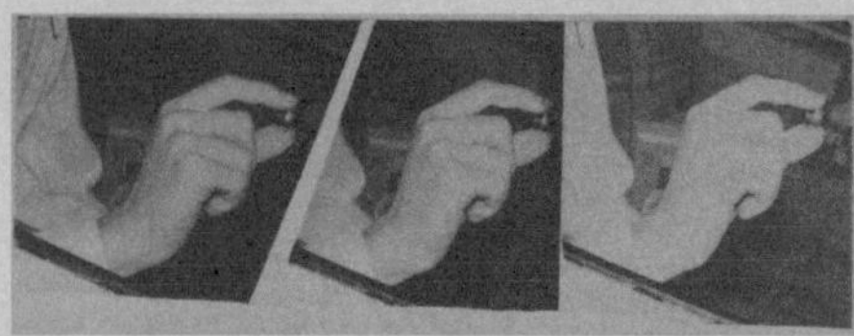

Anonymous, Hands, n.d., gelatin silver print, 4.5 x 14 cm, Collection FOMU 2023/15

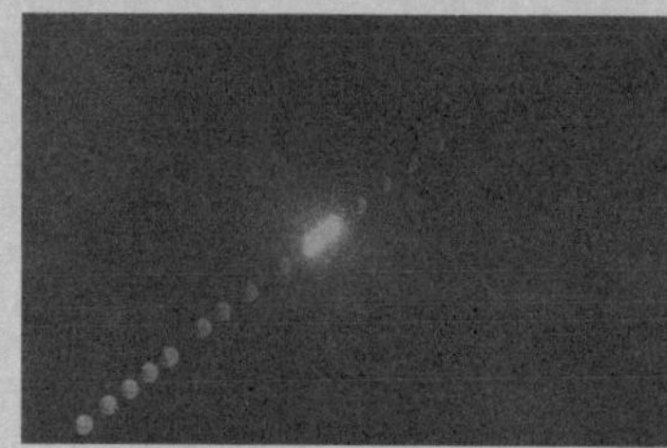

Anonymous, Total lunar eclipse, 16/09/1978, gelatin silver print, 8.9 x 13.9 cm, Collection FOMU 2023/13

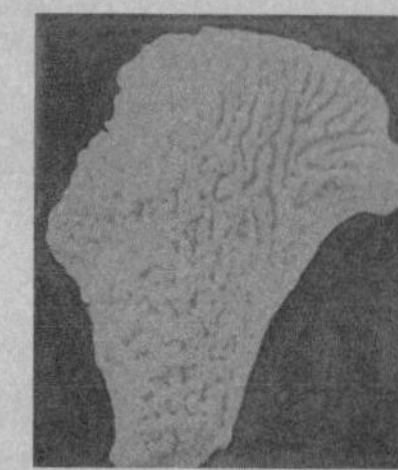

Anonymous, Sponge, 1840-60, salted paper print, 20 x 17.3 cm, Collection FOMU 2023/18

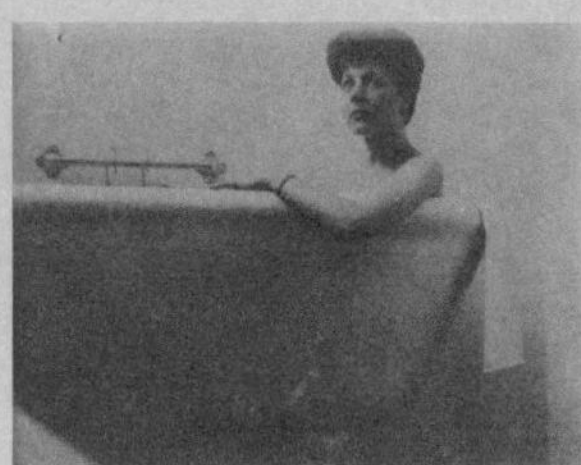

Anonymous, Portrait of a woman in a bathtub, ca. 1905, gelatin printing-out paper, 8 x 10.3 cm, Collection FOMU P/2003/360/1

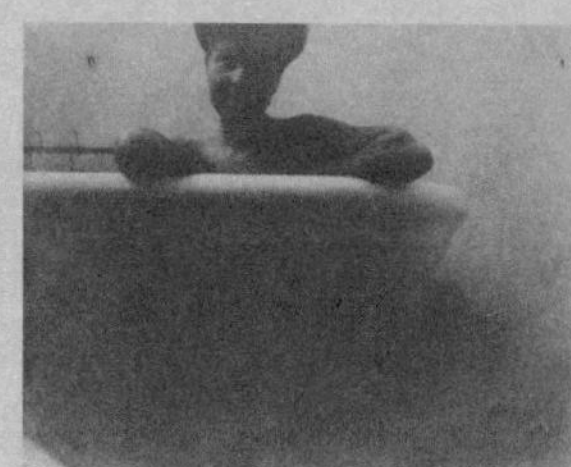

Anonymous, Portrait of a woman in a bathtub, ca. 1905, gelatin printing-out paper, 8 x 10.4 cm, Collection FOMU P/2003/360/2

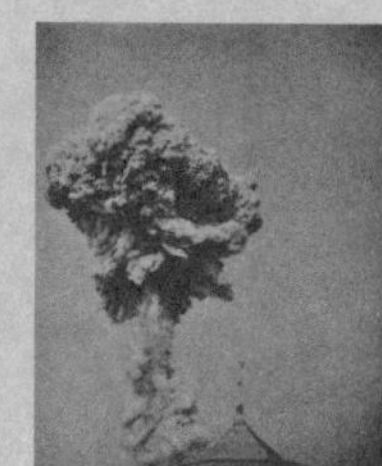

Ernest Huybrechts (BE, 1863-n.d.), The explosion, 1889, collotype, 17.5 x 14.7 cm, Collection FOMU P/1963/20/4

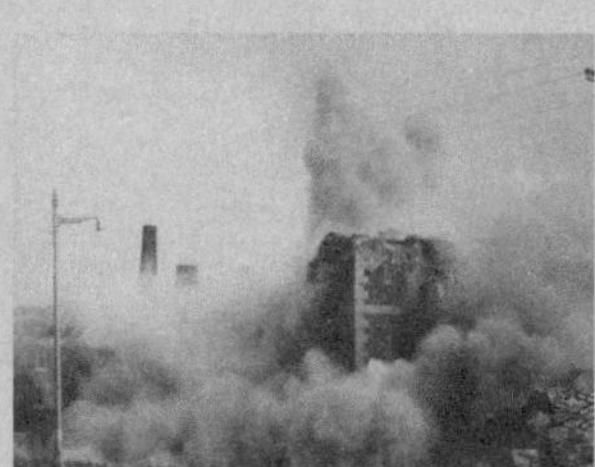

Anonymous, Blowing up the Berchem Gate, Antwerp, 1966, gelatin silver print, 18.2 x 24 cm, Collection FOMU P/2004/223

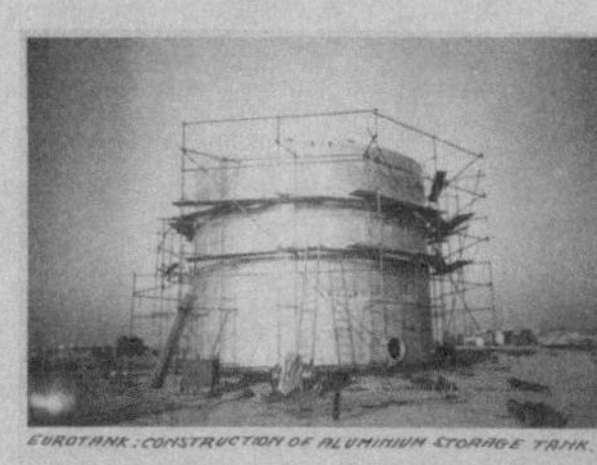

Anonymous, Construction of storage tank commissioned by Fulton Marine Engineering S.A., 1960-61, gelatin silver print, 13.2 x 18 cm, Collection FOMU P/2005/20/18

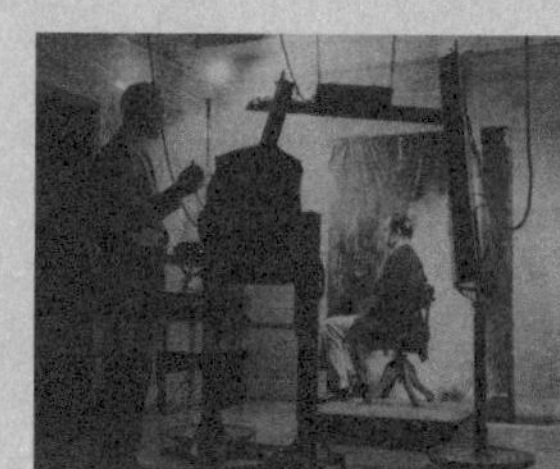

Anonymous, Police photo in the Missouri State Prison, USA, 1950, gelatin silver print, 19.4 x 24.2 cm, Collection FOMU P/2012/434

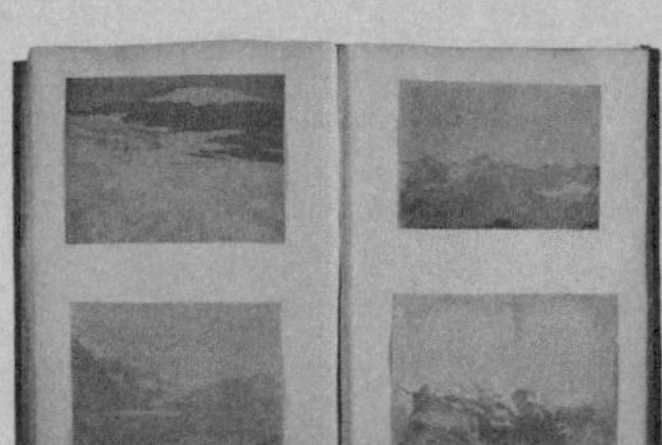

Anonymous, Photo album of the Antwerp family Osterrieth, 1890-1905, various techniques, 31.8 x 24.7 x 5 cm, Collection FOMU P/2013/32

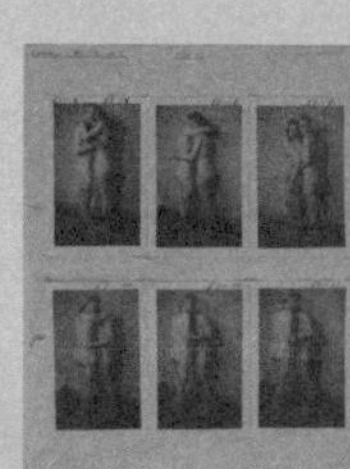

Willy Kessels (BE, 1898-1974), Studies of a nude embrace for 'The Couple', 1943, gelatin silver print, 27.4 x 21 cm, Collection FOMU P/2013/92/2

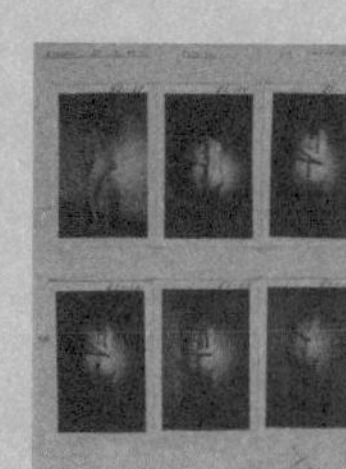

Willy Kessels (BE, 1898-1974), Studies of a nude embrace for 'The Couple', 1943, gelatin silver print, 27.4 x 21 cm, Collection FOMU P/2013/92/3

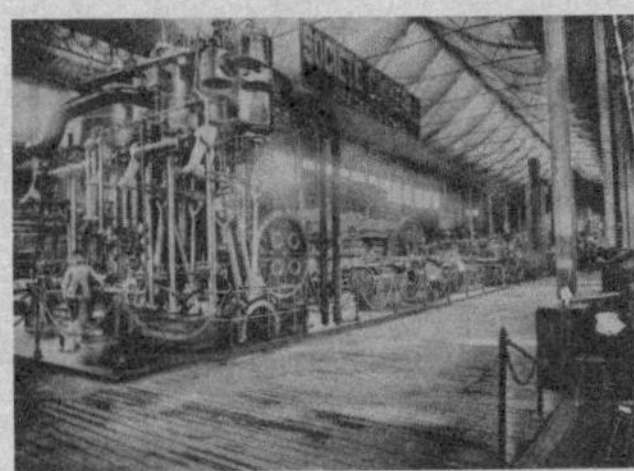

Charles Bernhoeft (LU, 1859-1933), Company John Cockerill Seraing, Antwerp International Exposition, 1894, collotype, 23.9 x 32 cm, Collection FOMU 2016/5/25

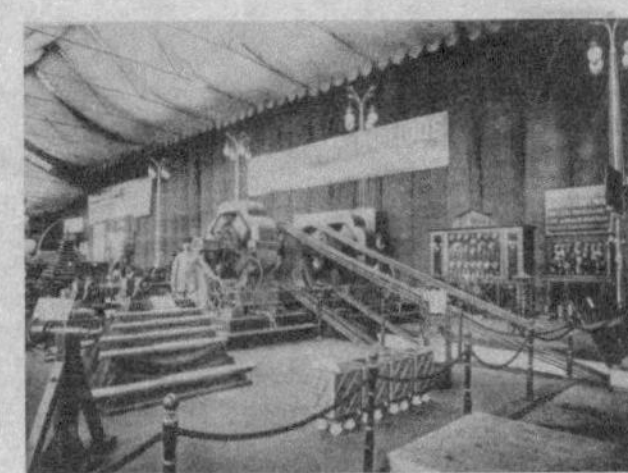

Charles Bernhoeft (LU, 1859-1933), Electricity and hydraulic engineering, Charleroi, Antwerp International Exposition, 1894, collotype, 23.8 x 32 cm, Collection FOMU 2016/5/31

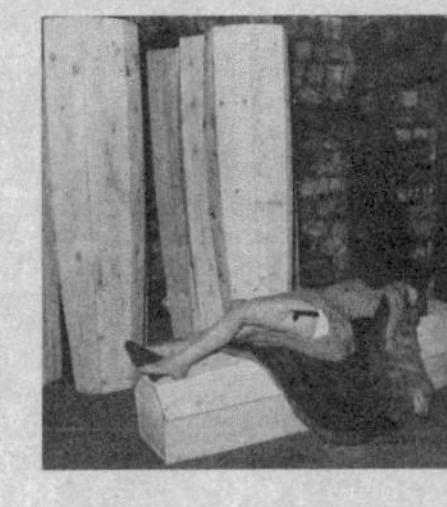

Walter Carone (IT, 1920-1982), Suicide at the morgue, ca. 1950, gelatin silver print, 19.1 x 18.6 cm, Collection FOMU 2019/9

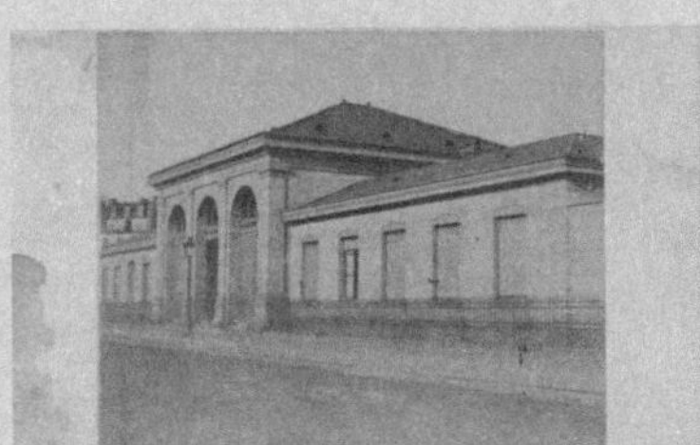

Anonymous, The morgue, Paris, ca. 1870, albumen print, 6.3 x 10.4 cm, Collection FOMU P/1971/299/15

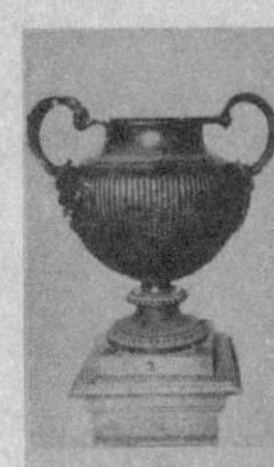

Enrico Verzaschi (IT, 1814-1878), Crater of Mithridates V Eupator, Rome, ca. 1860, albumen print, 10.5 x 6.3 cm, Collection FOMU P/1971/312/30

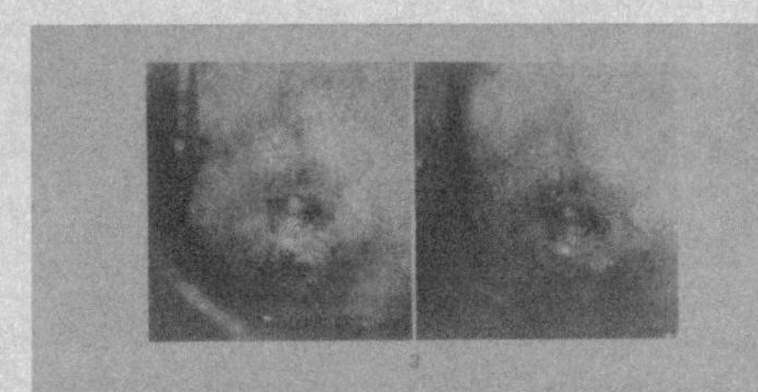

Leo Drüner (DE, 1870-1940), Stereophotograph of colposcopic findings, ca. 1935, gelatin silver print, 6.3 x 12.9 cm, Collection FOMU P/1998/65/22

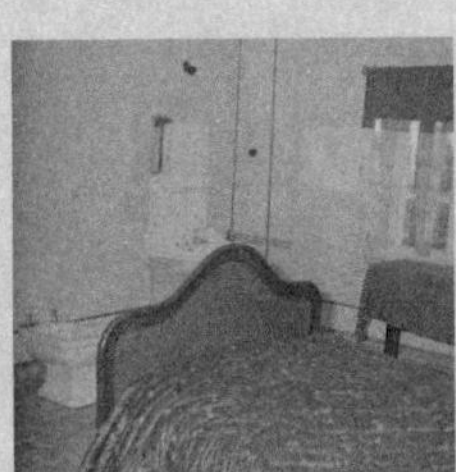

Rik Selleslags (BE, 1911-1982), Retirement home Karlee, Waasmunster, ca. 1944, plastic film negative, 6 x 6 cm, Collection FOMU 2018/45/190/21

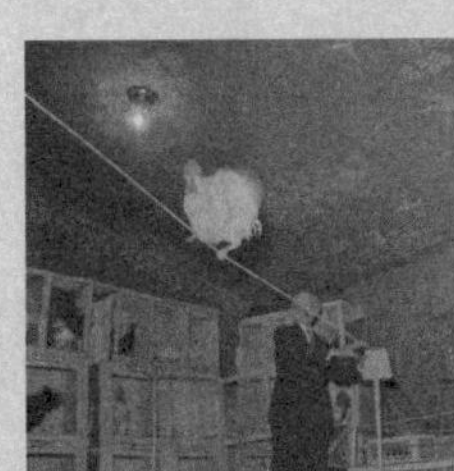

Rik Selleslags (BE, 1911-1982), Coq Savant, 1944, plastic film negative, 6 x 6 cm, Collection FOMU 2018/45/193/9

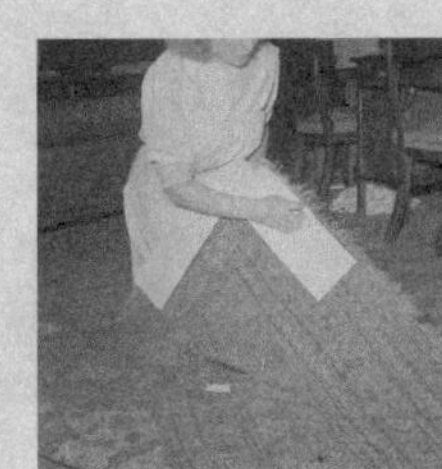

Rik Selleslags (BE, 1911-1982), Household goods, ca. 1944, plastic film negative, 6 x 6 cm, Collection FOMU 2018/45/219/1

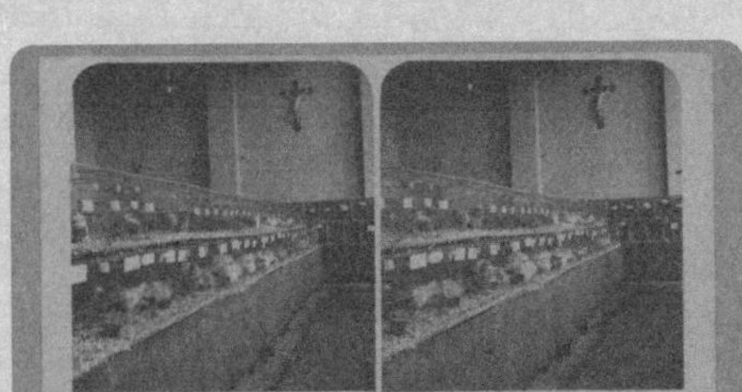

Frans Van De Poel (BE, 1865-1949), Exhibition 'Neerhof', Borgerhout, 1910, gelatin silver print, 9 x 17.8 cm, Collection FOMU P/1984/22/2

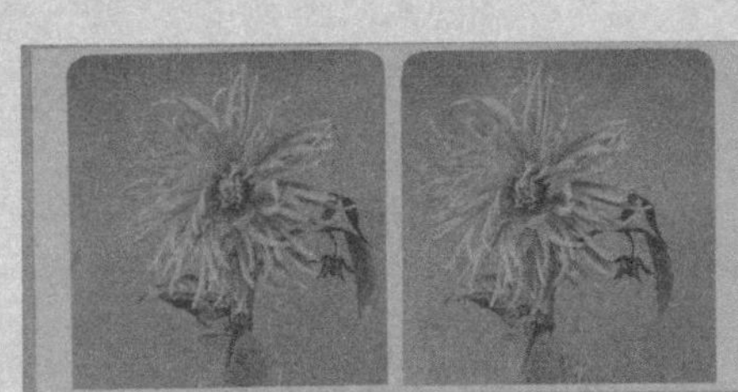

Frans Van De Poel (BE, 1865-1949), Dahlia cactus, ca. 1910, gelatin silver print, 8.4 x 17.5 cm, Collection FOMU P/1985/225/7

Frans Van De Poel (BE, 1865-1949), Spider web, ca. 1910, gelatin silver print, 8.4 x 17.5 cm, Collection FOMU P/1985/225/55

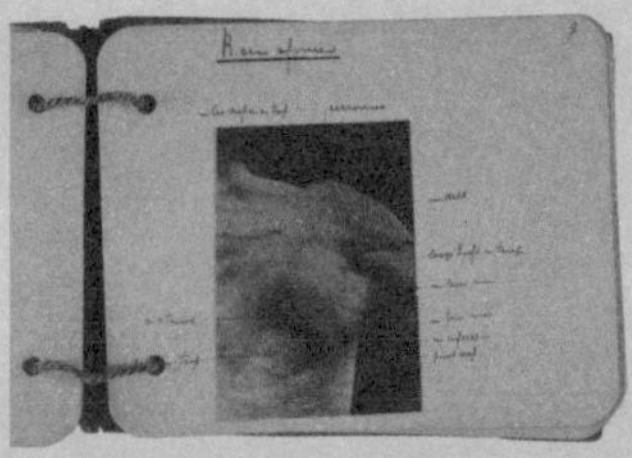

Anonymous, Photo album with studies of the human body, n.d., gelatin silver prints, 11.4 x 14.5 x 1.5 cm, Collection FOMU 2023/32

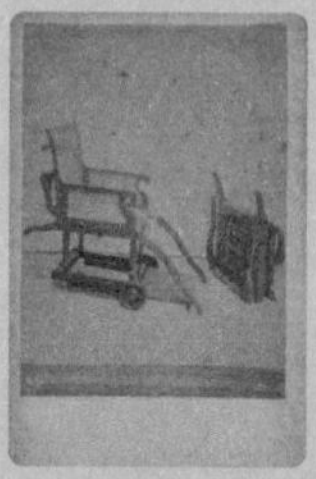

François Smeesters (BE, 1839-1922), Wheelchair, 1888-90, albumen print, 17.1 x 11 cm, Collection FOMU 2023/33/11

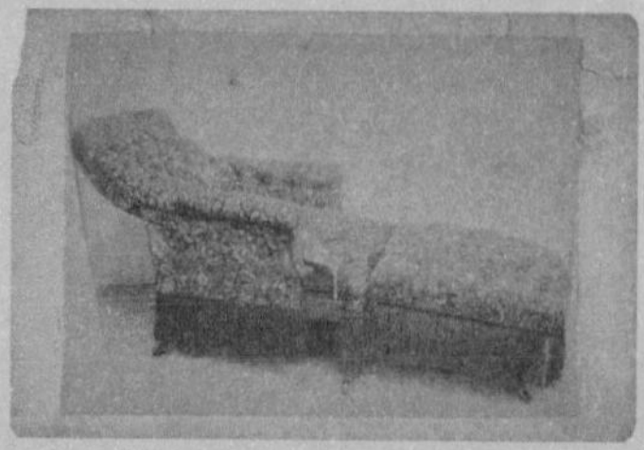

François Smeesters (BE, 1839-1922), Chaise longue, 1888-90, albumen print, 11 x 17.1 cm, Collection FOMU 2023/33/3

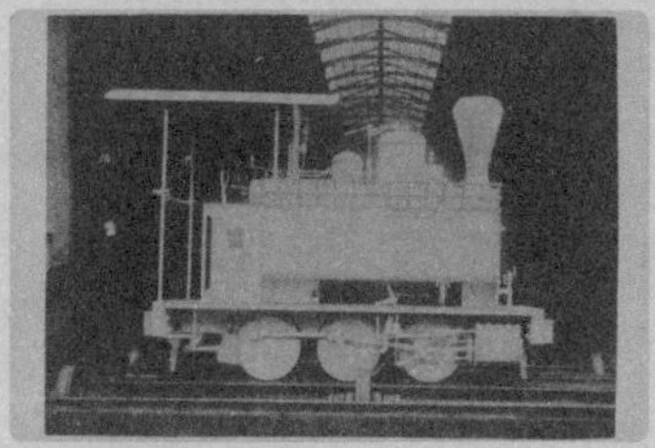

Anonymous, Locomotive, Société Anonyme de Marcinelle & Couillet, ca. 1880, gelatin printing-out paper, 10.3 x 14.5 cm, Collection FOMU P/1965/499/7

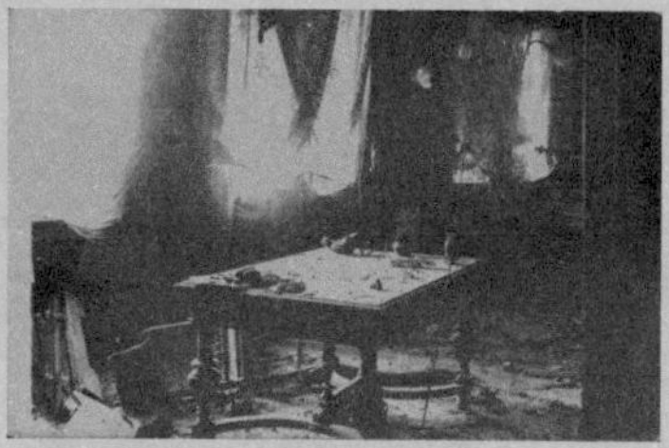

Anonymous, Damaged interior during the First World War, 1914, gelatin silver print, 8.8 x 13.9 cm, Collection FOMU P/1974/43/376/1

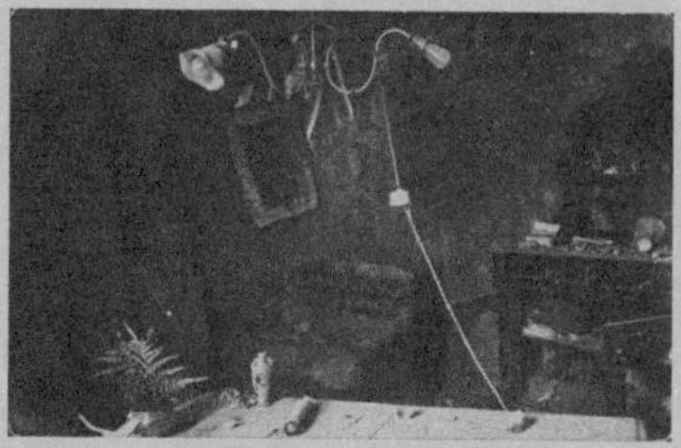

Anonymous, Damaged interior during the First World War, 1914, gelatin silver print, 8.8 x 13.9 cm, Collection FOMU P/1974/43/376/2

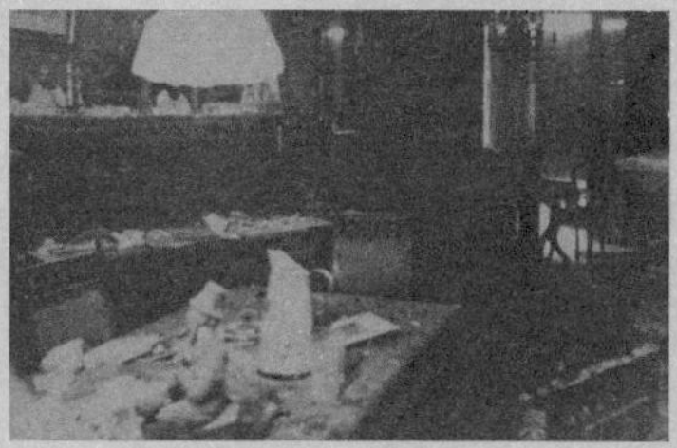

Anonymous, Damaged interior during the First World War, 1914, gelatin silver print, 8.8 x 13.9 cm, Collection FOMU P/1974/43/376/3

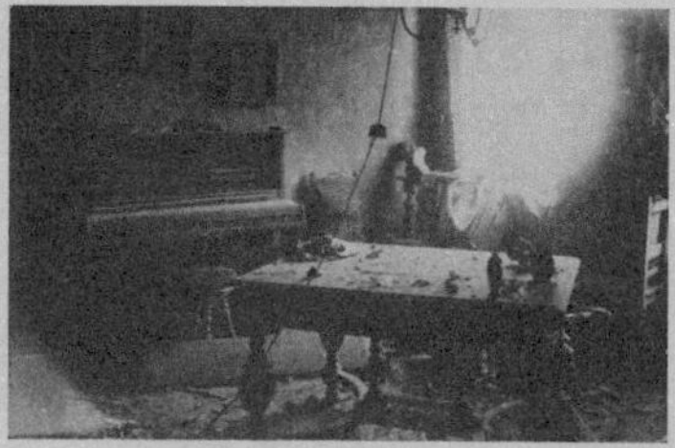

Anonymous, Damaged interior during the First World War, 1914, gelatin silver print, 8.8 x 13.9 cm, Collection FOMU P/1974/43/376/4

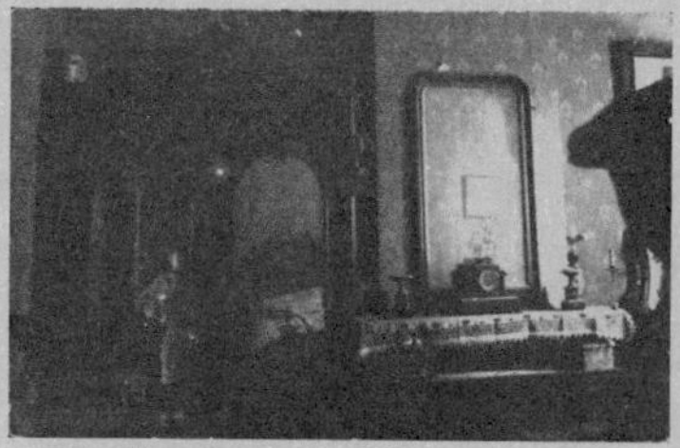

Anonymous, Damaged interior during the First World War, 1914, gelatin silver print, 8.8 x 13.9 cm, Collection FOMU P/1974/43/376/5

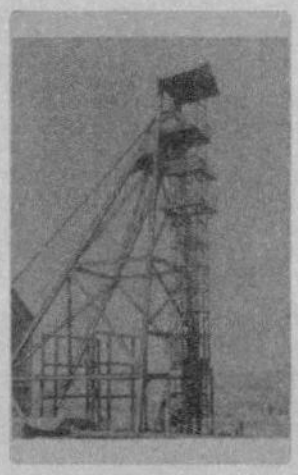

Anonymous, Headframe, Société Anonyme de Marcinelle & Couillet, ca. 1880, gelatin printing-out paper, 14.3 x 10.2 cm, Collection FOMU P/1965/499/8

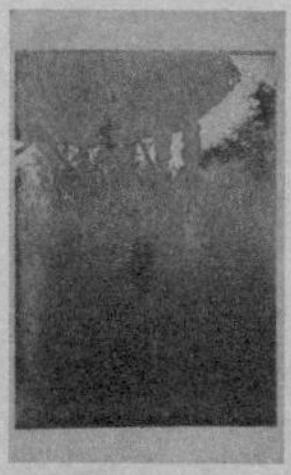

Anonymous, Portait of a woman, 1910-20, gelatin silver print, 13.8 x 8.7 cm, Collection FOMU P/1980/244/31

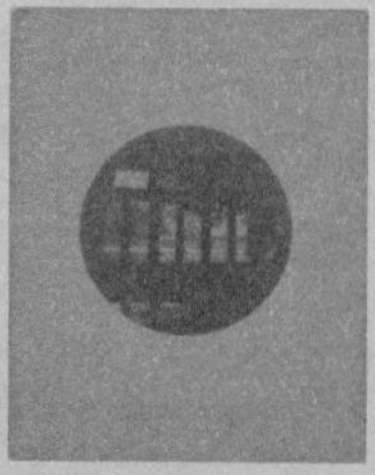

Anonymous, View through windows, 1888-99, gelatin printing-out paper, 13.4 x 10.8 cm, Collection FOMU P/1967/112/1

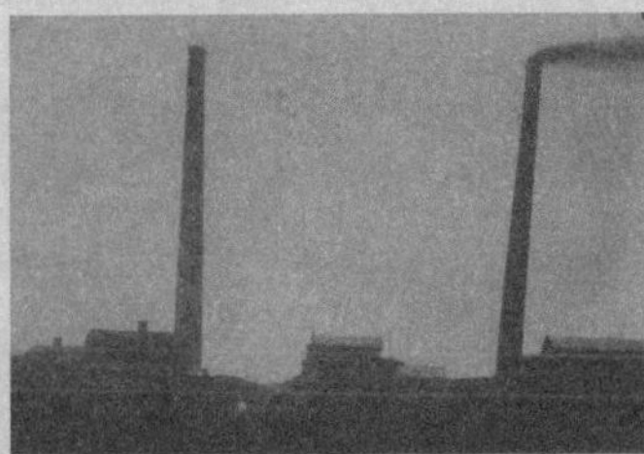

Anonymous, Two chimneys, 1910-20, gelatin silver print, 8.8 x 12.9 cm, Collection FOMU P/1980/243/749

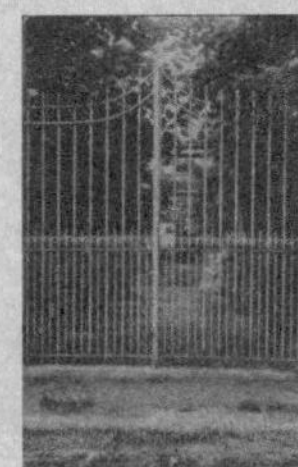

Anonymous, A woman in a fenced garden, 1910-20, gelatin silver print, 13.8 x 8.8 cm, Collection FOMU P/1980/243/767

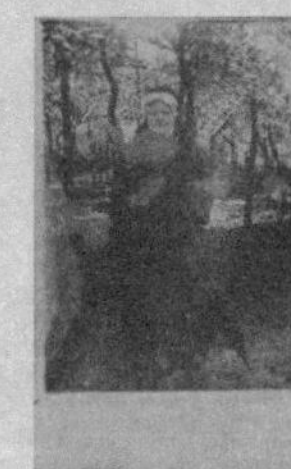

Anonymous, Portrait of a woman, 1910-20, gelatin silver print, 13.8 x 8.8 cm, Collection FOMU P/1980/244/43

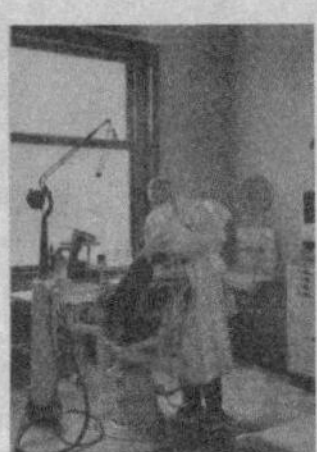

Anonymous, Dentist's room, Sanatorium Elisabeth, Sijsele, ca. 1963, collotype, 14.9 x 10.4 cm, Collection FOMU P/1981/24/21

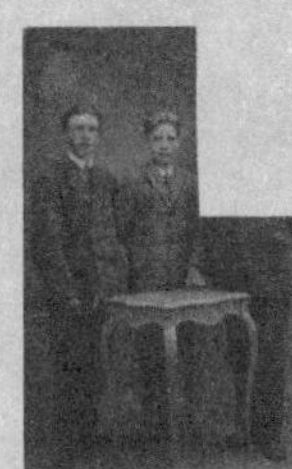

Anonymous, Studio portrait, ca. 1930, gelatin silver print, 13.6 x 8.6 cm, Collection FOMU P/1983/235/4

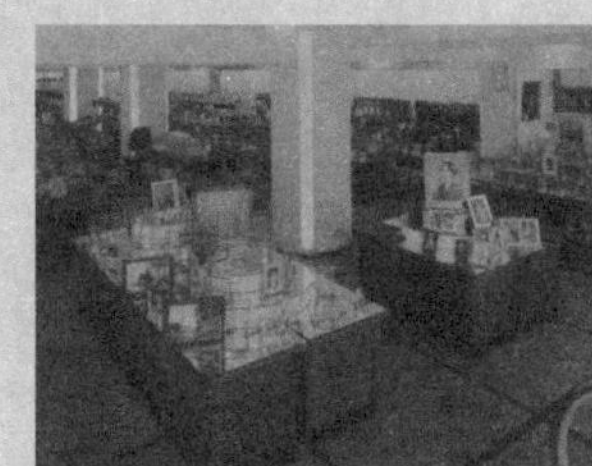

Emile Sergysels (BE, 1889-1967), Interior of the Grand Bazar department store in Antwerp, n.d., gelatin silver print, 16.4 x 21.8 cm, Collection FOMU 2021/39/2

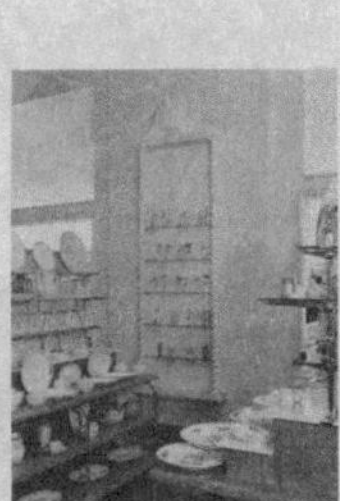

Emile Sergysels (BE, 1889-1967), Interior of the Grand Bazar department store in Antwerp, n.d., gelatin silver print, 22.5 x 16.9 cm, Collection FOMU 2021/39/3

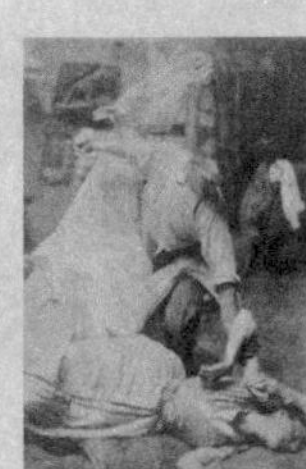

Jacques de Lalaing (BE, 1858-1917), Study of a woman, man and horse, 1883-1914, albumen print, 17.1 x 11.9 cm, Collection FOMU 2015/59/162

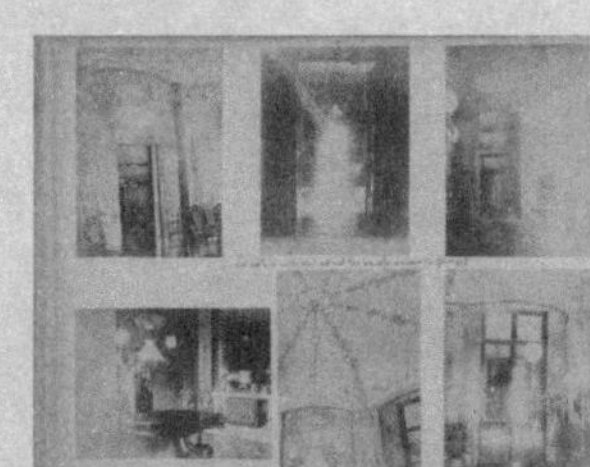

Anonymous, Photo album of the Belgian noble family Vilain XIIII, 1896-1924, various techniques, 27 x 37 x 7 cm, Collection FOMU 2022/13

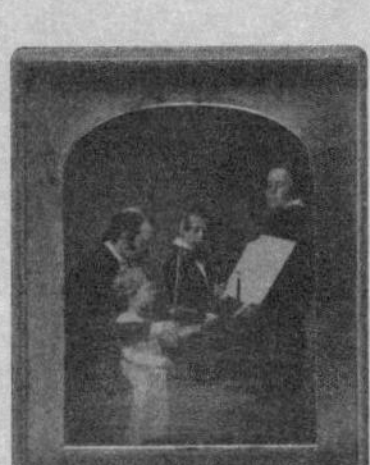

Anonymous, A man and three children with a violin, 1839-60, daguerreotype, 14 x 11.5 cm, Collection FOMU 2022/46

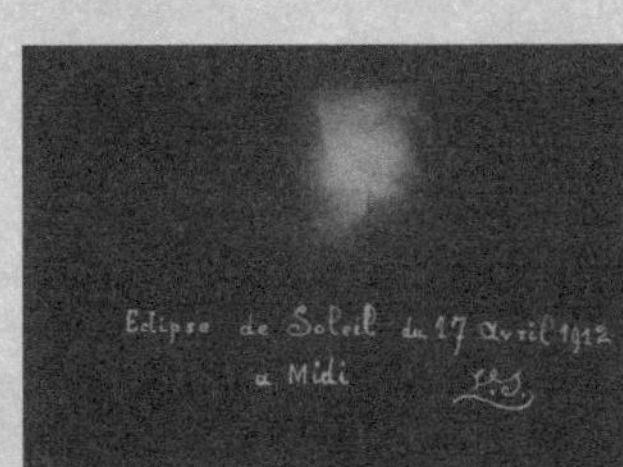

Anonymous, Solar eclipse, 17/04/1912, gelatin printing-out paper, 8 x 11 cm, Collection FOMU 2023/8/2

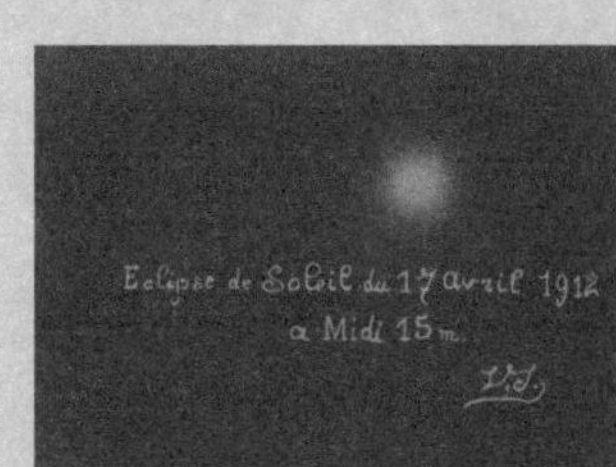

Anonymous, Solar eclipse, 17/04/1912, gelatin printing-out paper, 8 x 11 cm, Collection FOMU 2023/8/1

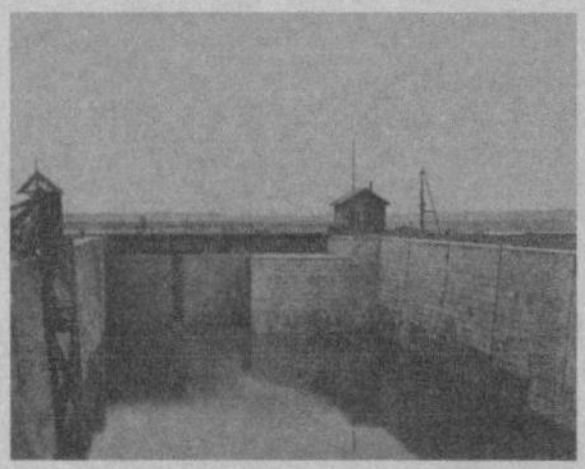

Gustave Hergaux (FR, 1821-1893), New maritime constructions in Antwerp by Couvreux & Hersent, 1877-84, albumen prints, 36.5 x 51 x 6 cm, Collection FOMU P/1992/191

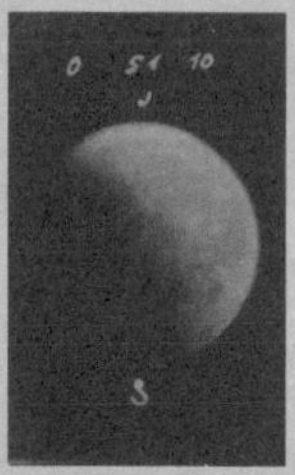

Anonymous, Lunar eclipse, n.d., gelatin silver print, 13.7 x 8.8 cm, Collection FOMU 2023/9/6

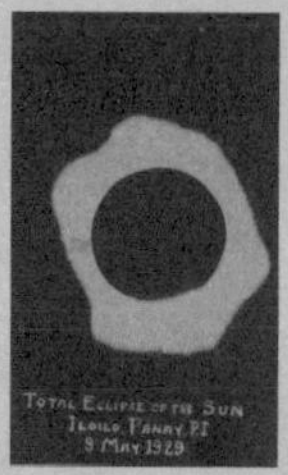

Anonymous, Total solar eclipse, Iloilo, Panay, 09/05/1929, gelatin silver print, 13.8 x 8.7 cm, Collection FOMU 2023/10

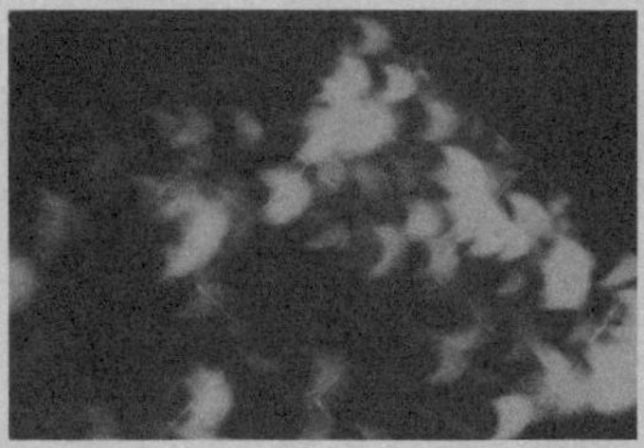

Anonymous, Solar eclipse, 29/04/1976, gelatin silver print, 8.5 x 12.7 cm, Collection FOMU 2023/11

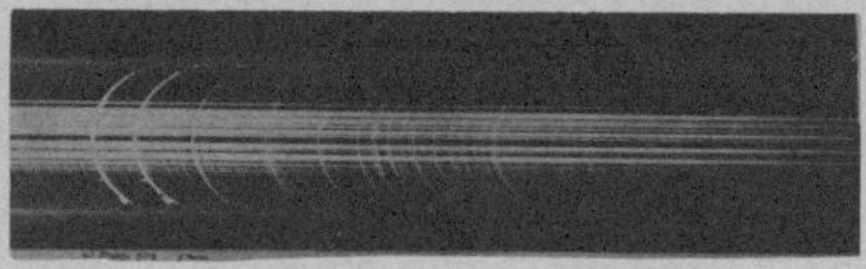

Anonymous, Gas, n.d., gelatin silver print, 5.7 x 20.8 cm, Collection FOMU 2023/14

Anonymous, Saturn, s.d., gelatin silver print, 12.4 x 18 cm, Collection FOMU 2023/12

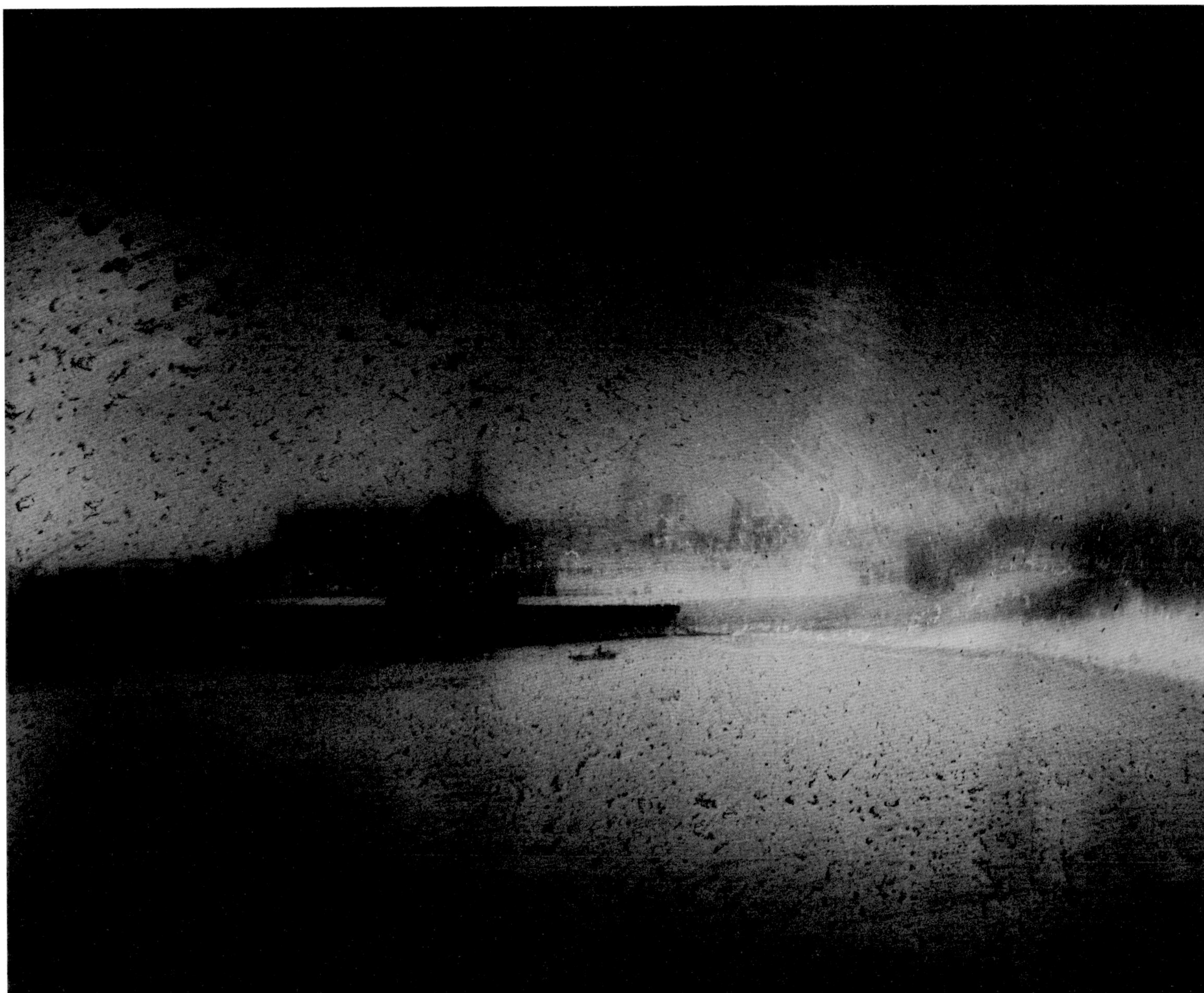

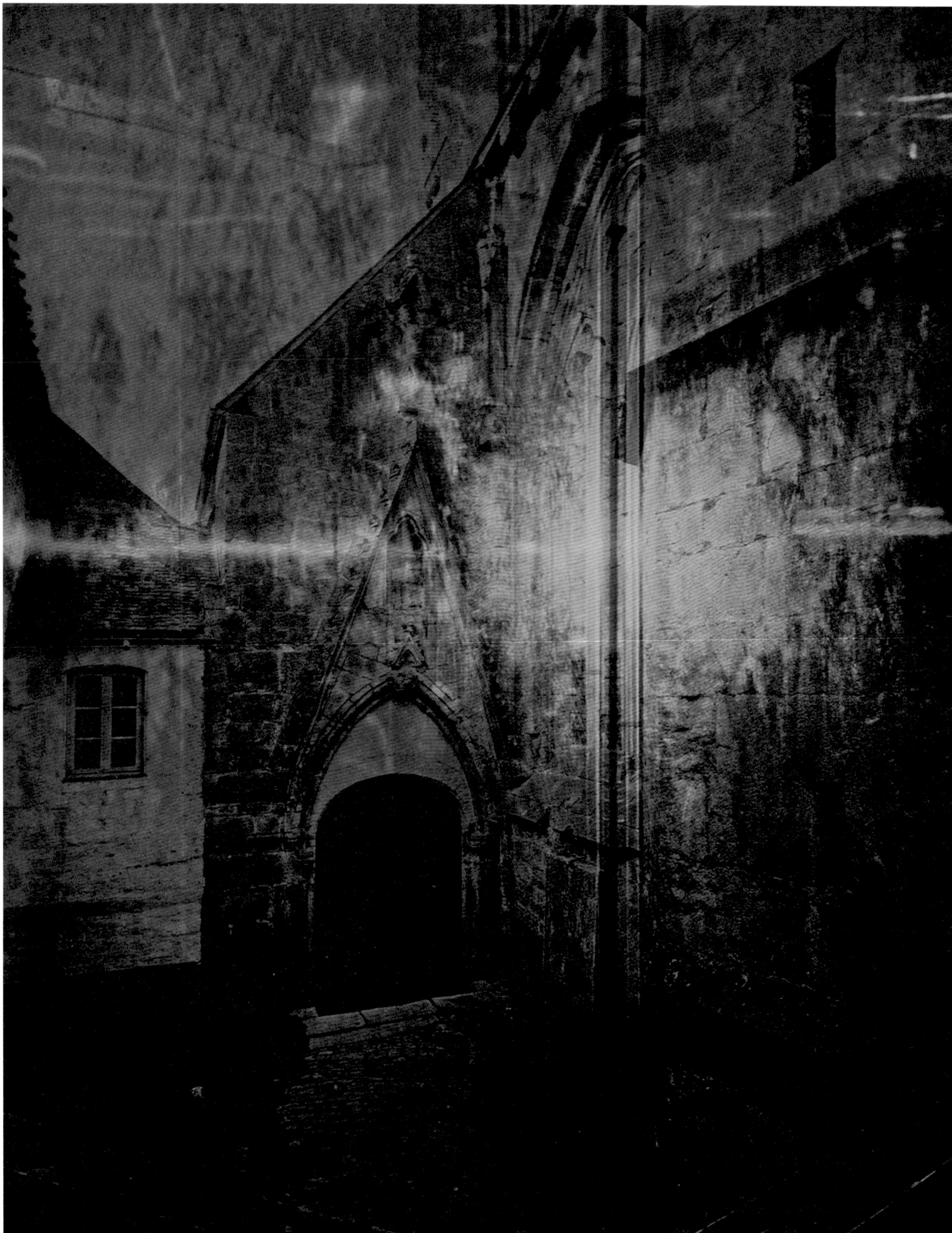

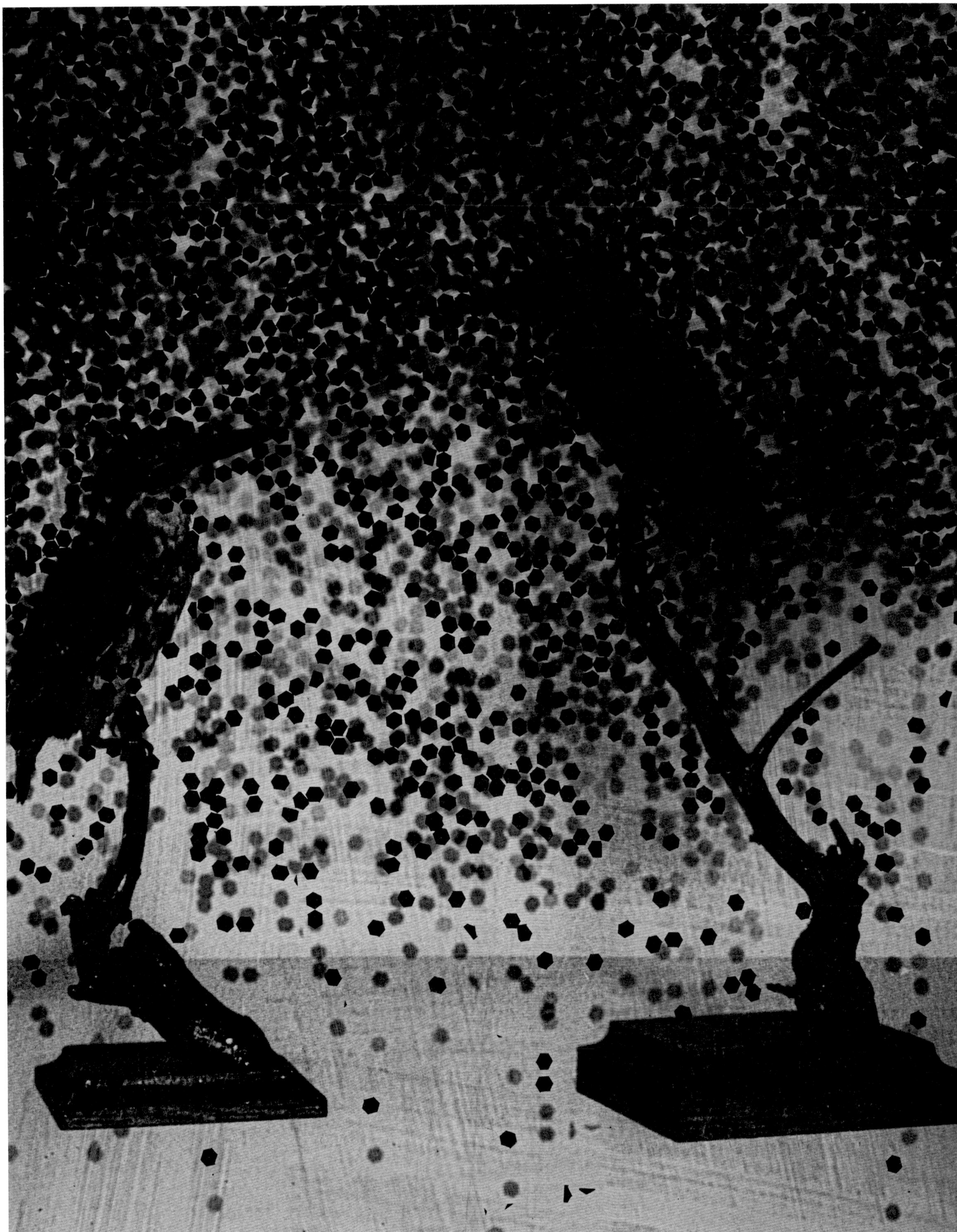

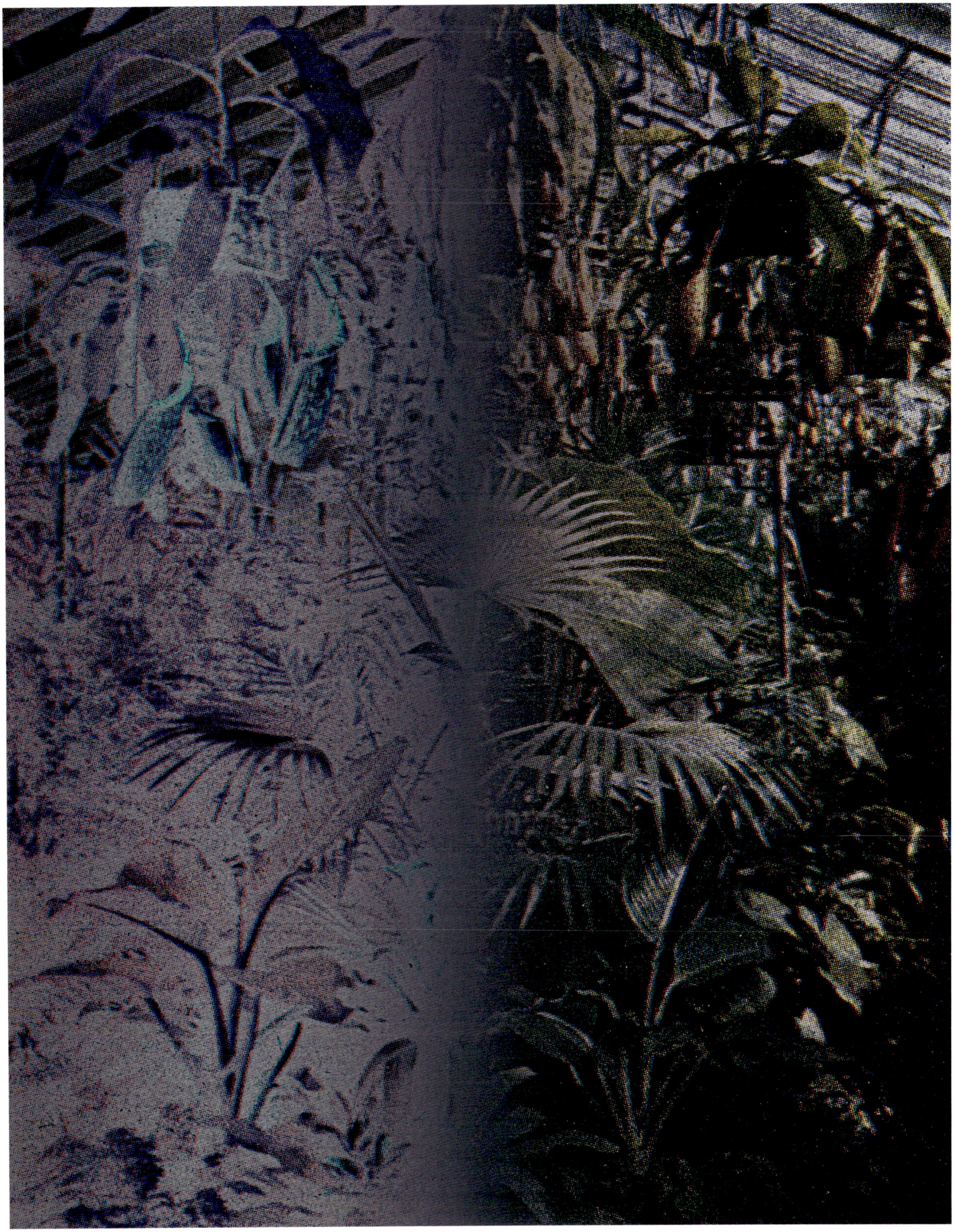

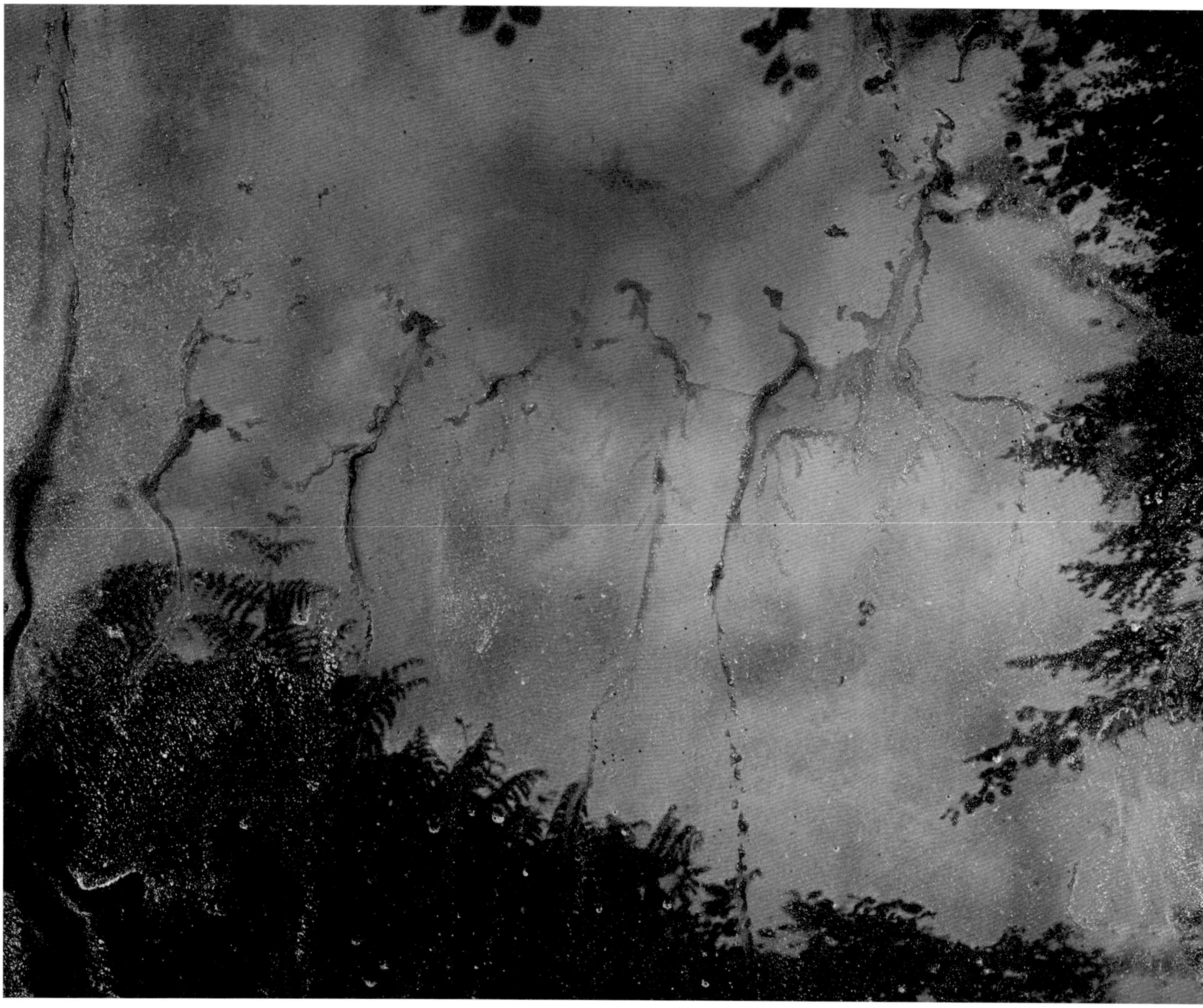

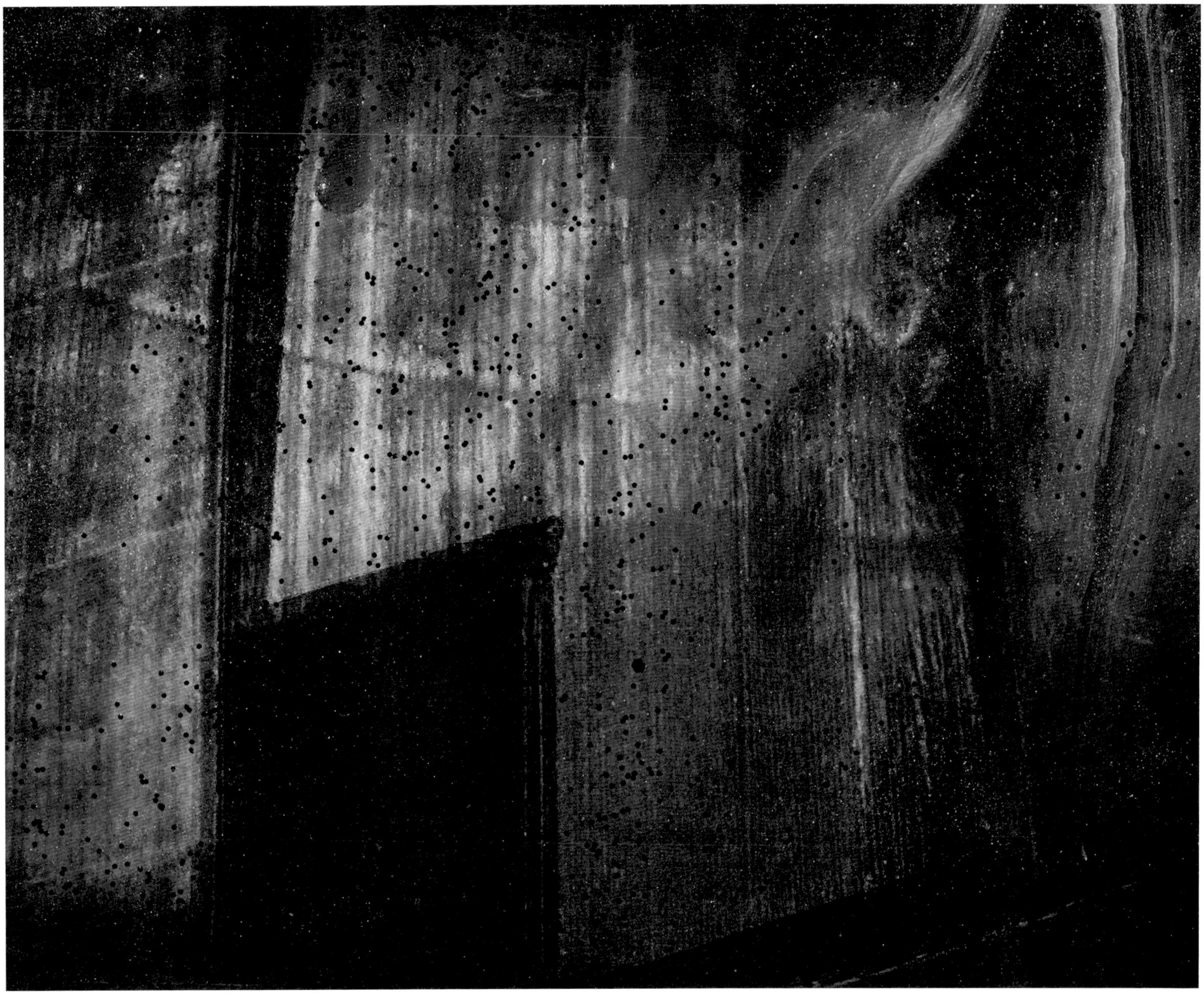

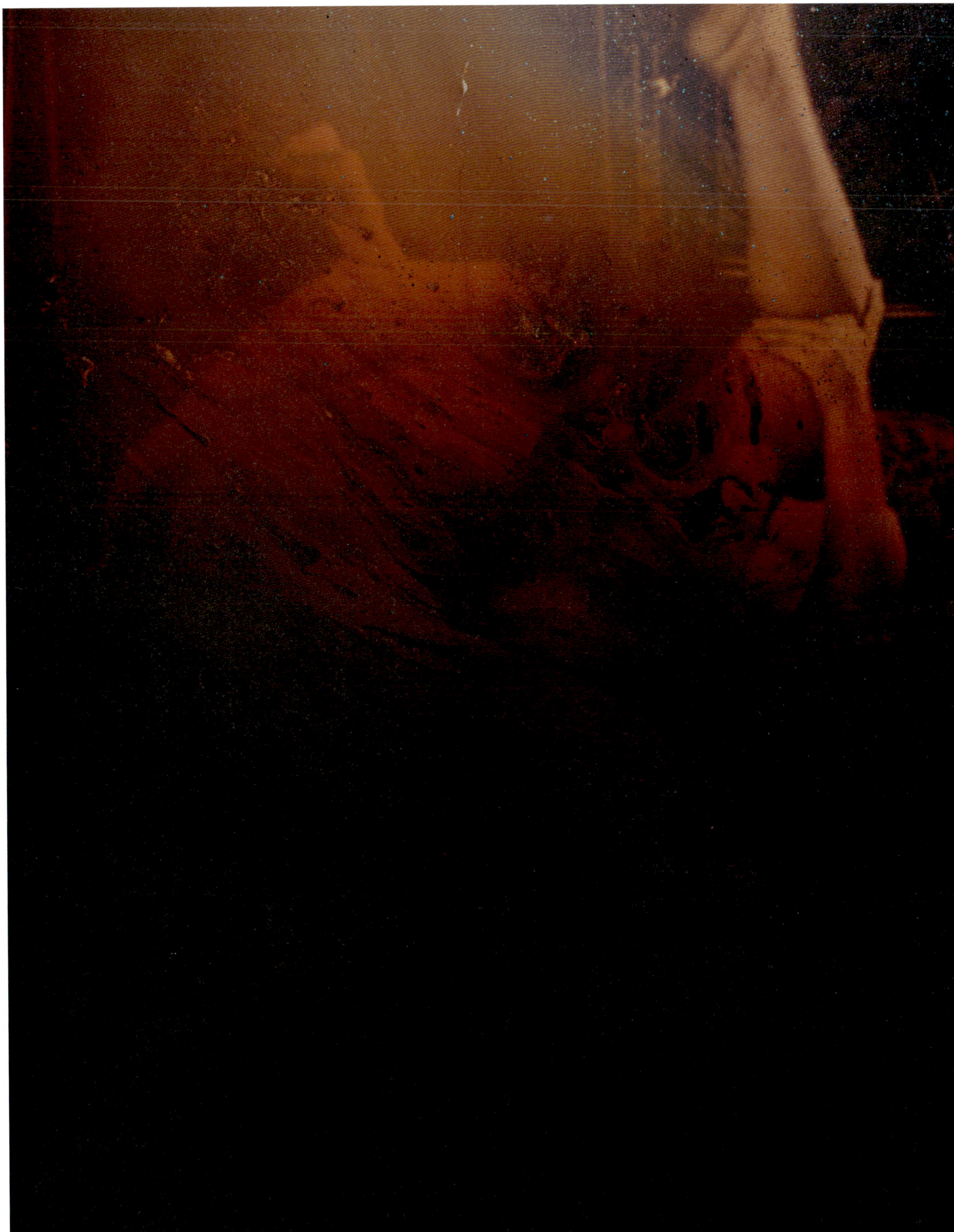

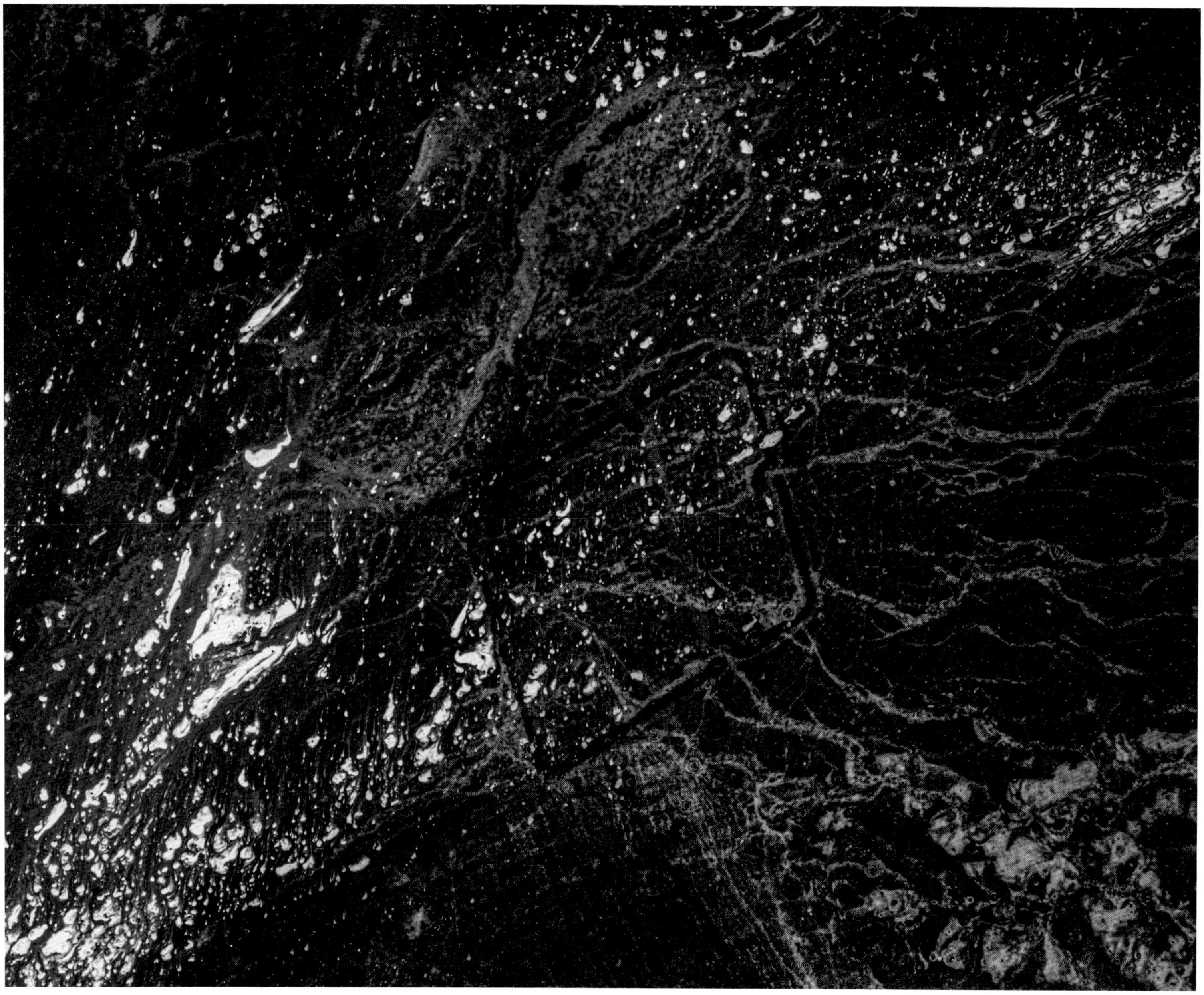

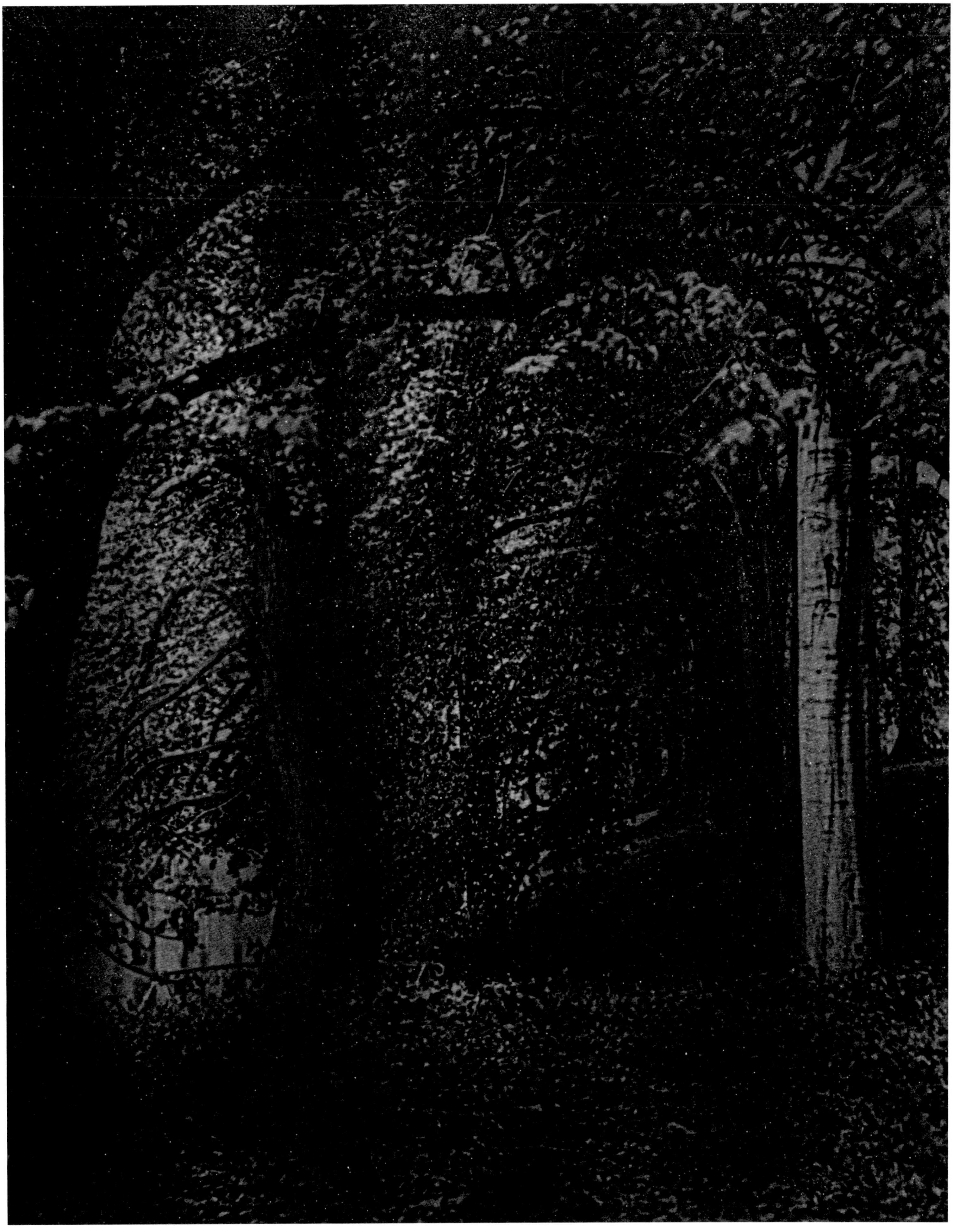

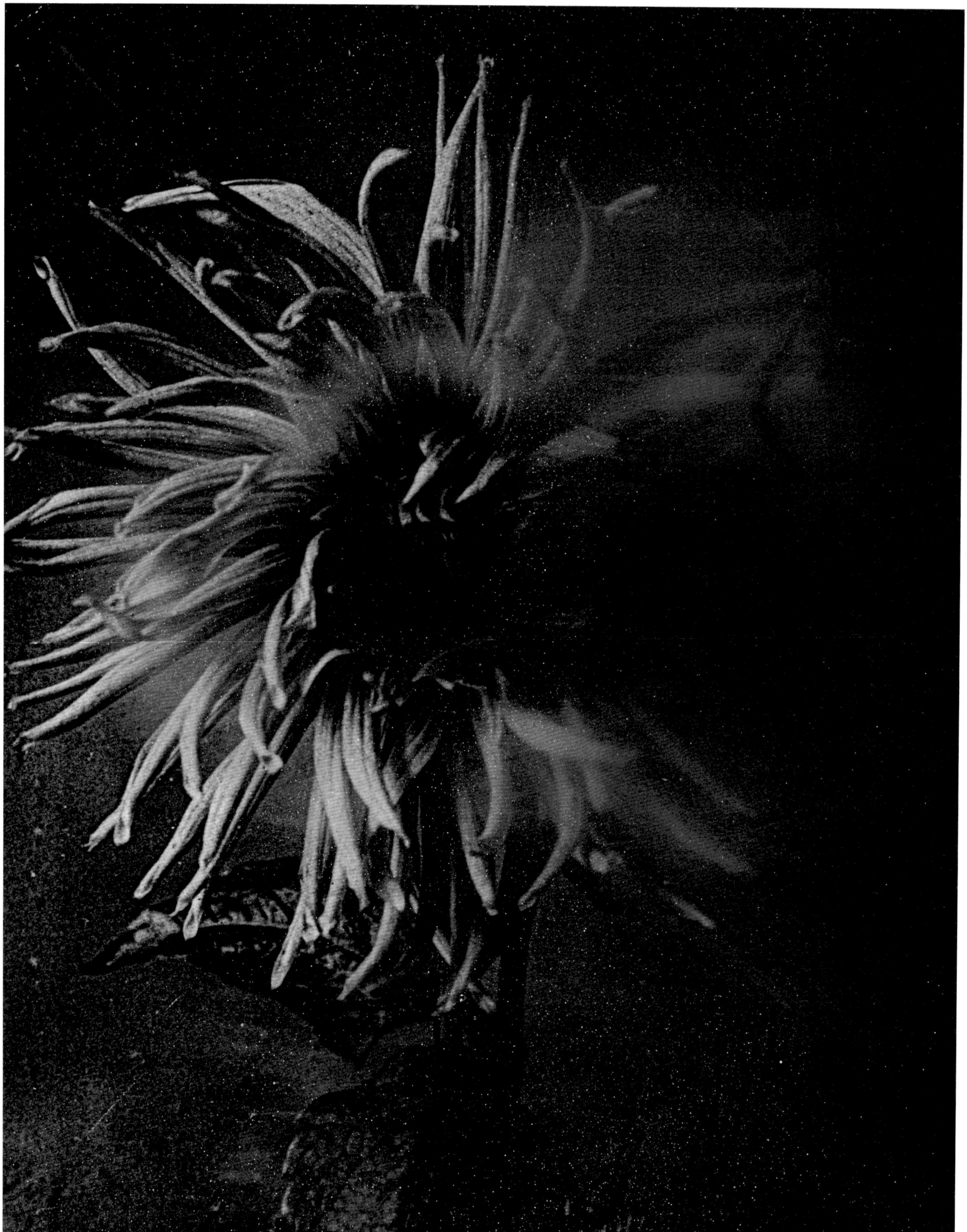

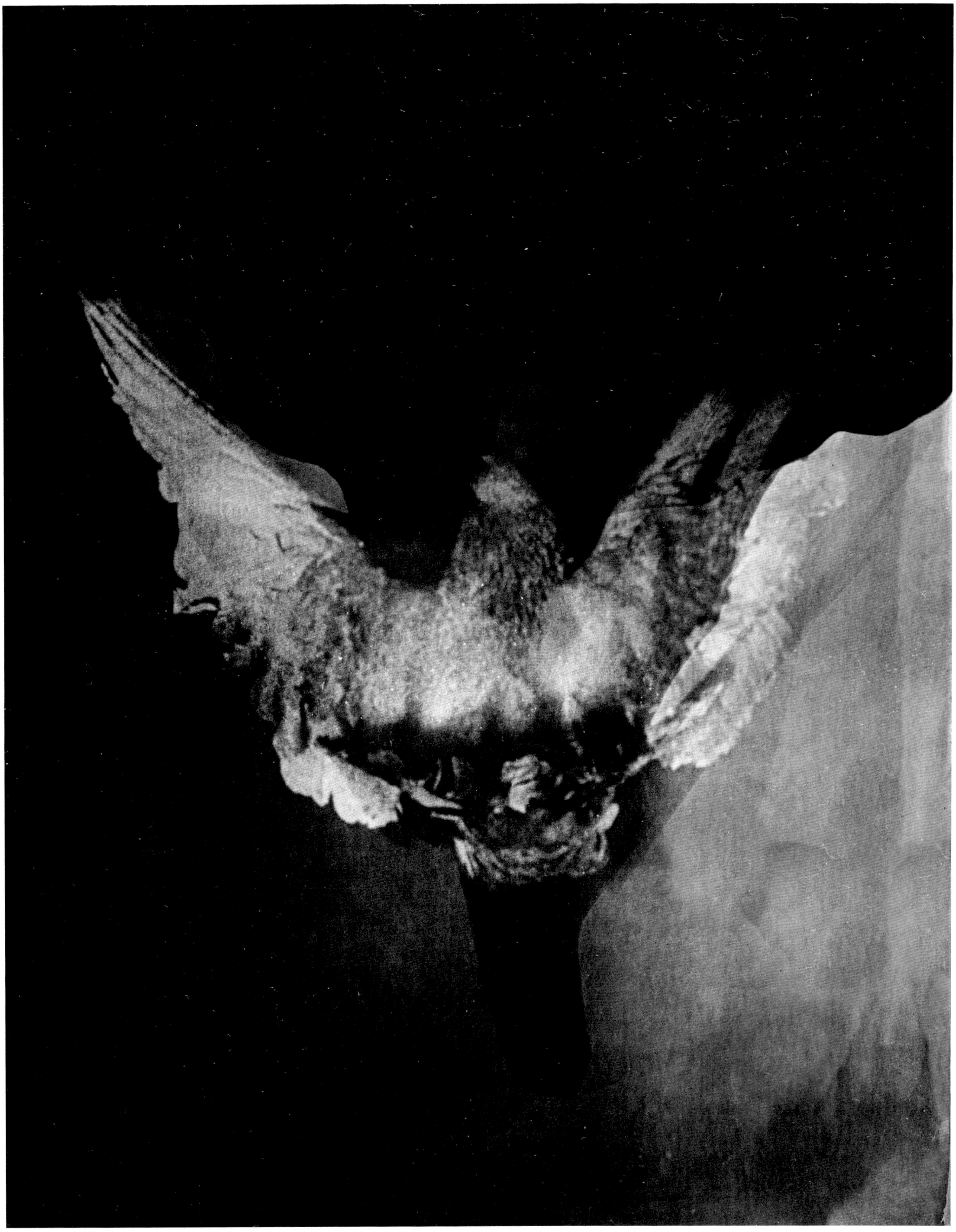

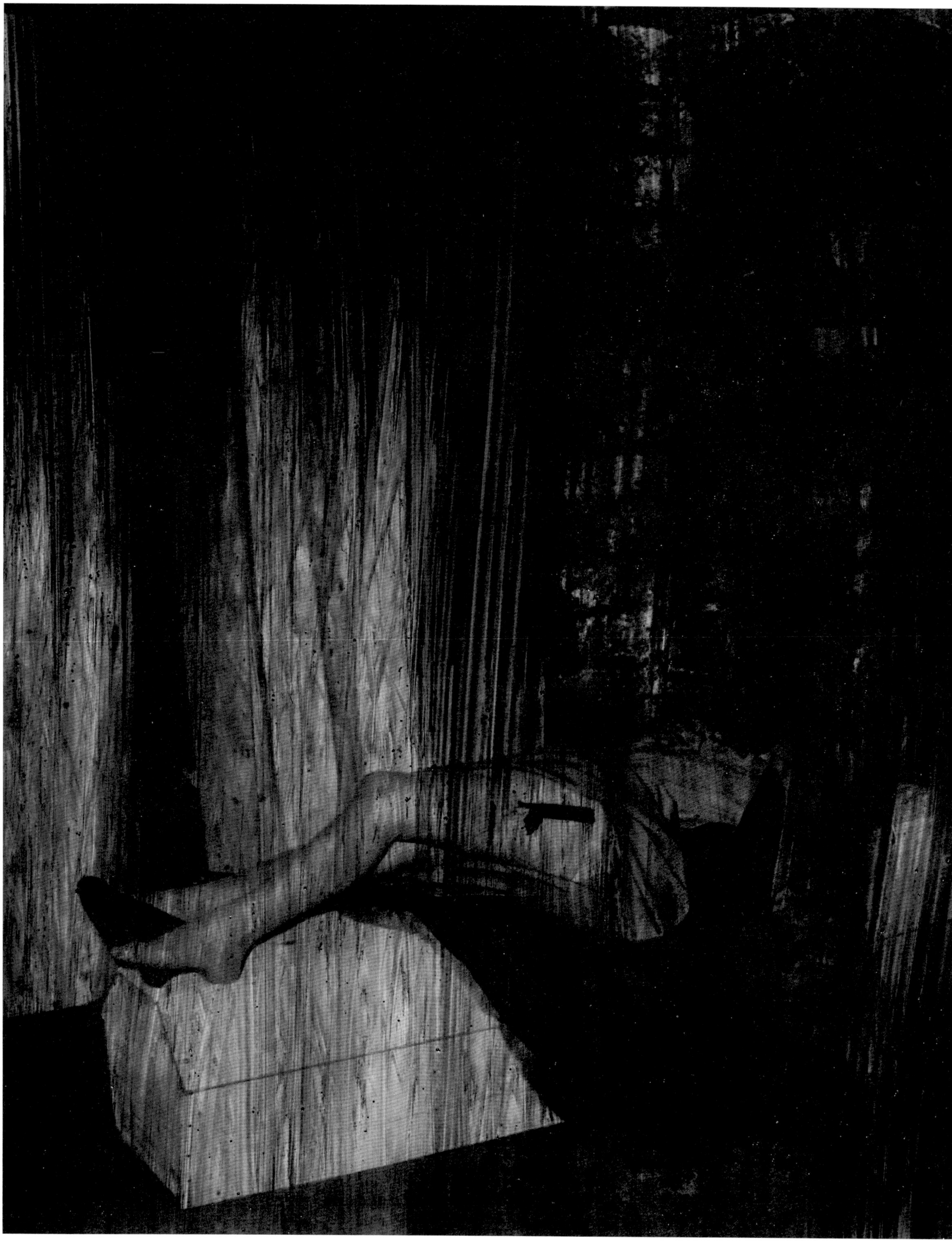

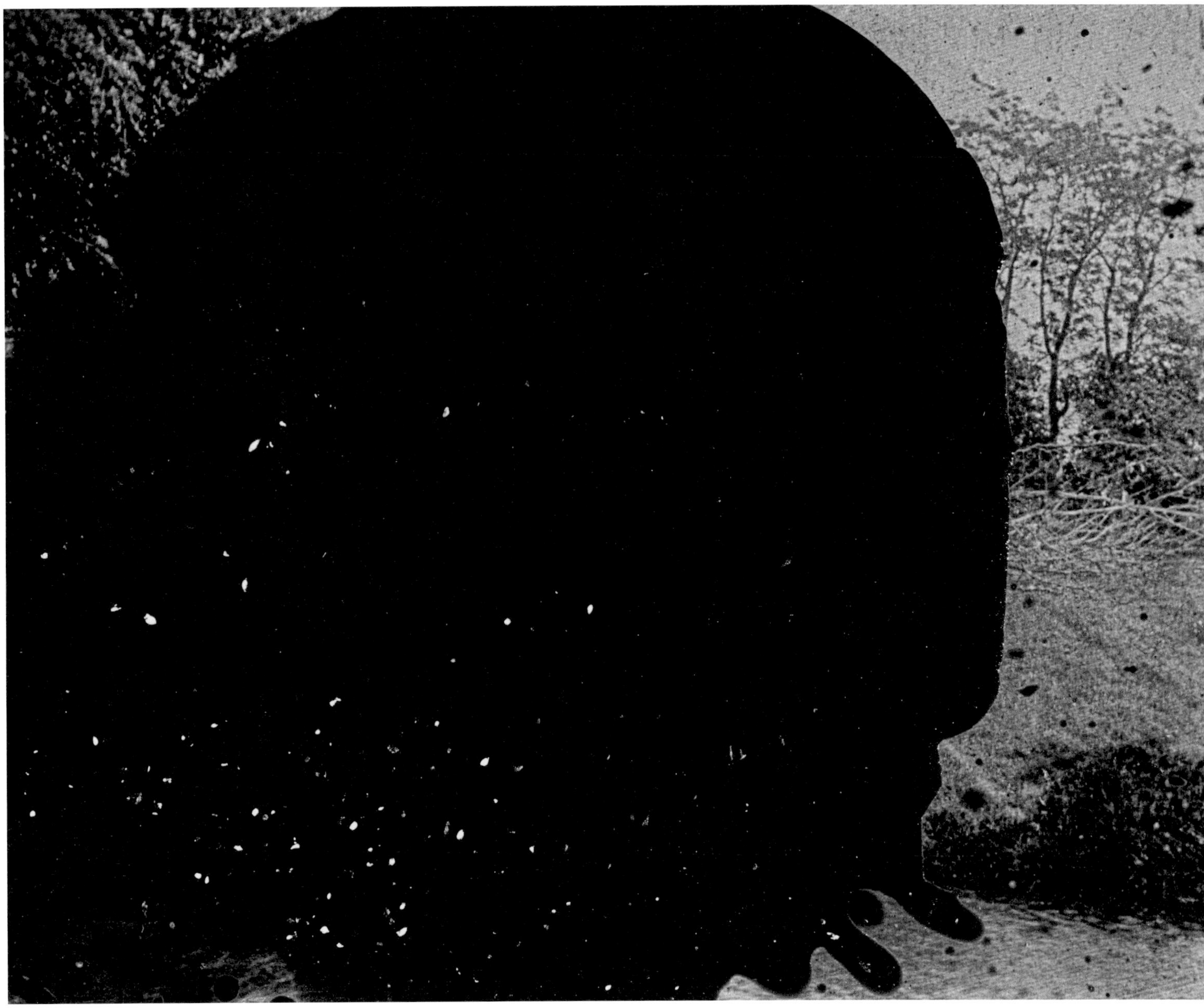

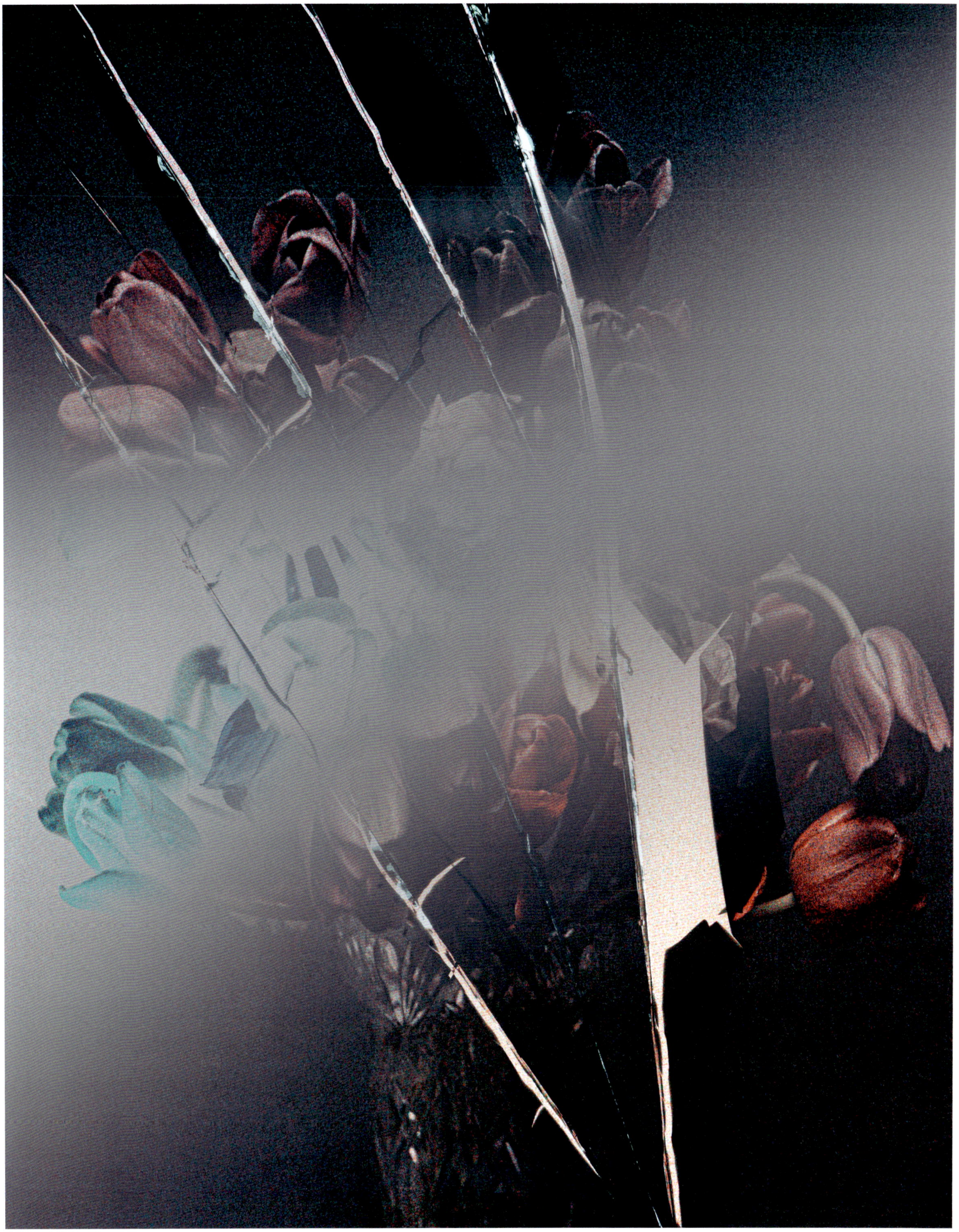

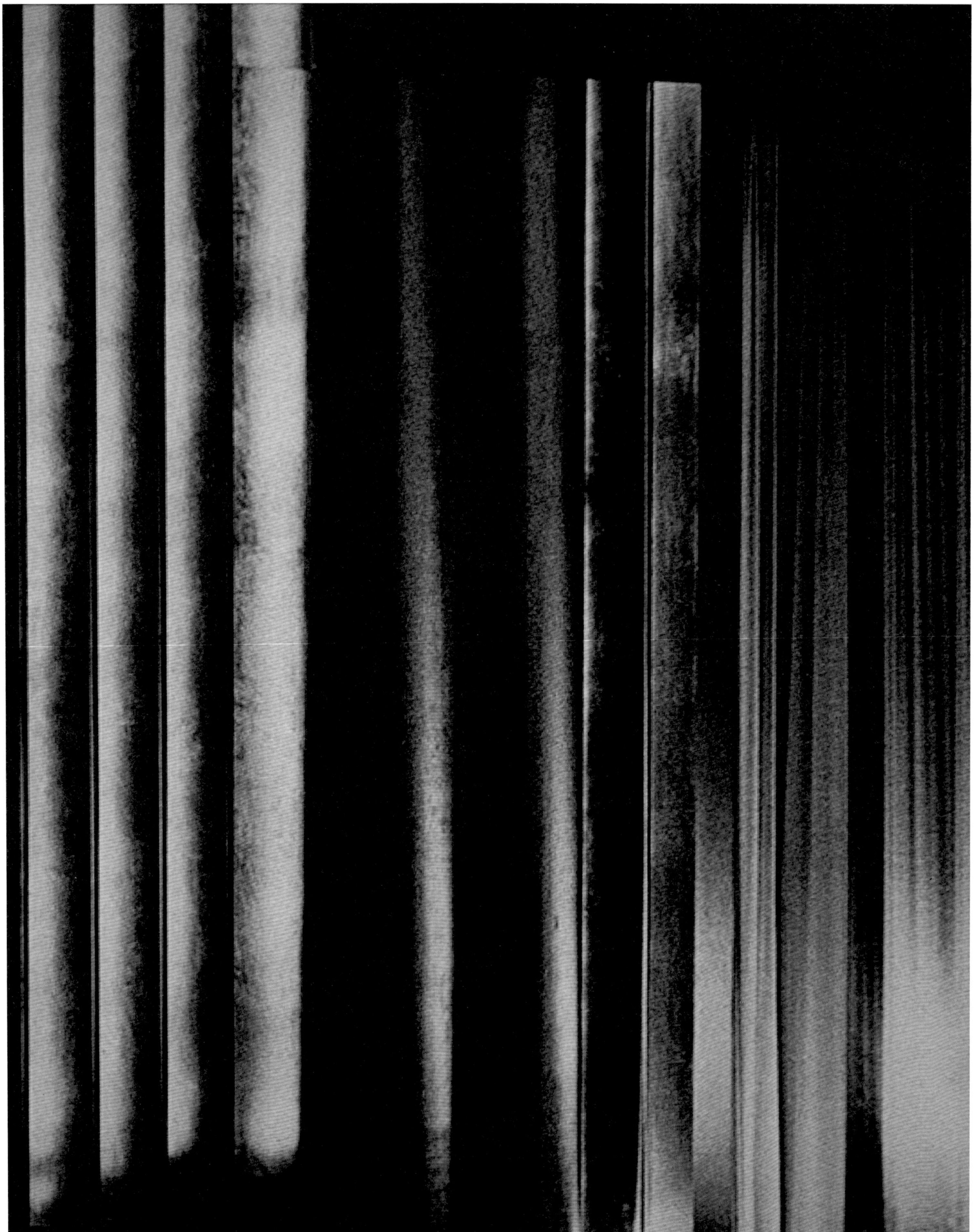

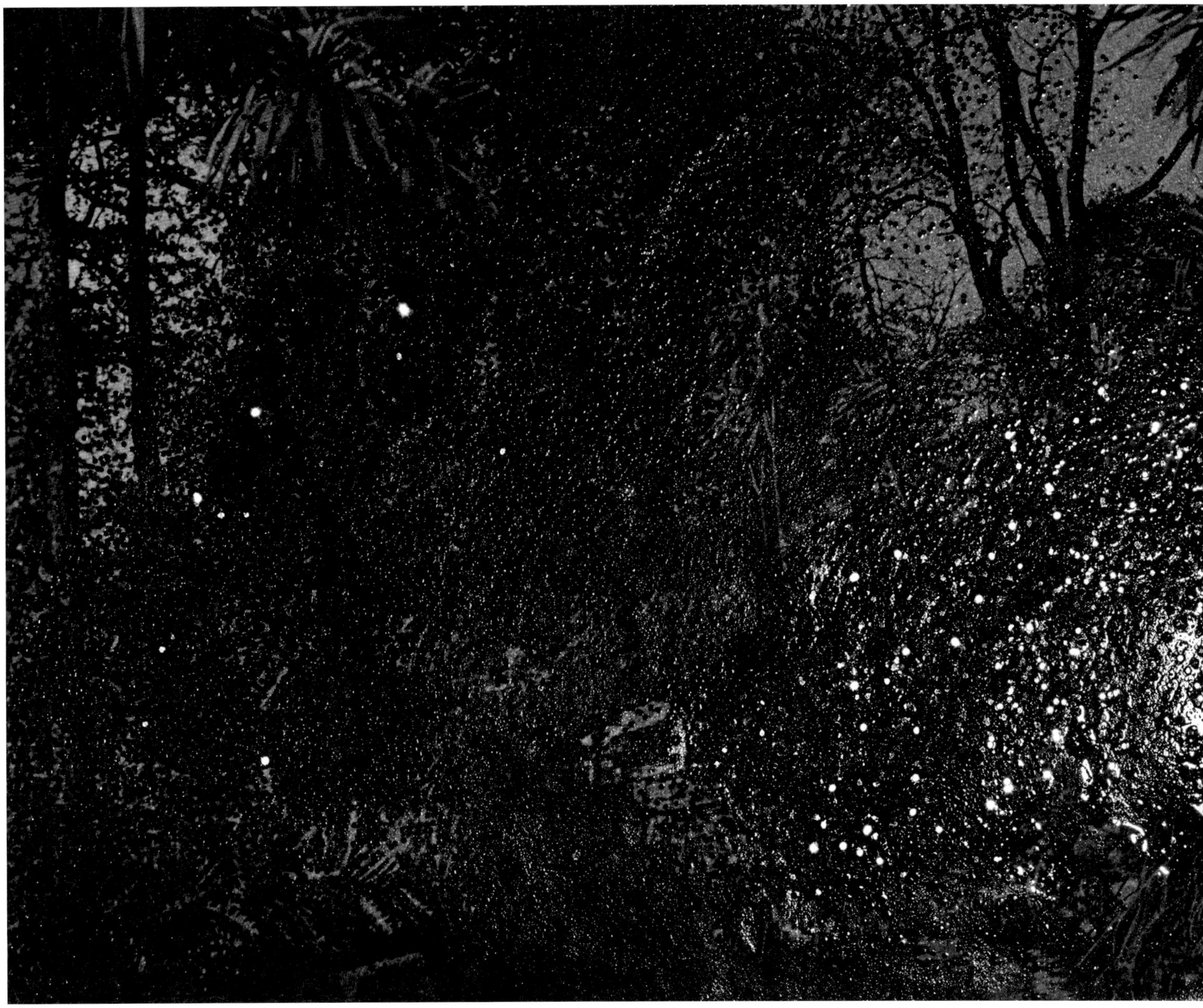

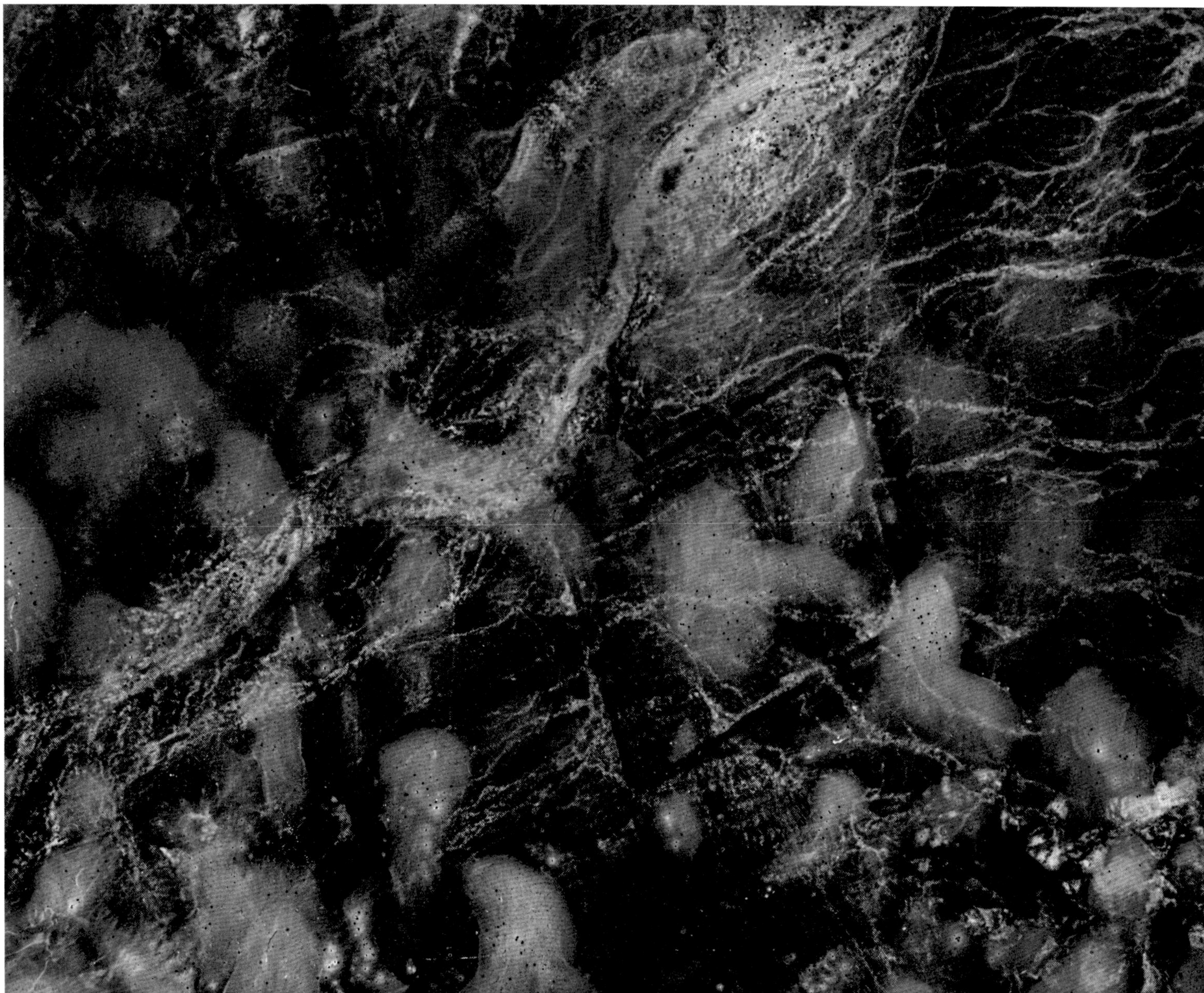

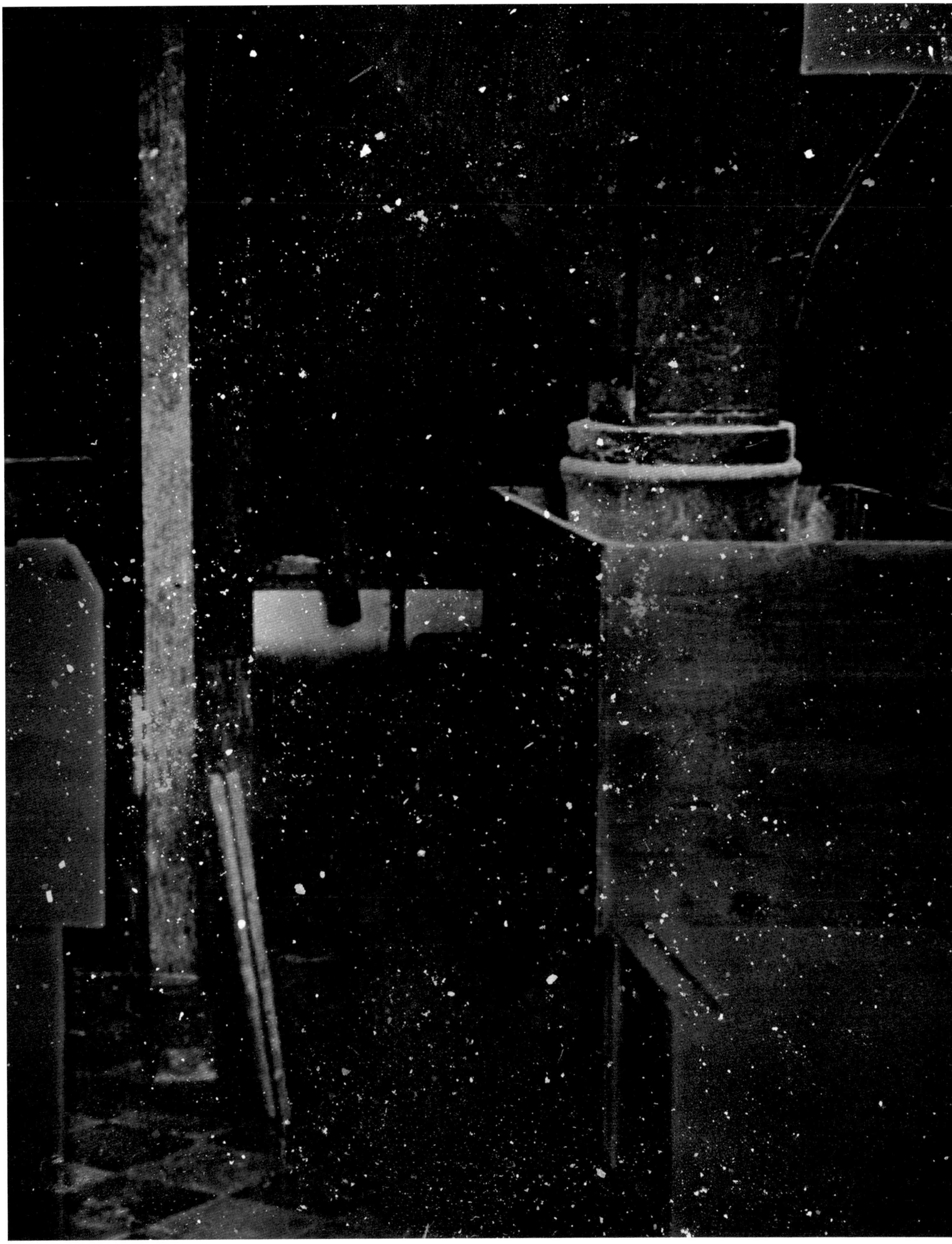

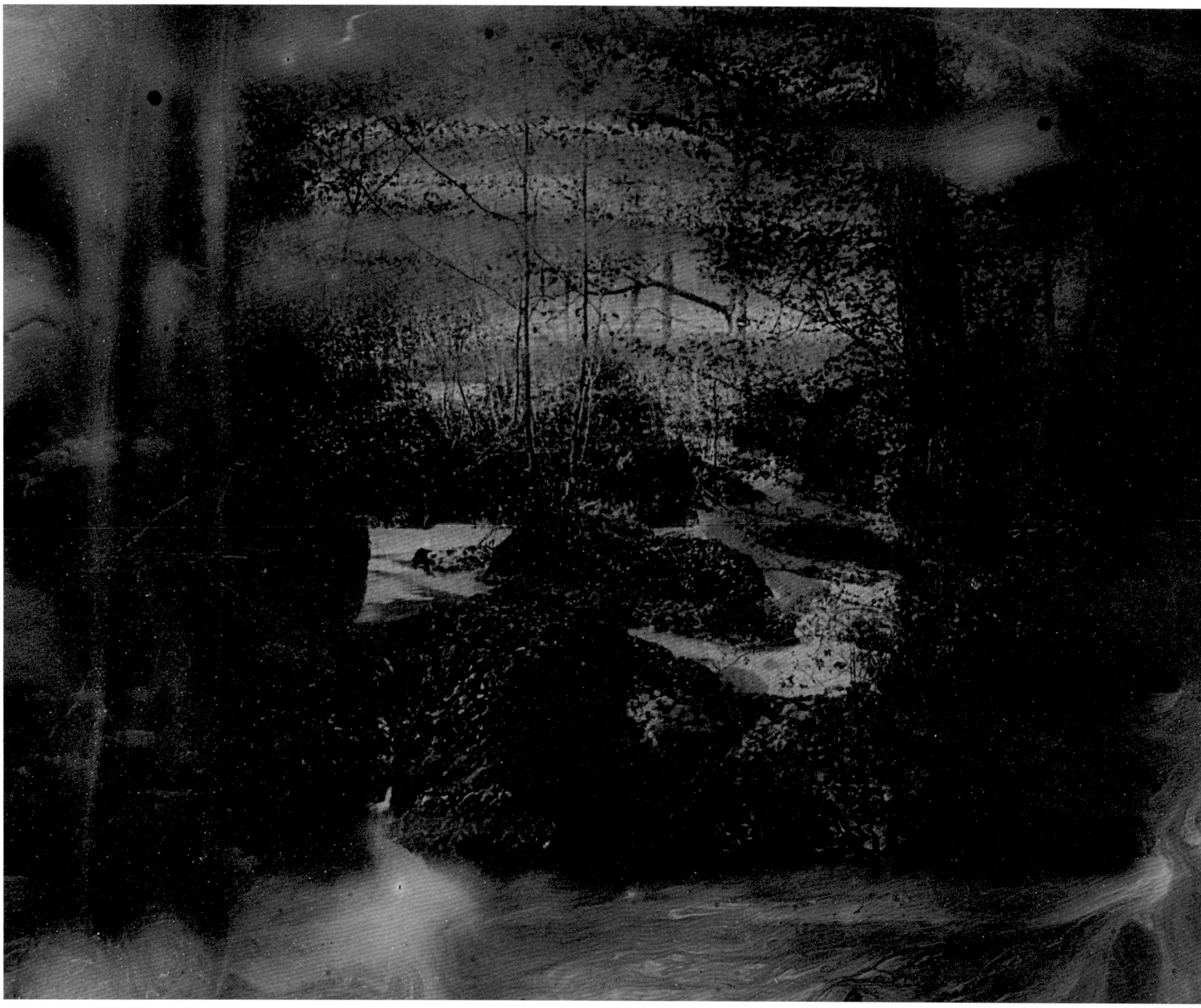

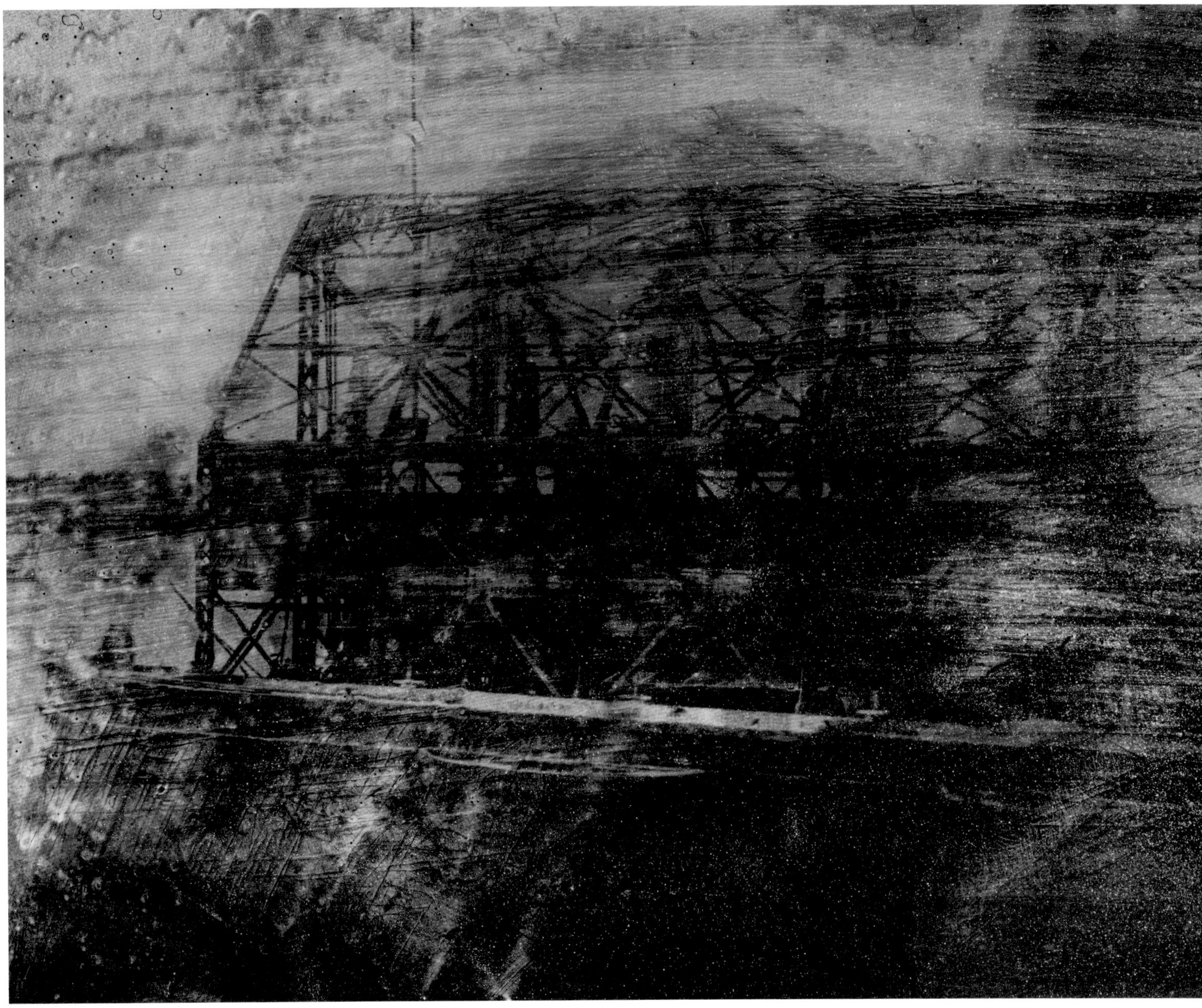

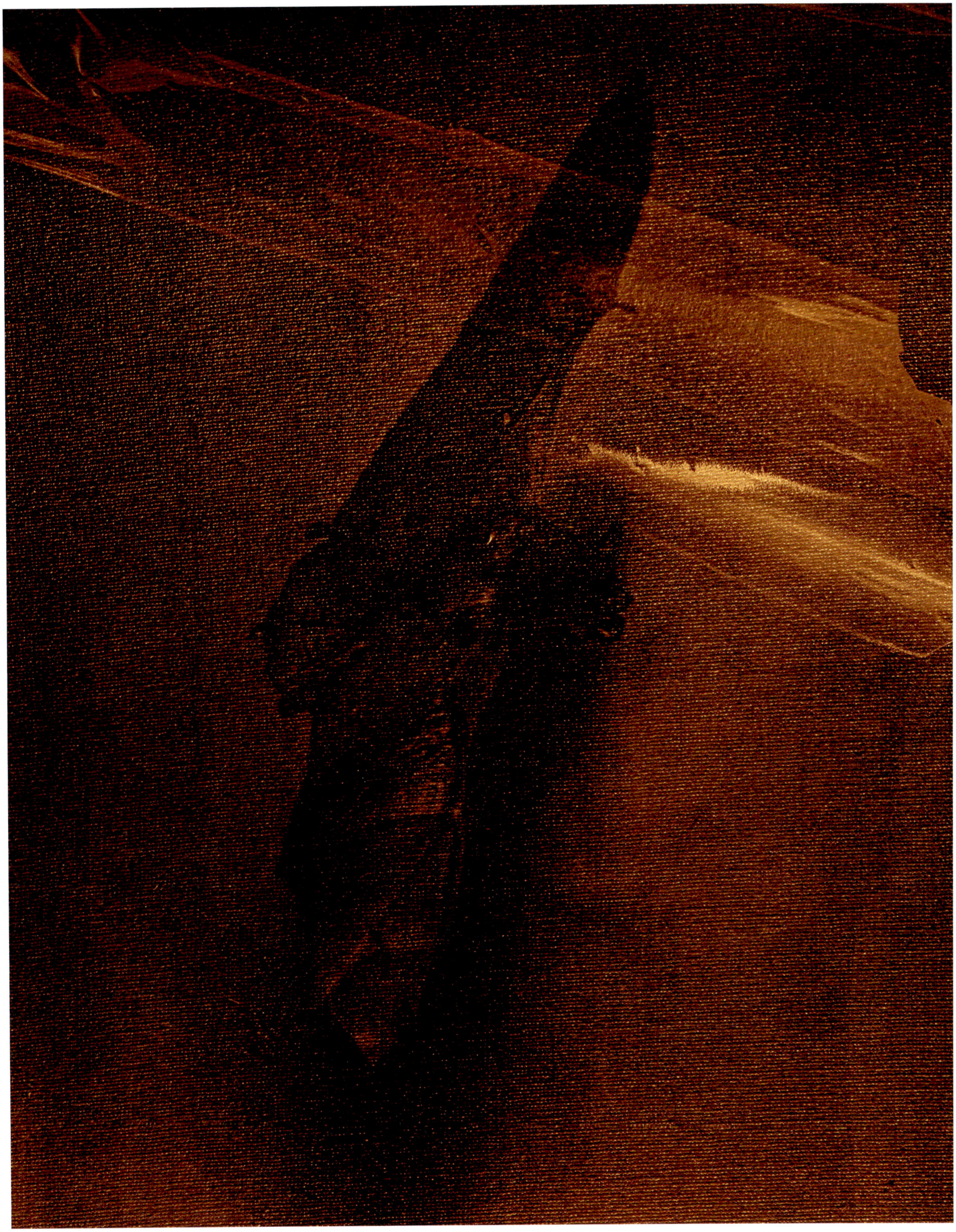

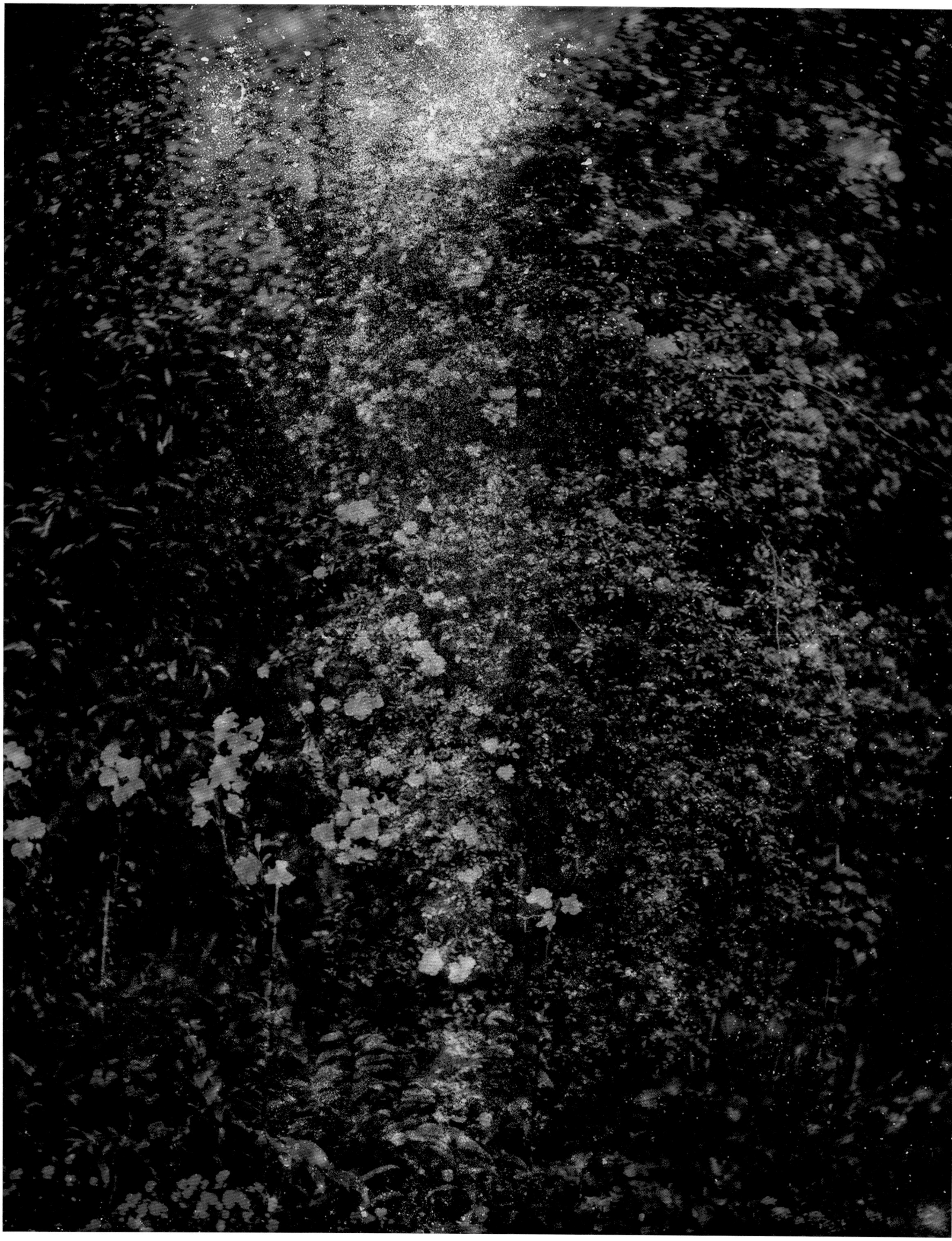

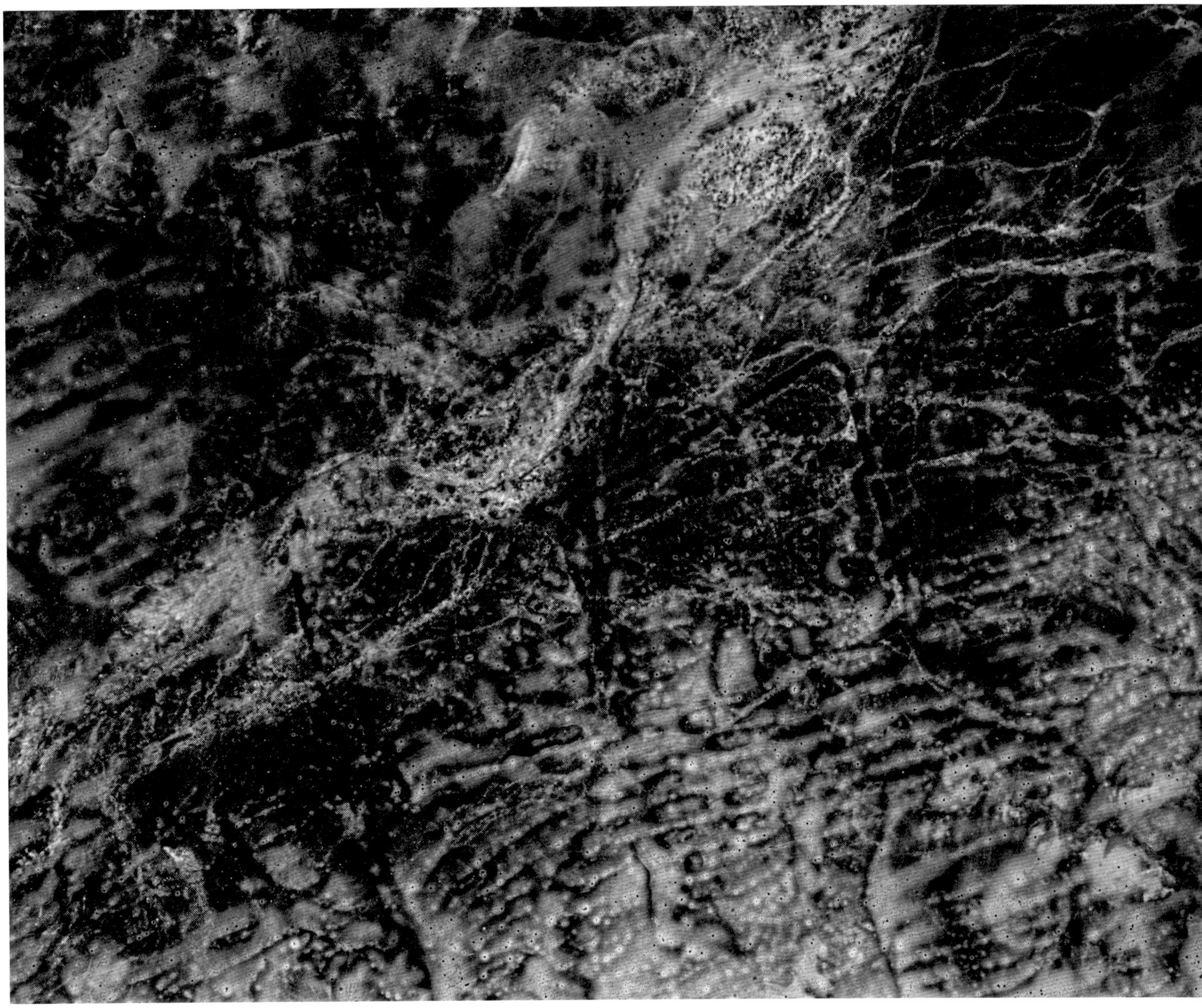

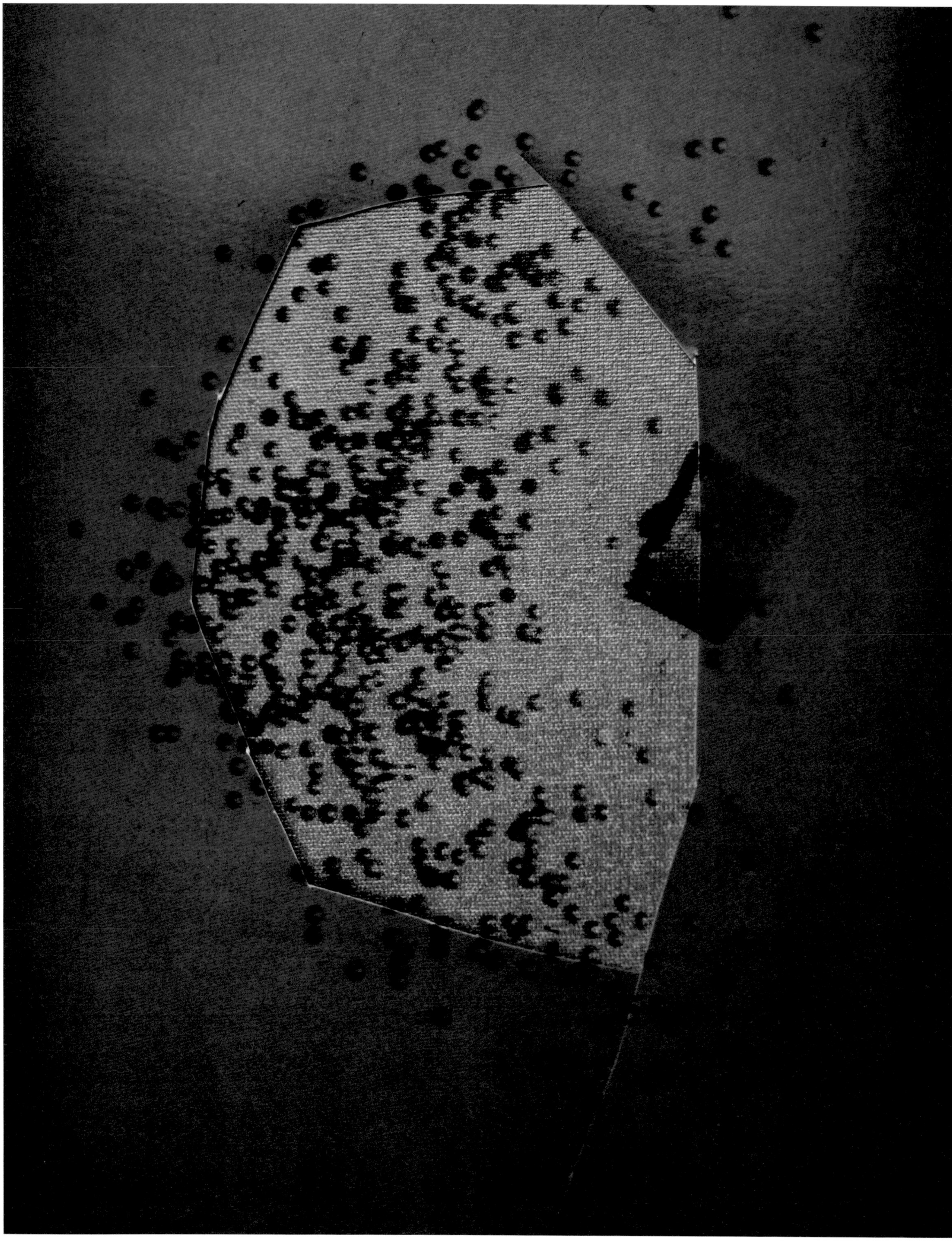

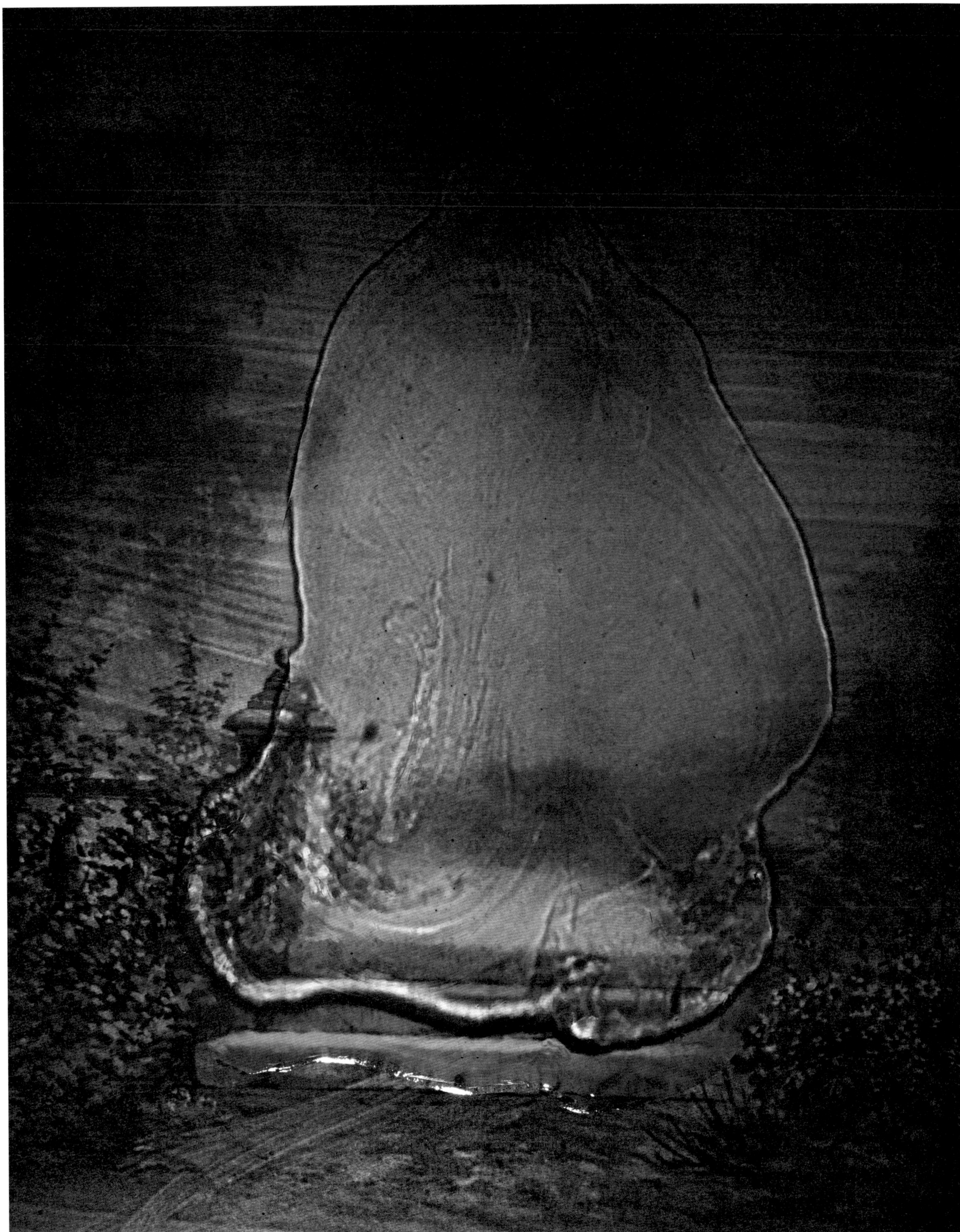

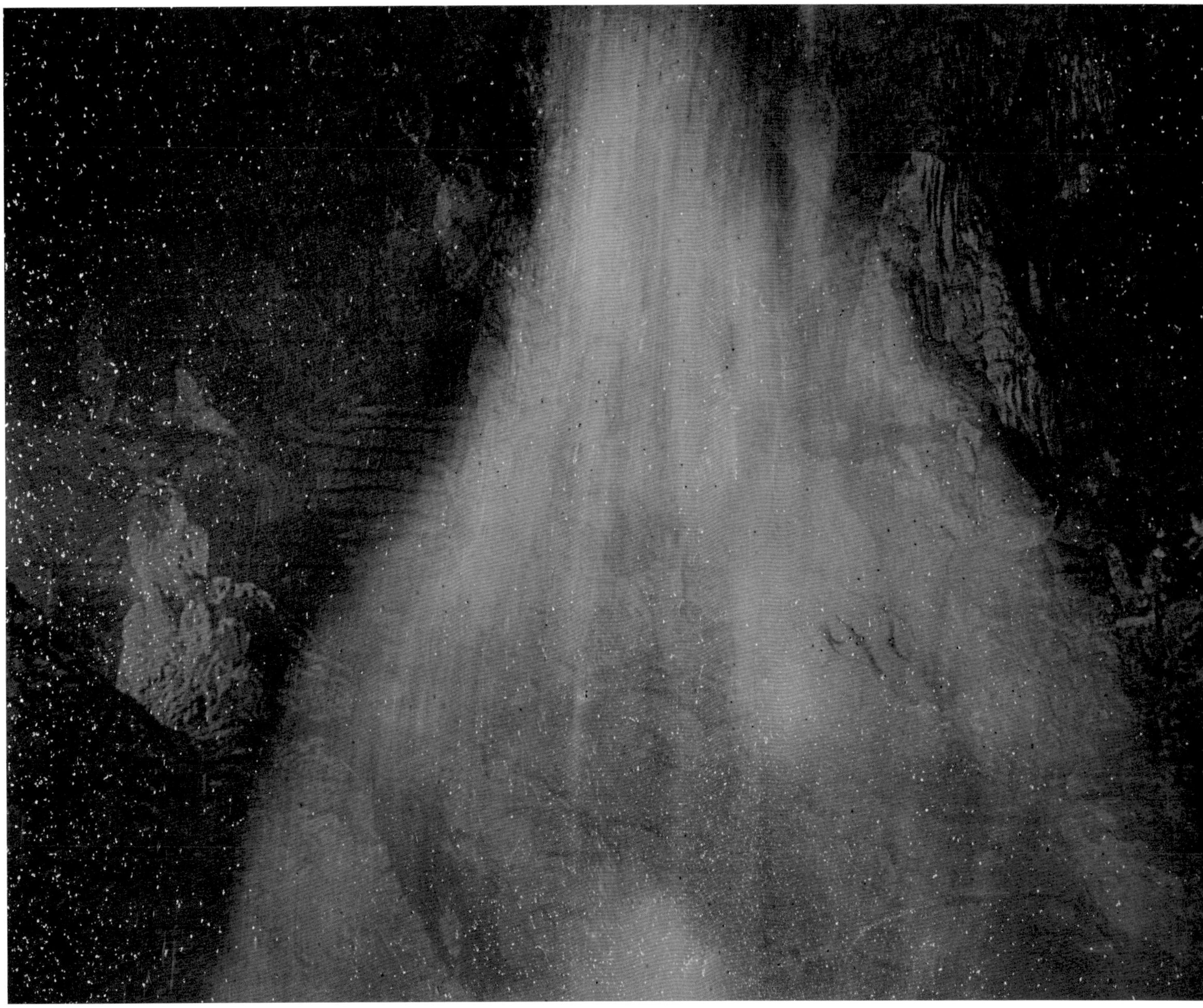

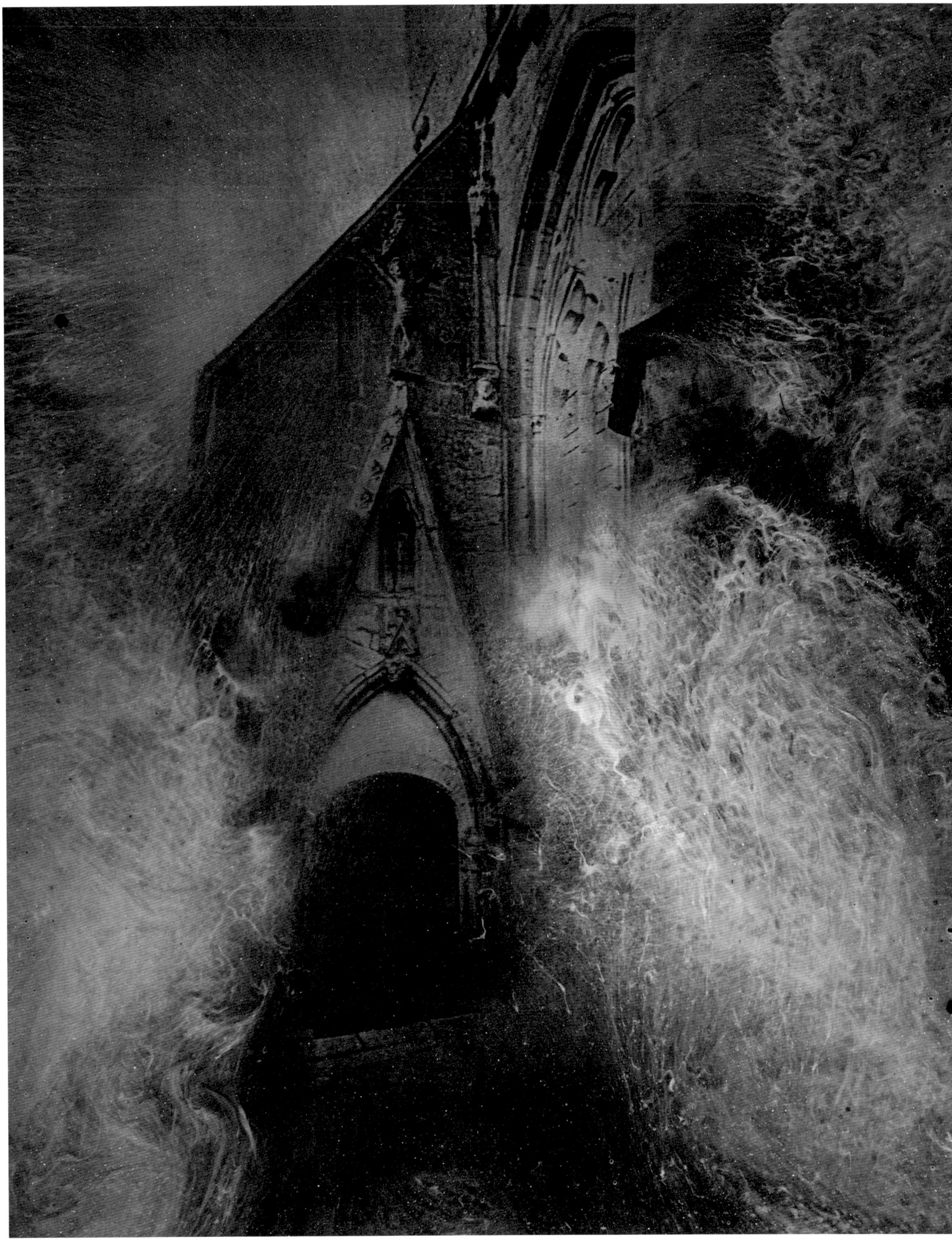

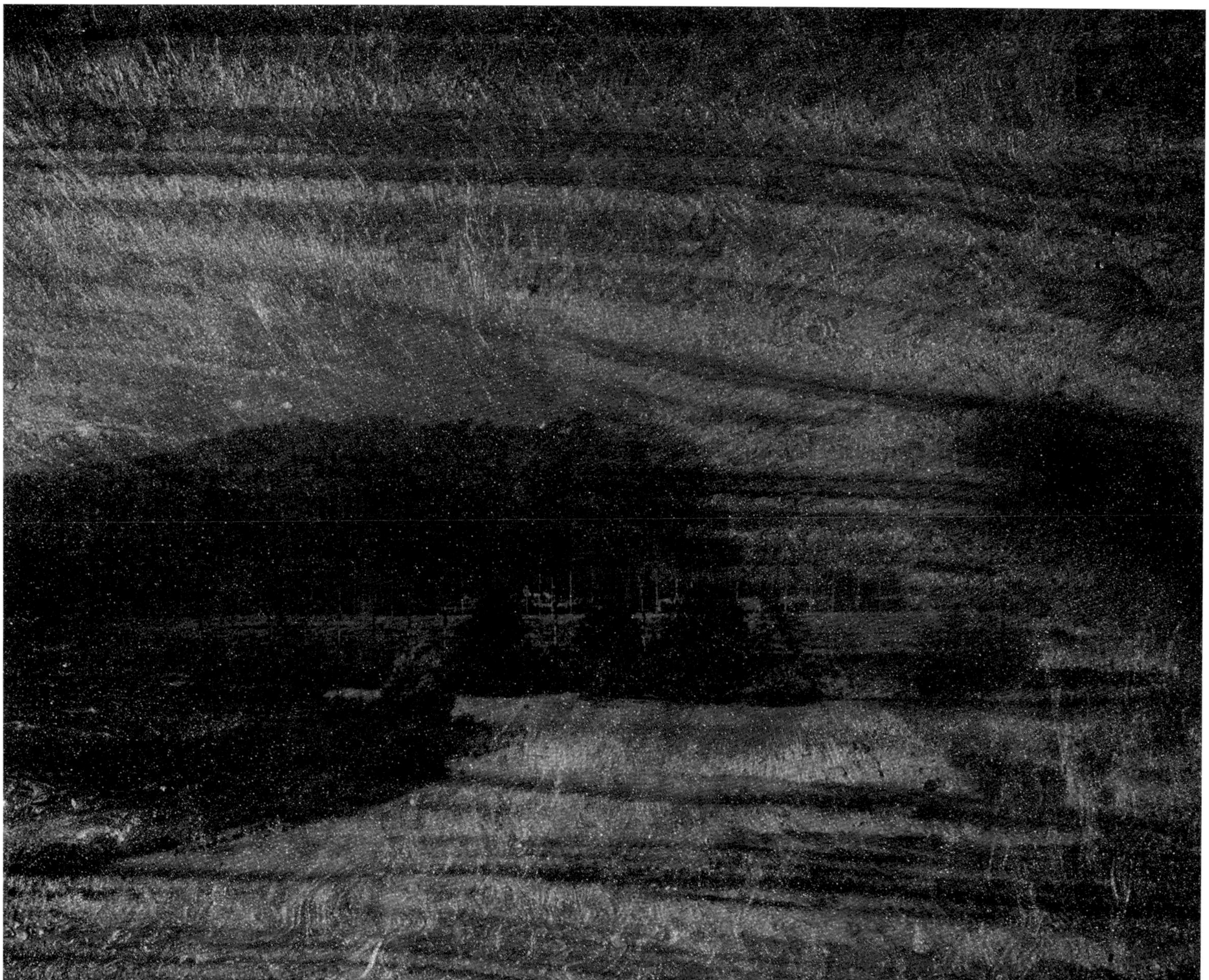

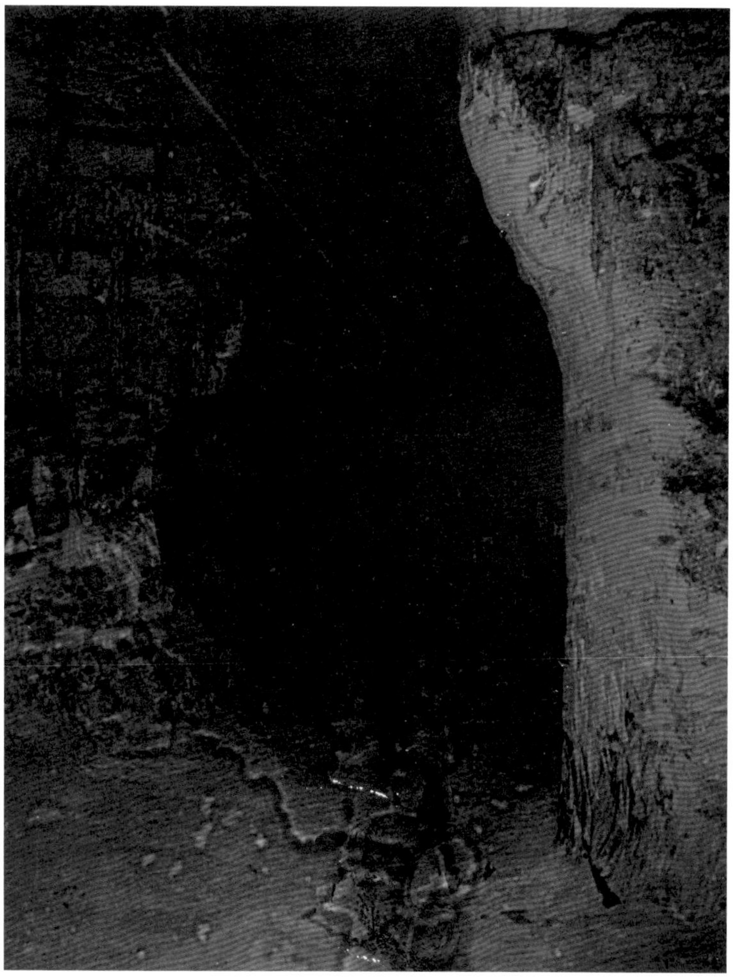
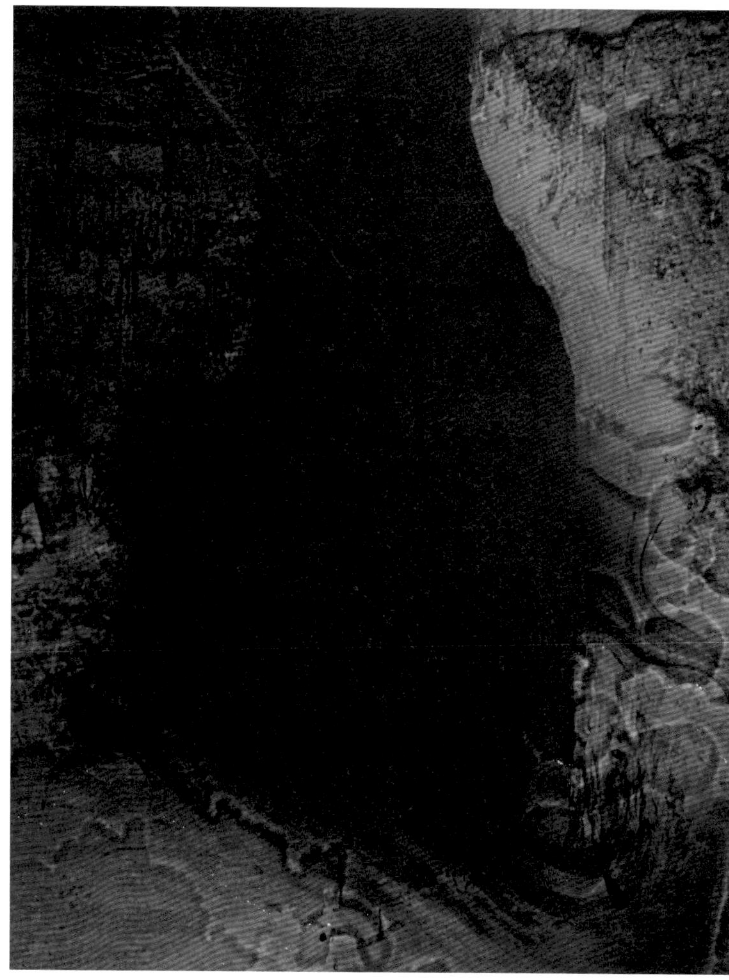

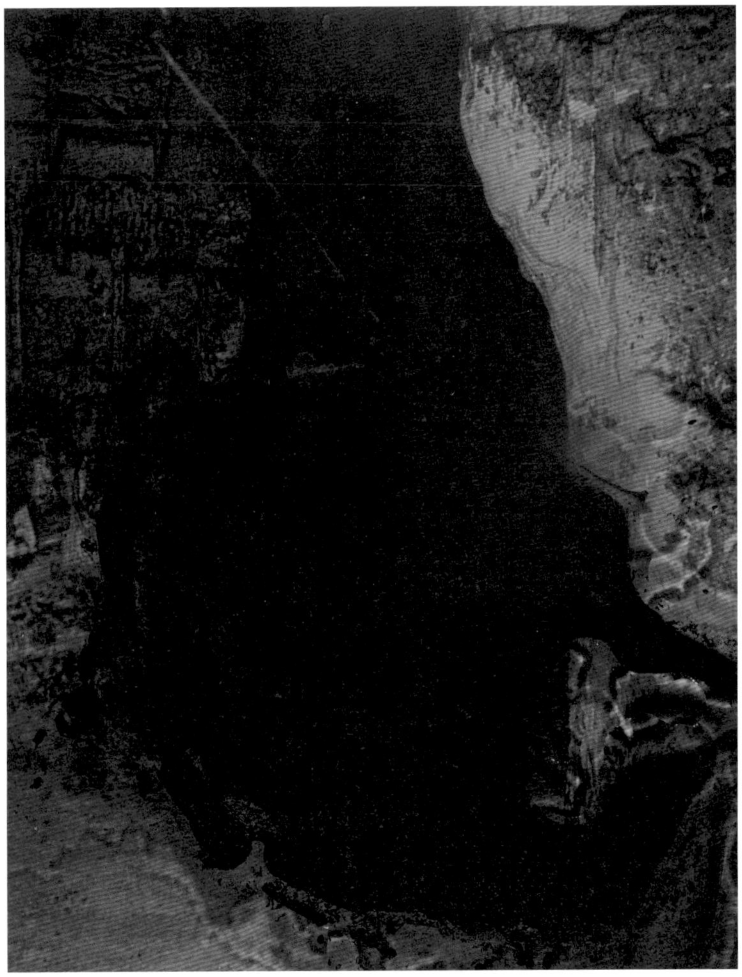

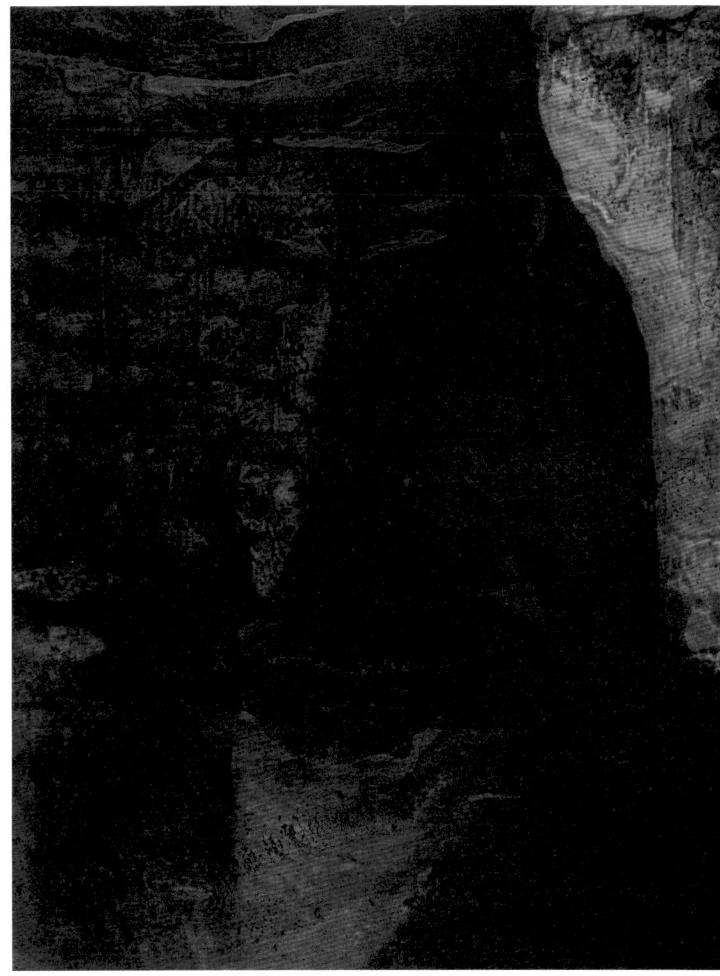

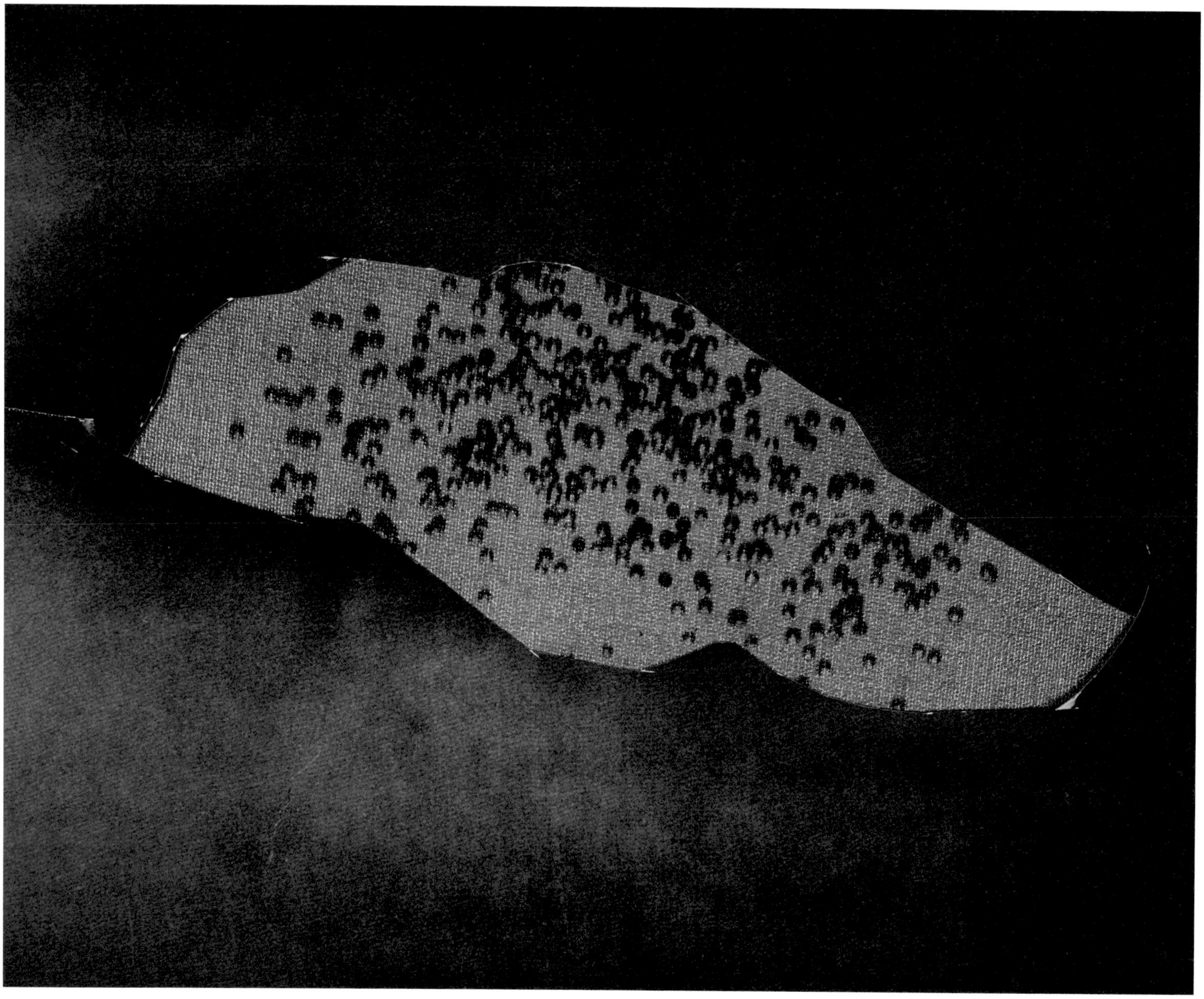

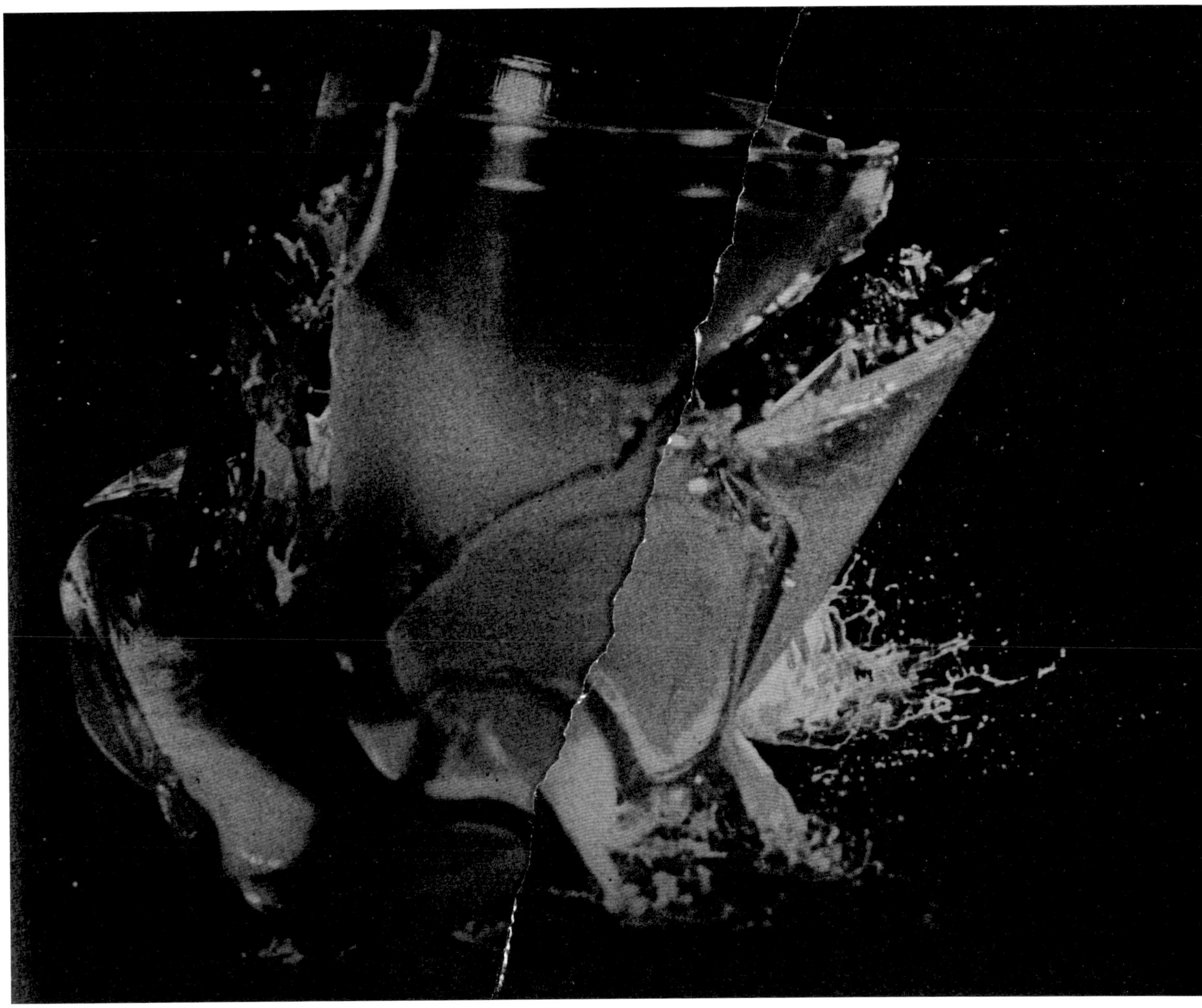

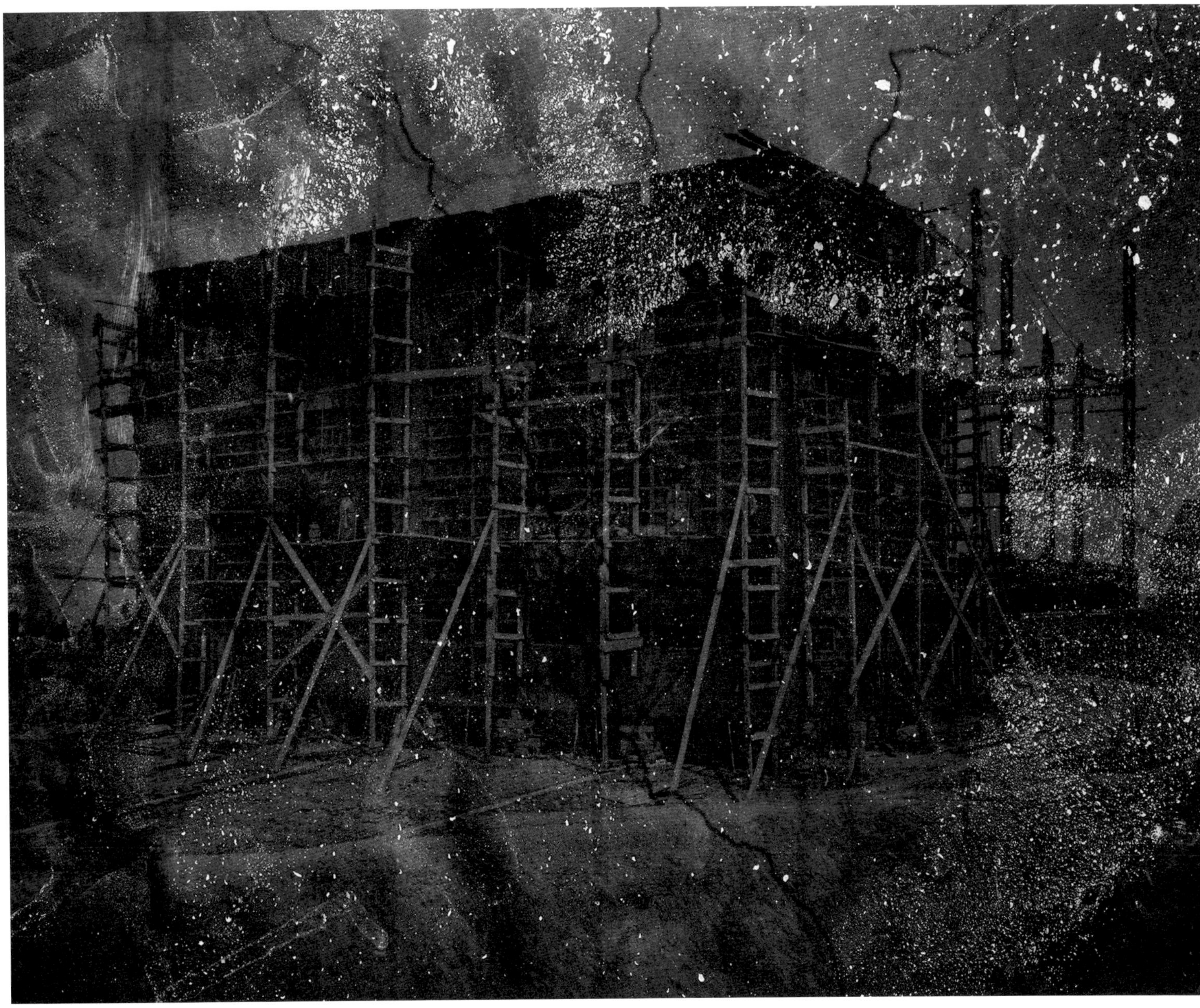

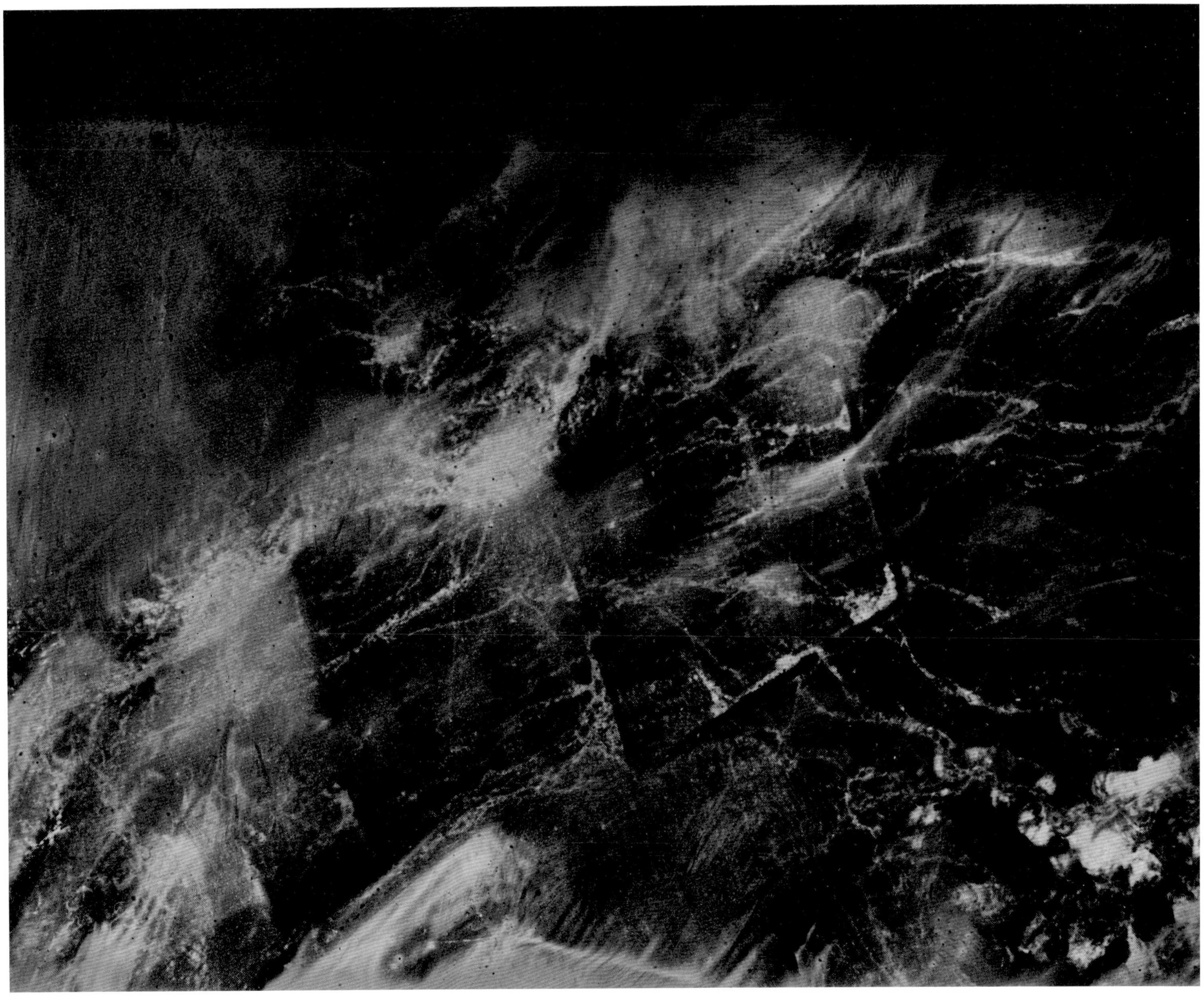

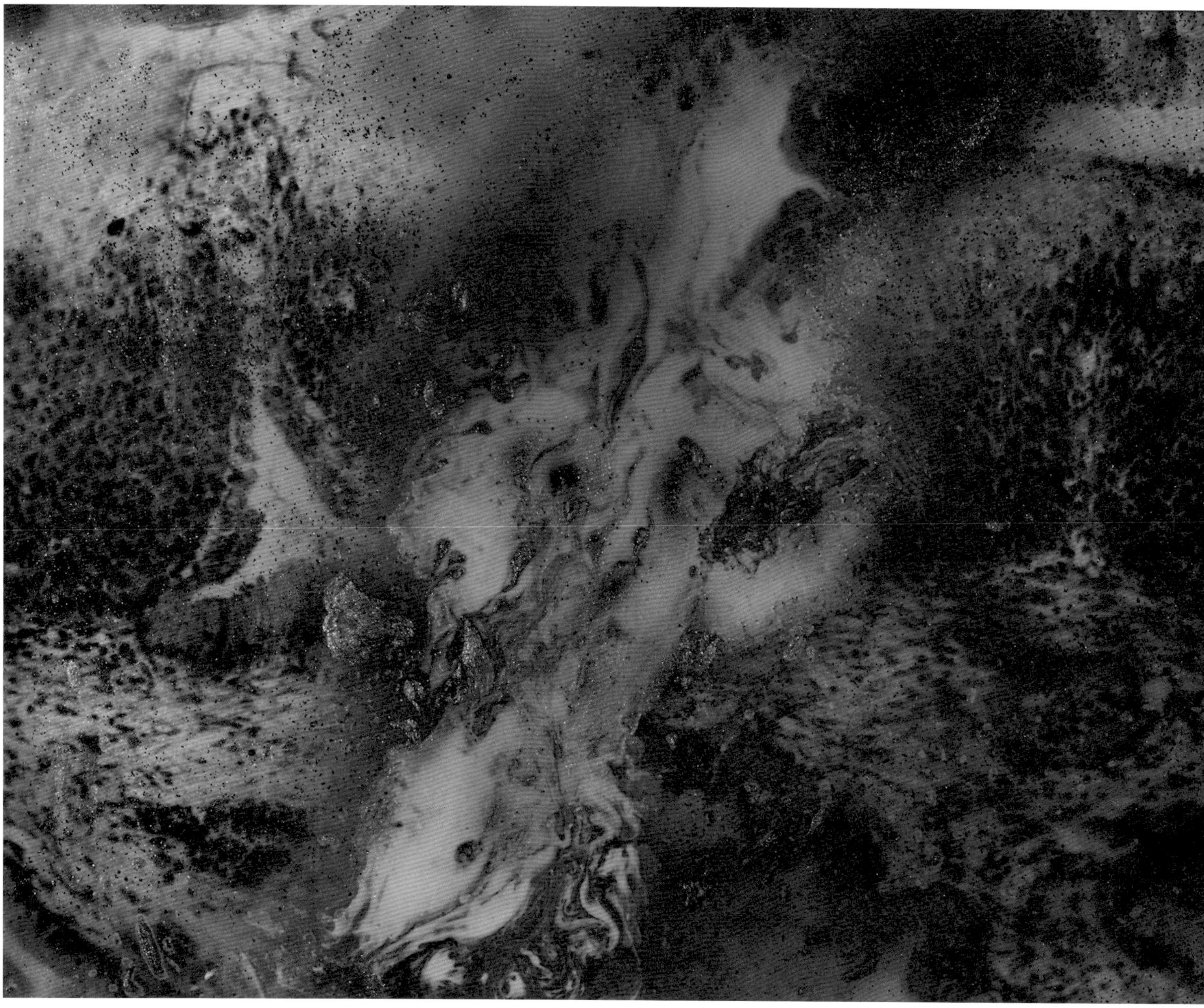

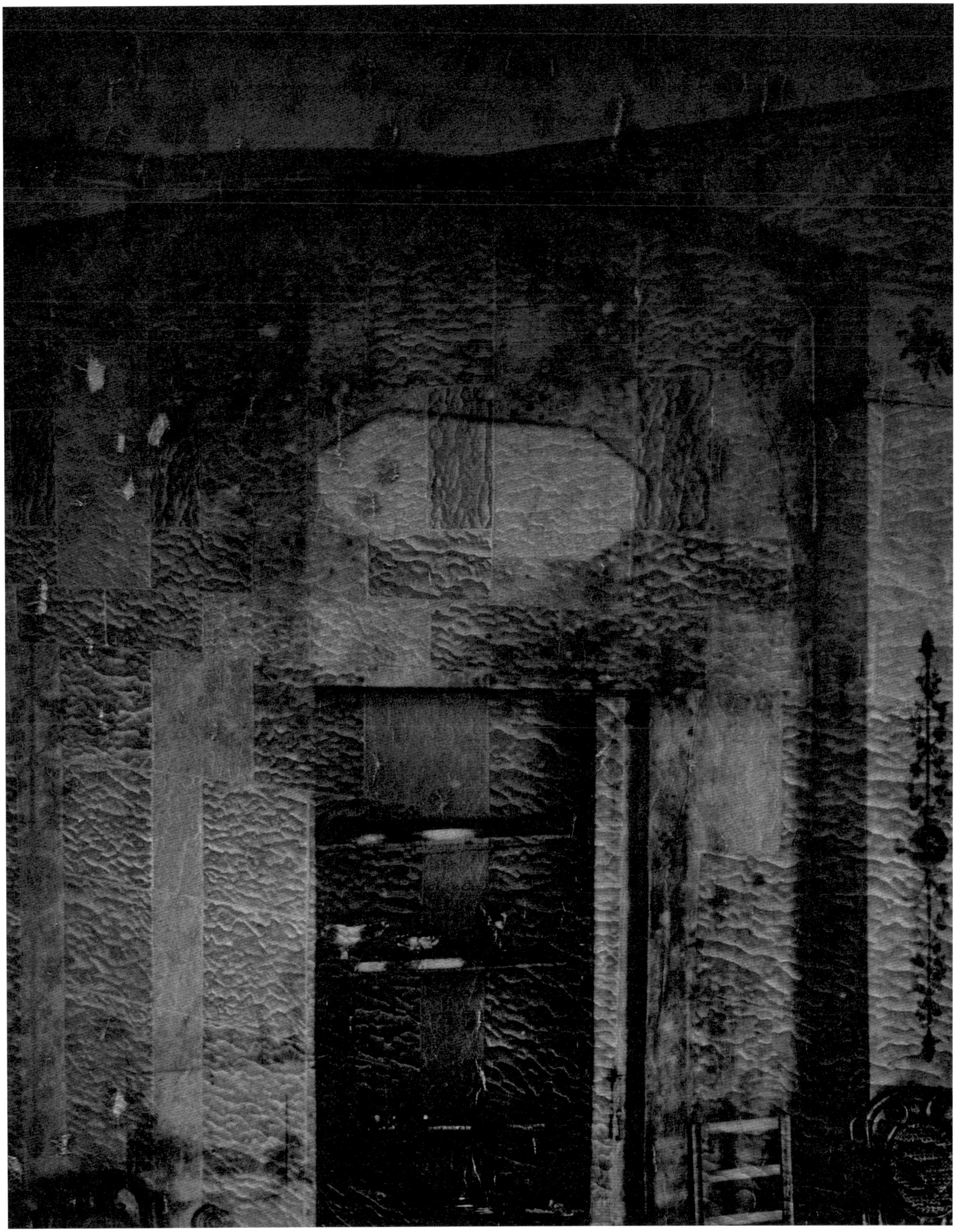

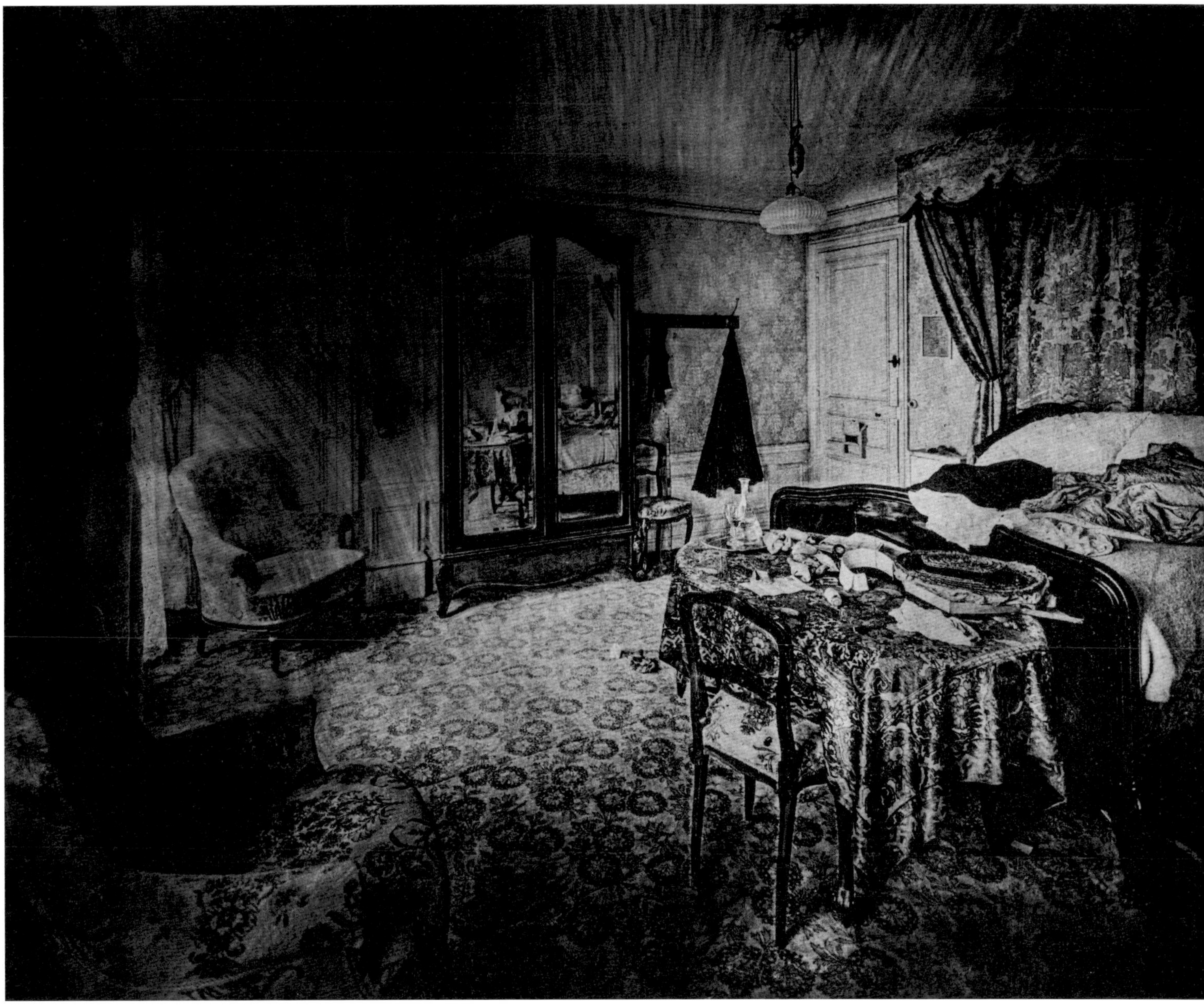

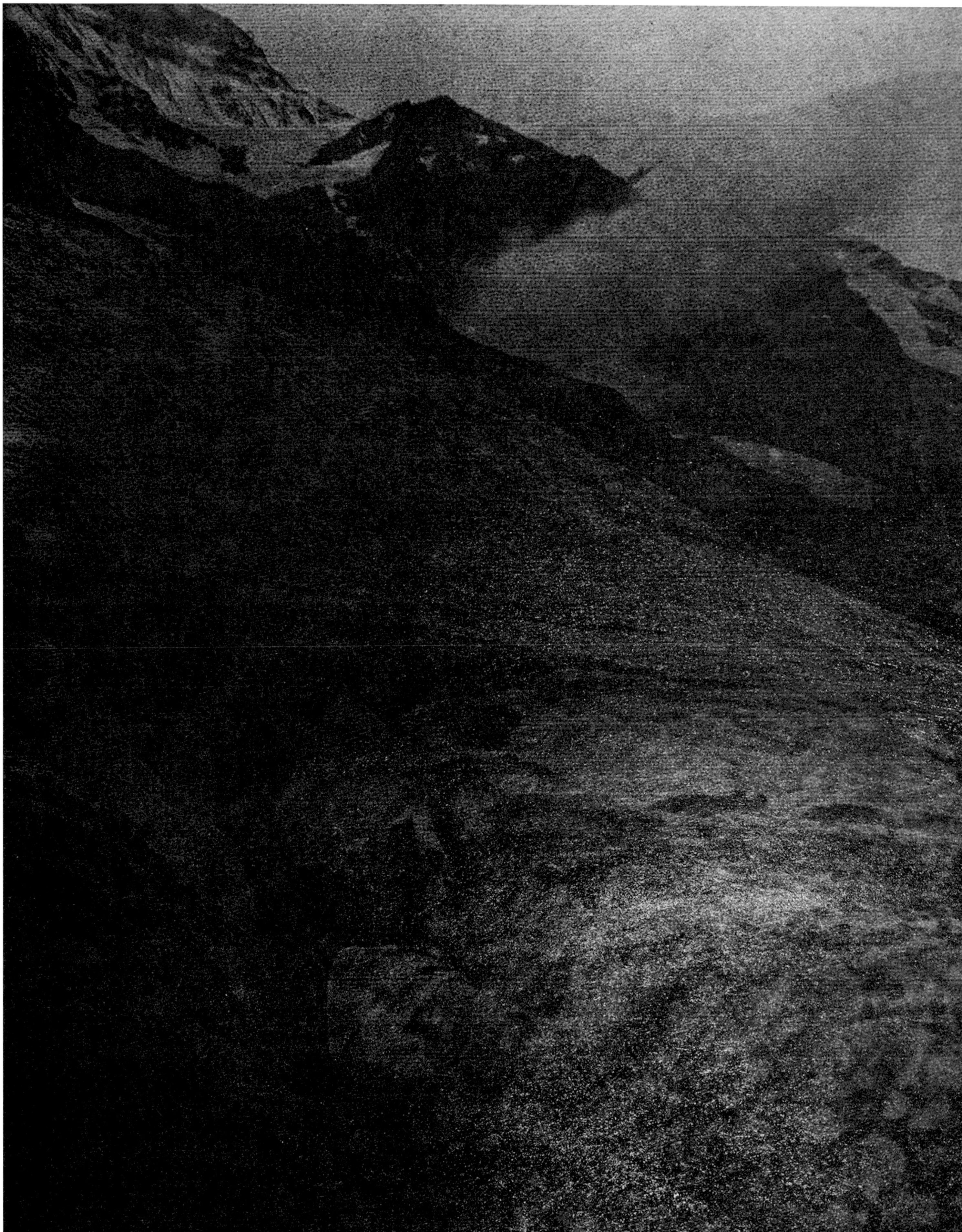

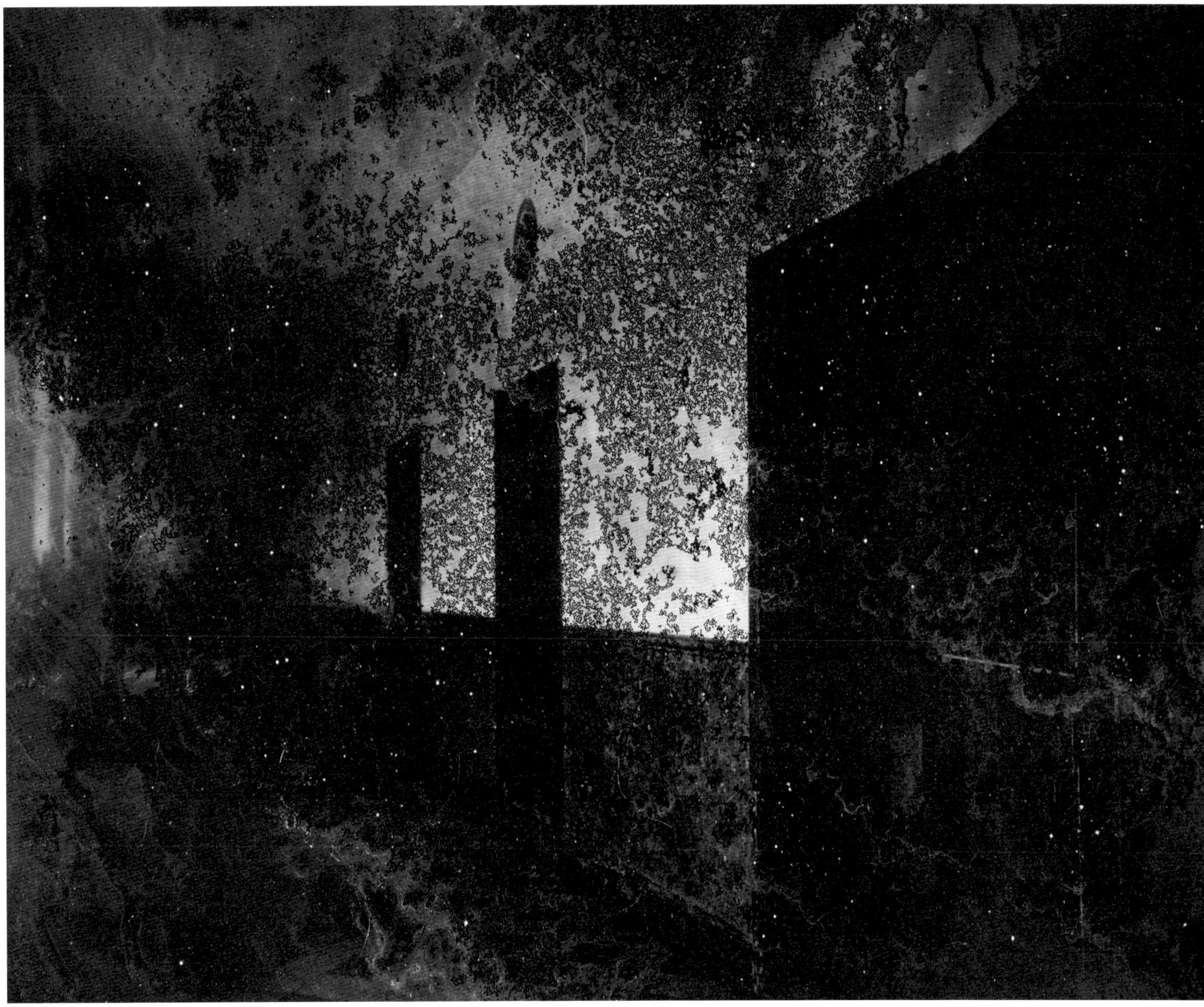

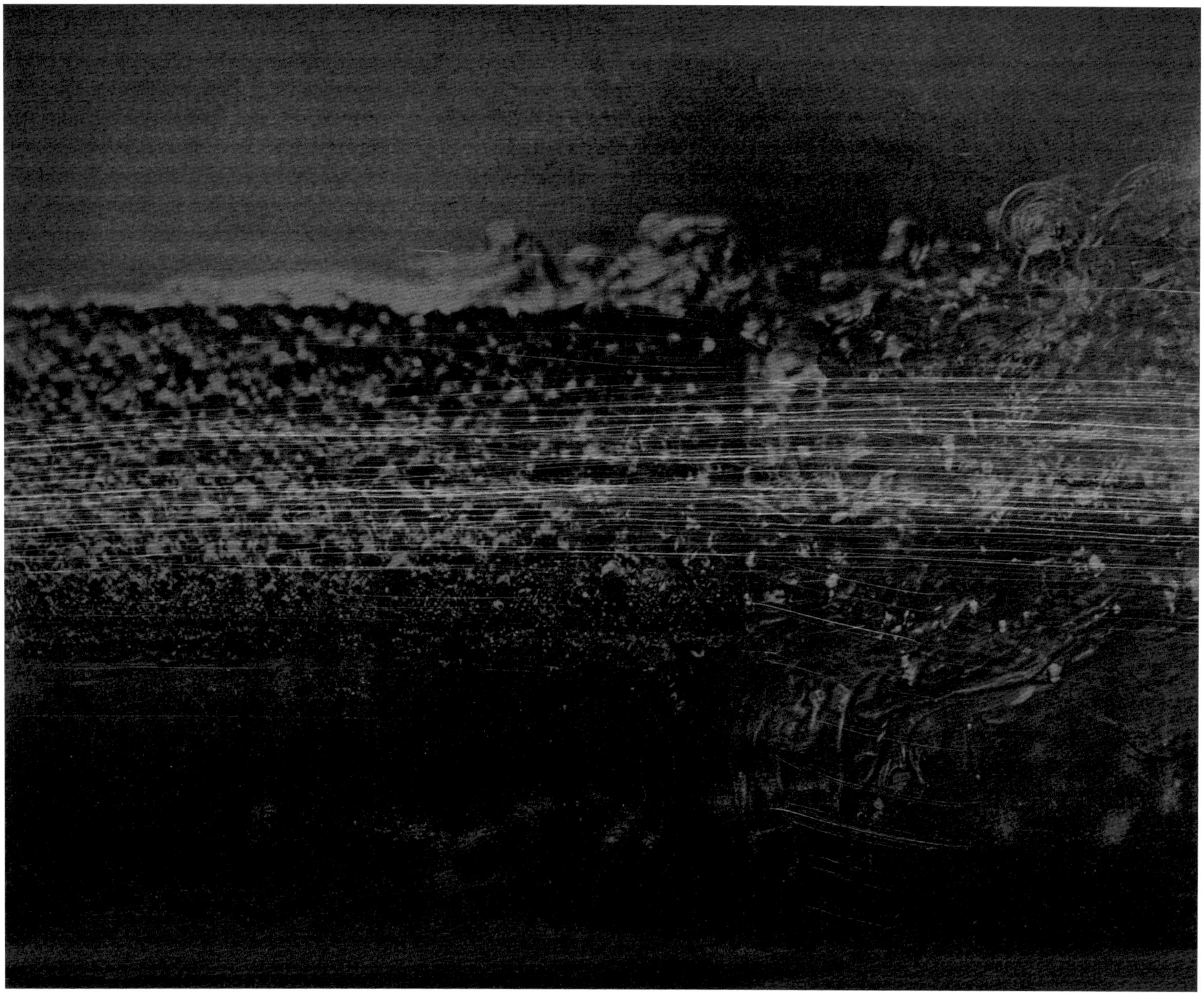

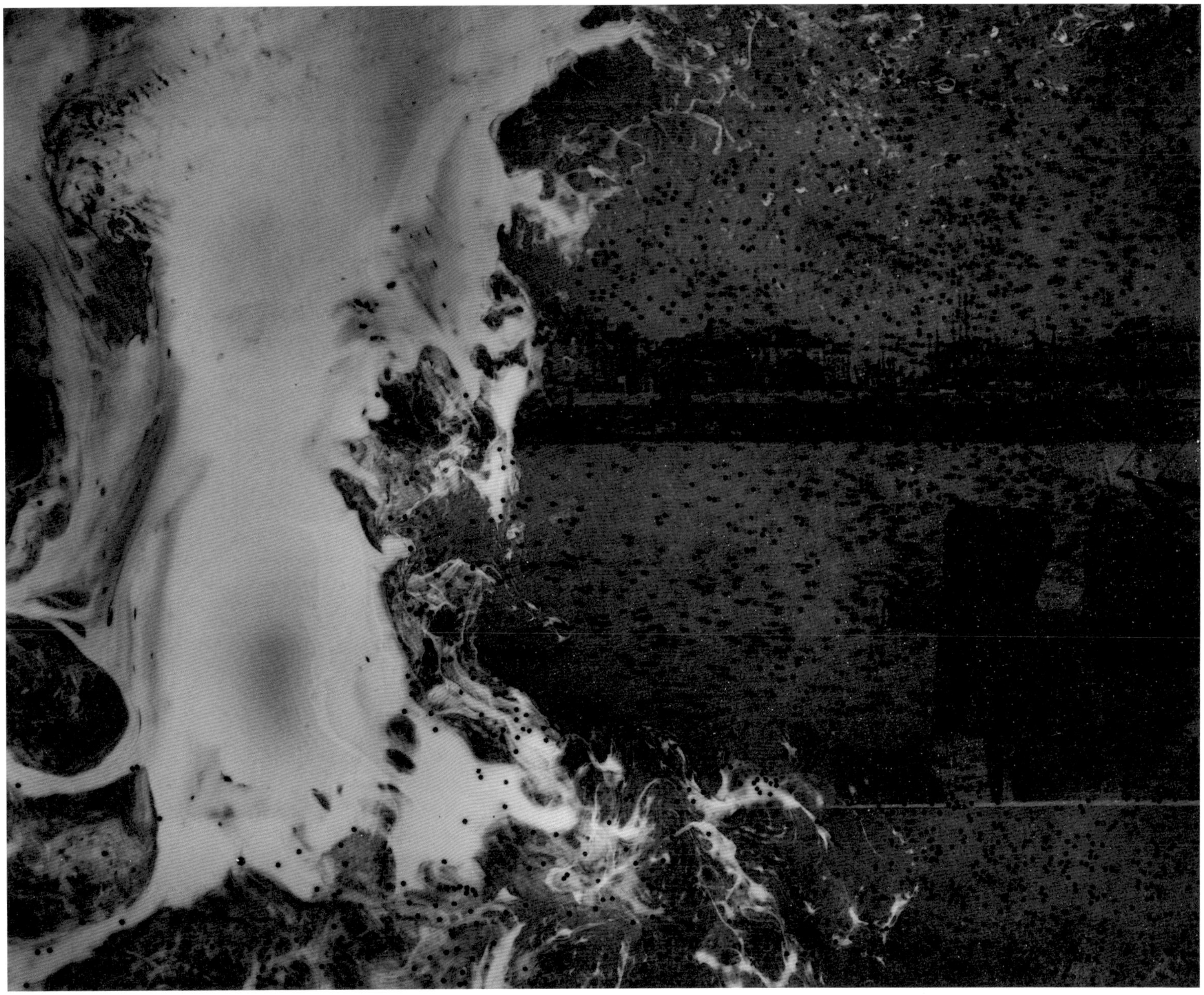

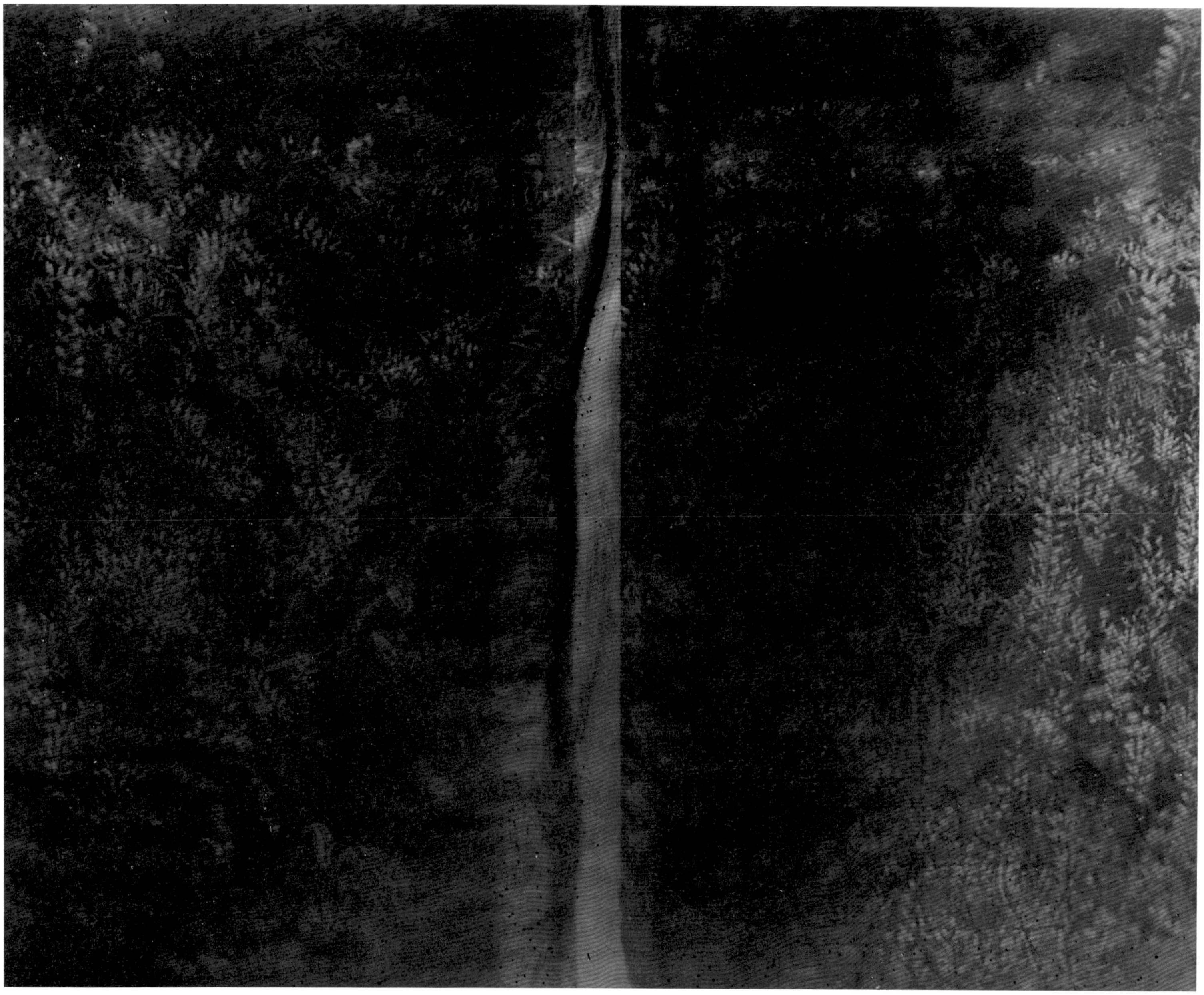

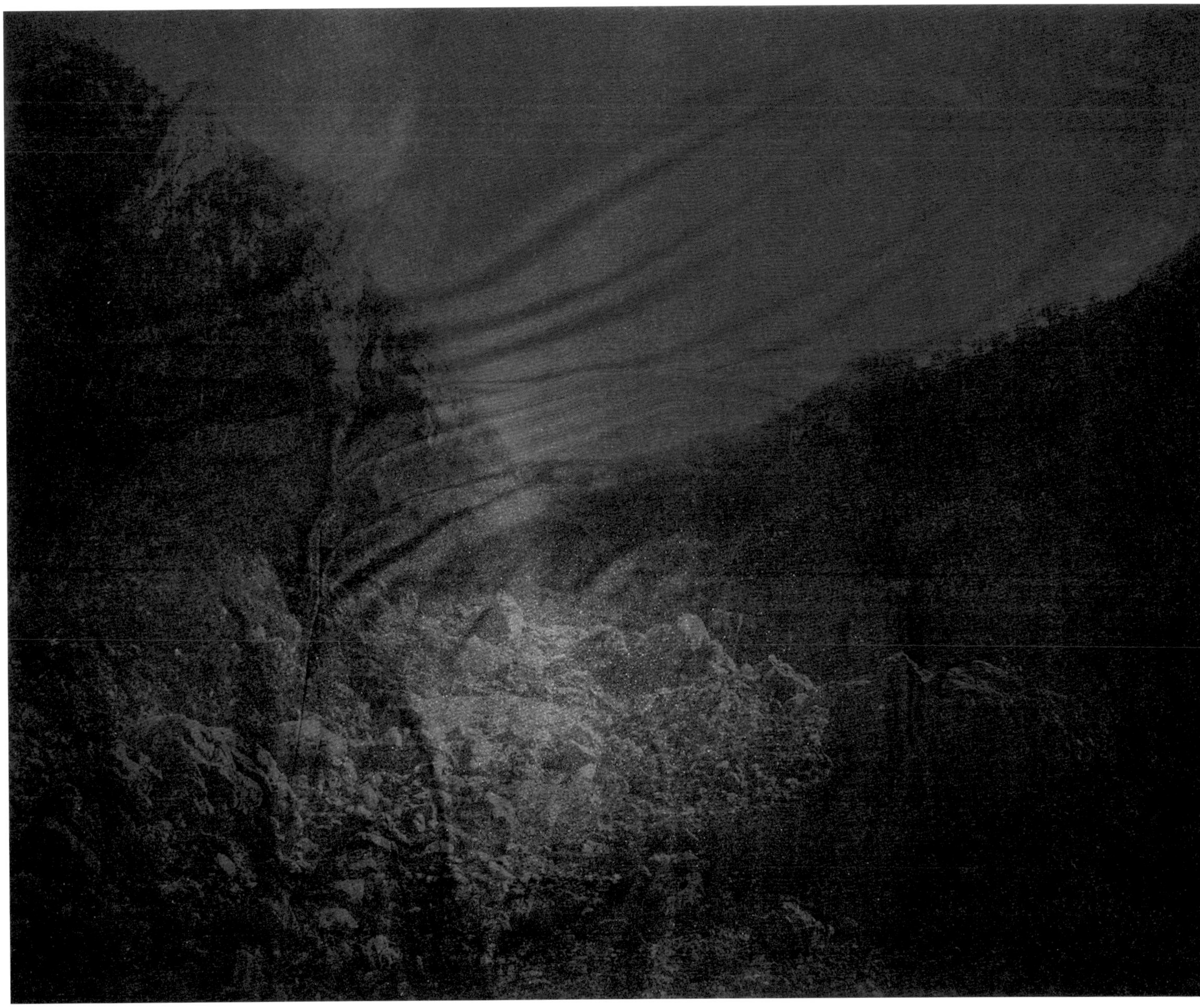

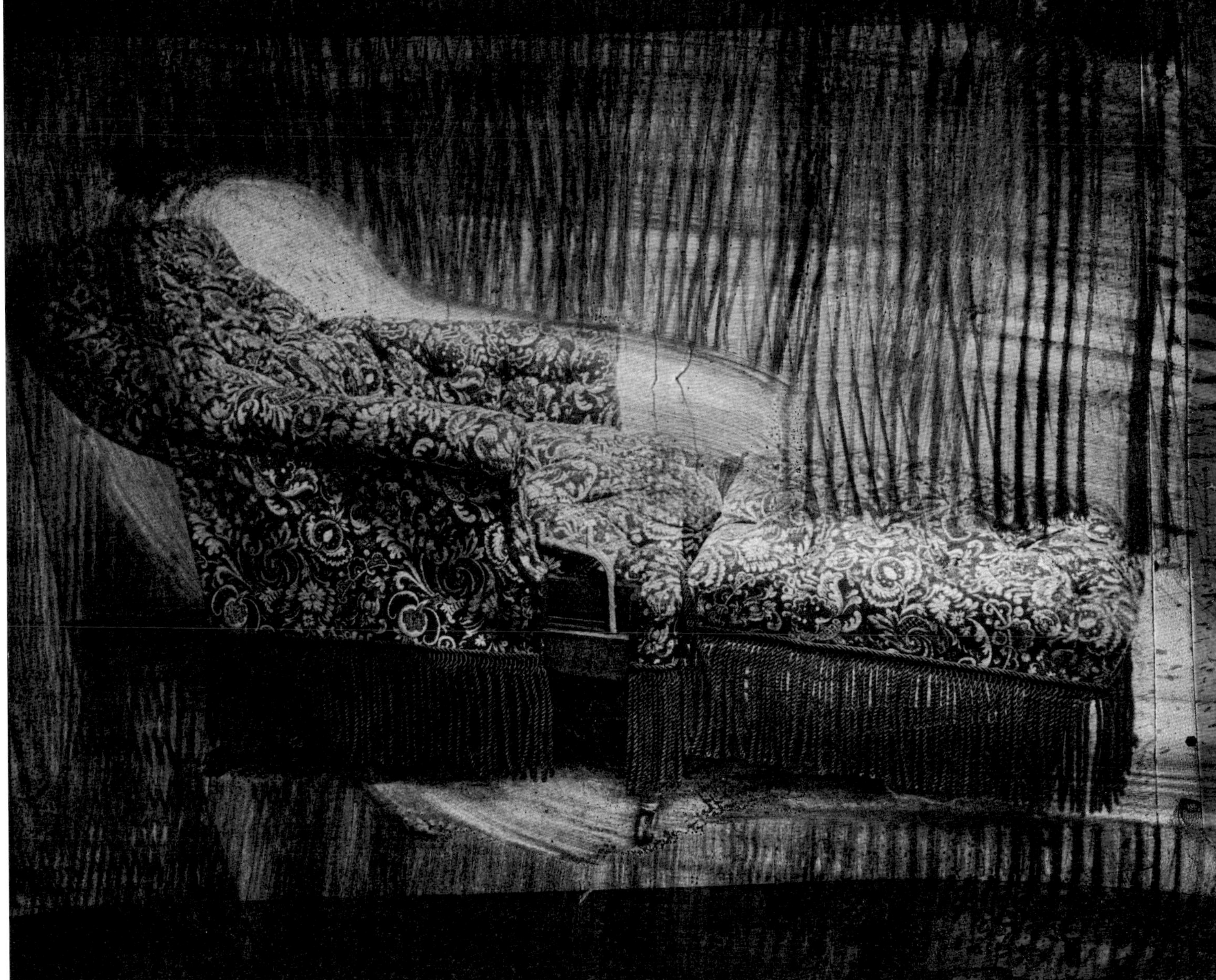

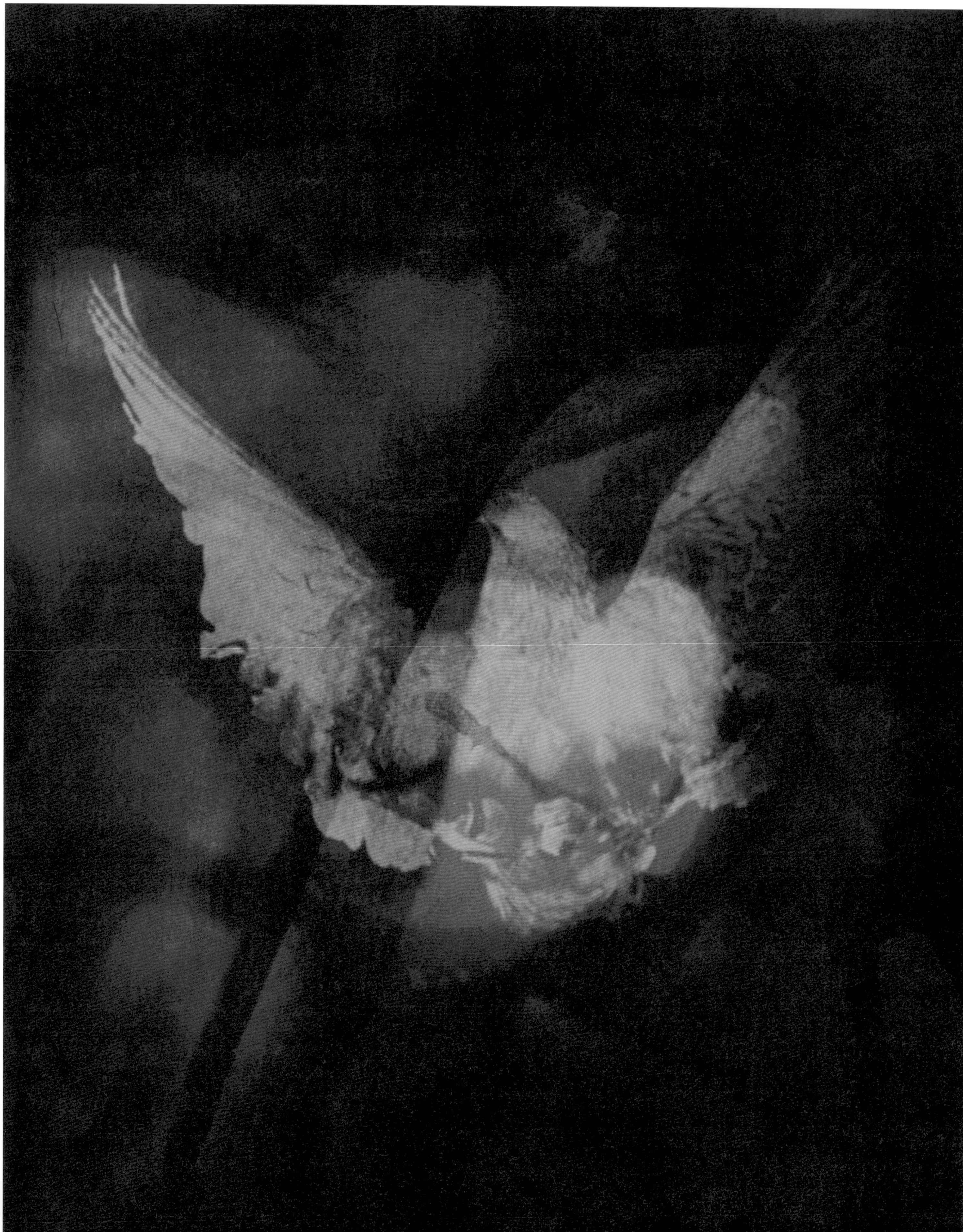

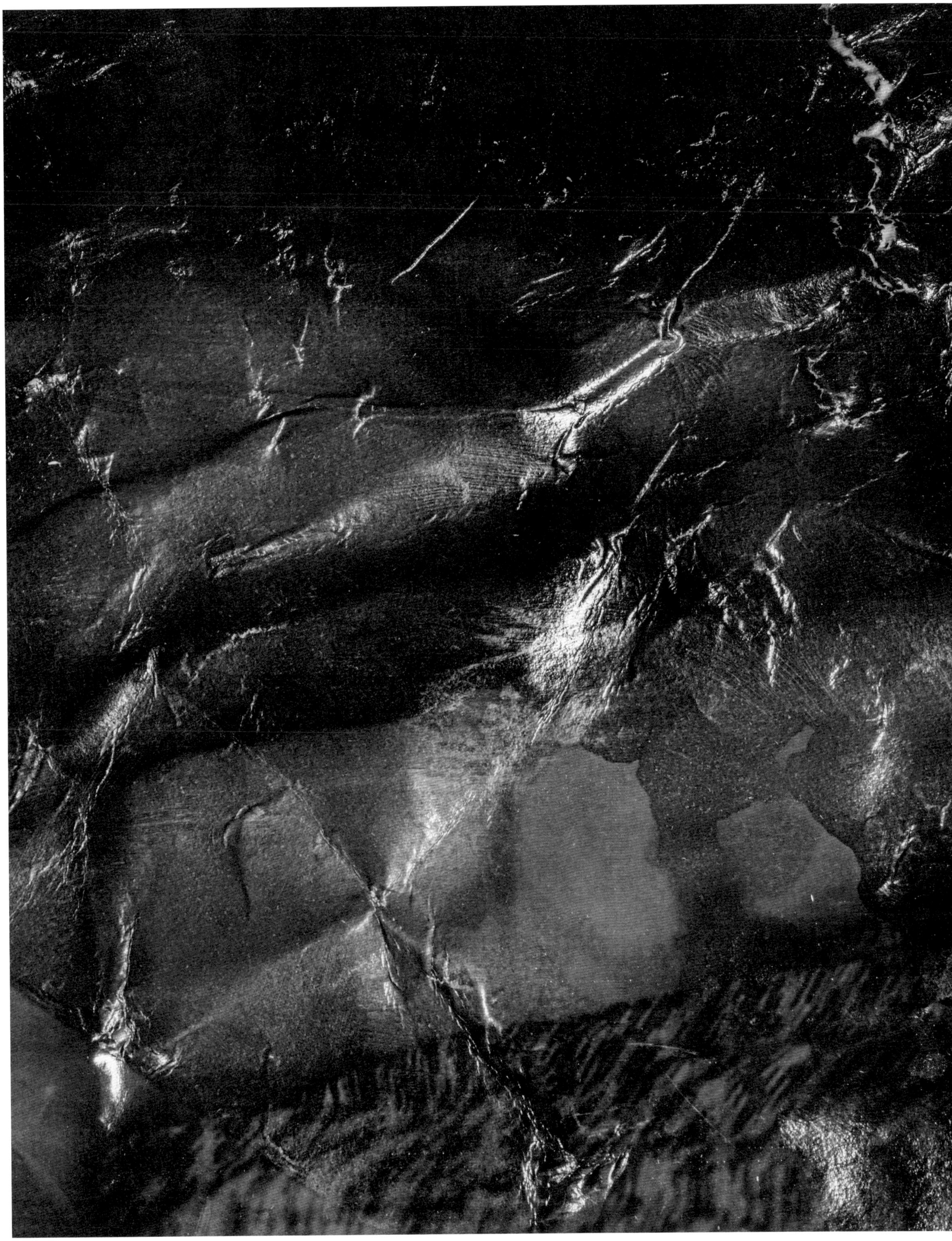

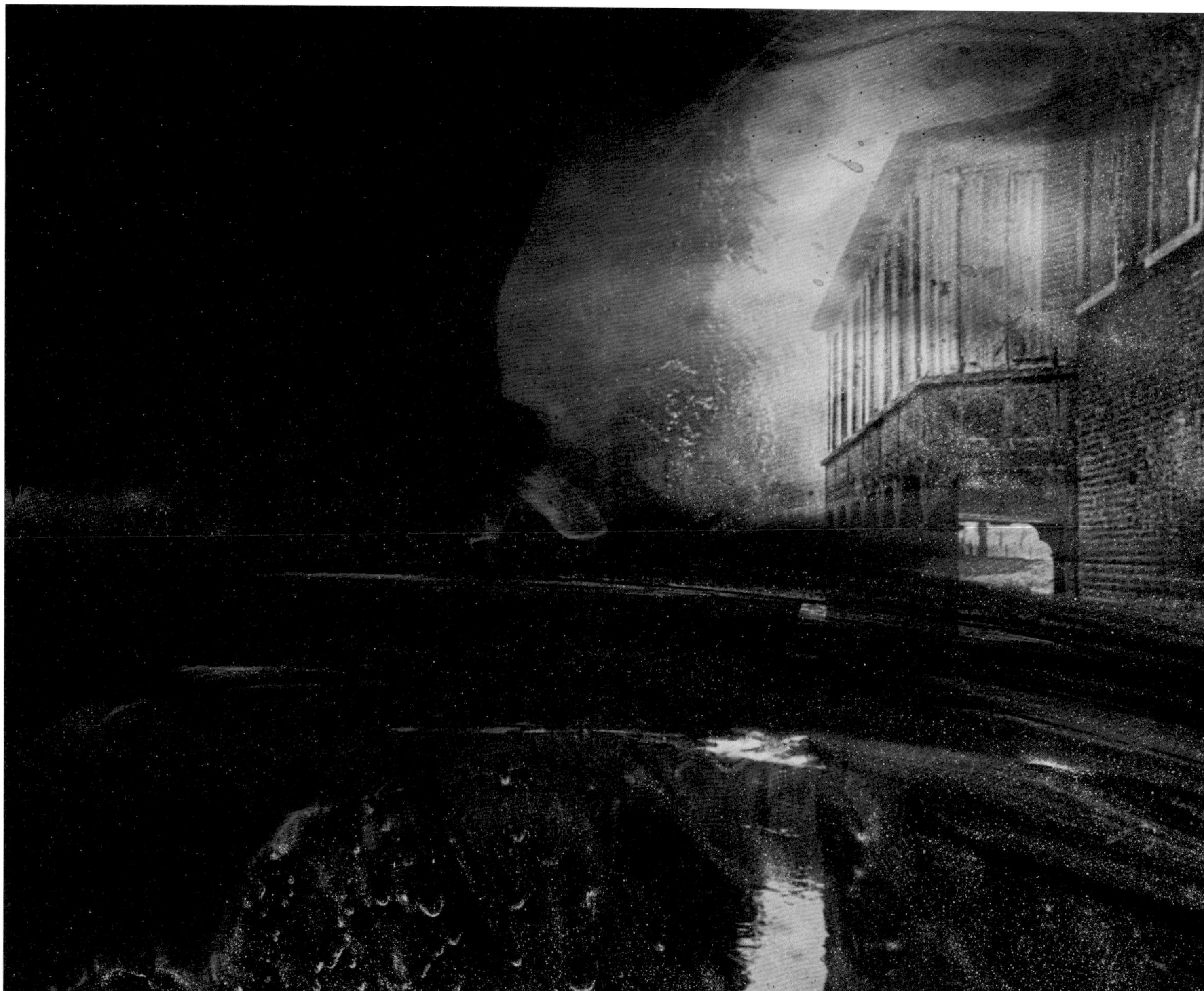

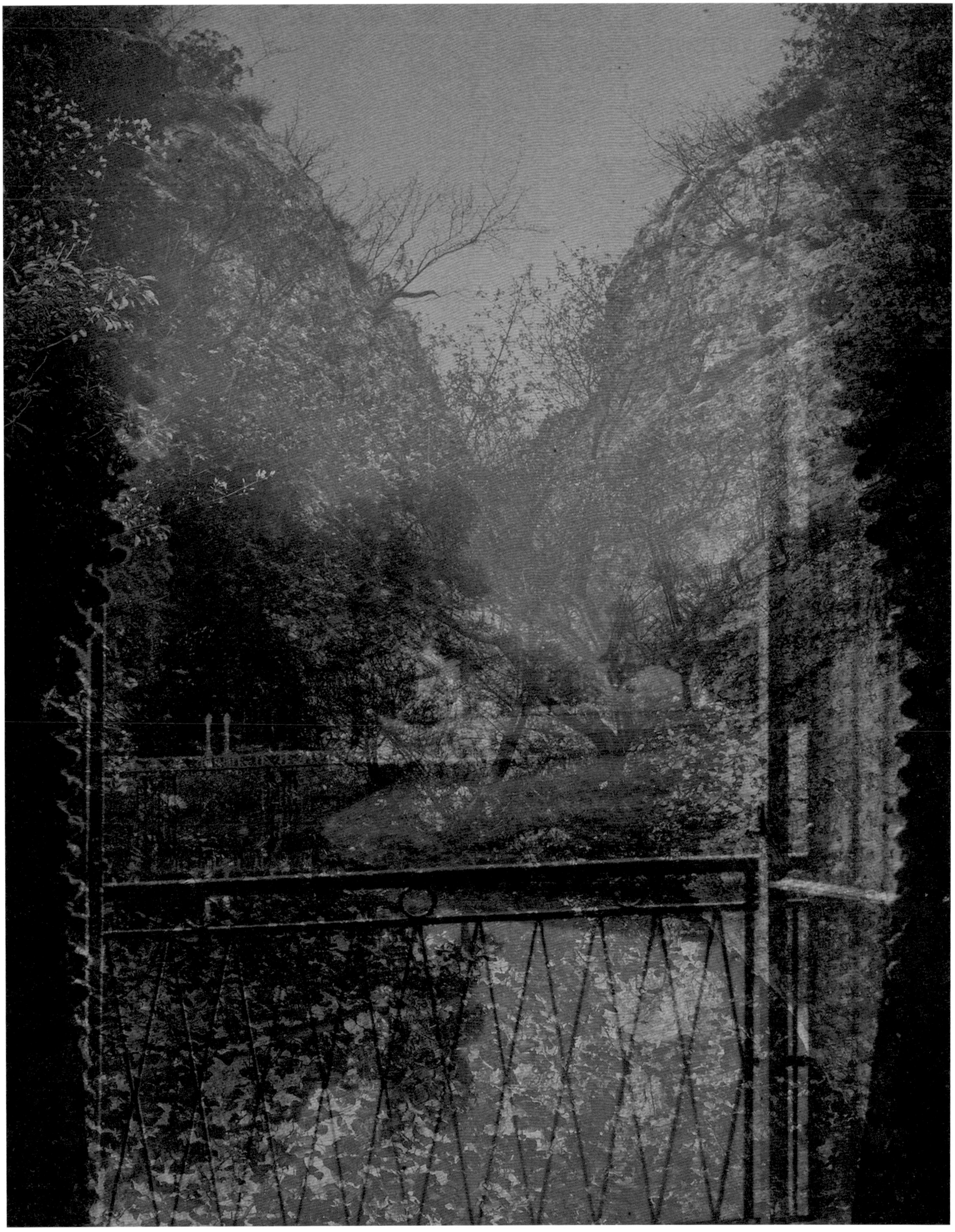

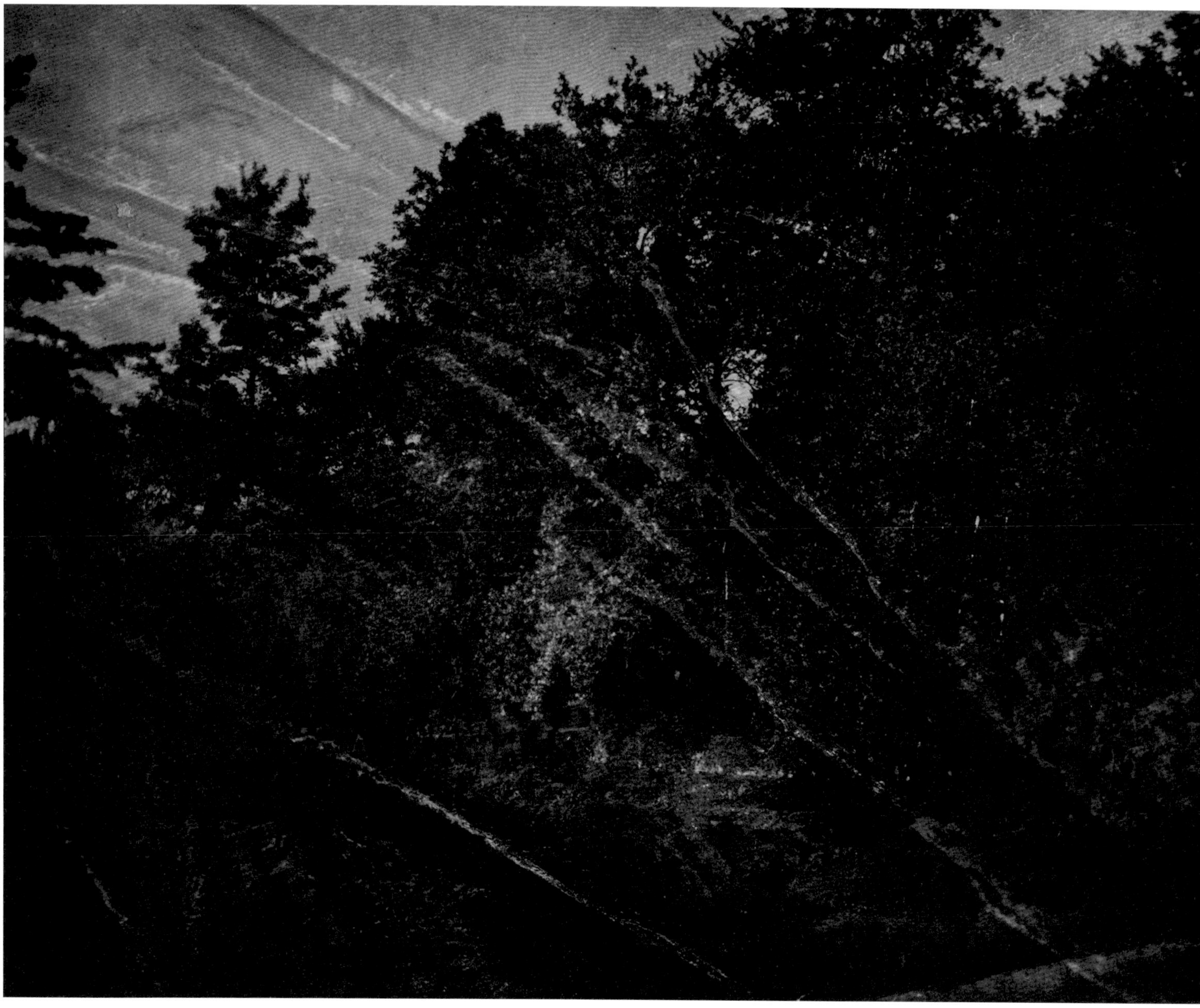

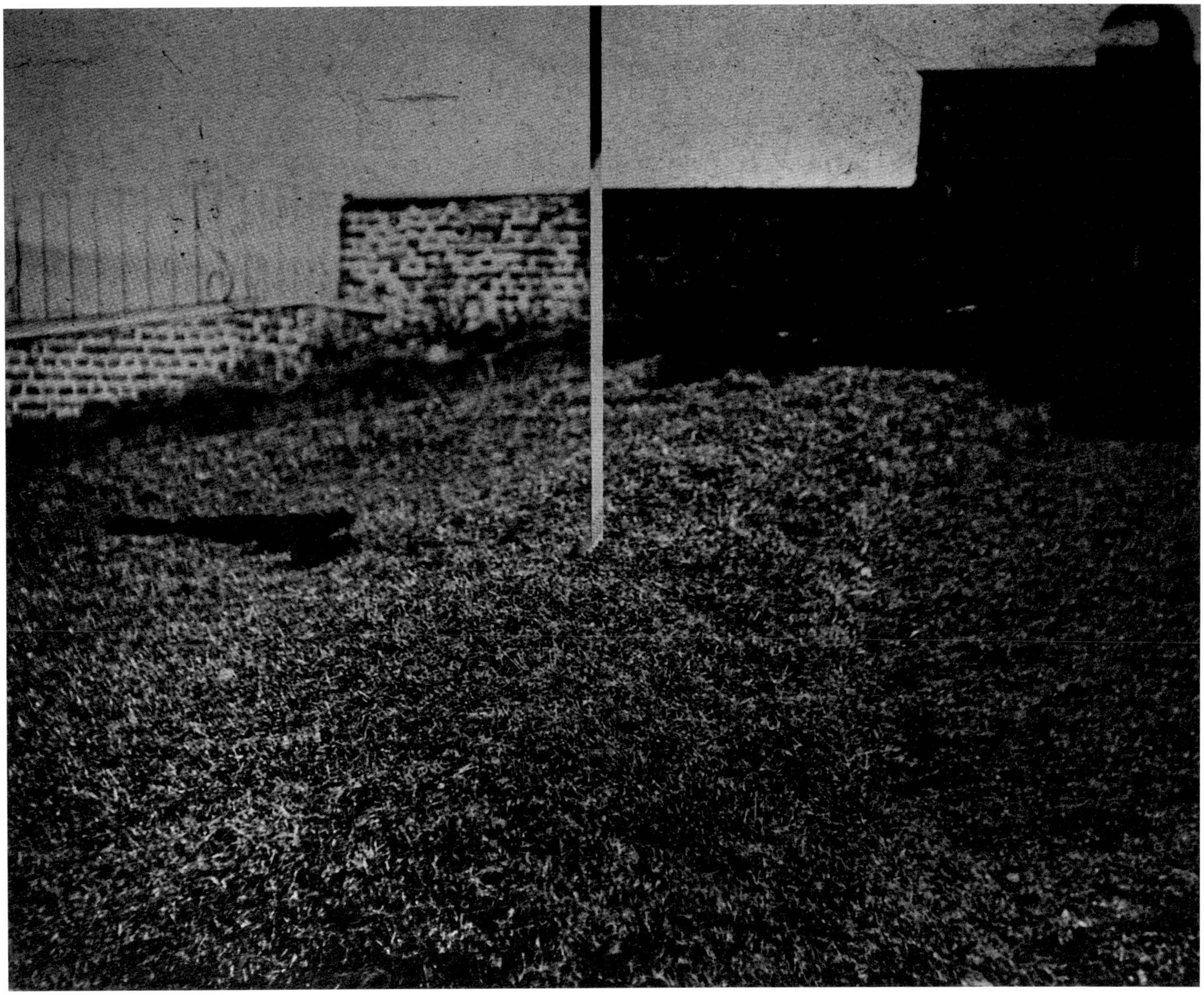

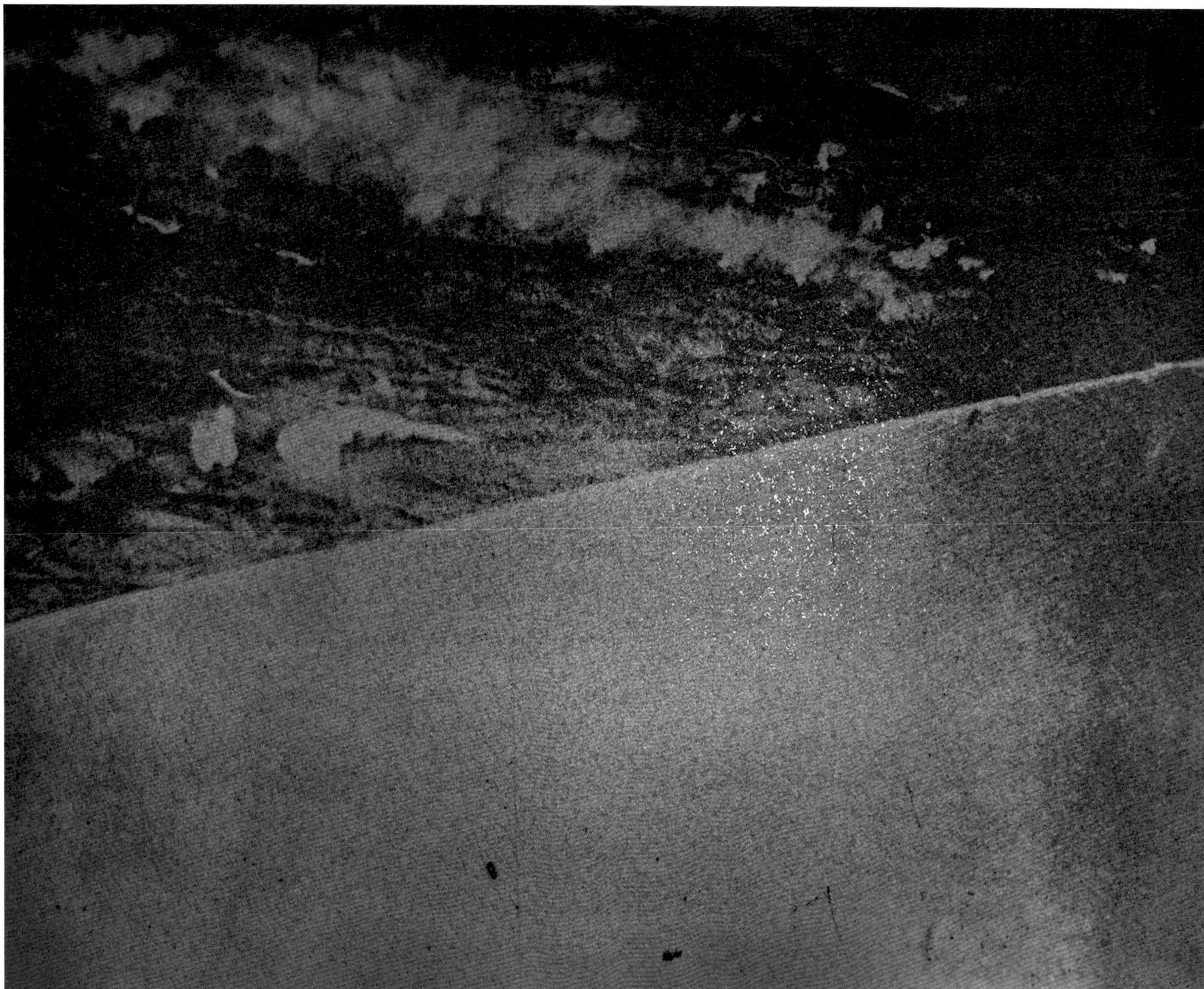

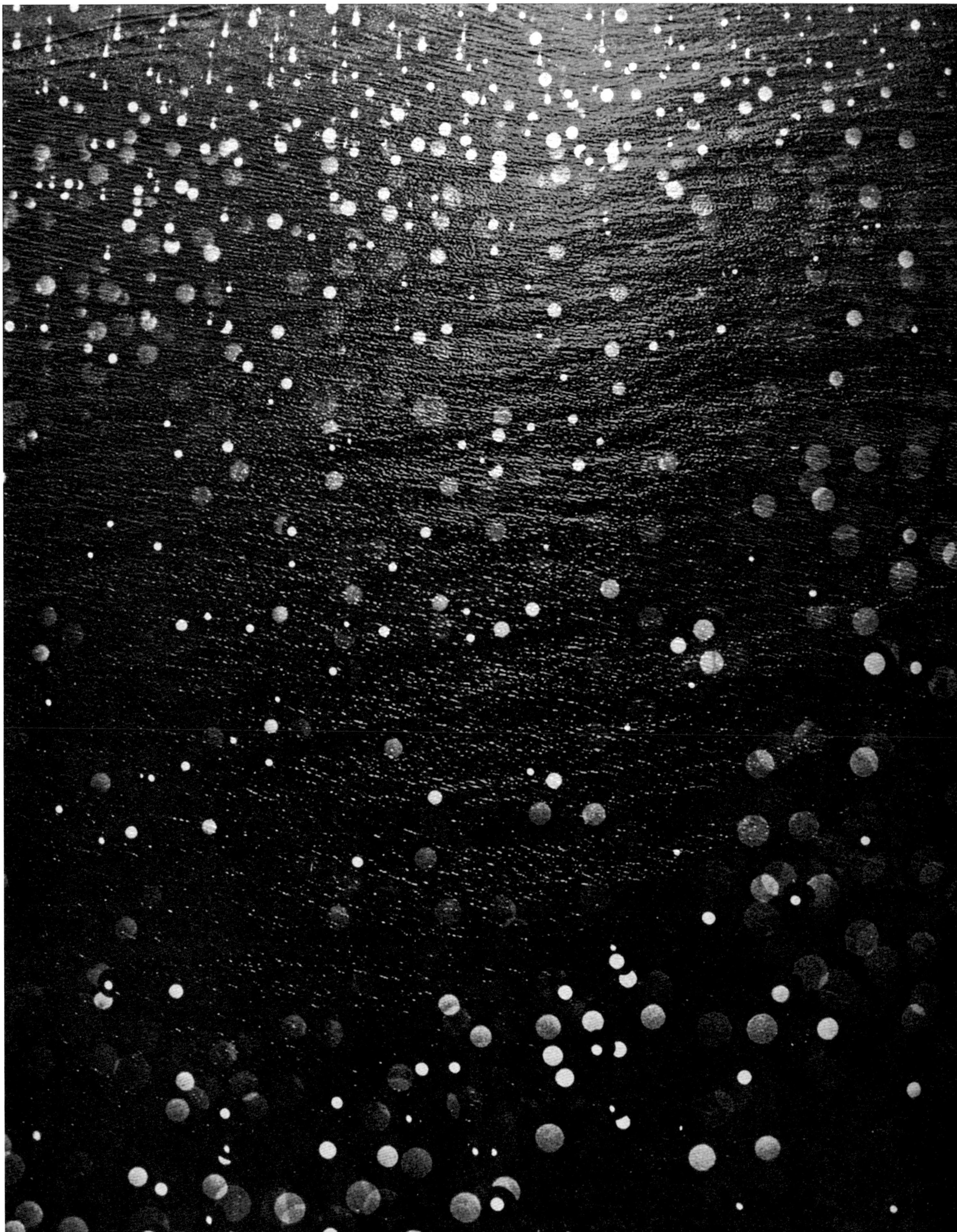

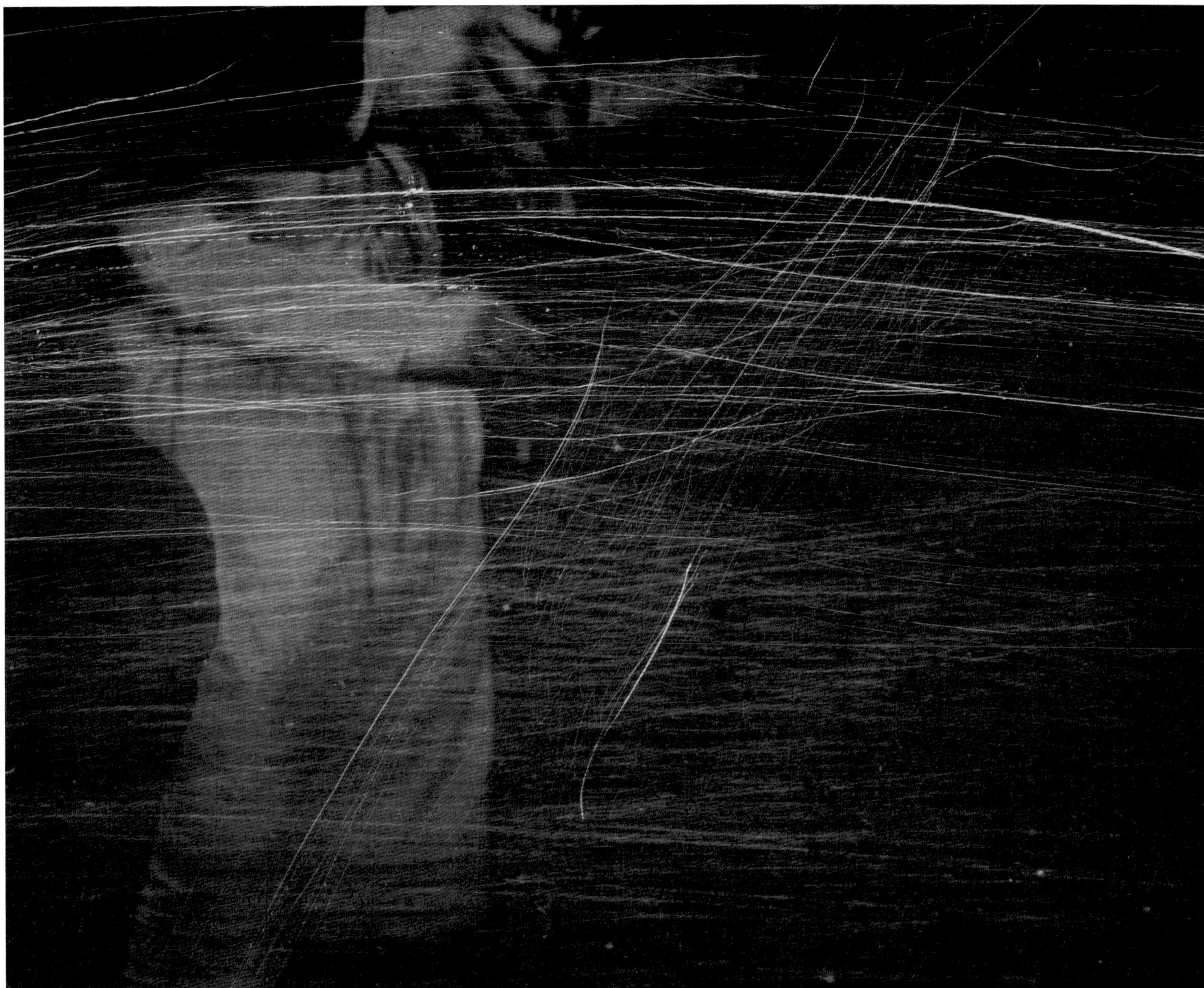

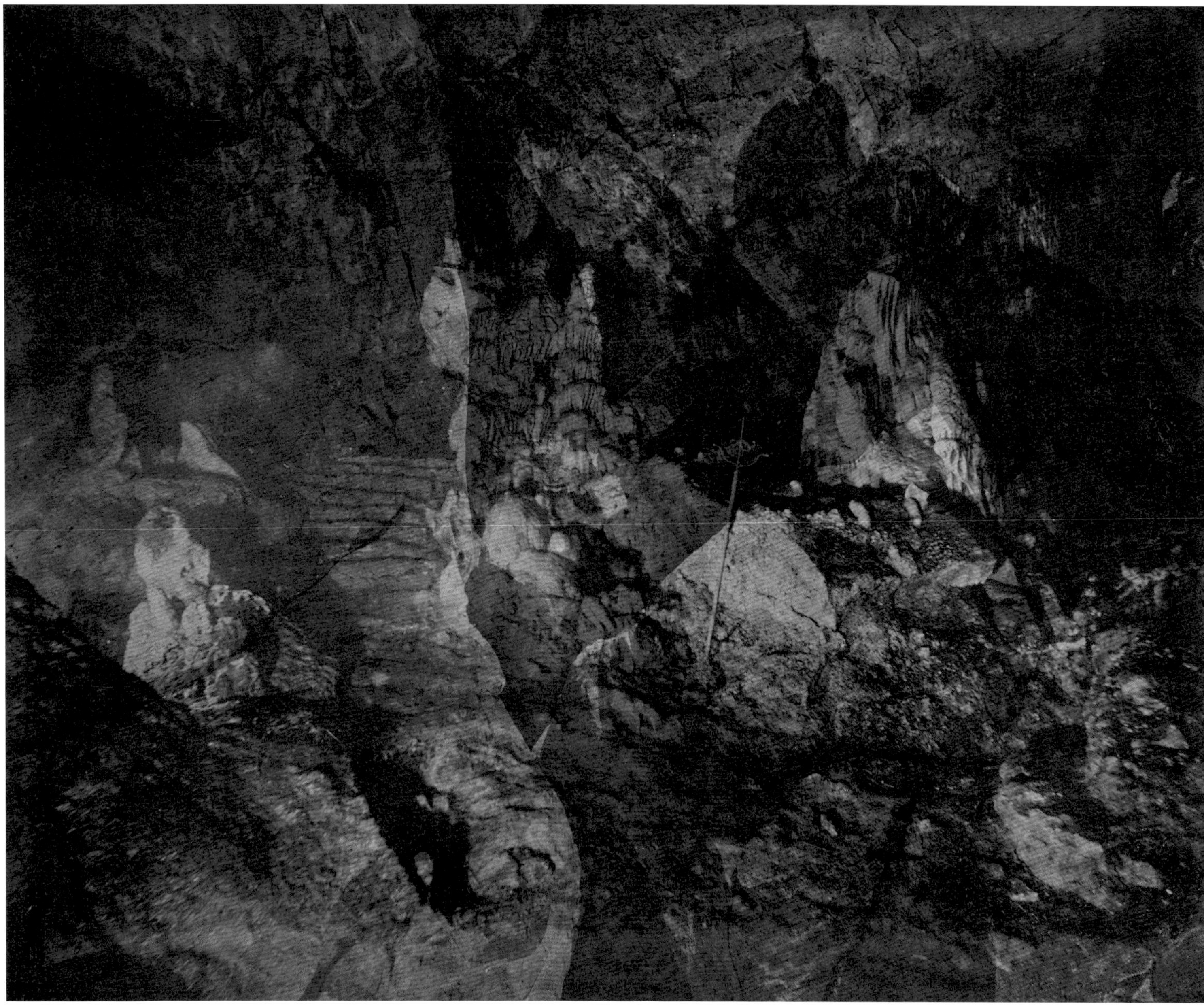

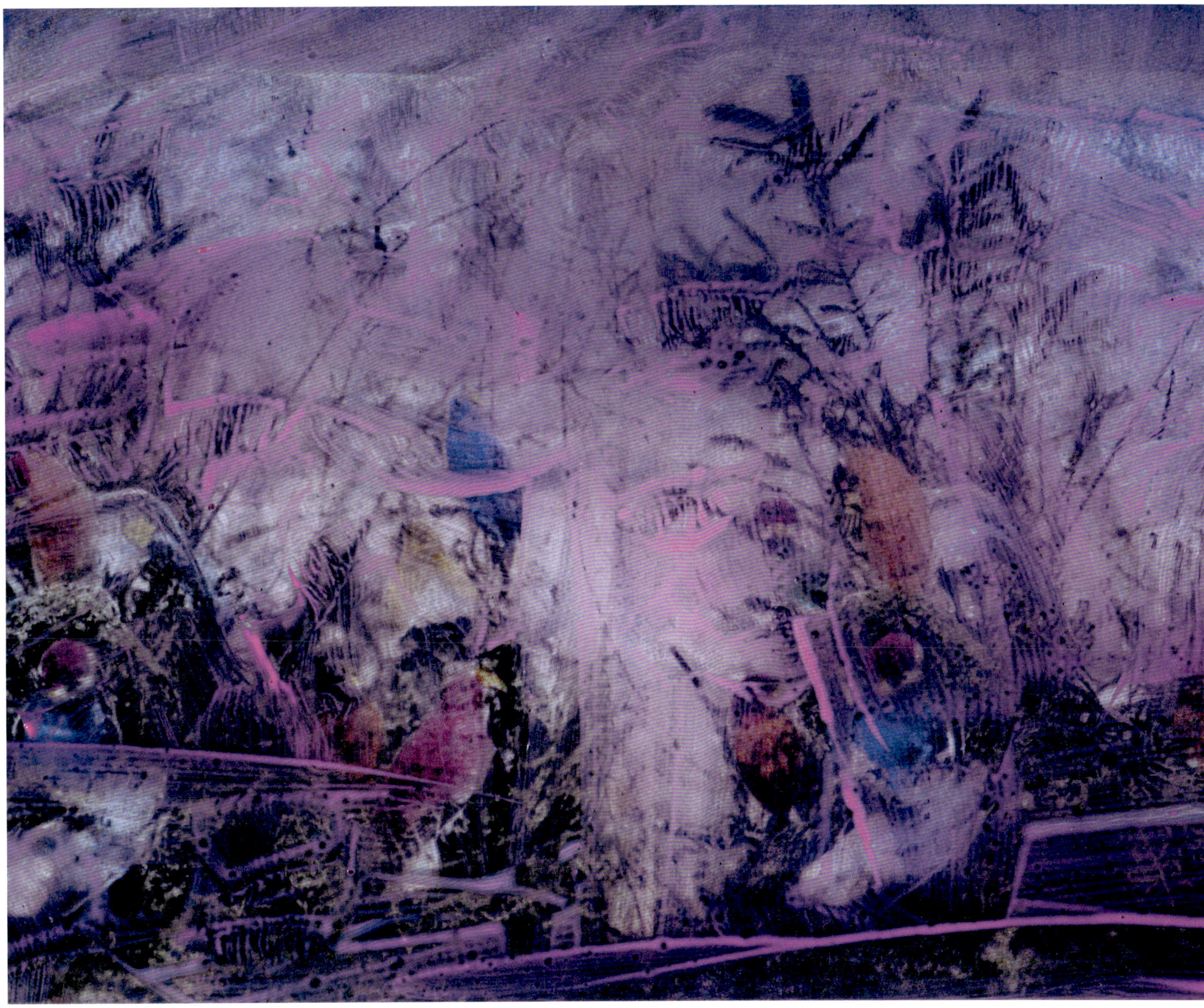

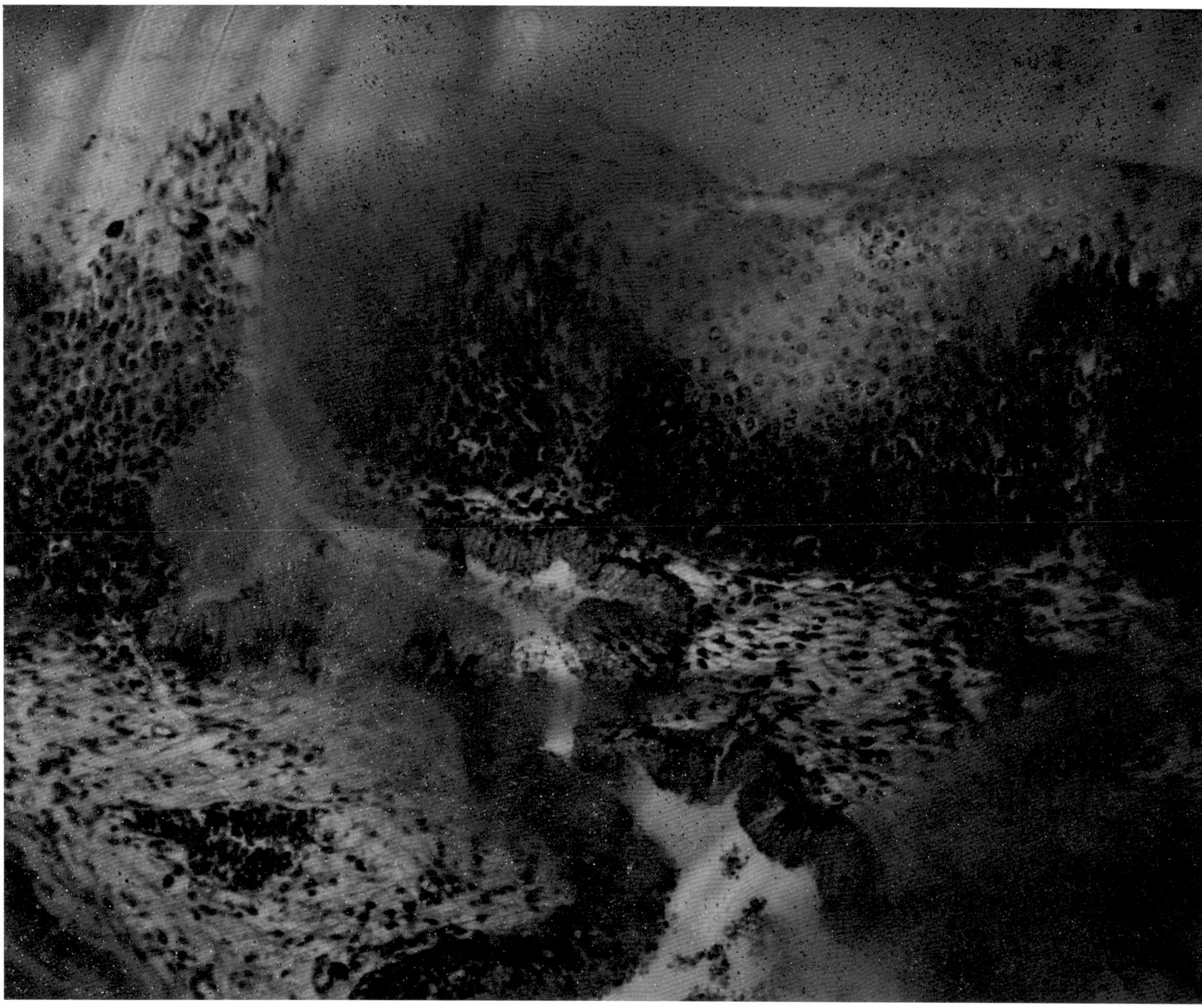

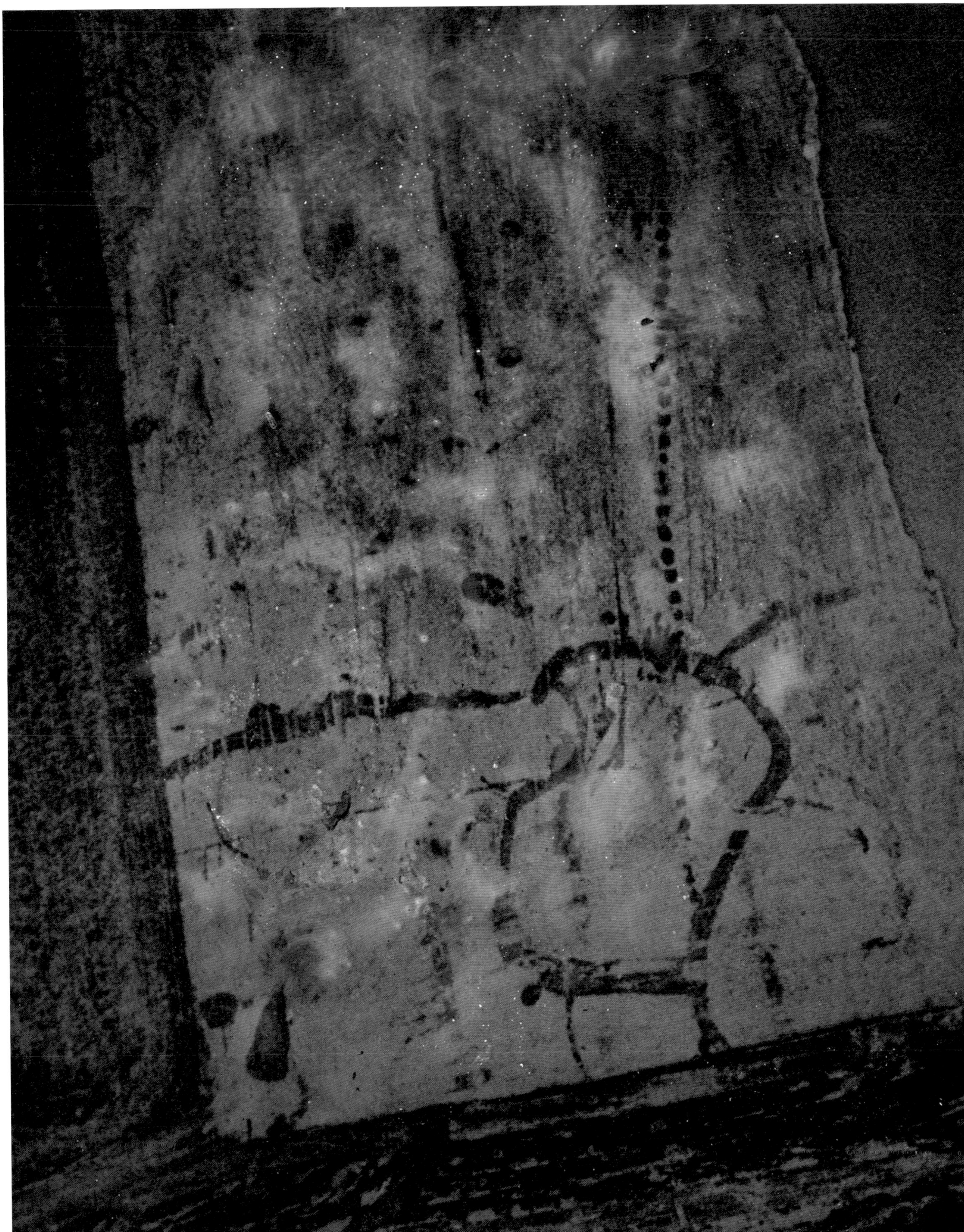

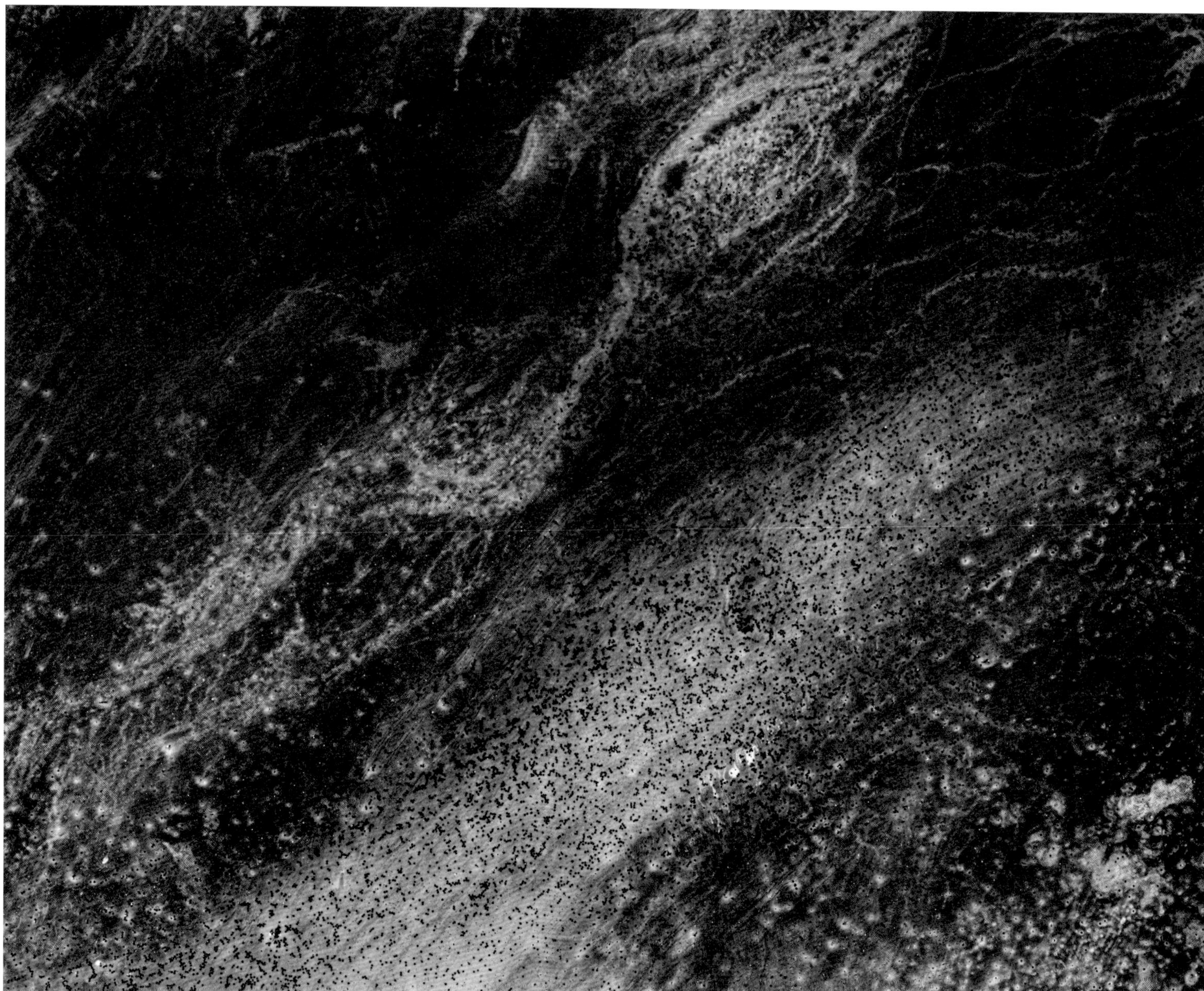

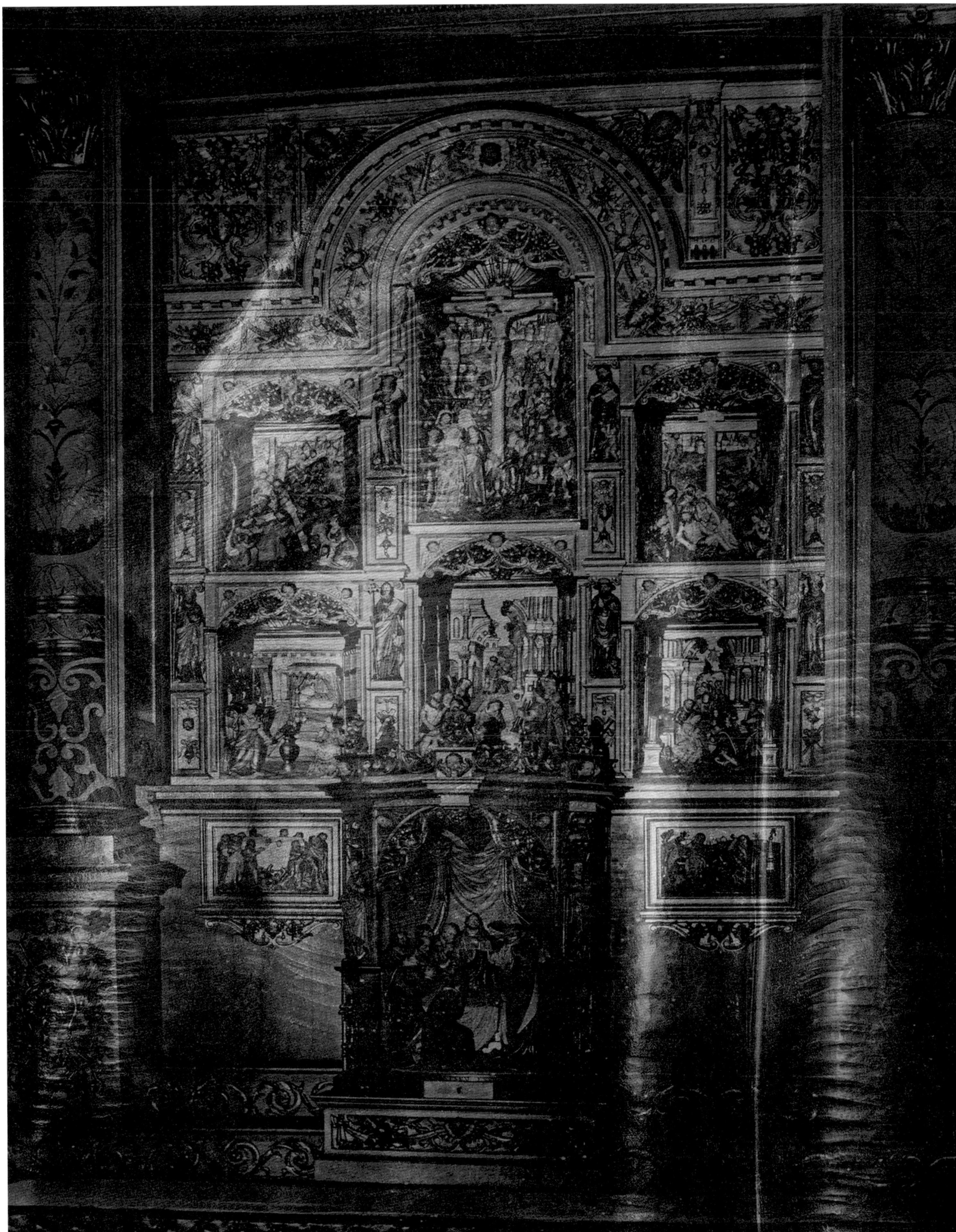

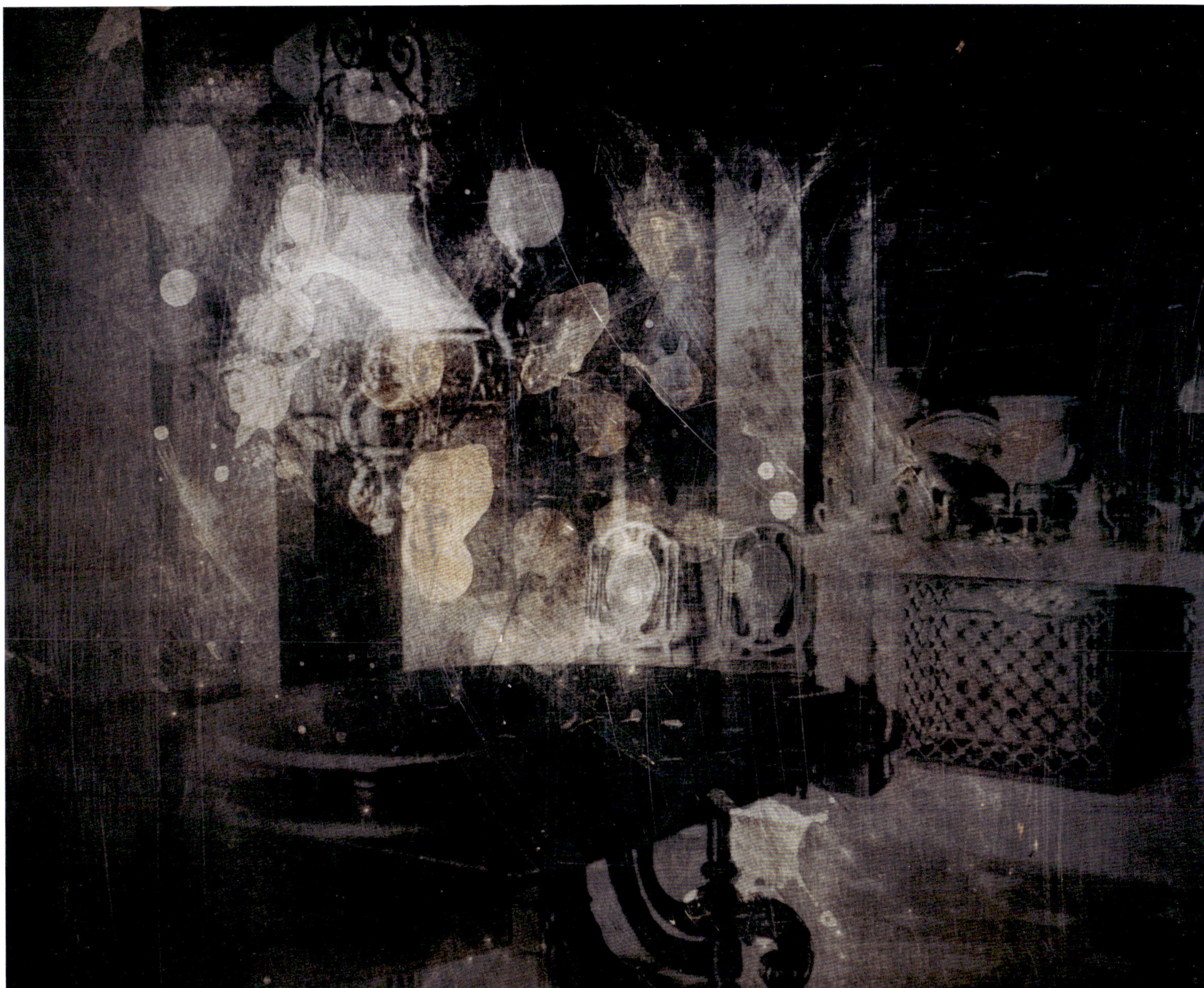

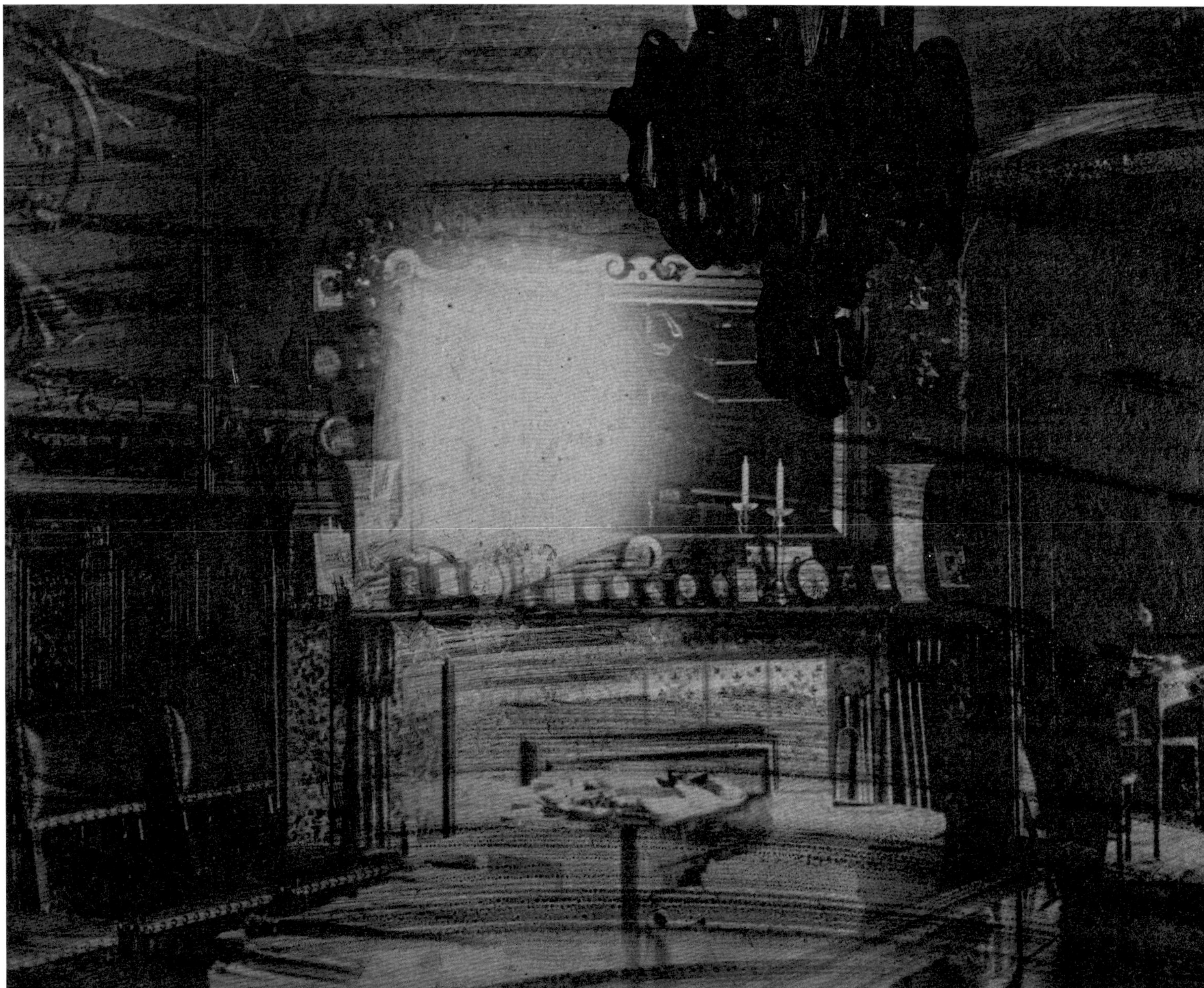

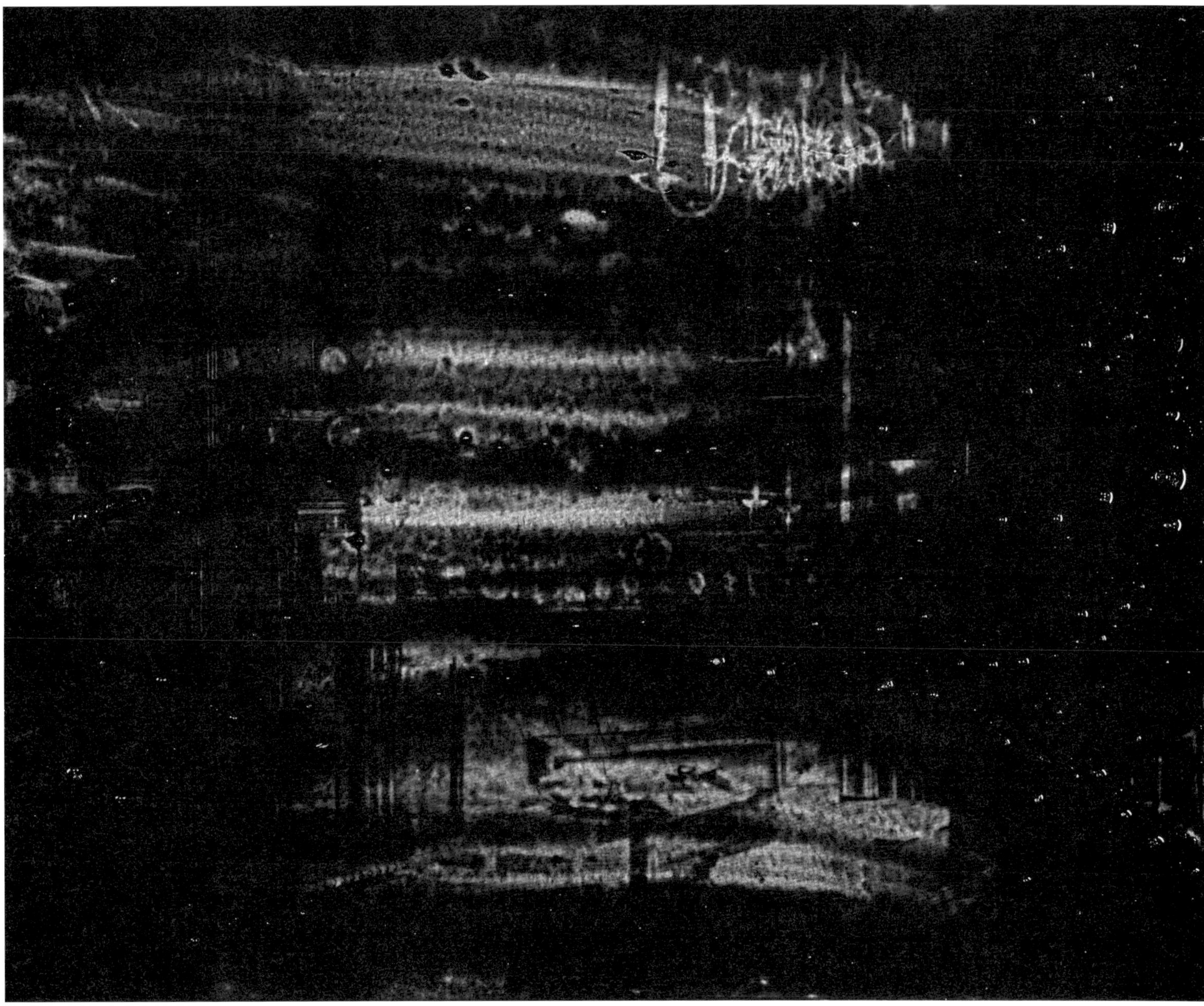

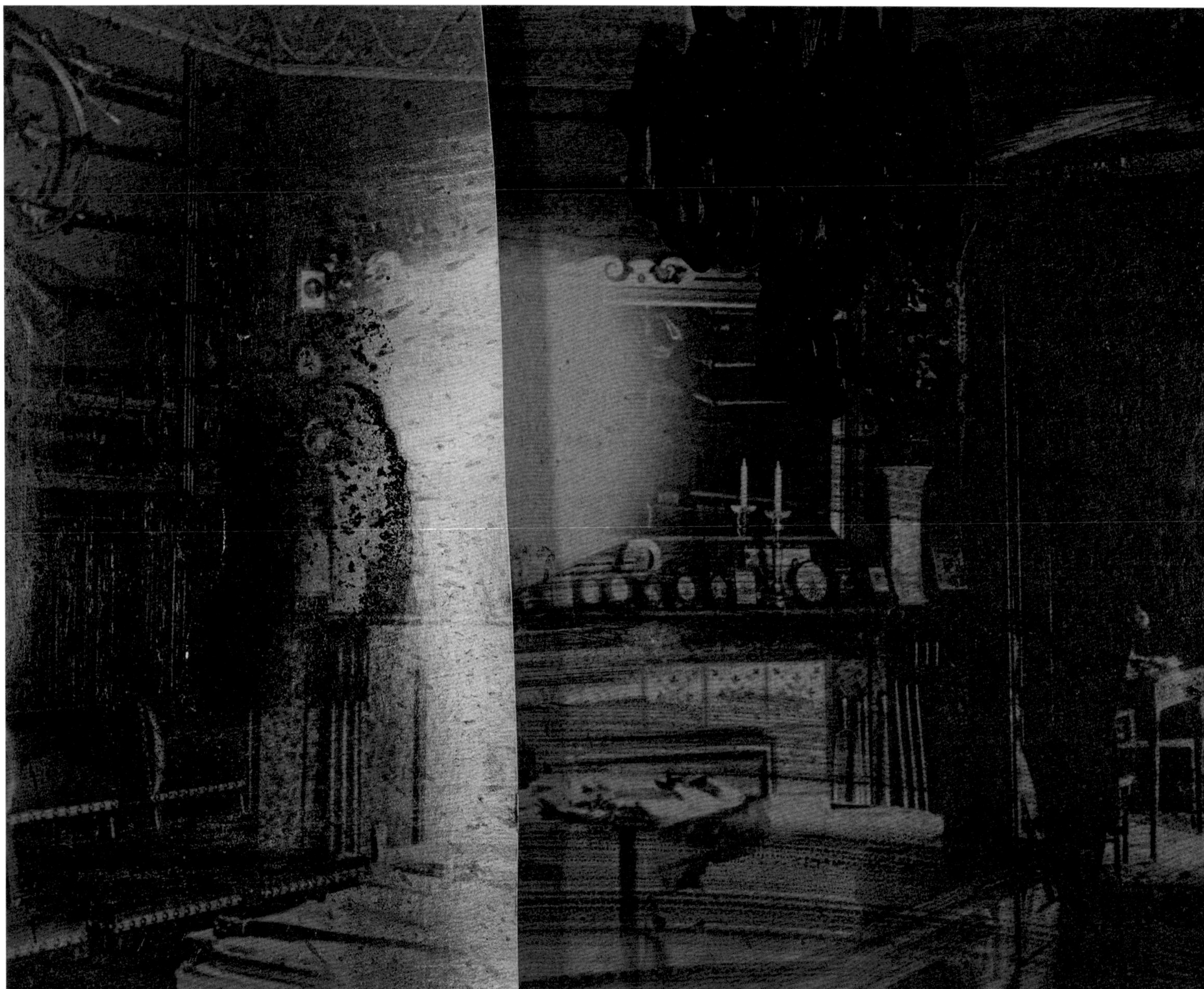

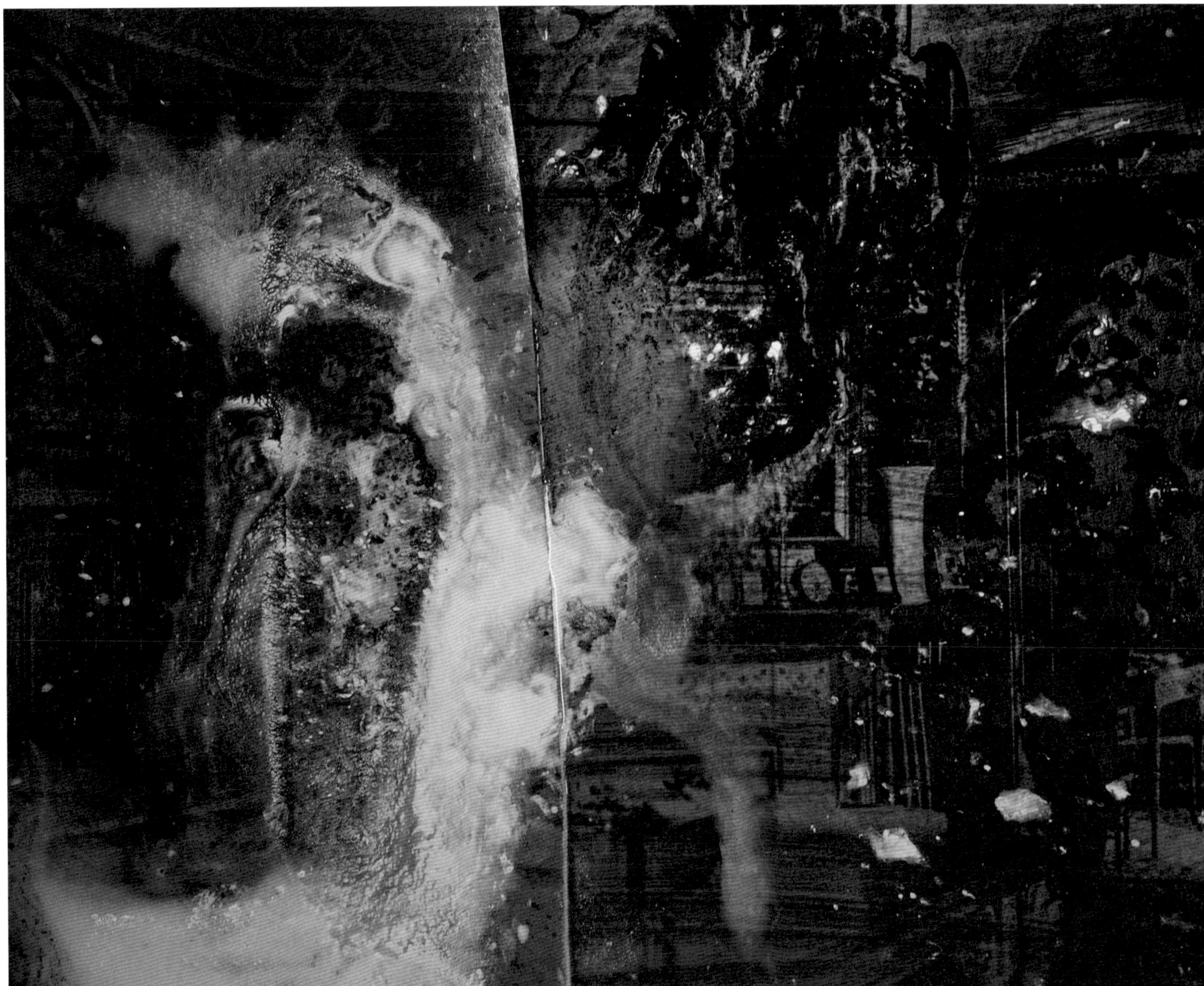

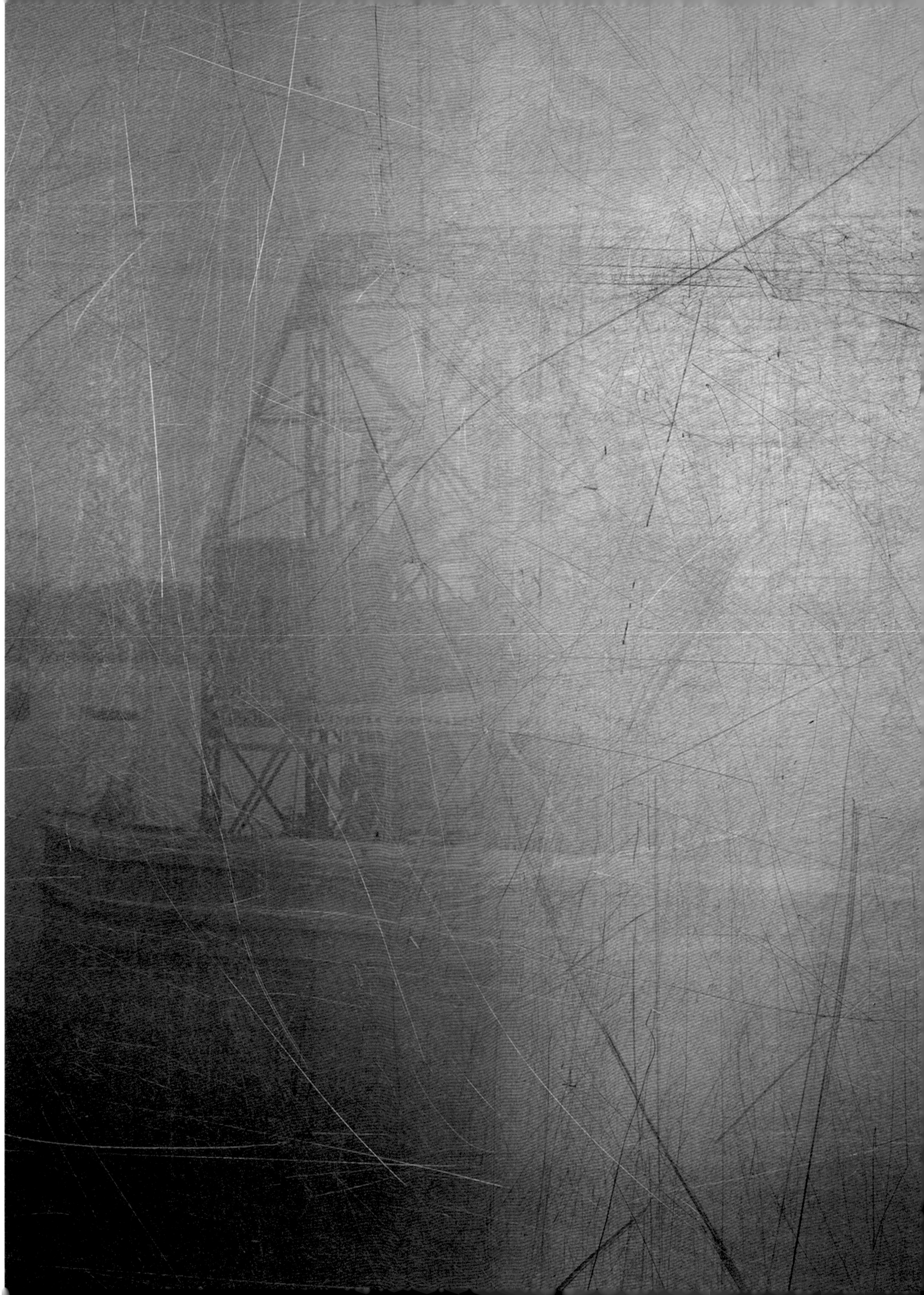

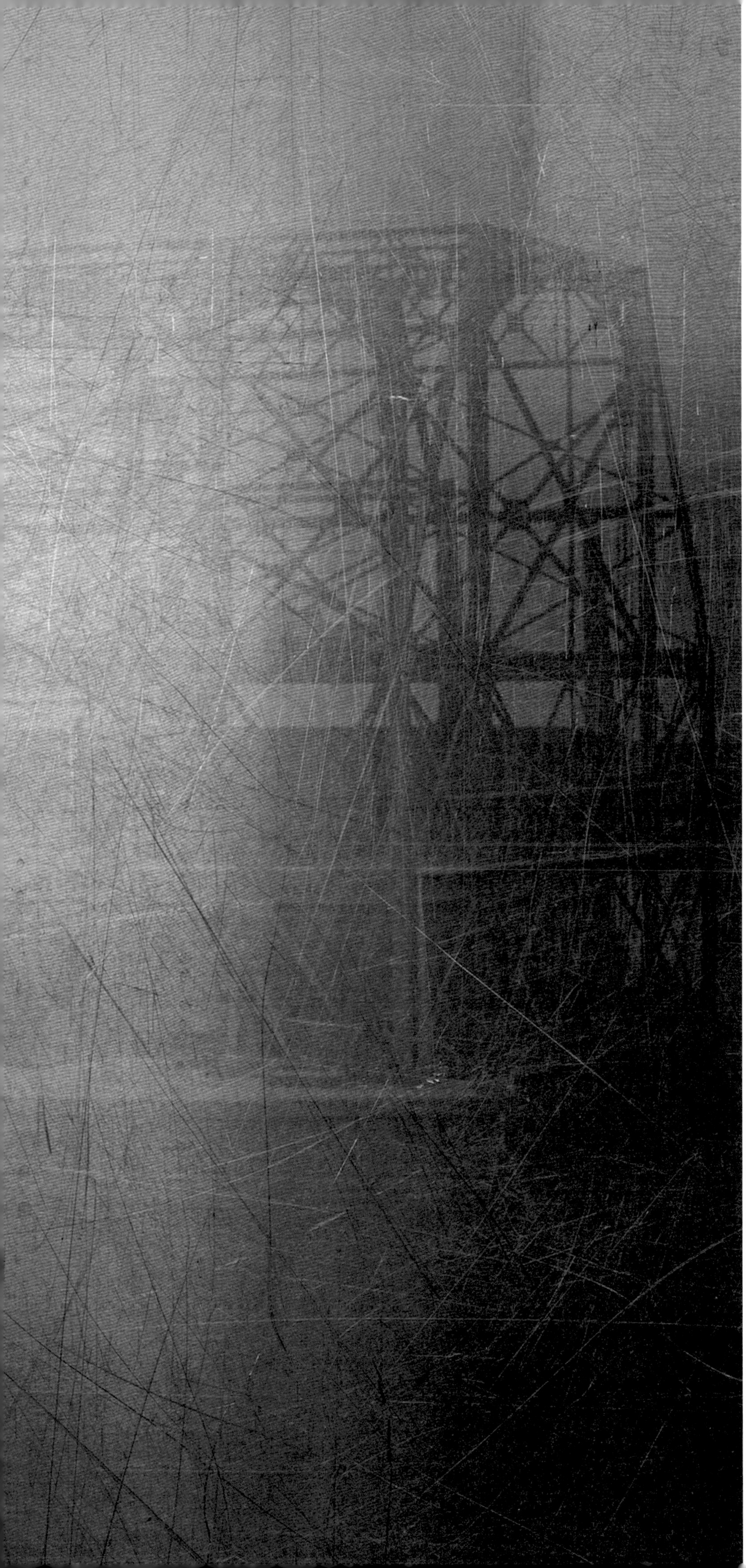

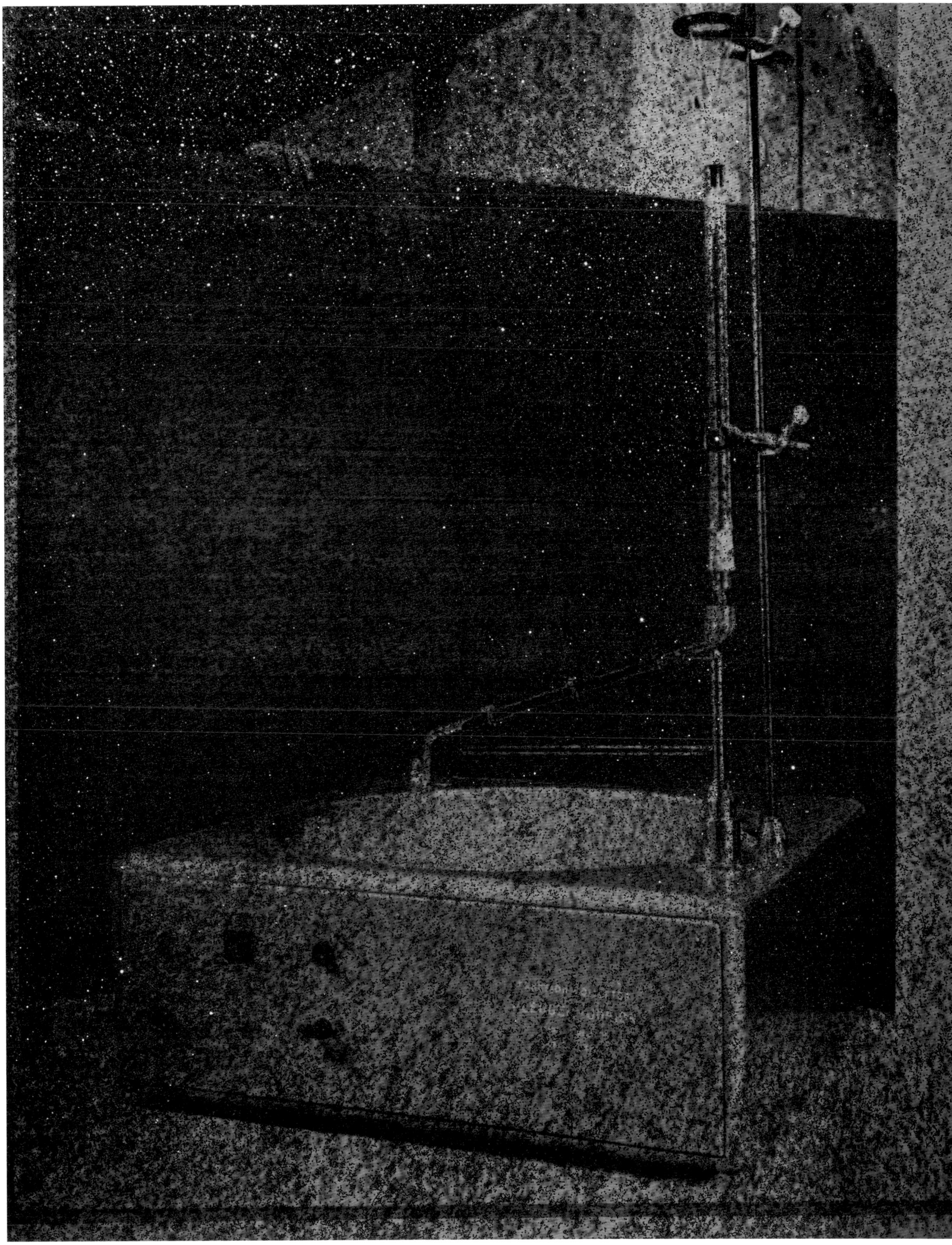

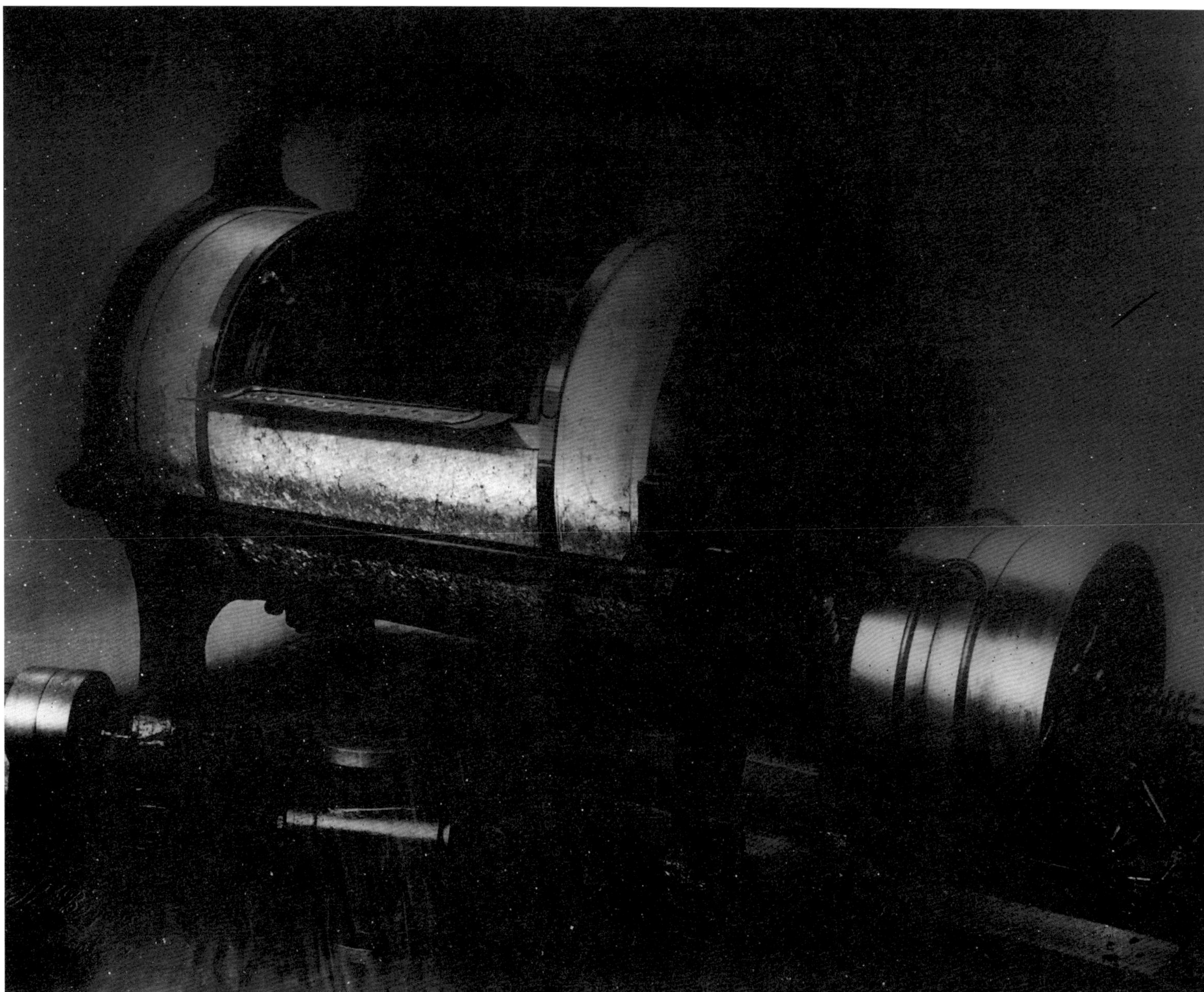

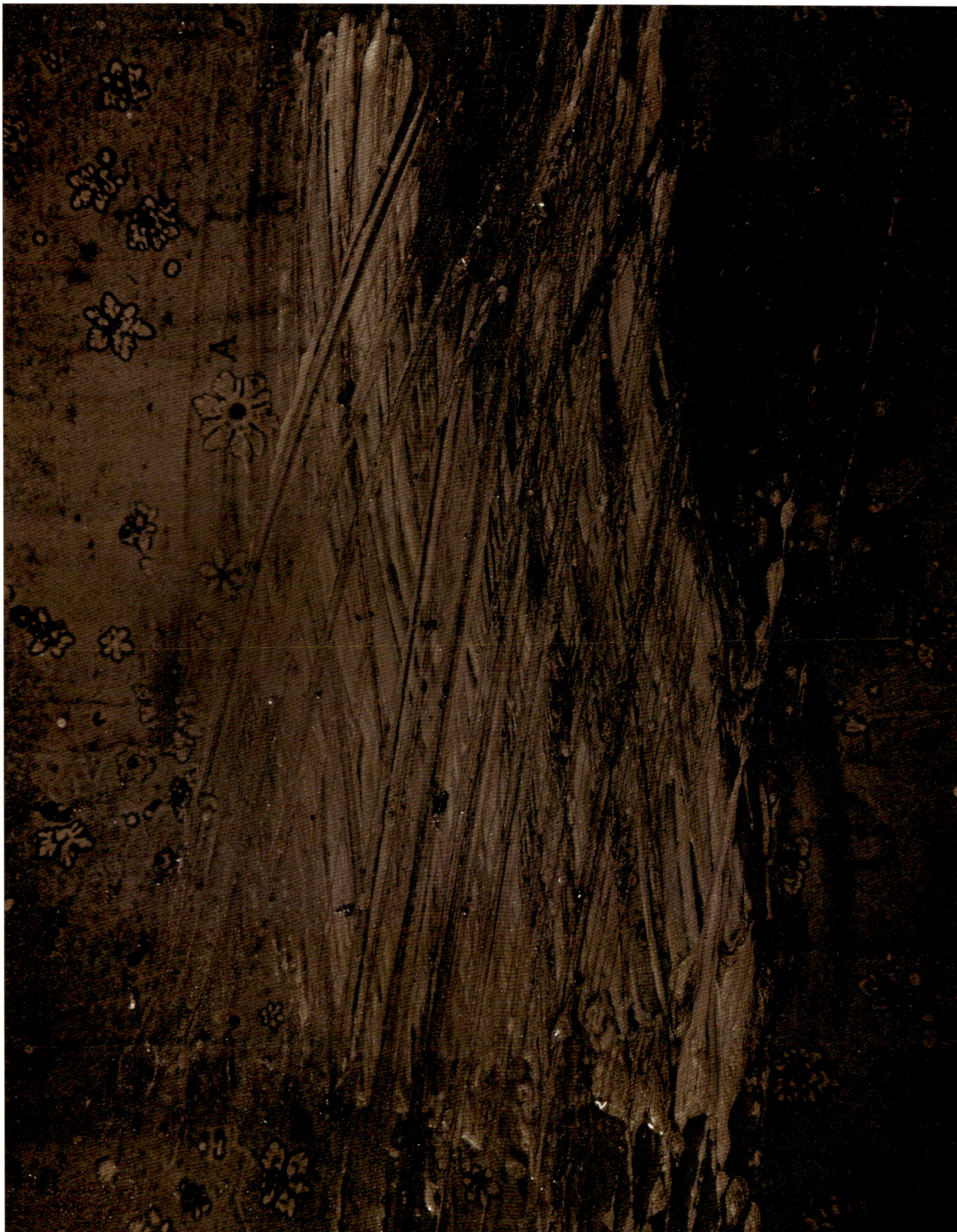

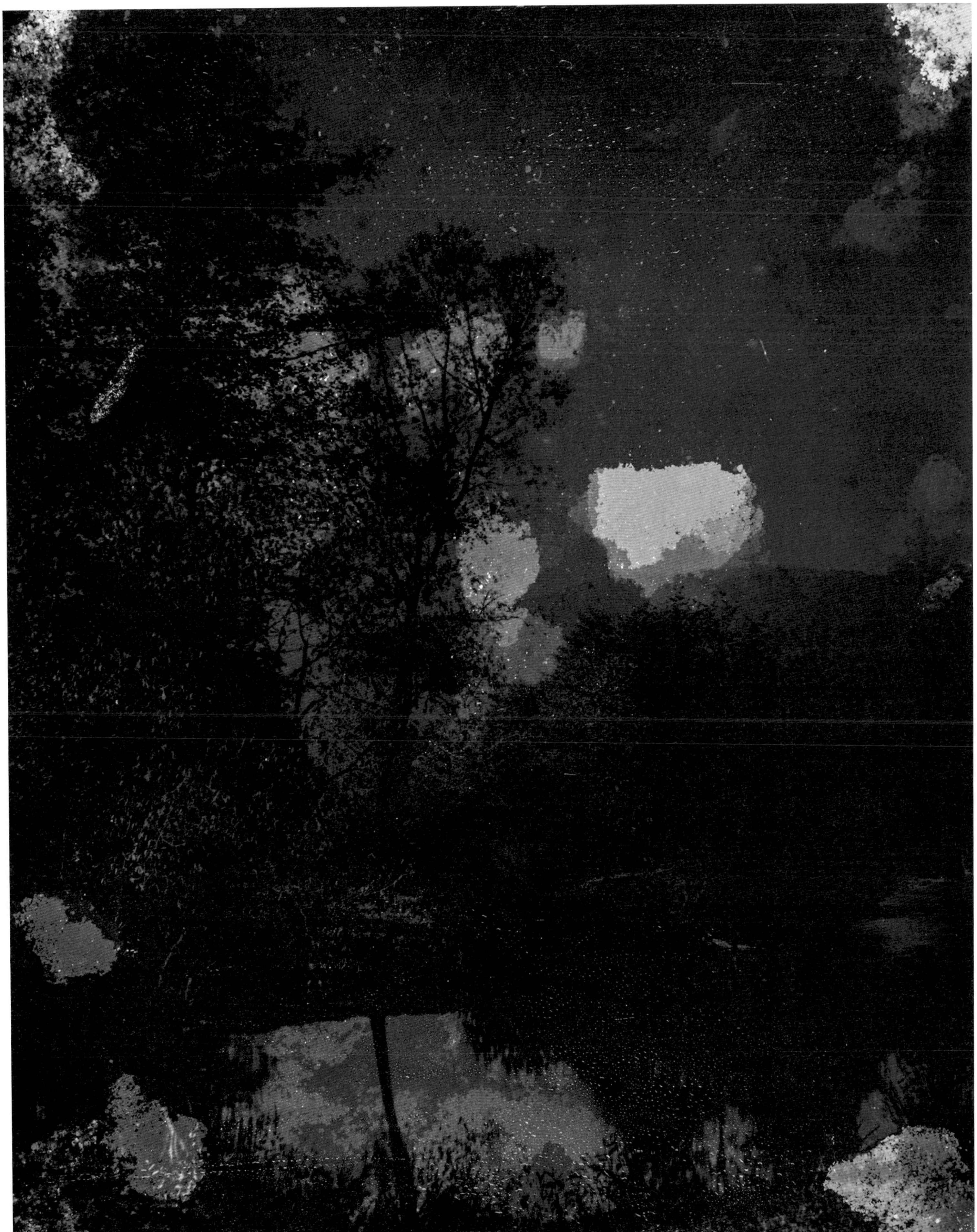

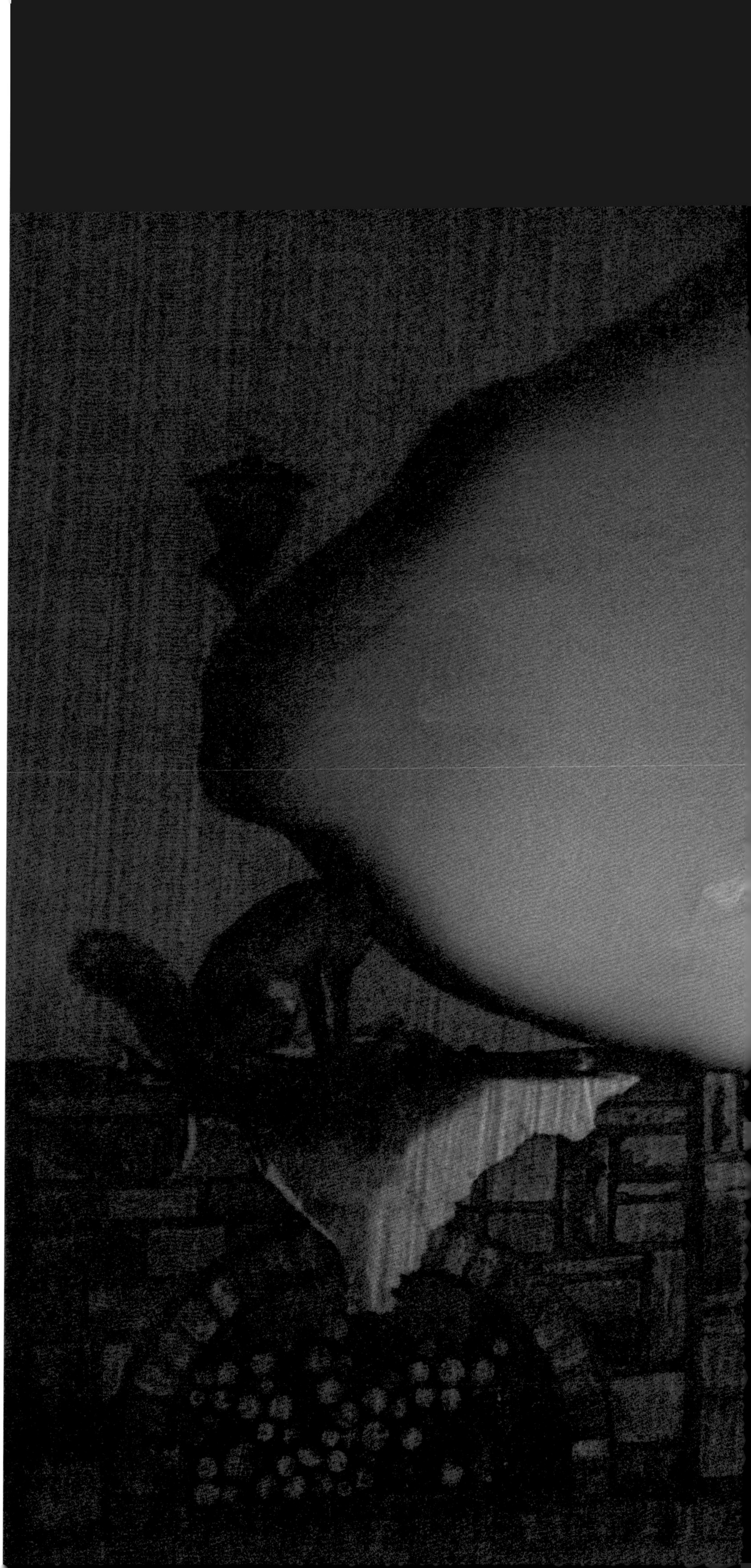

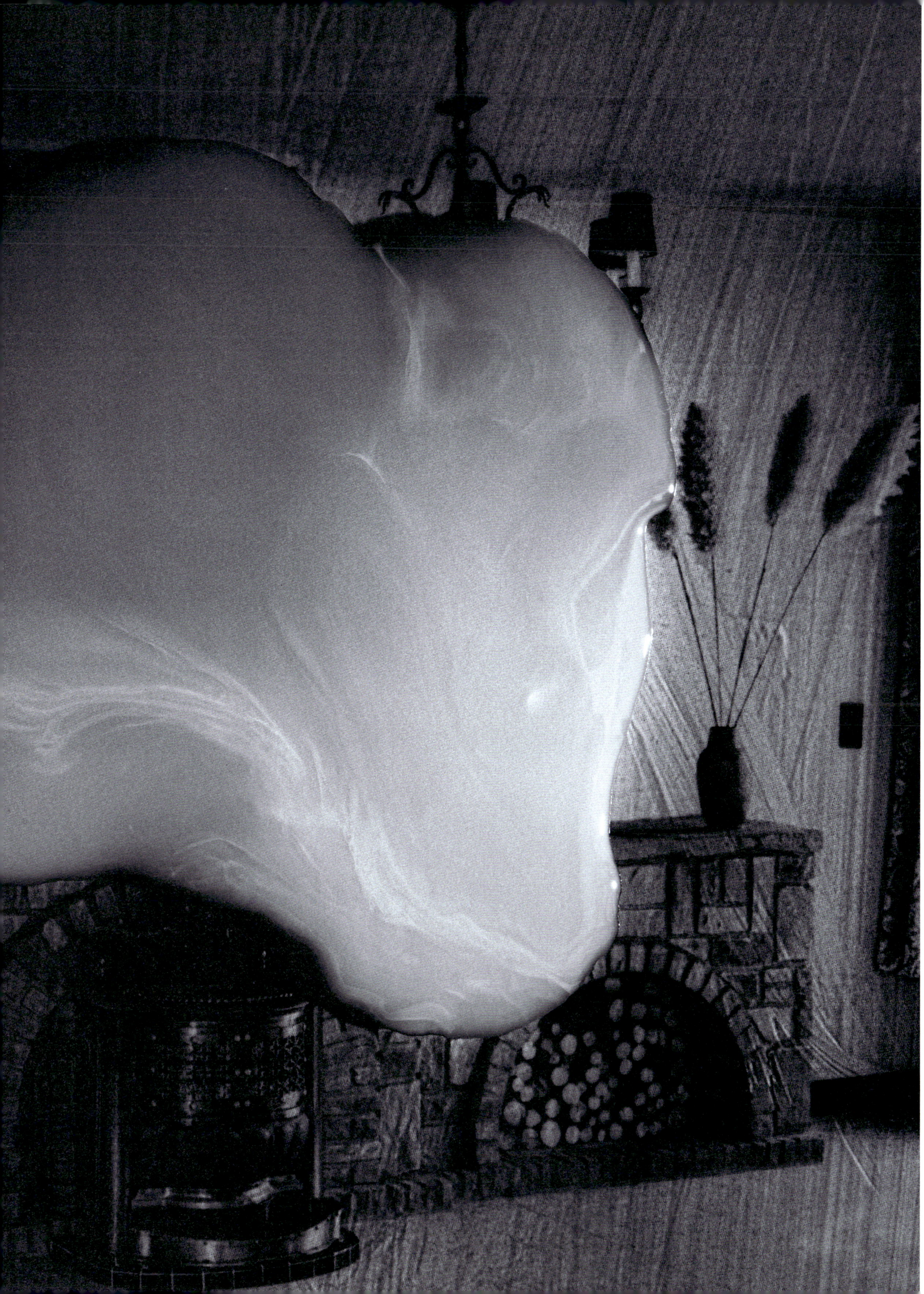

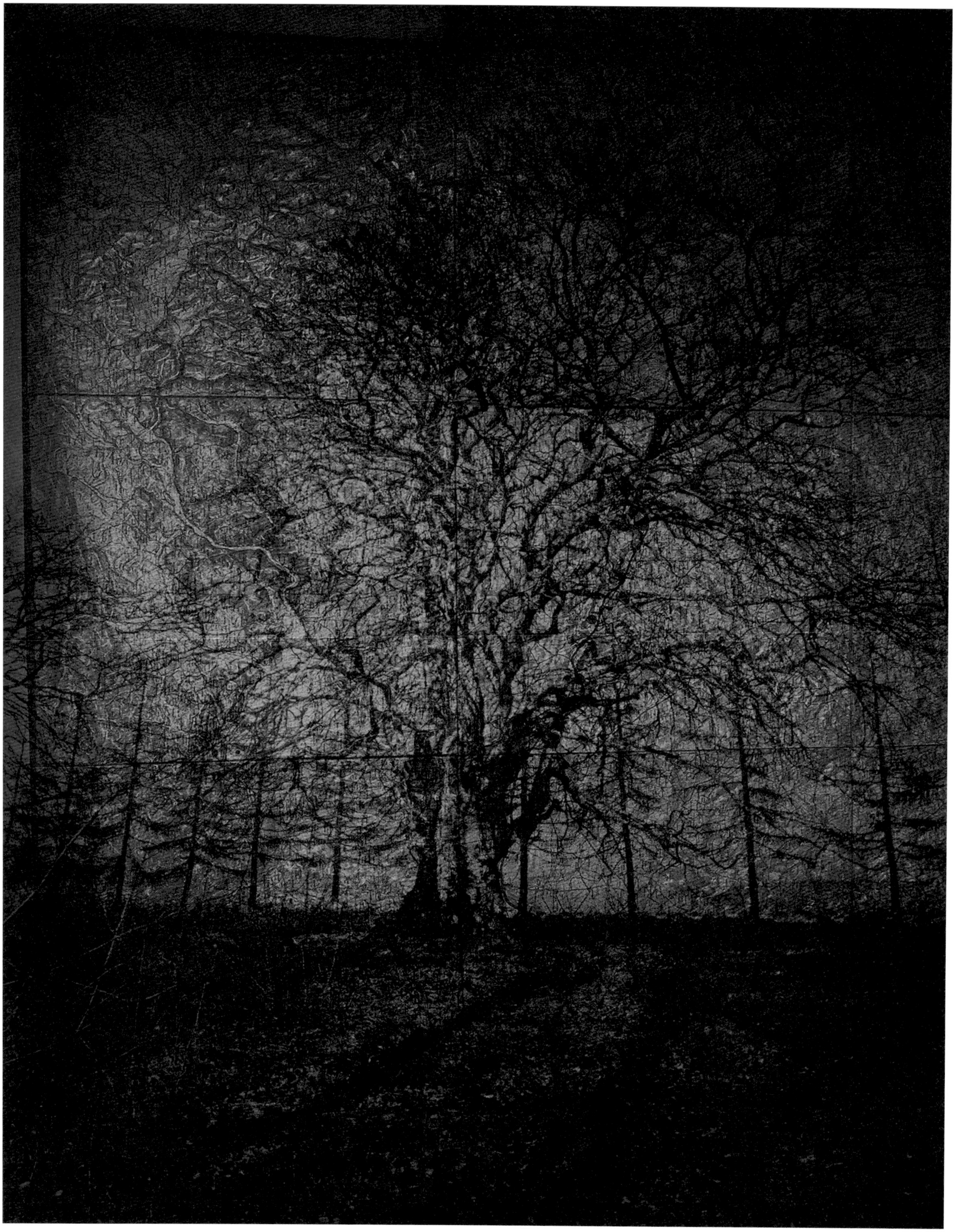

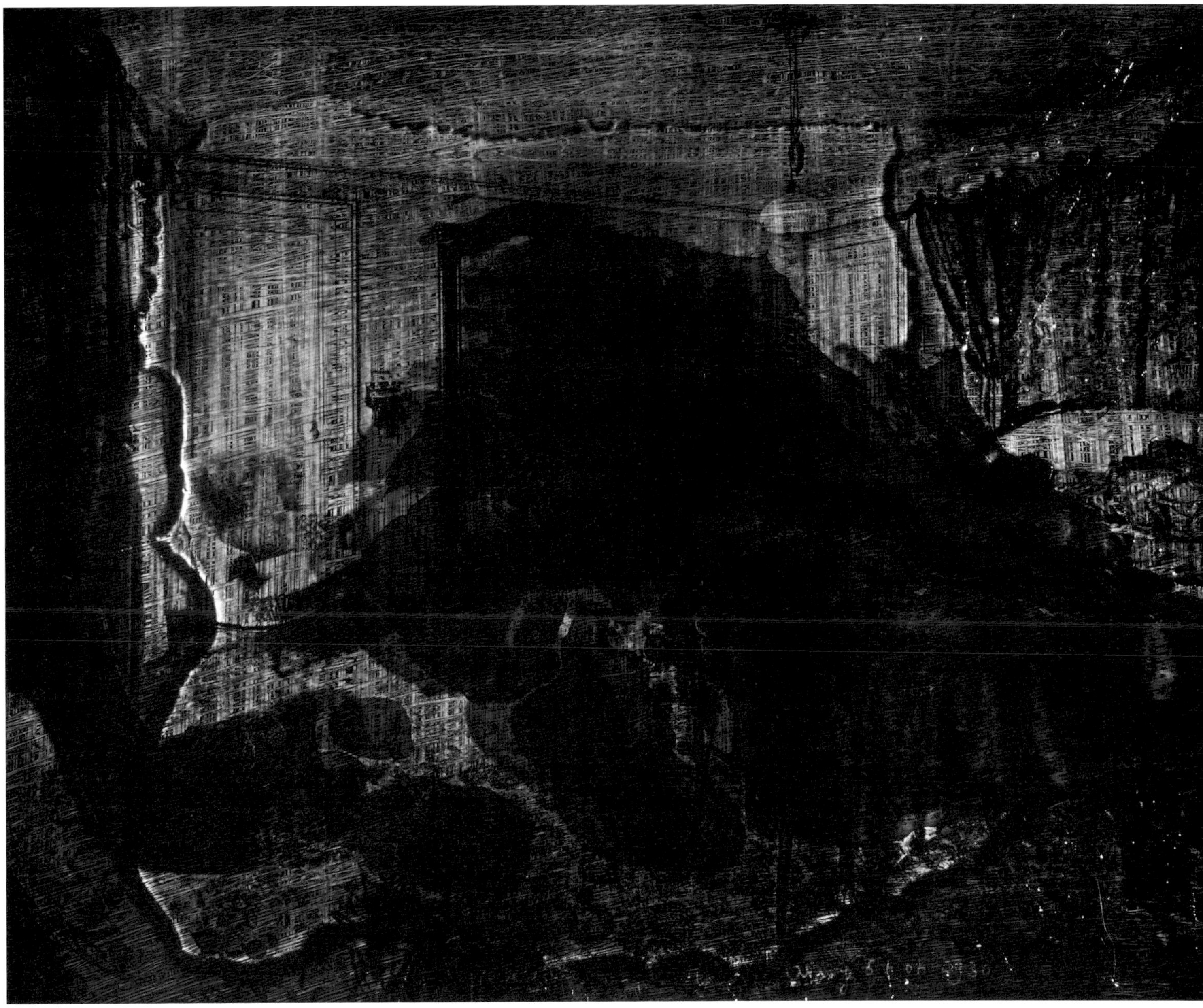

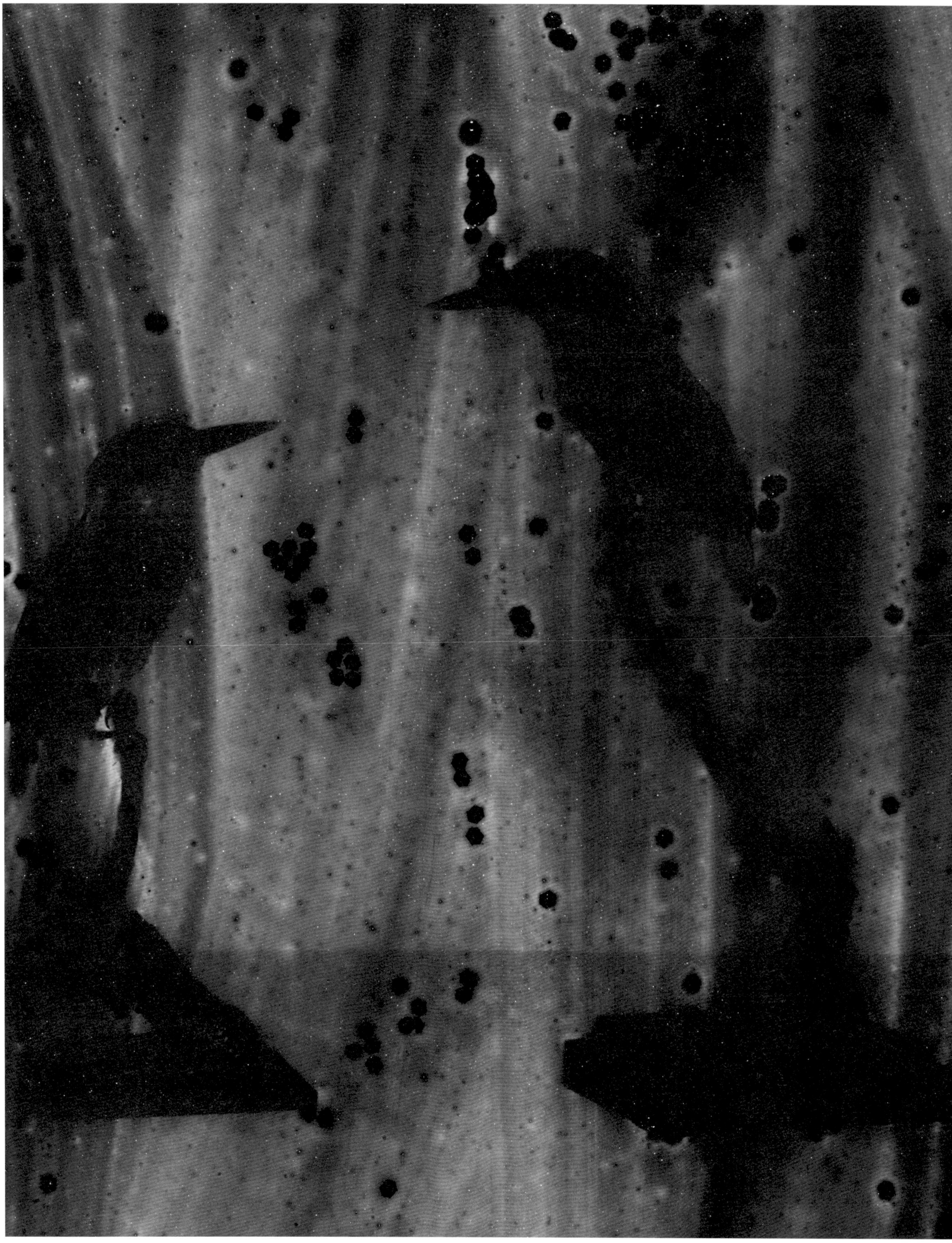

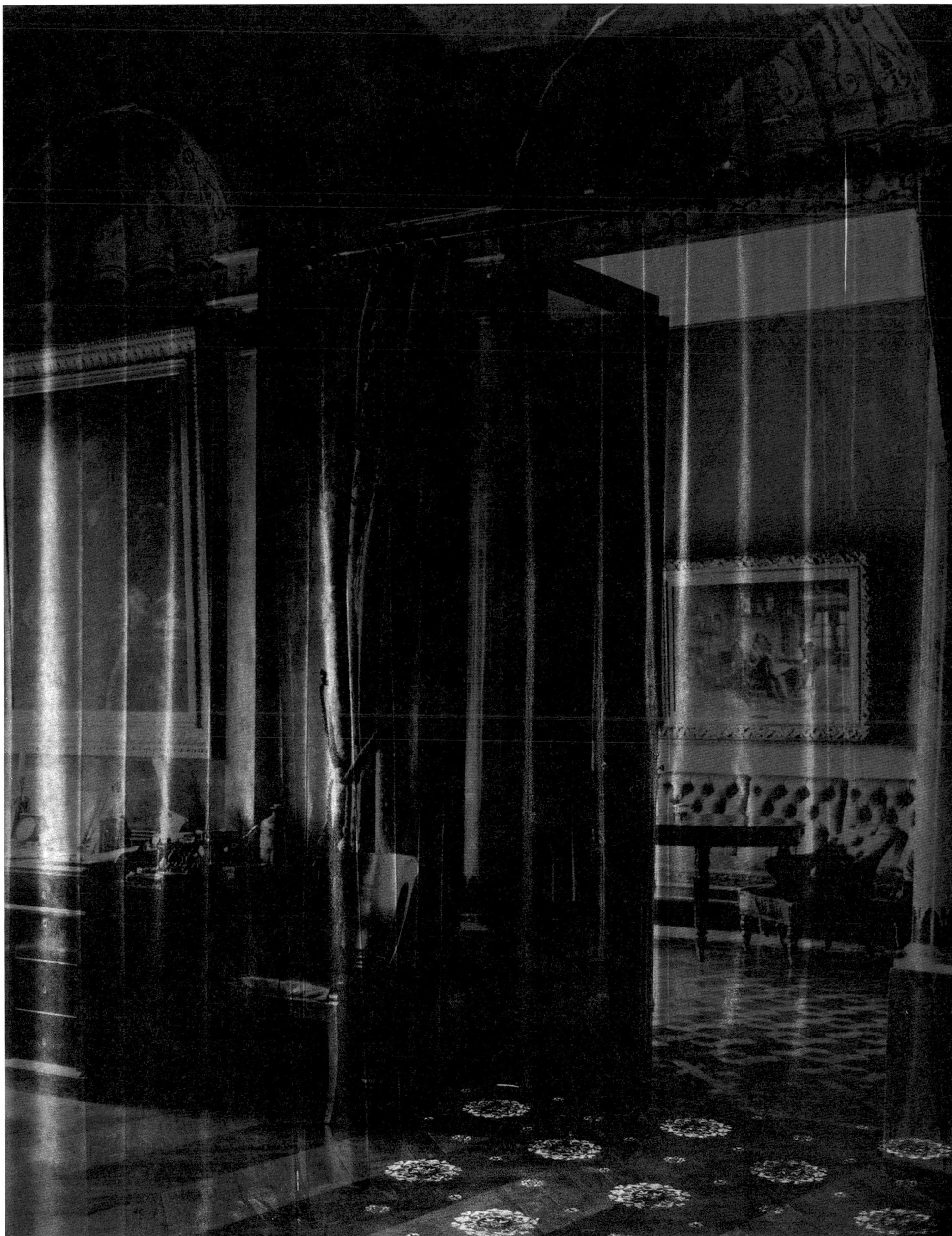

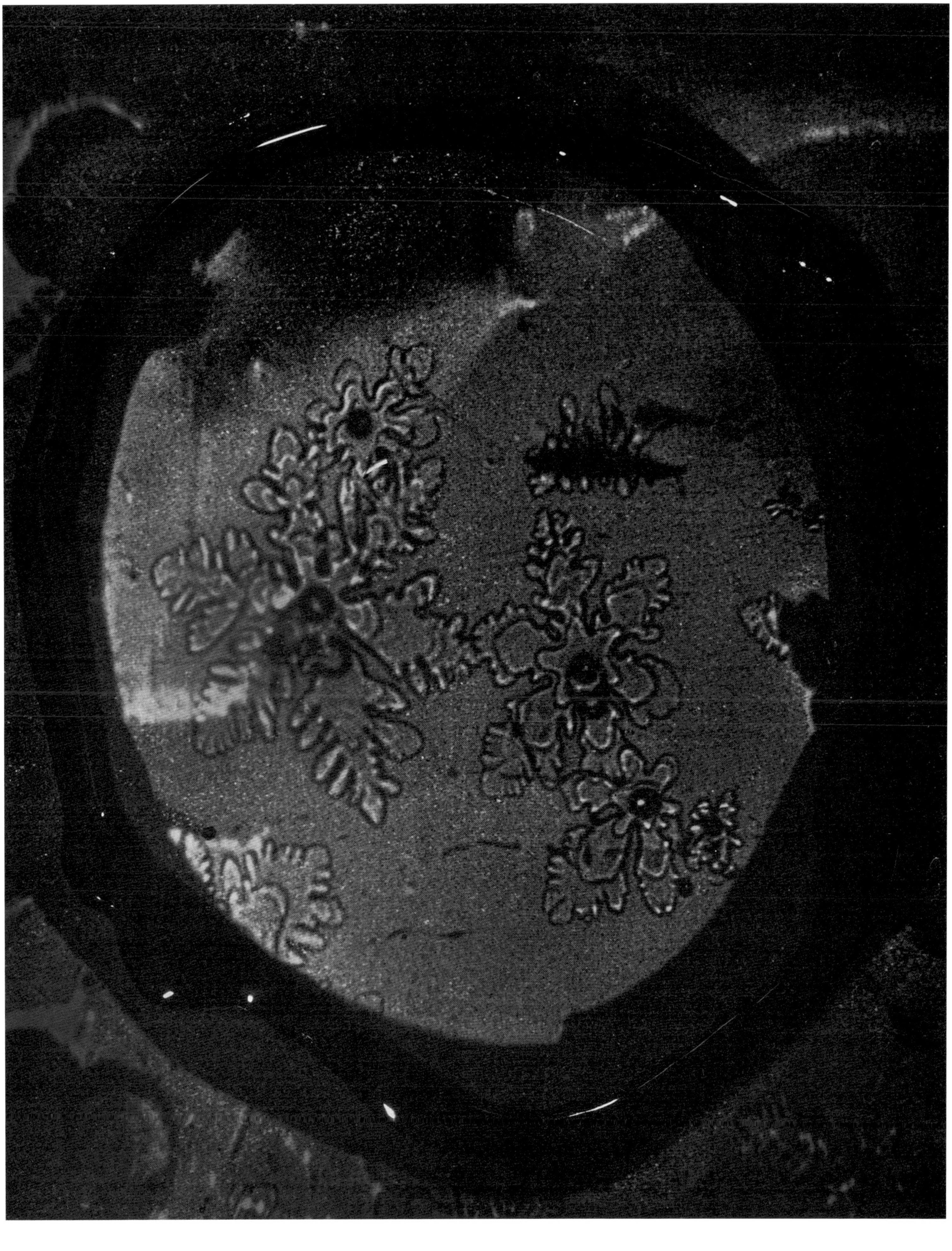

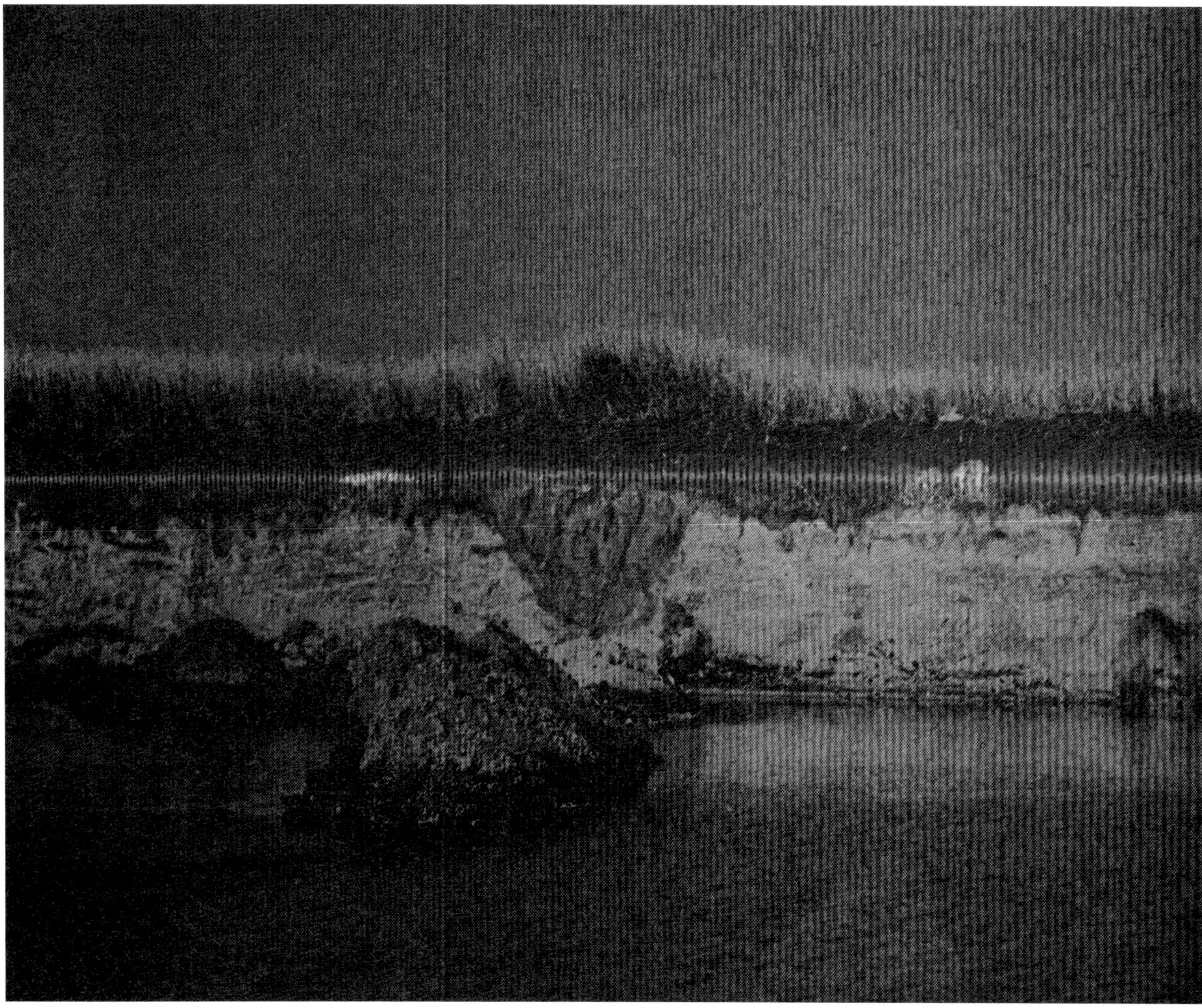

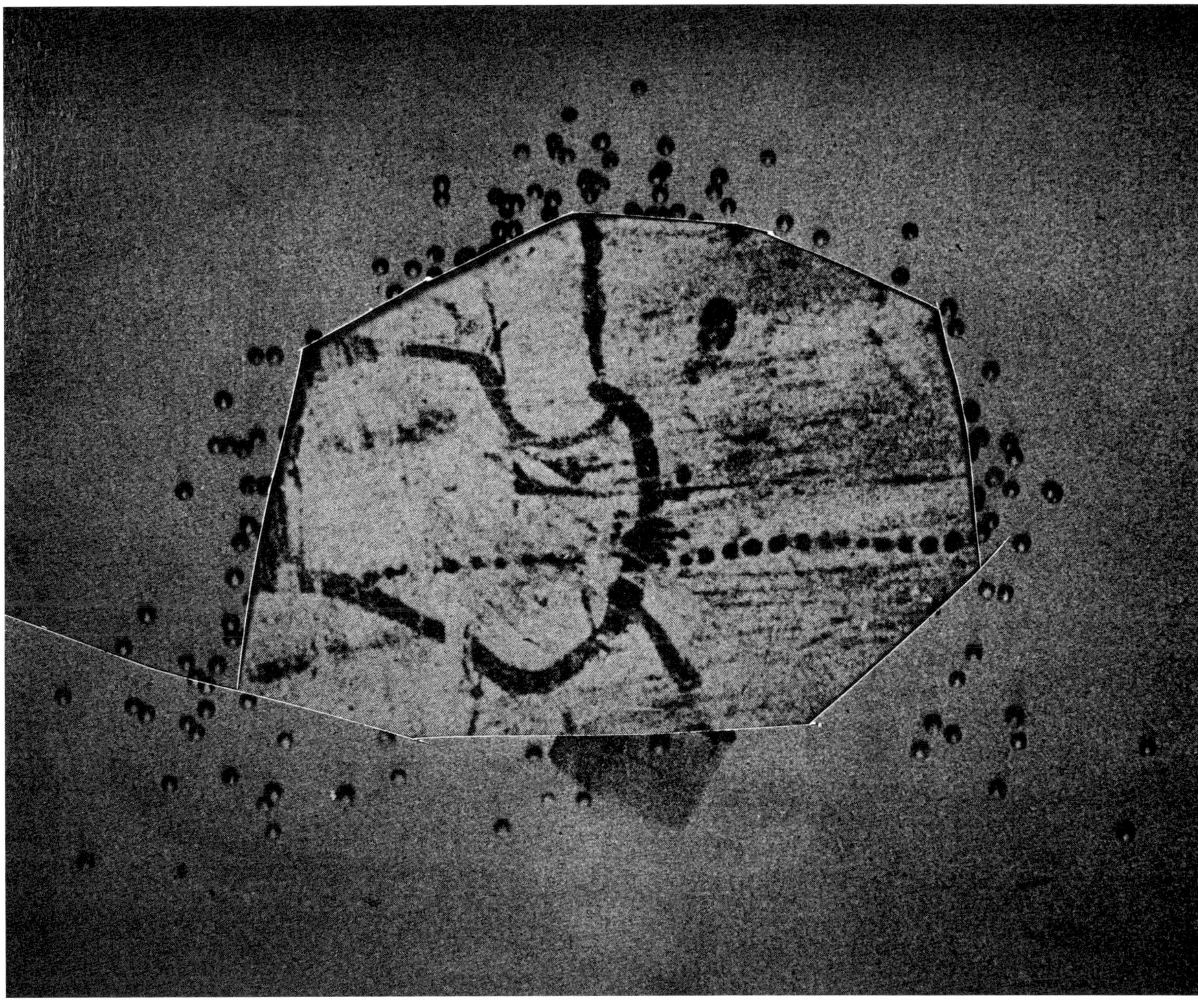

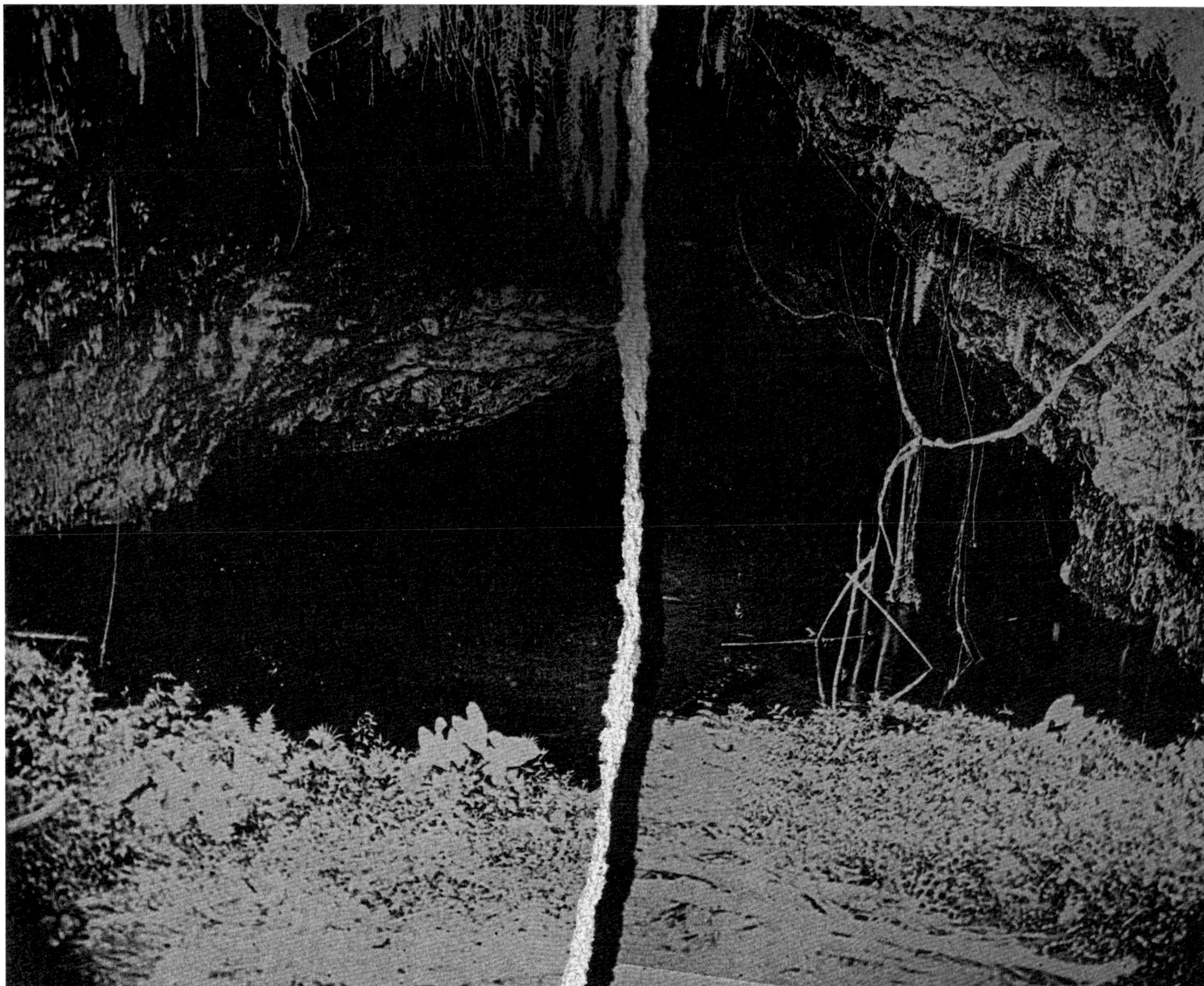

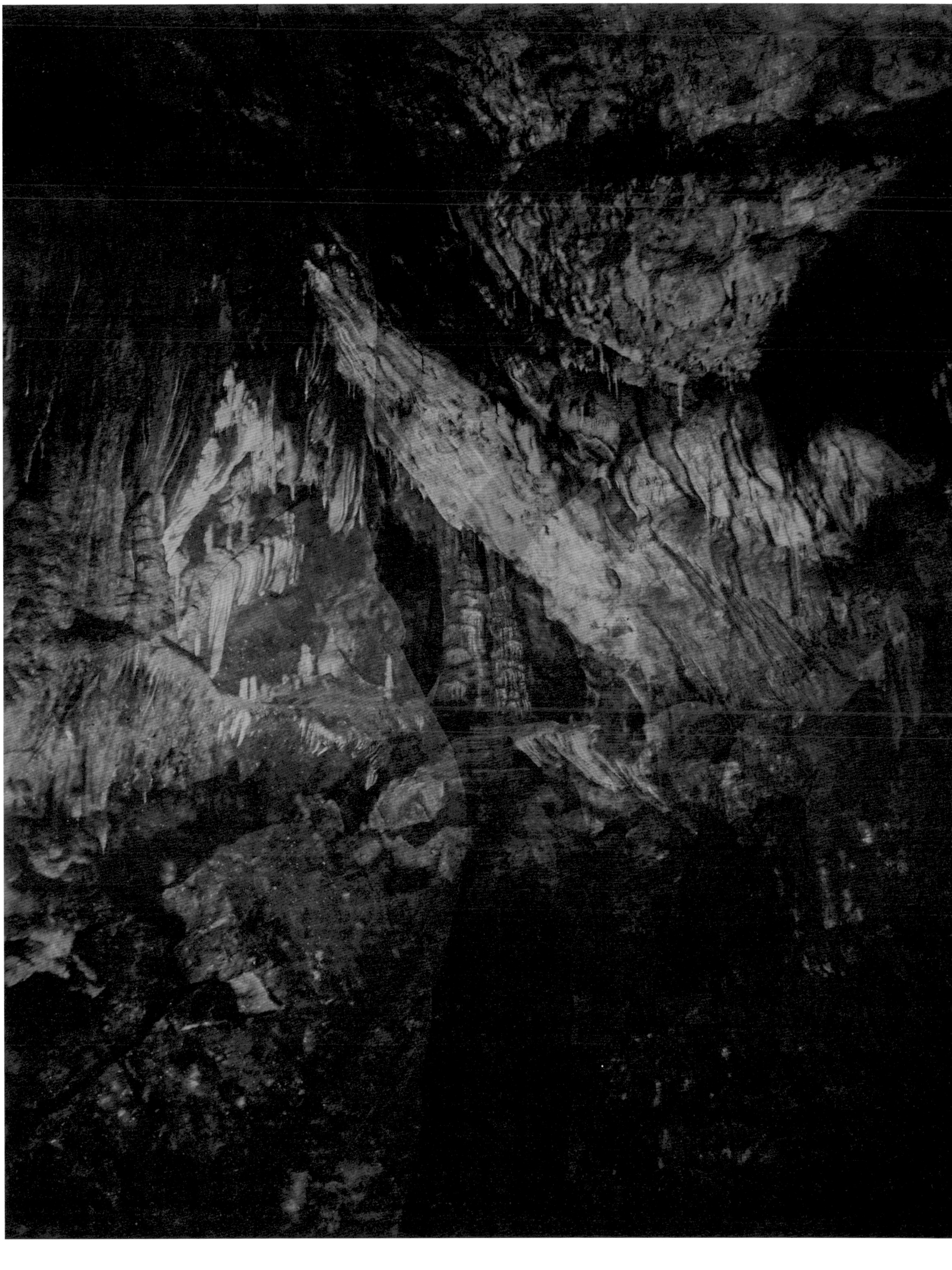

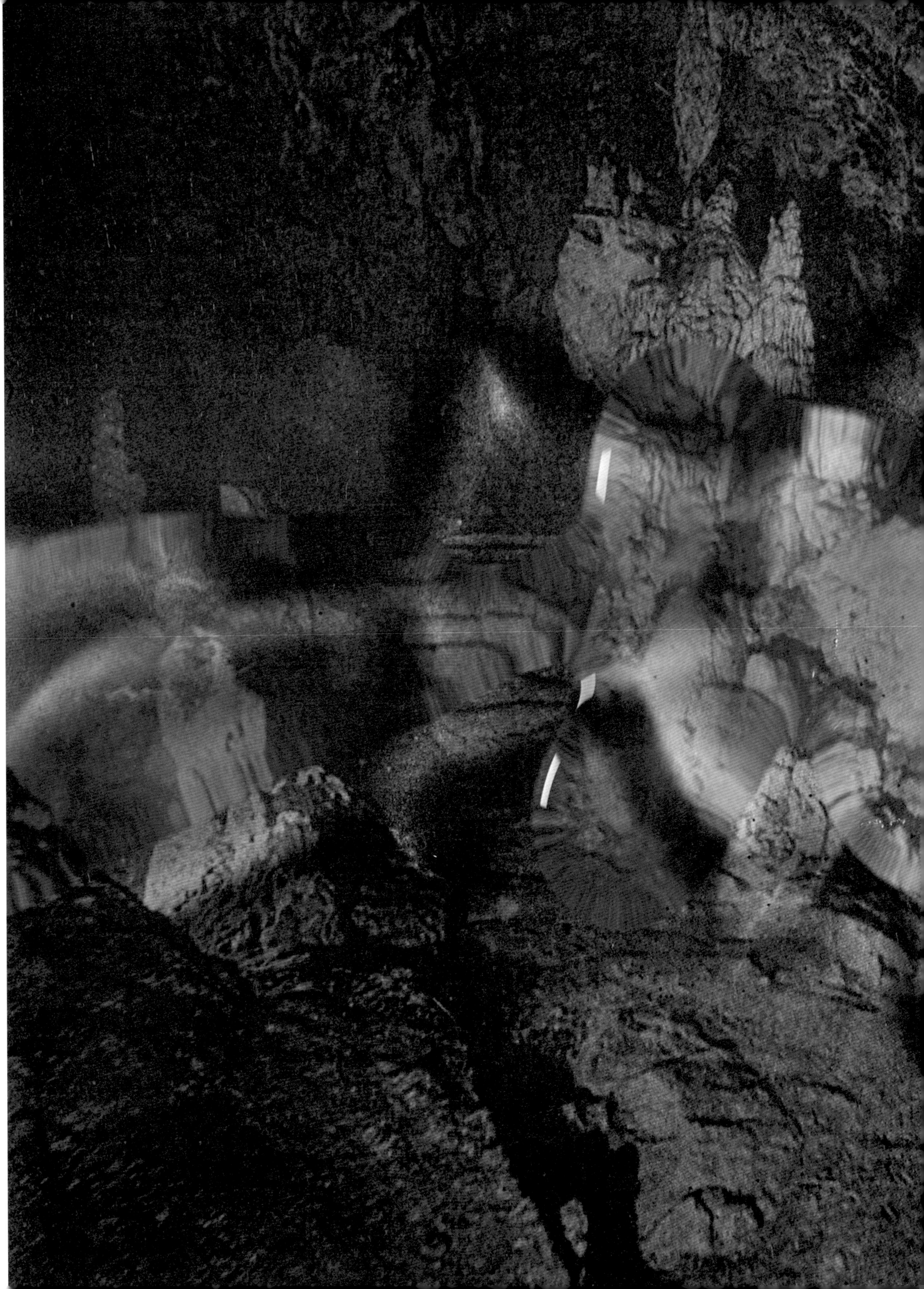

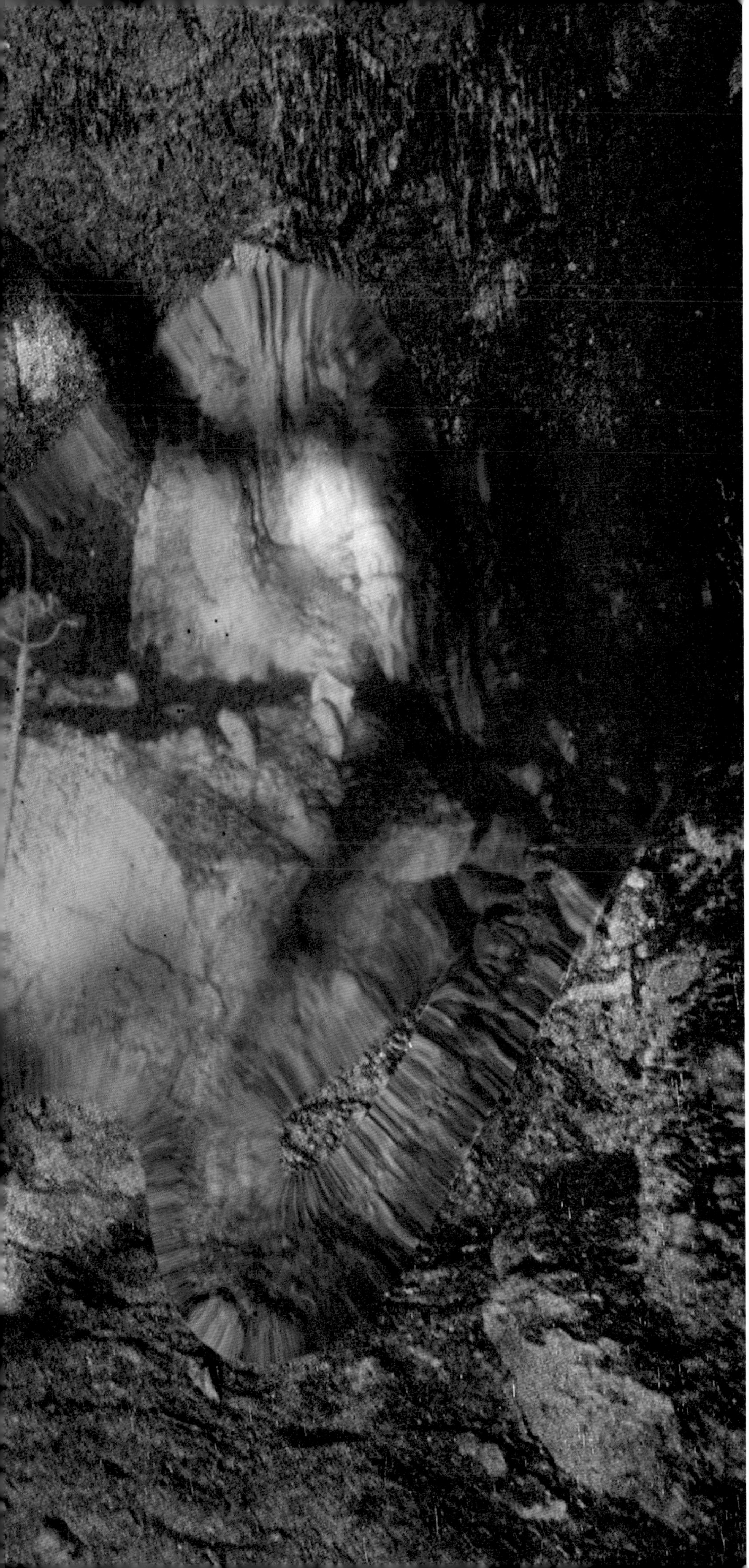

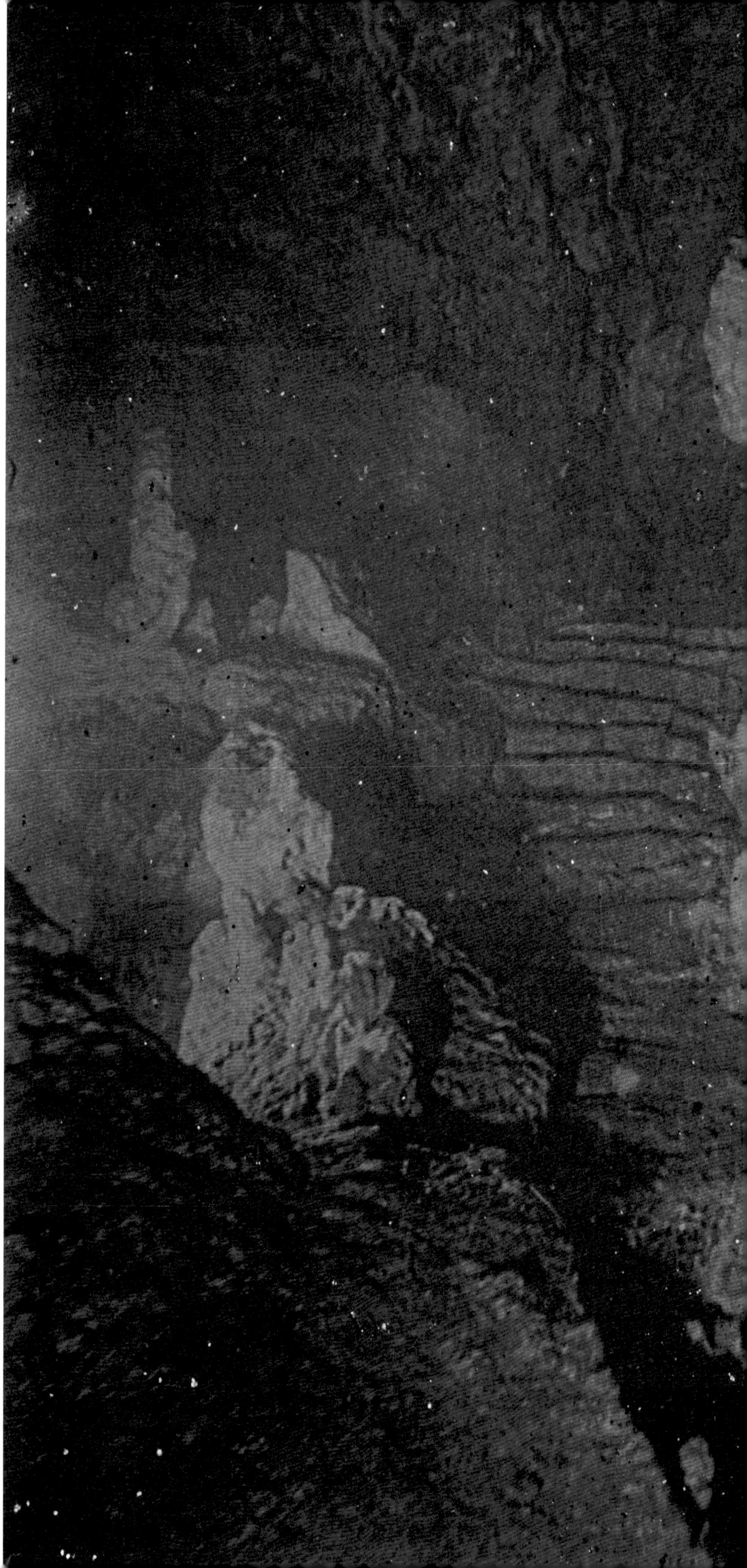

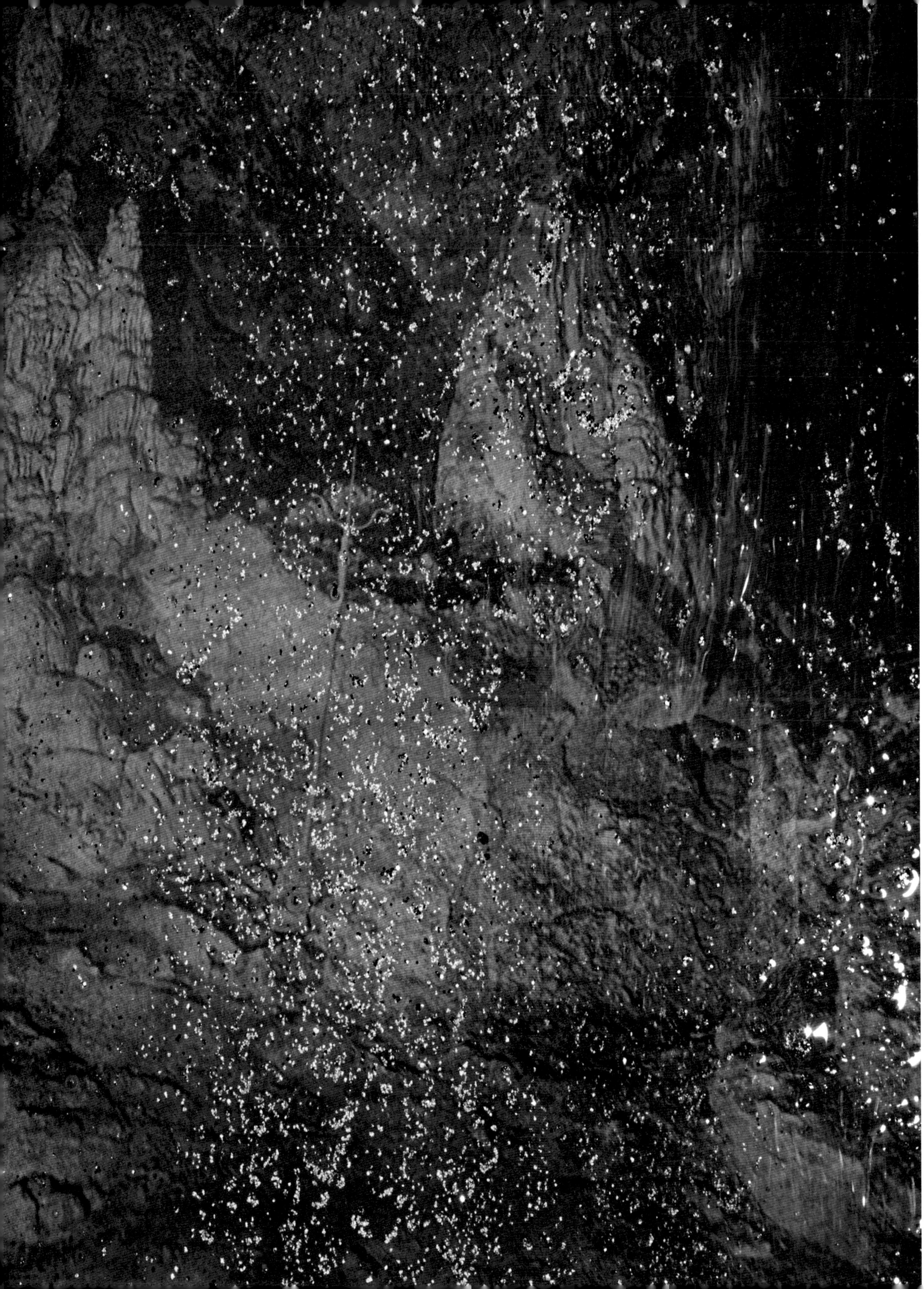

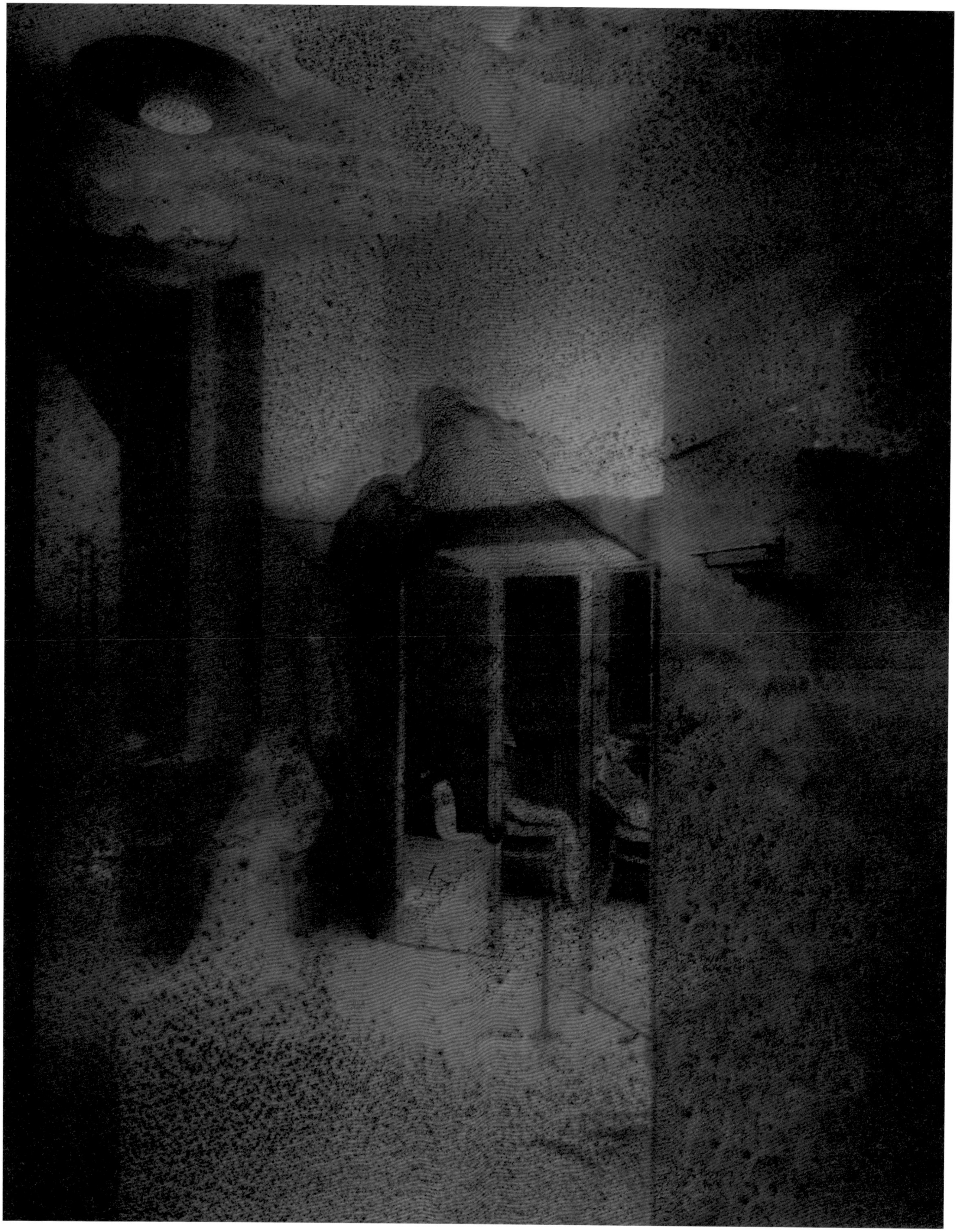

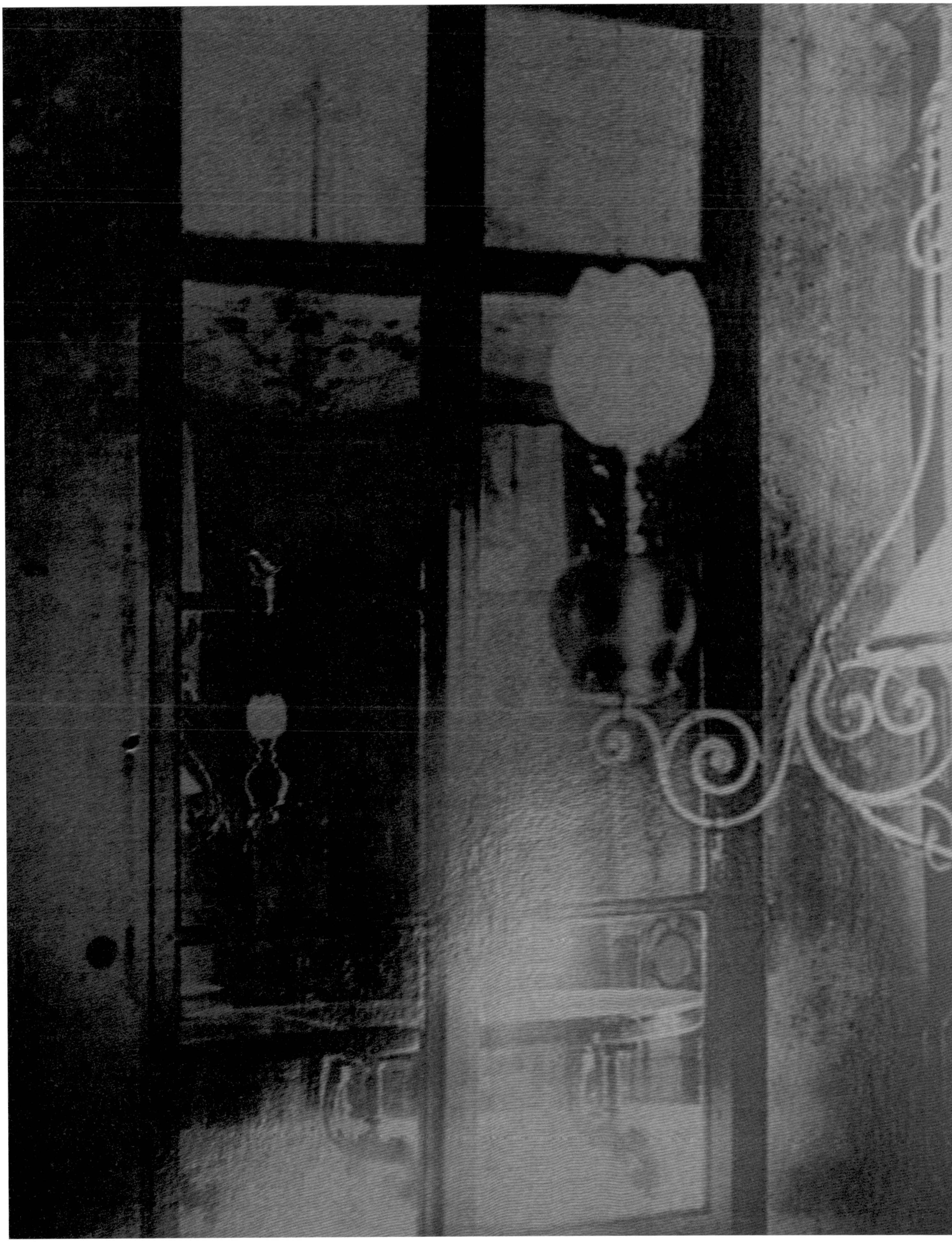

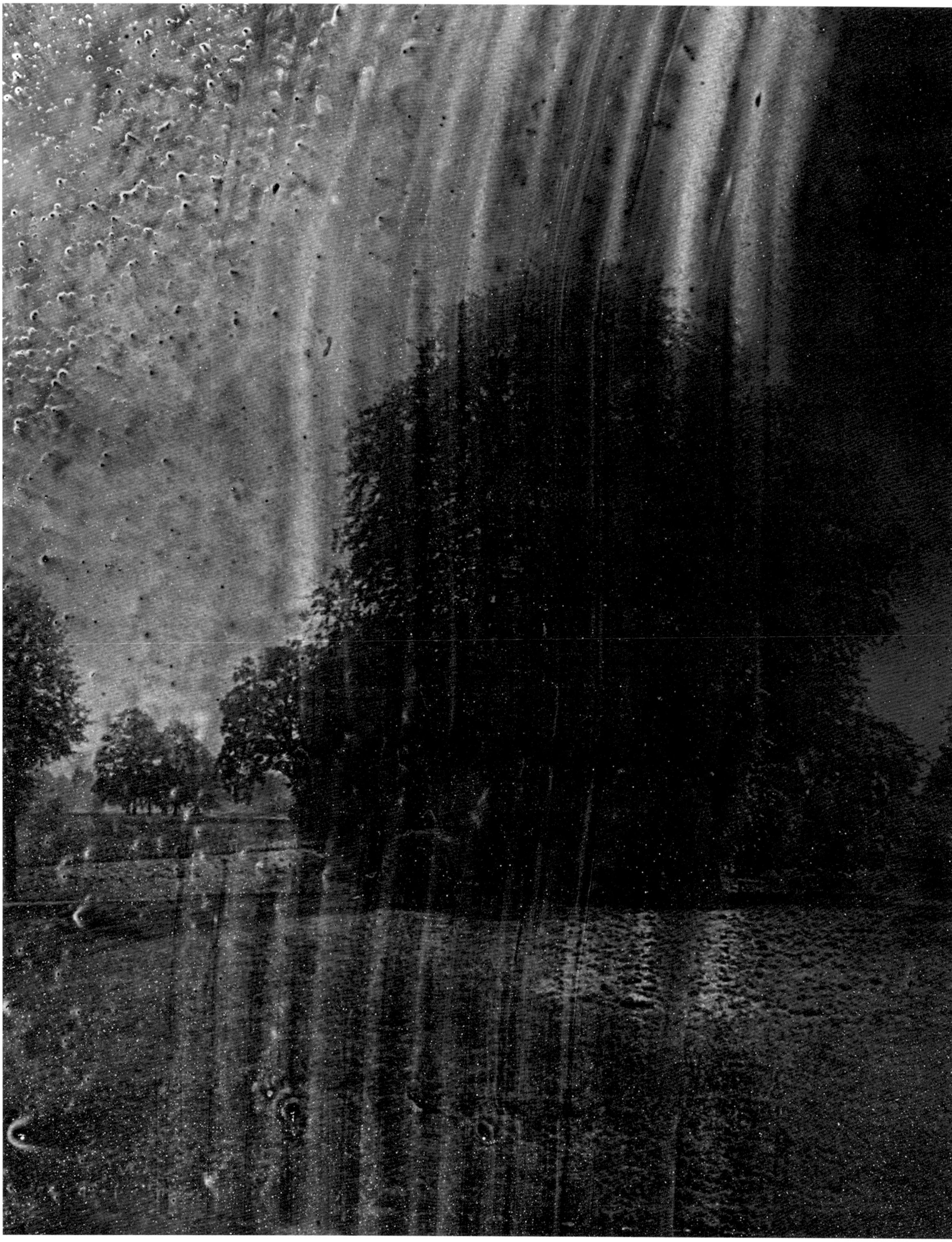

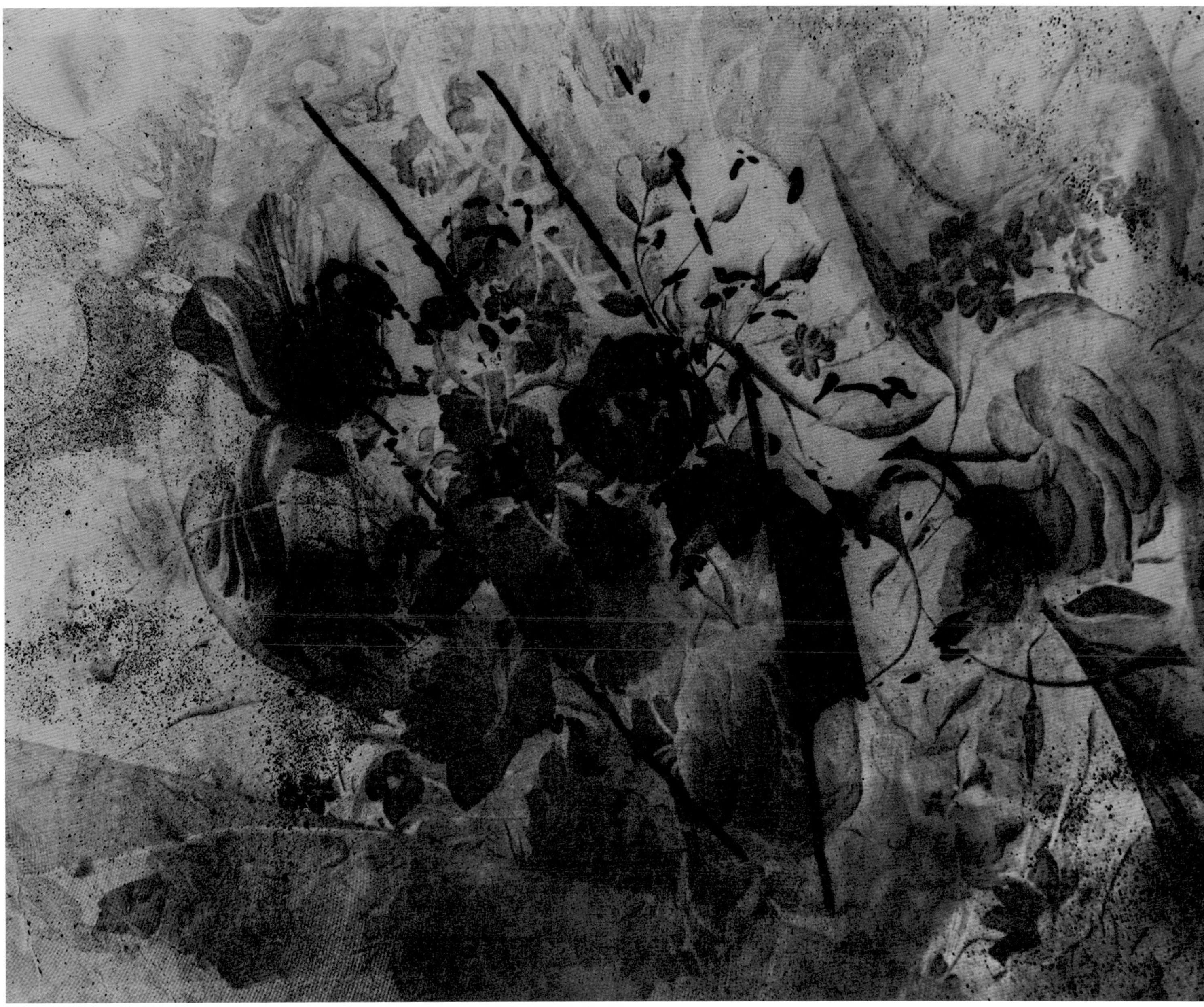

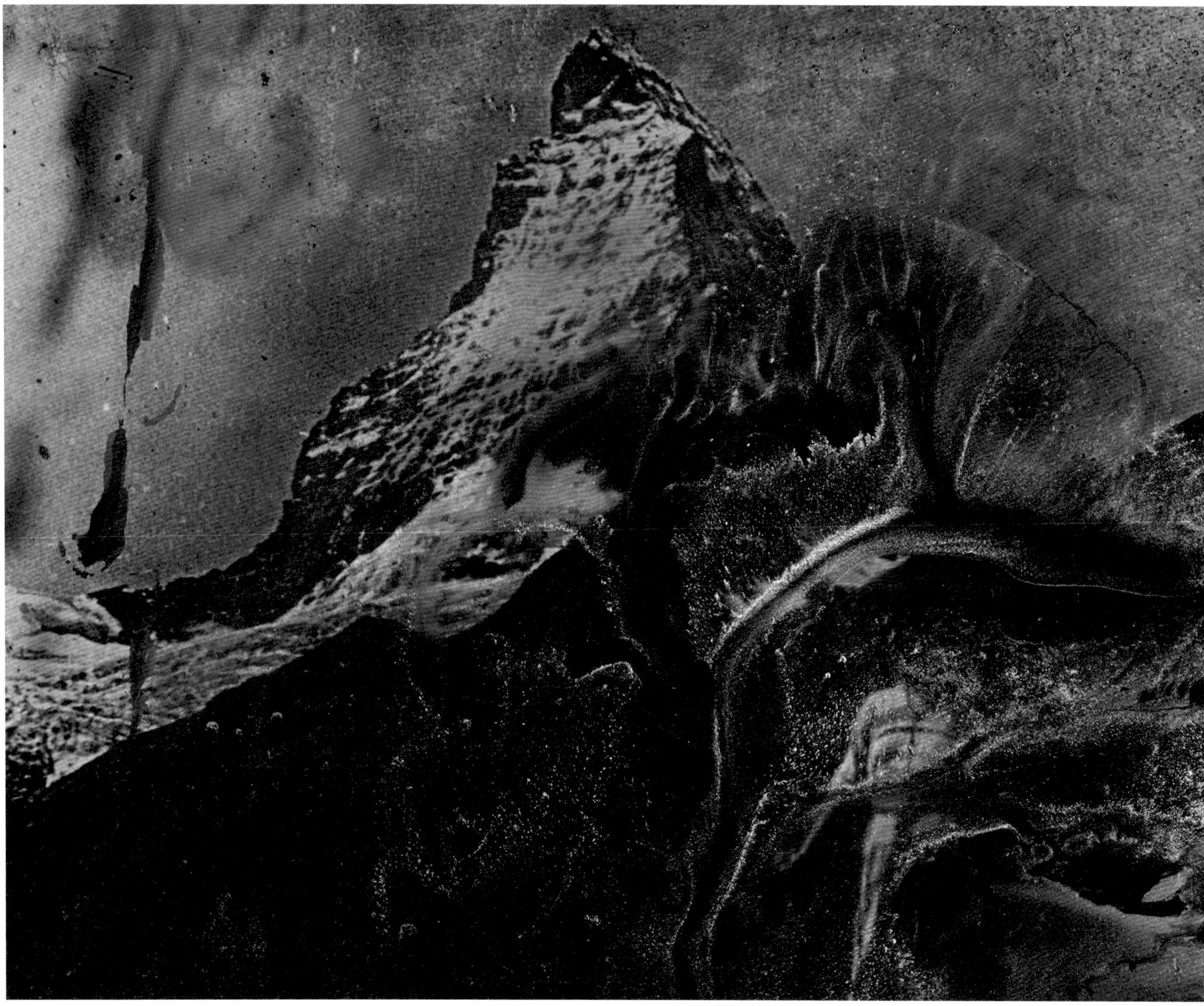

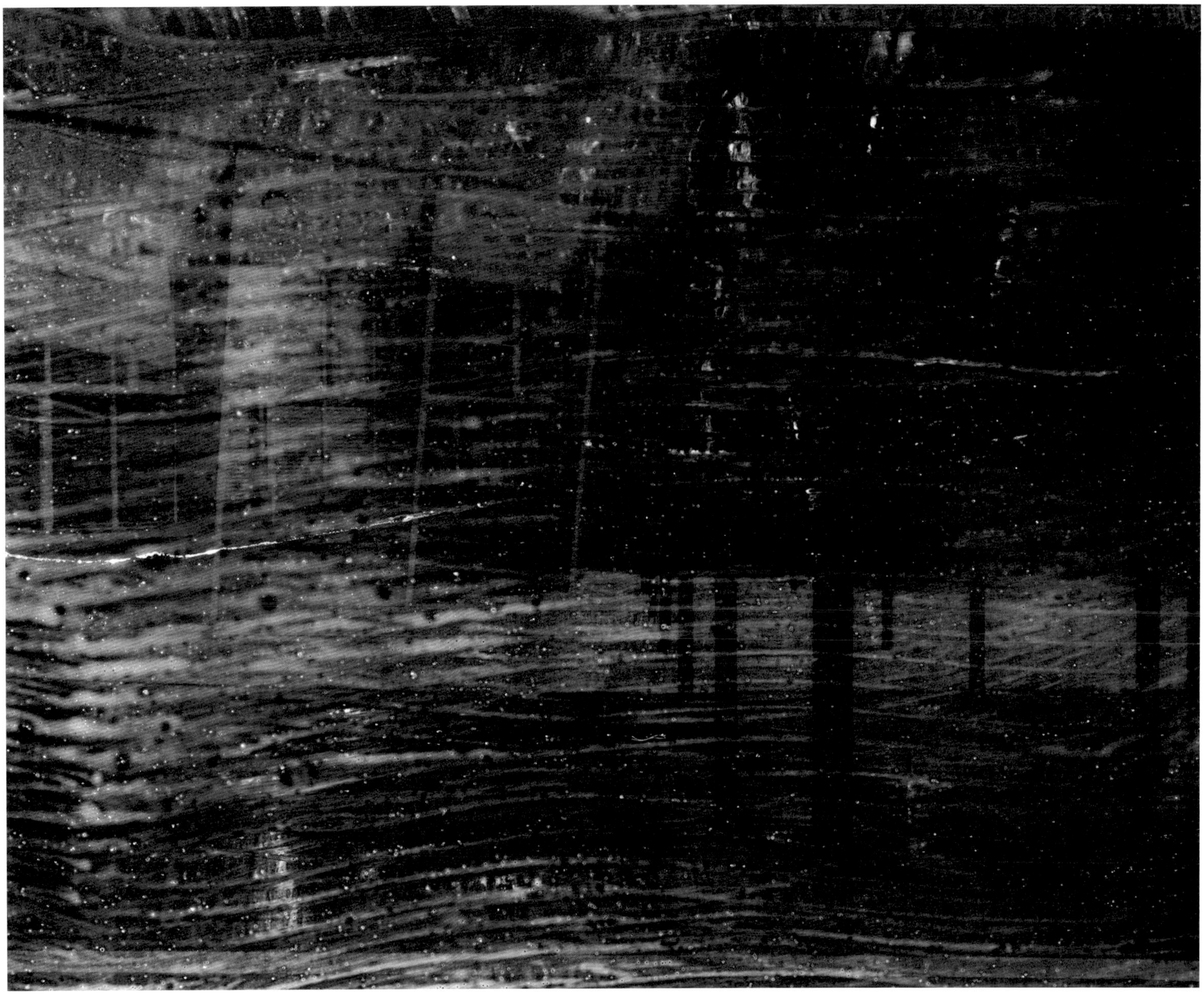

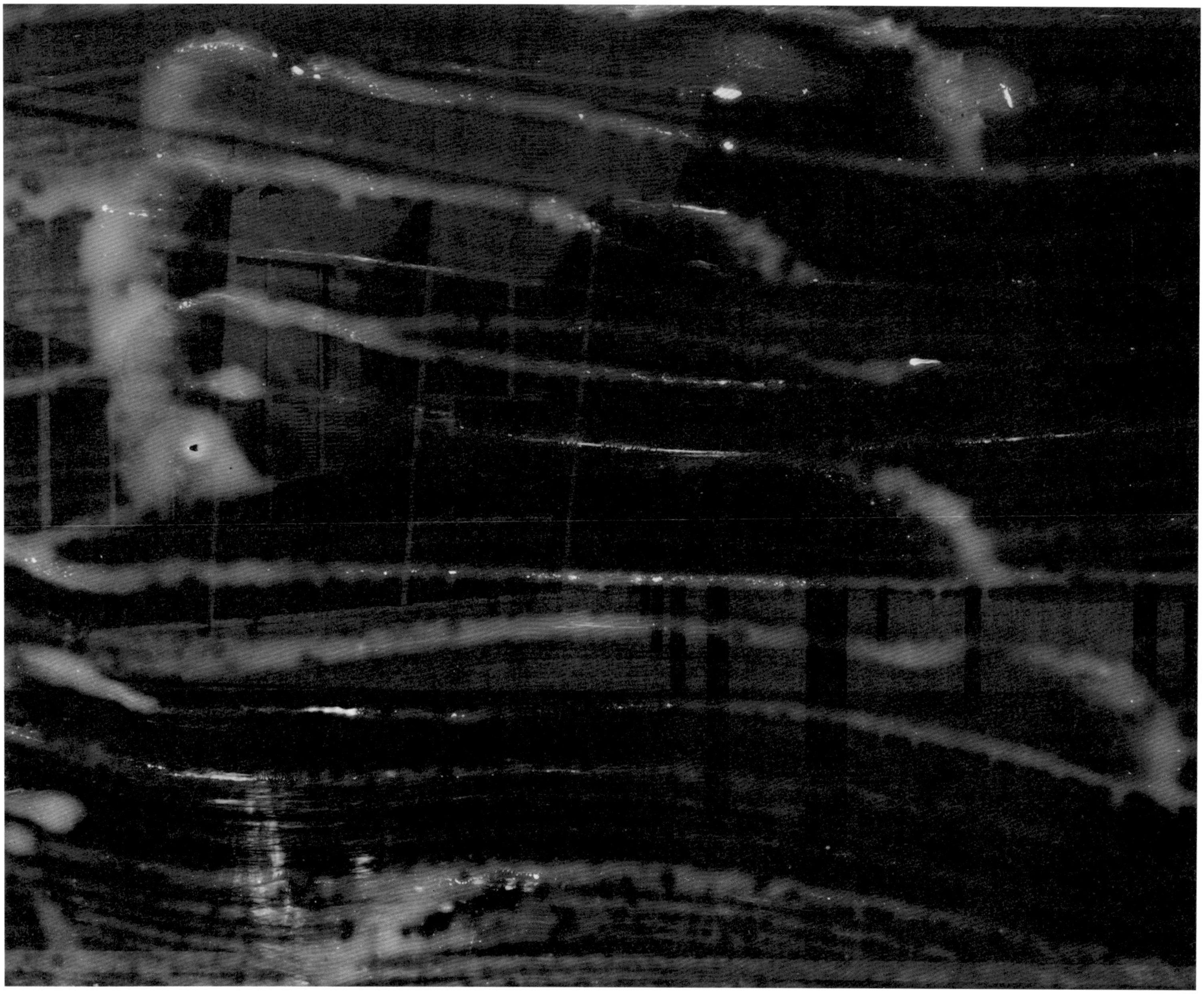

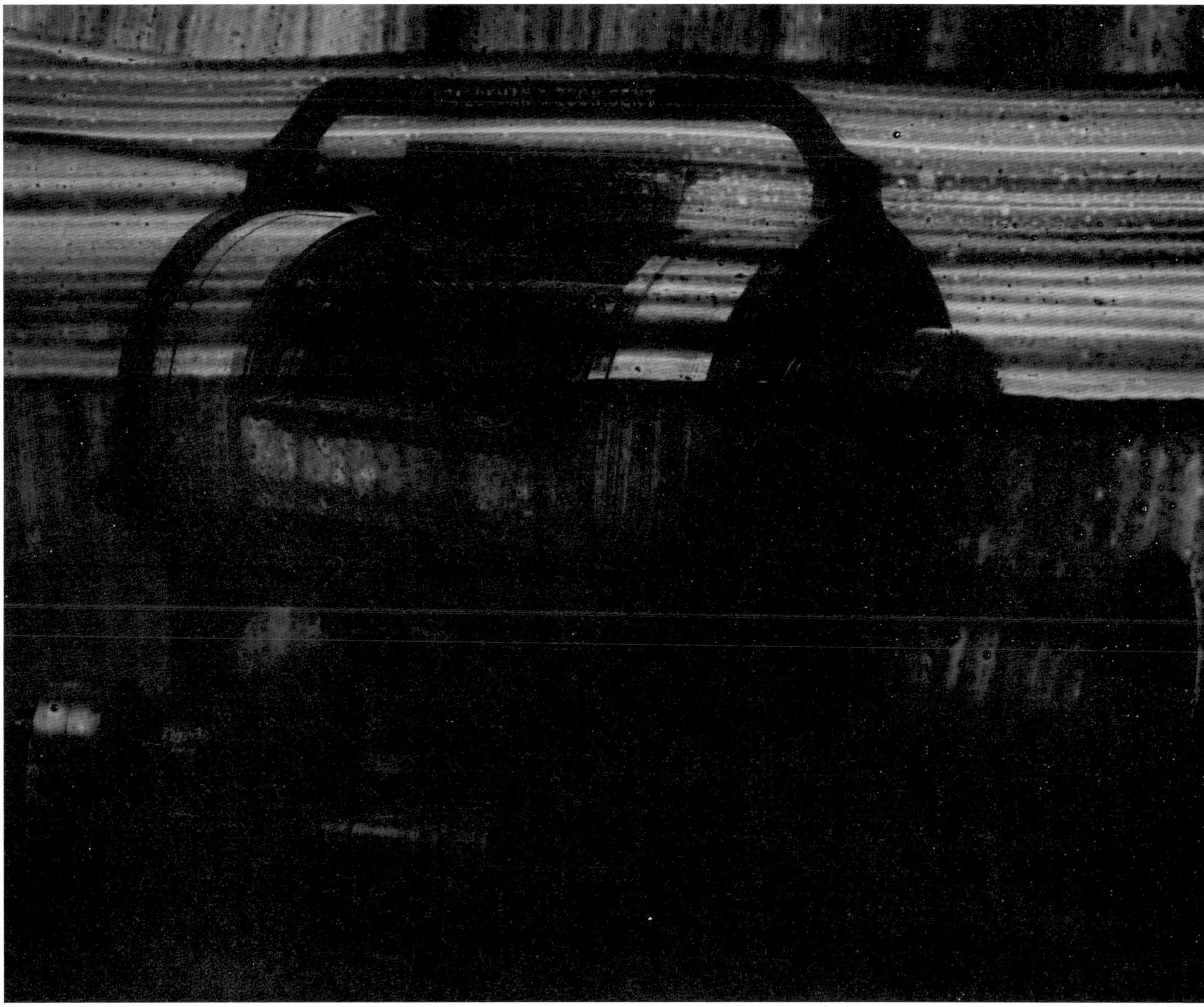

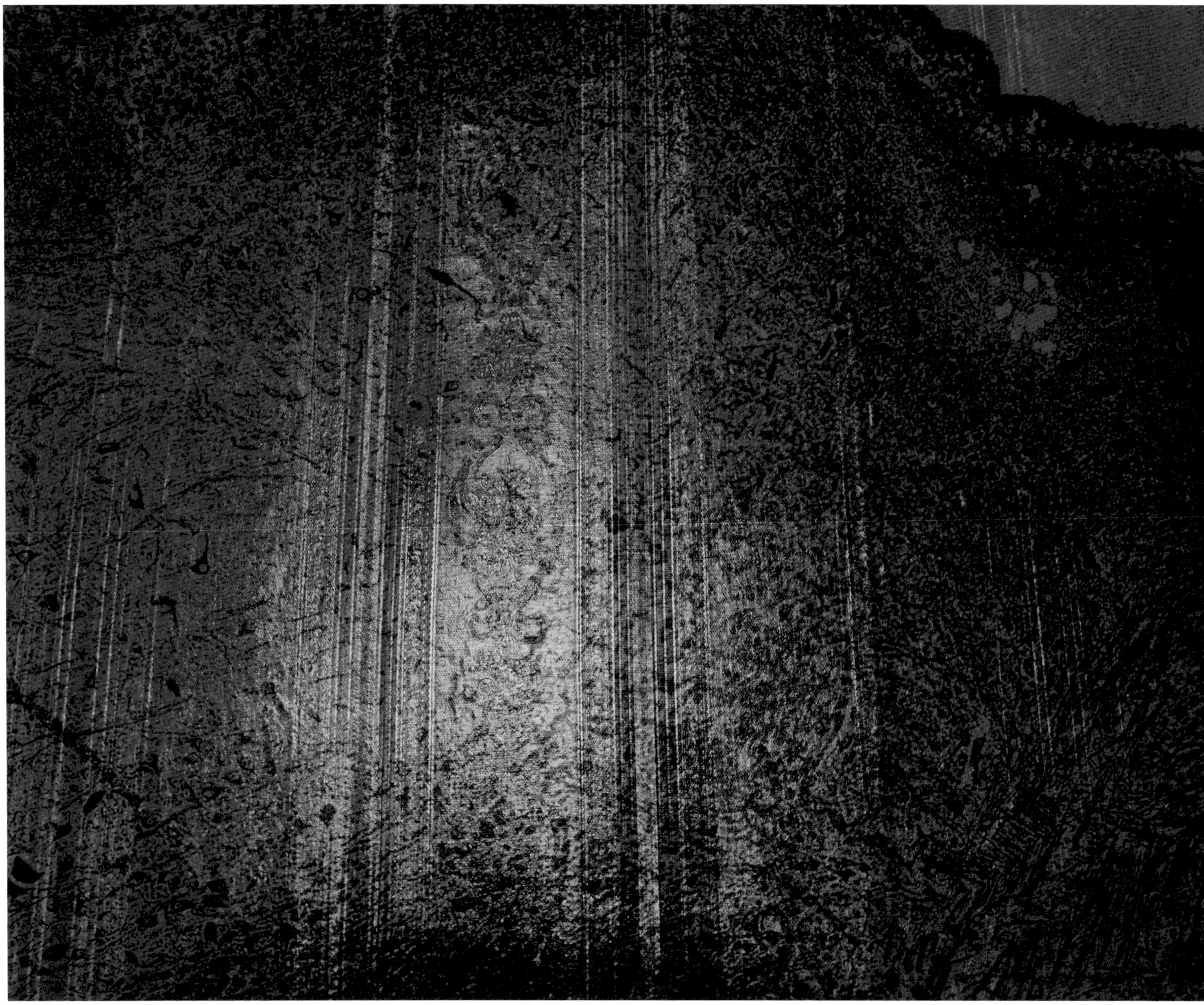

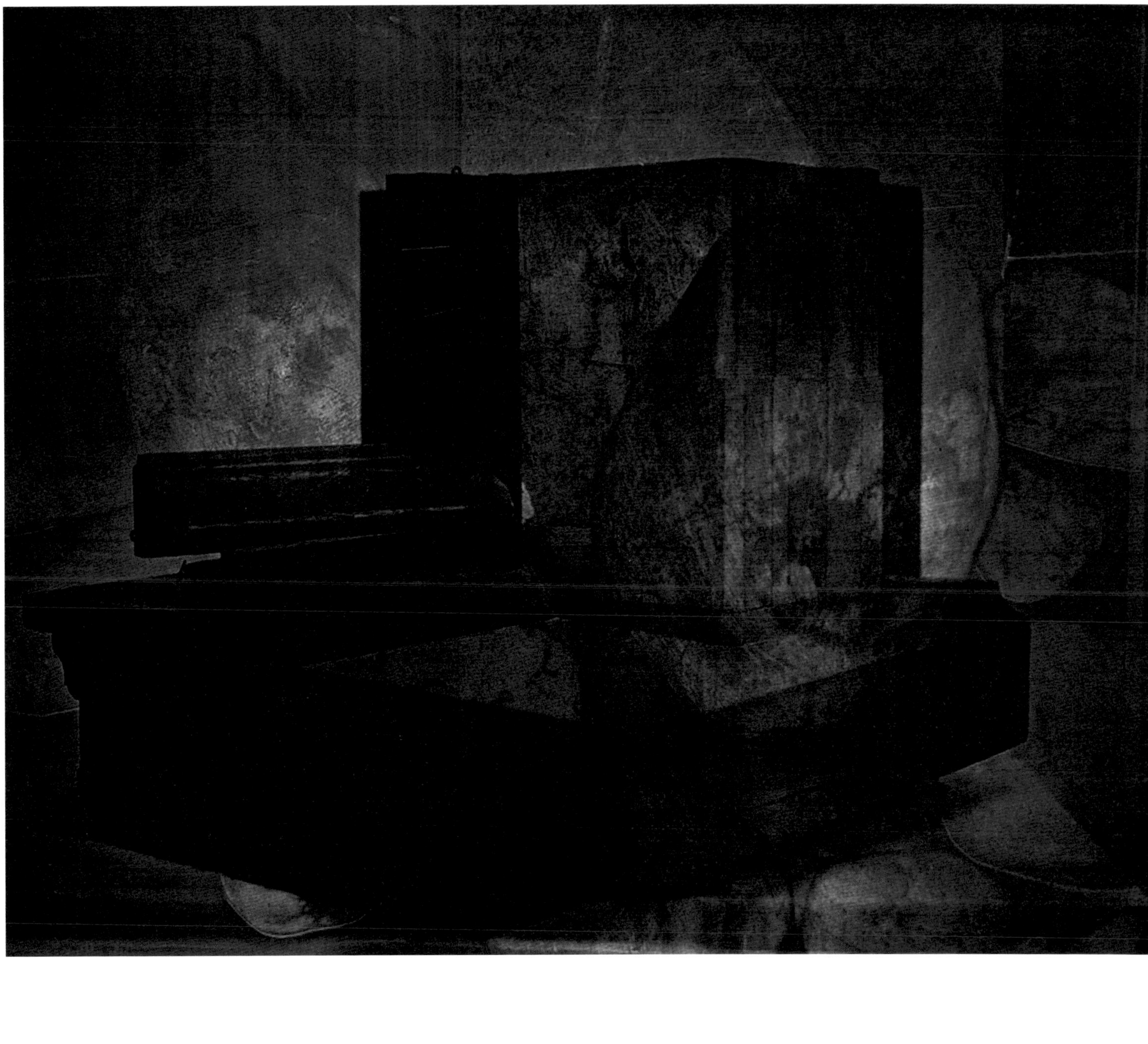

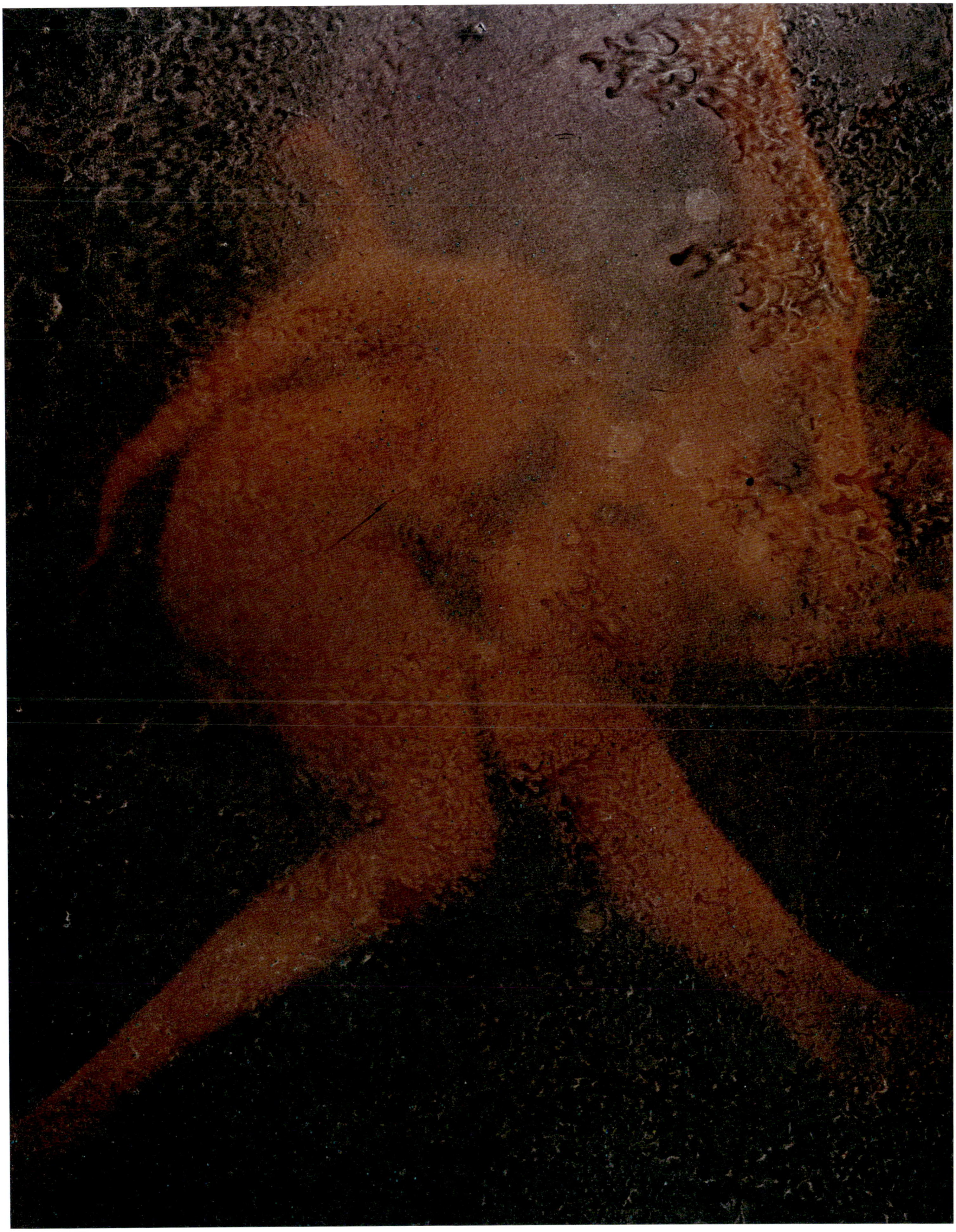

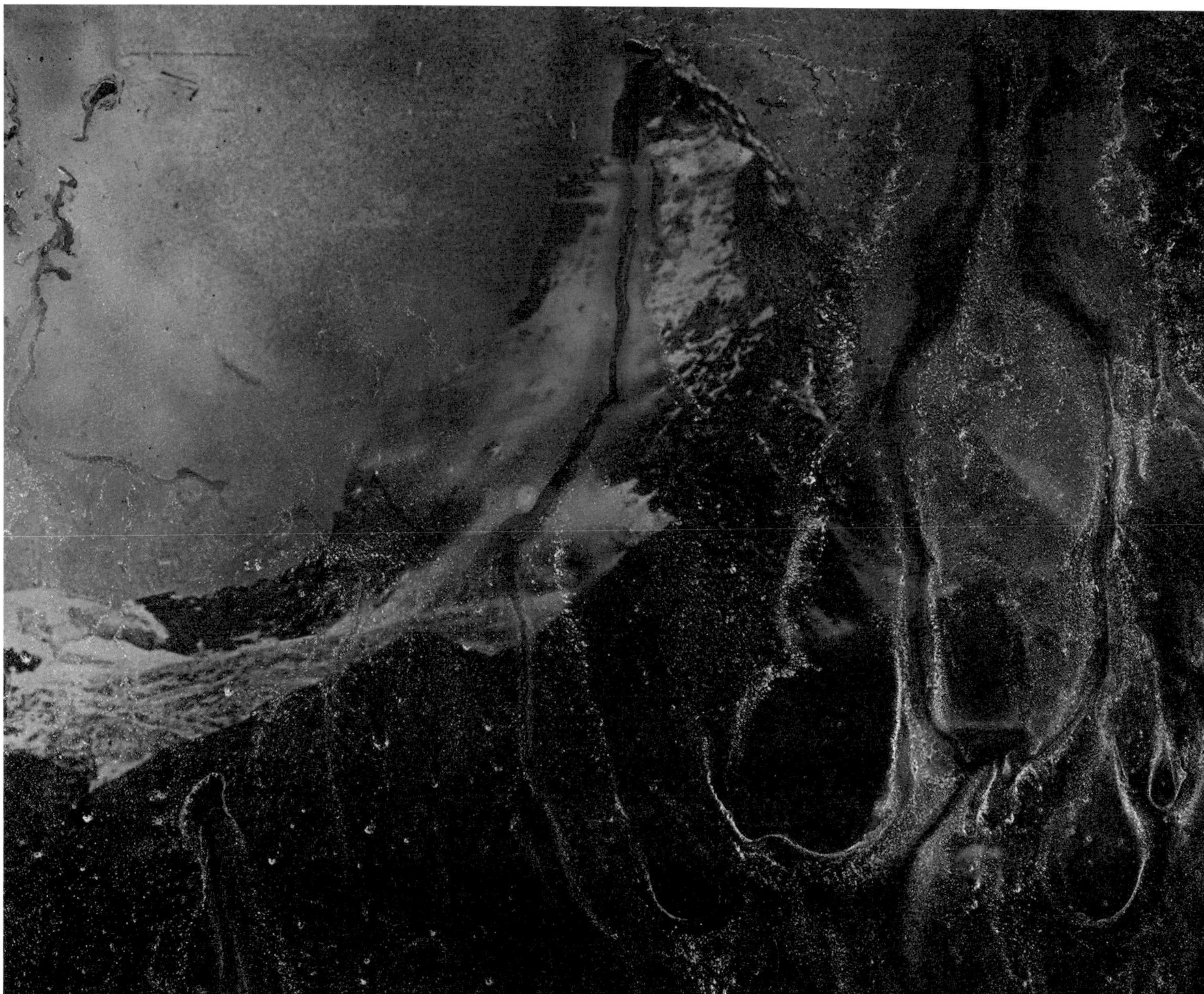

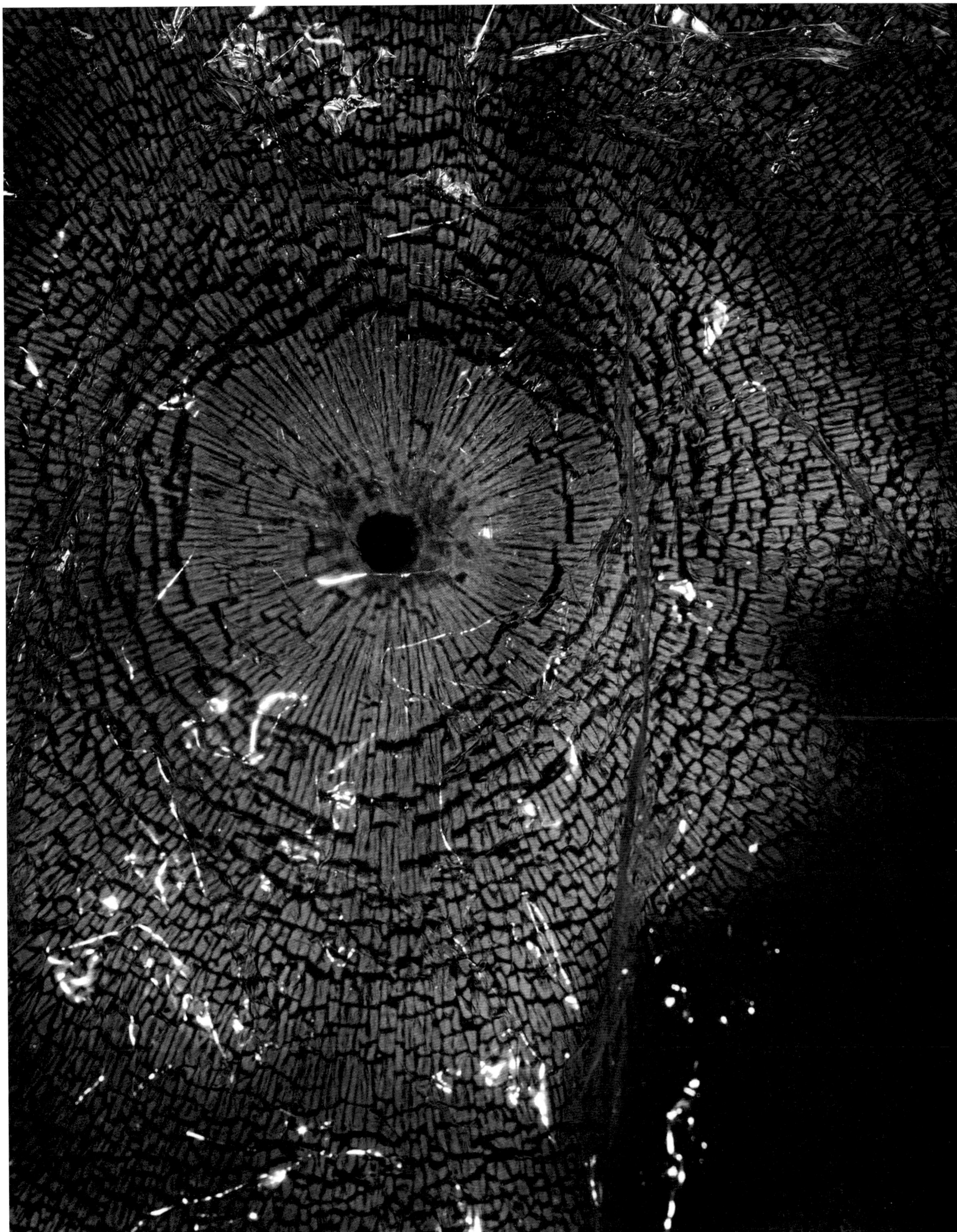

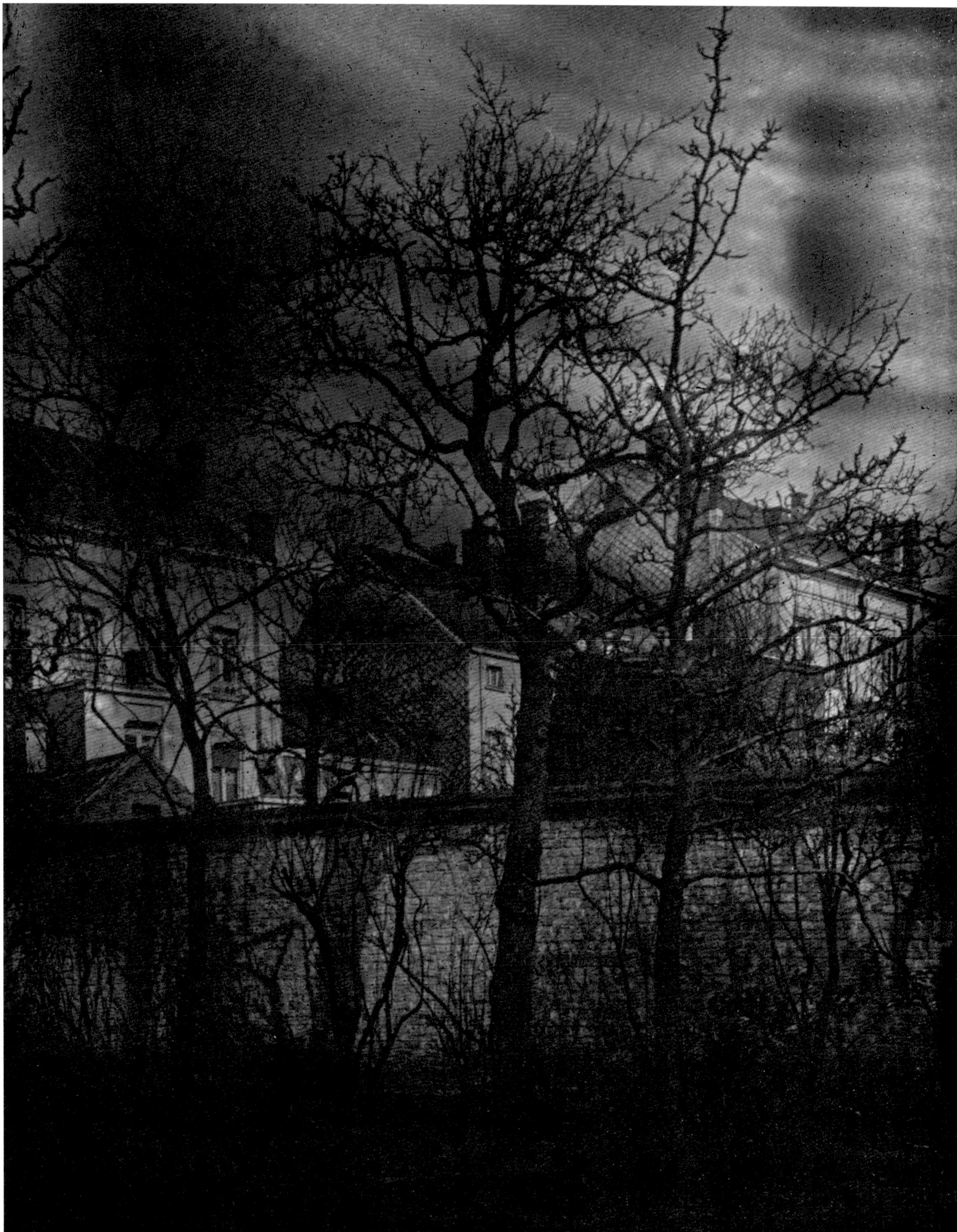

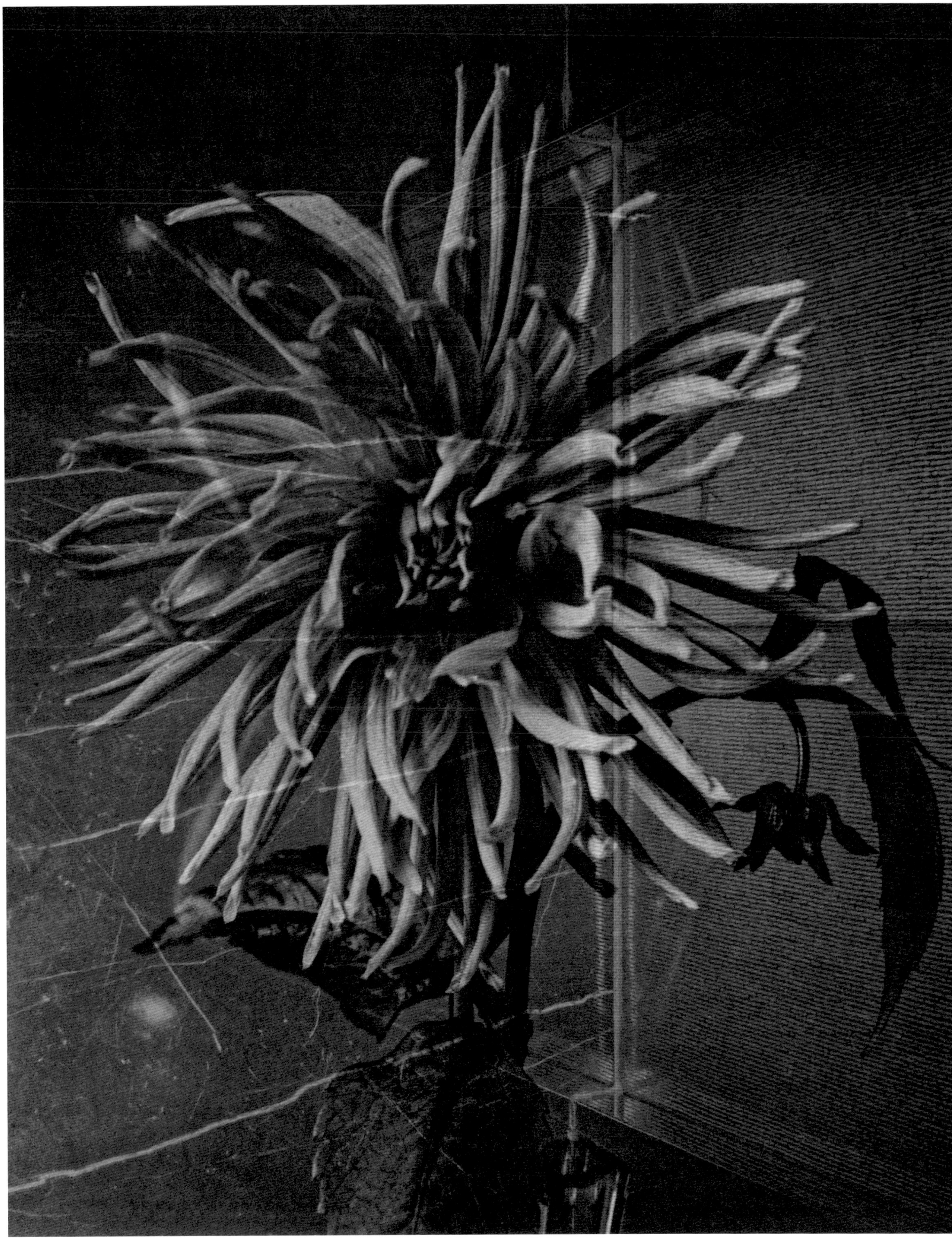

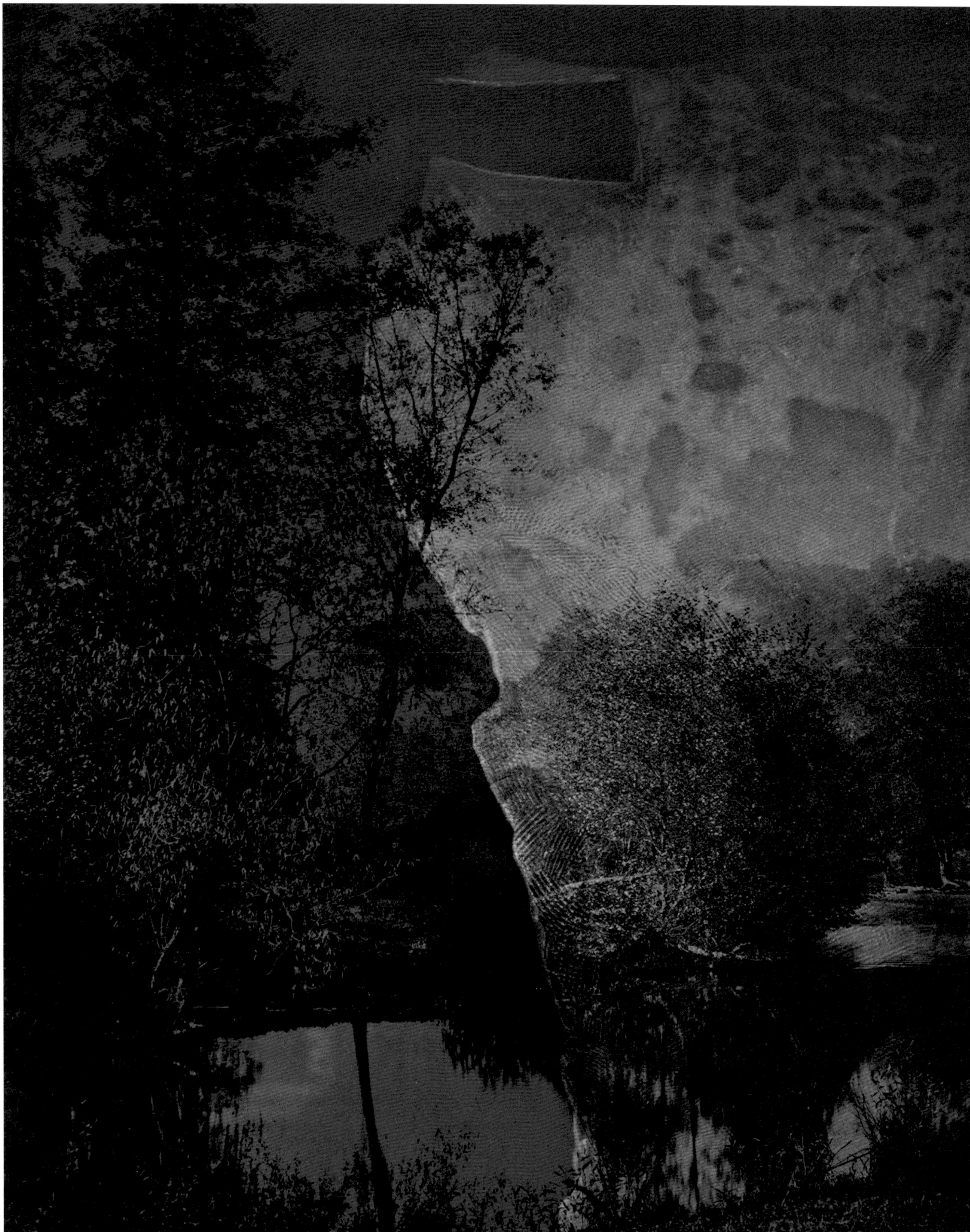

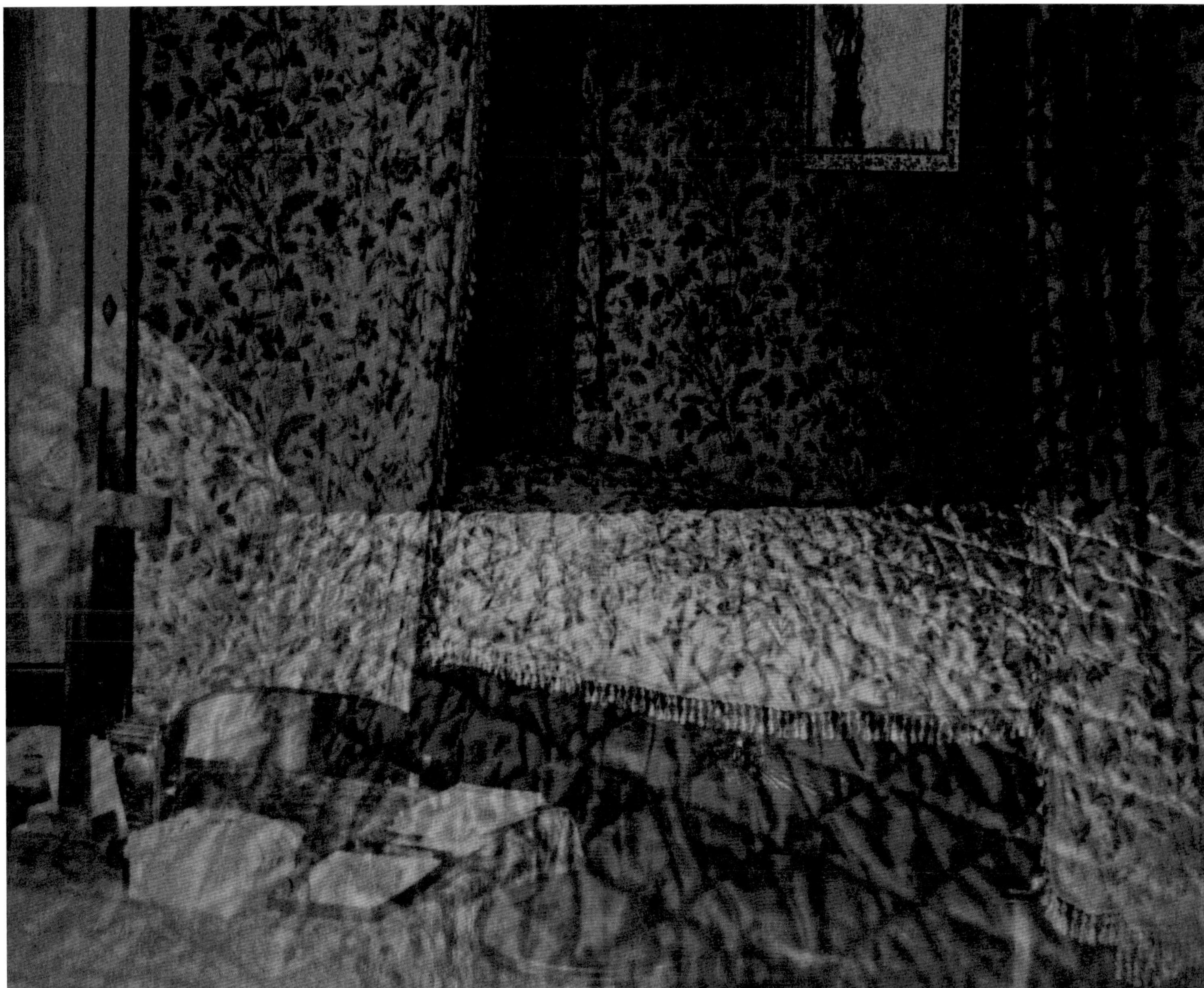

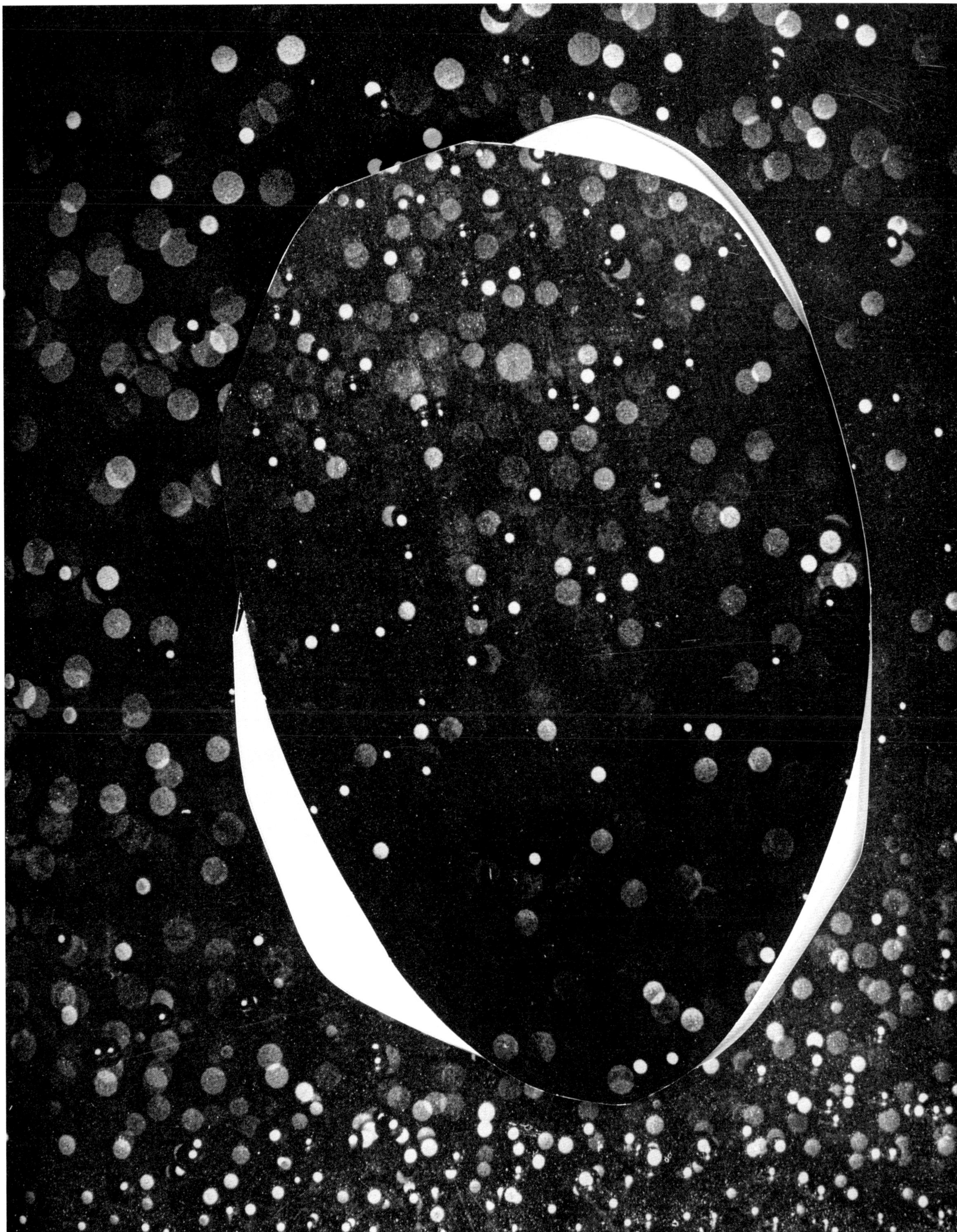

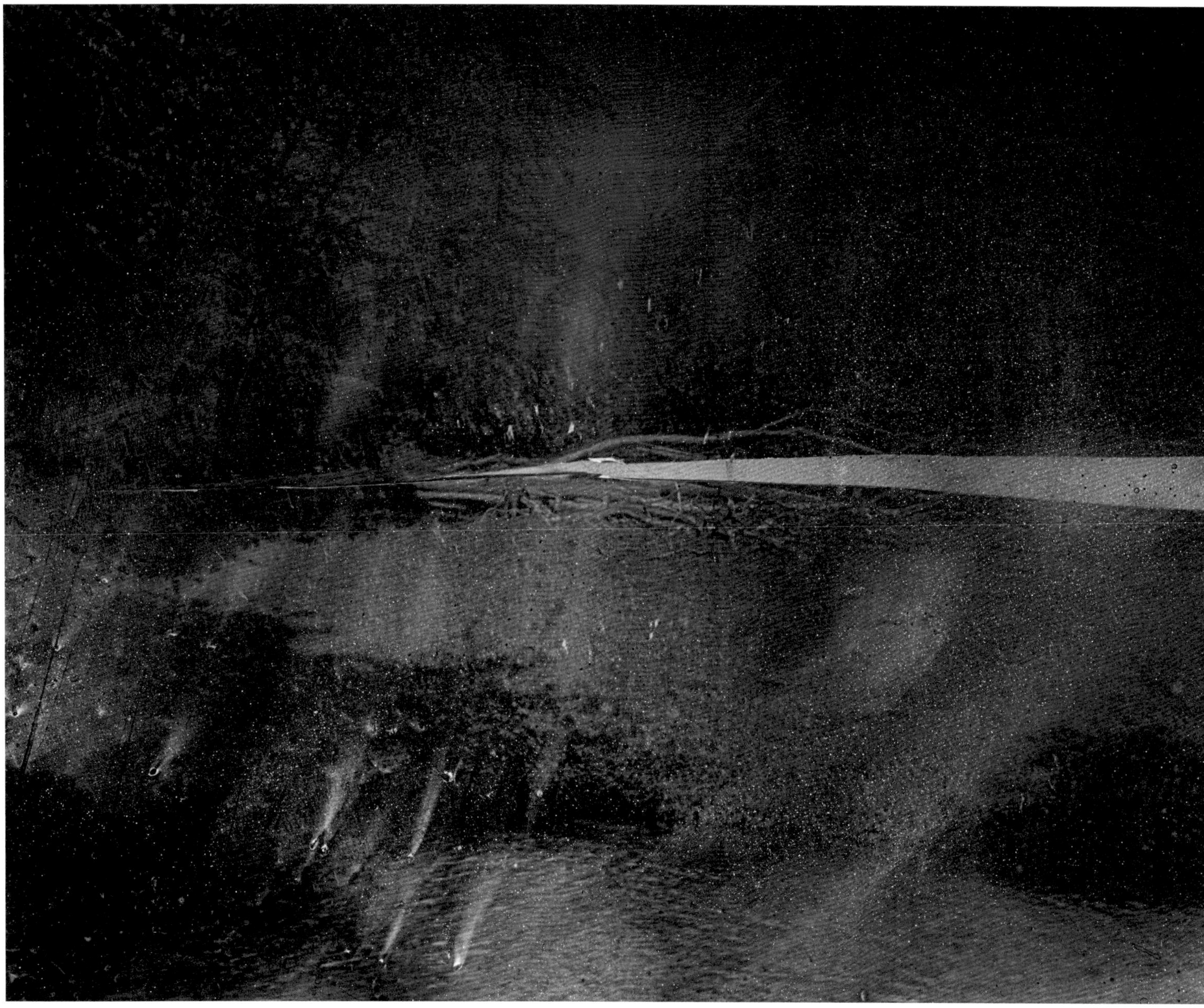

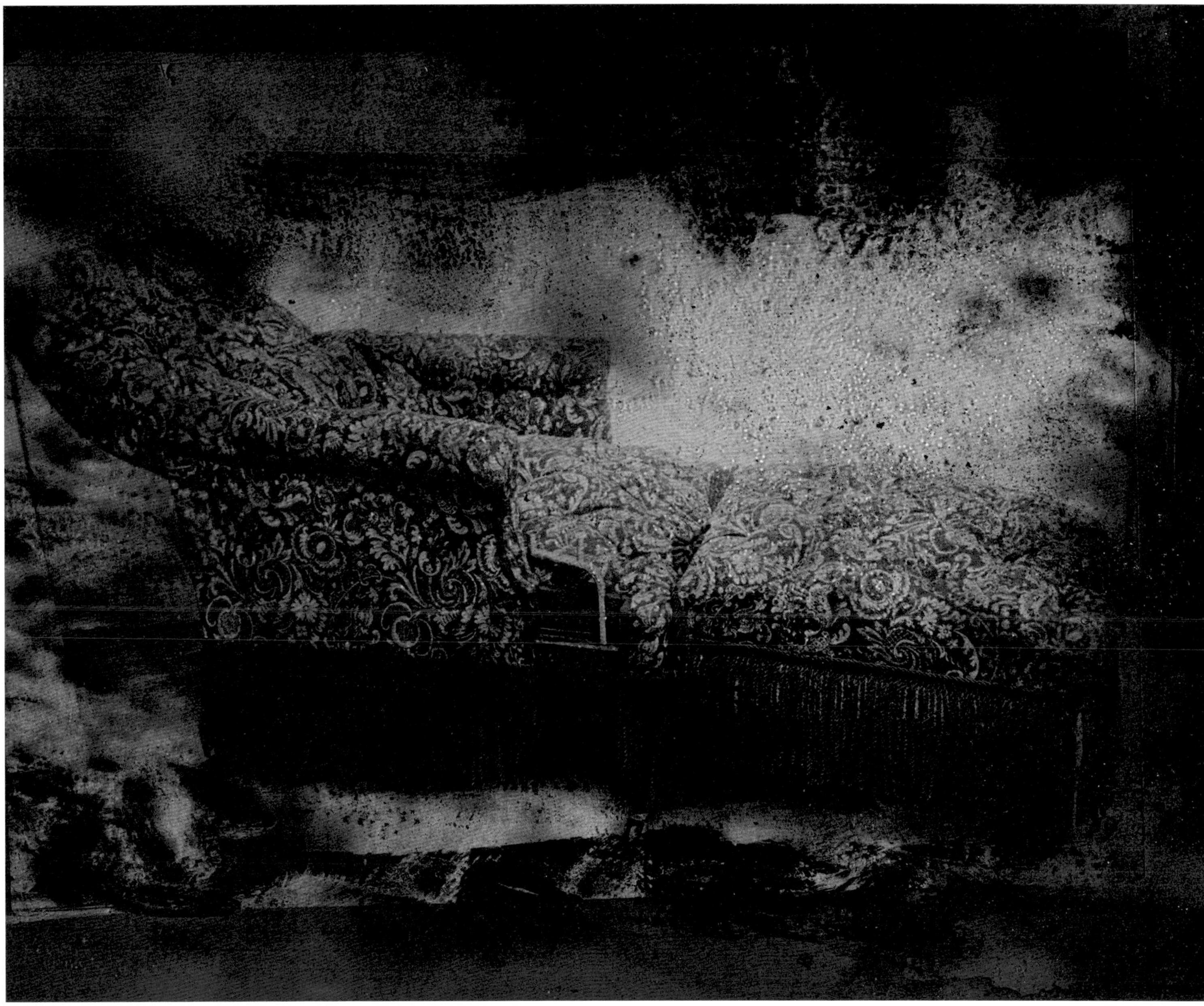

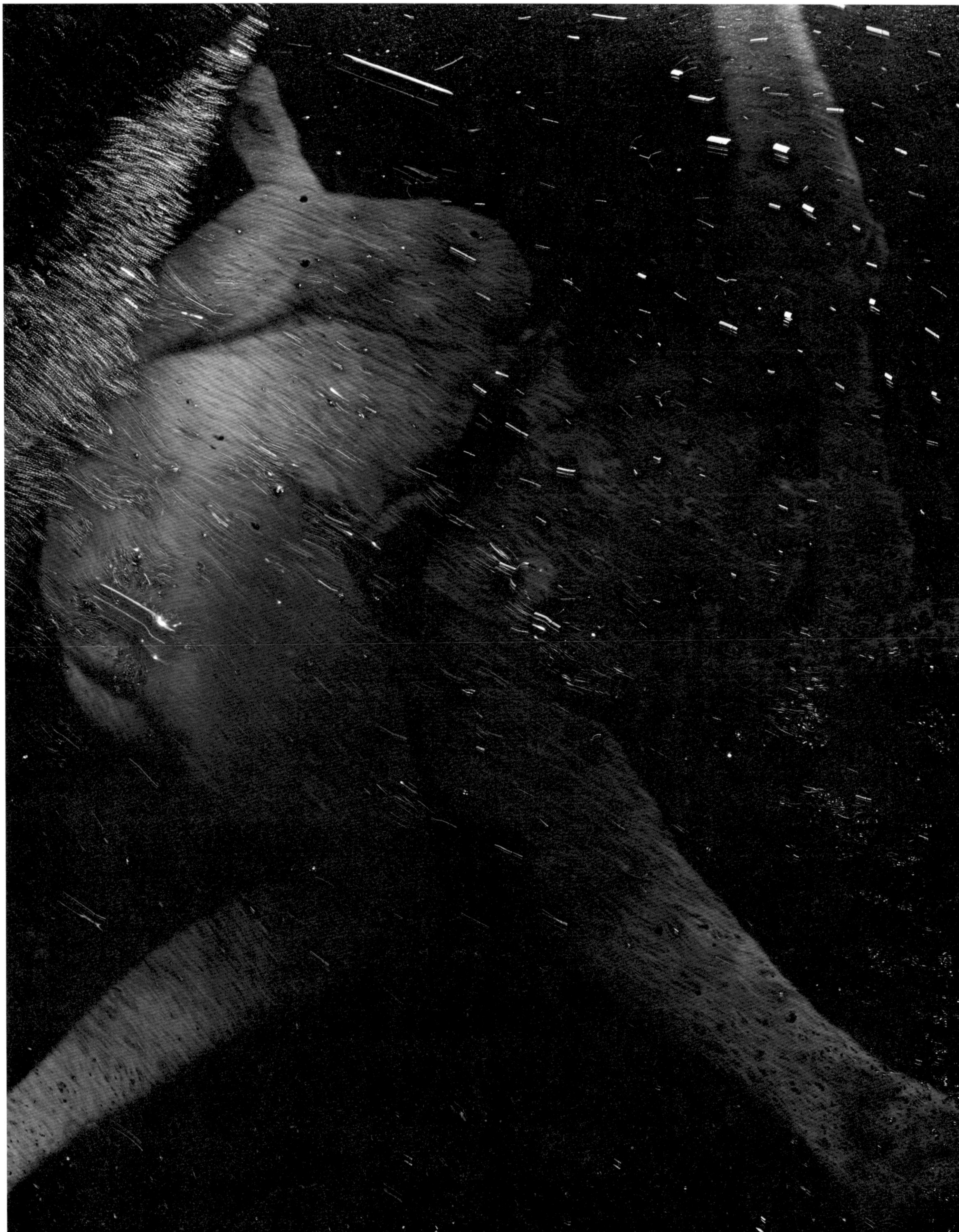

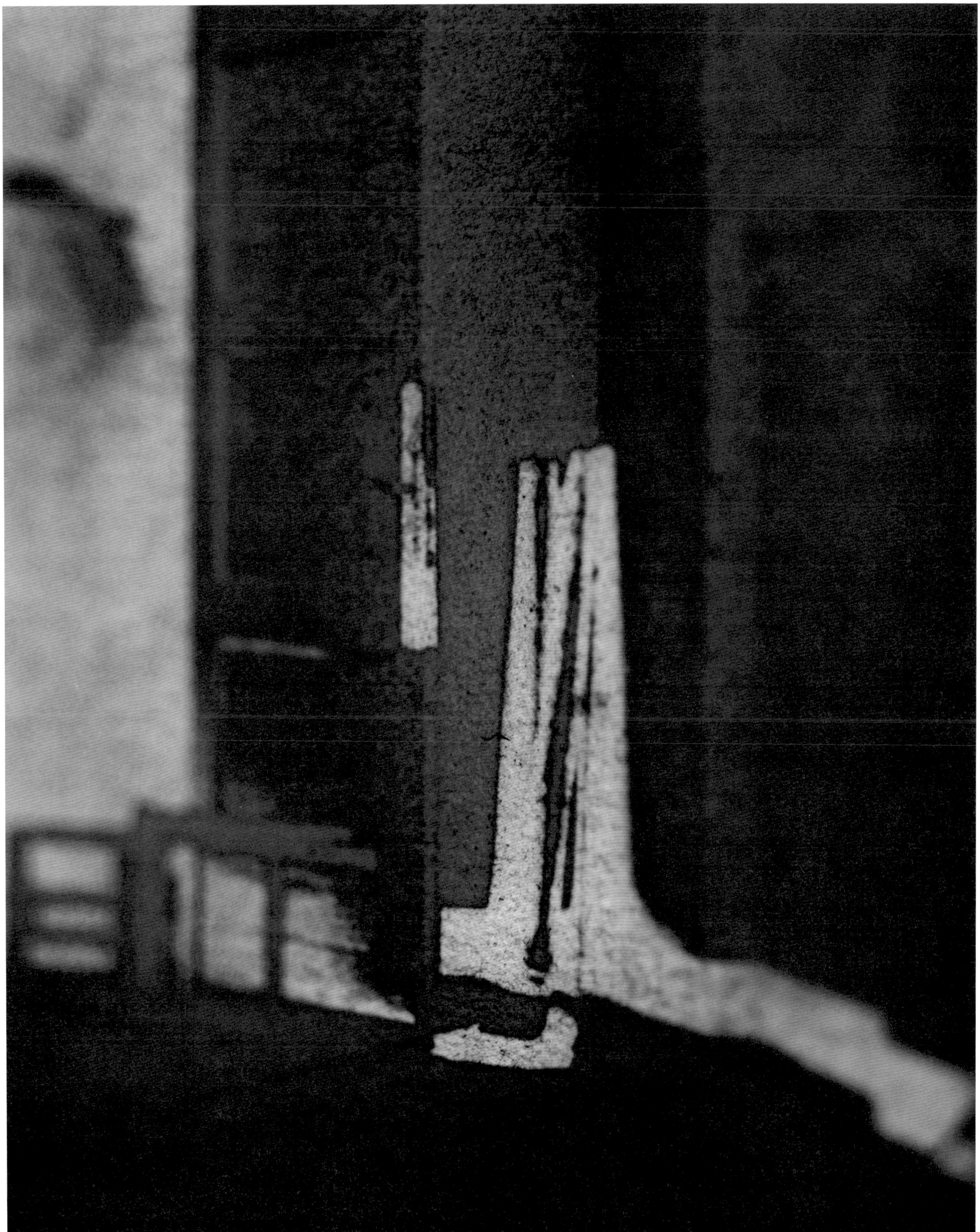

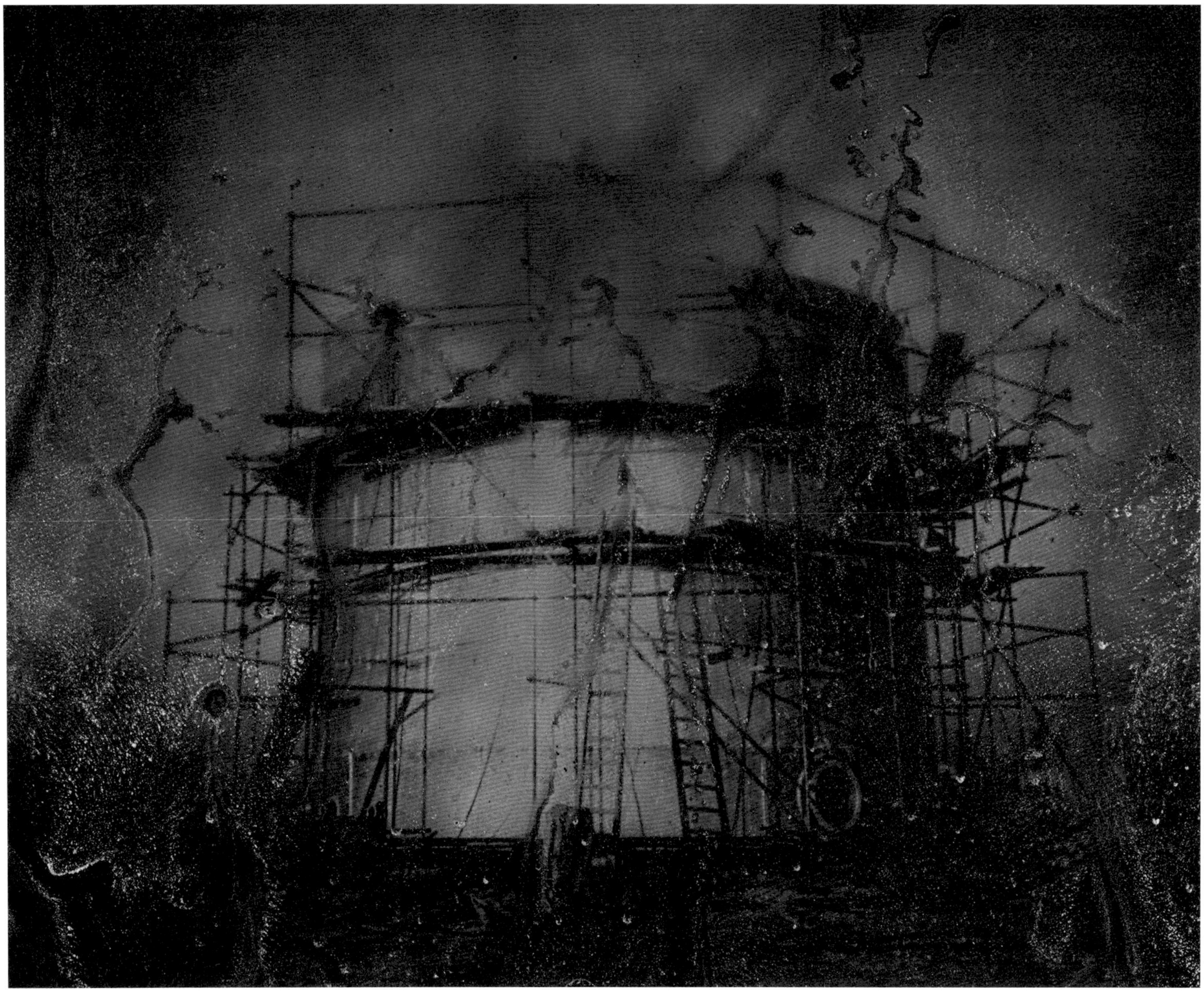

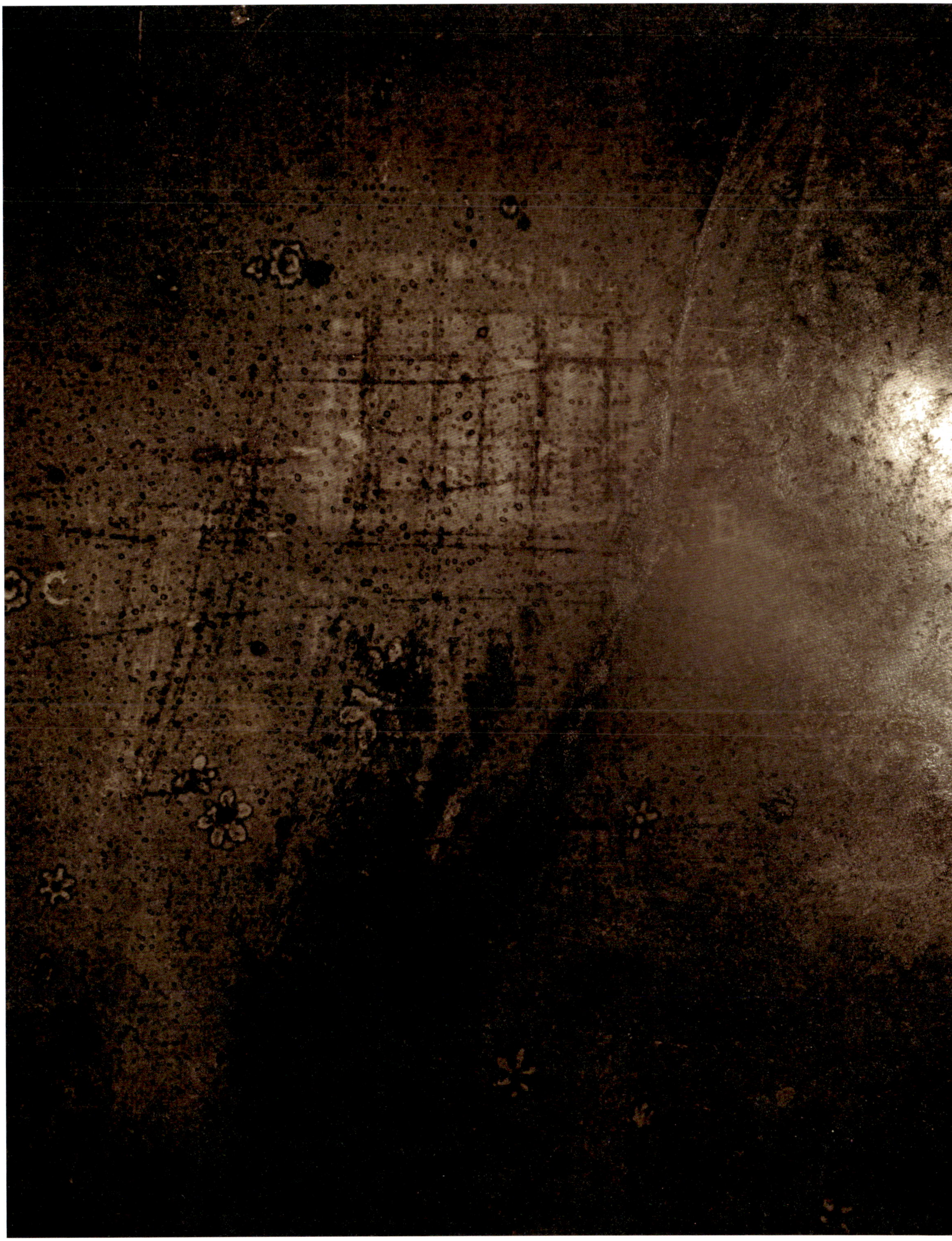

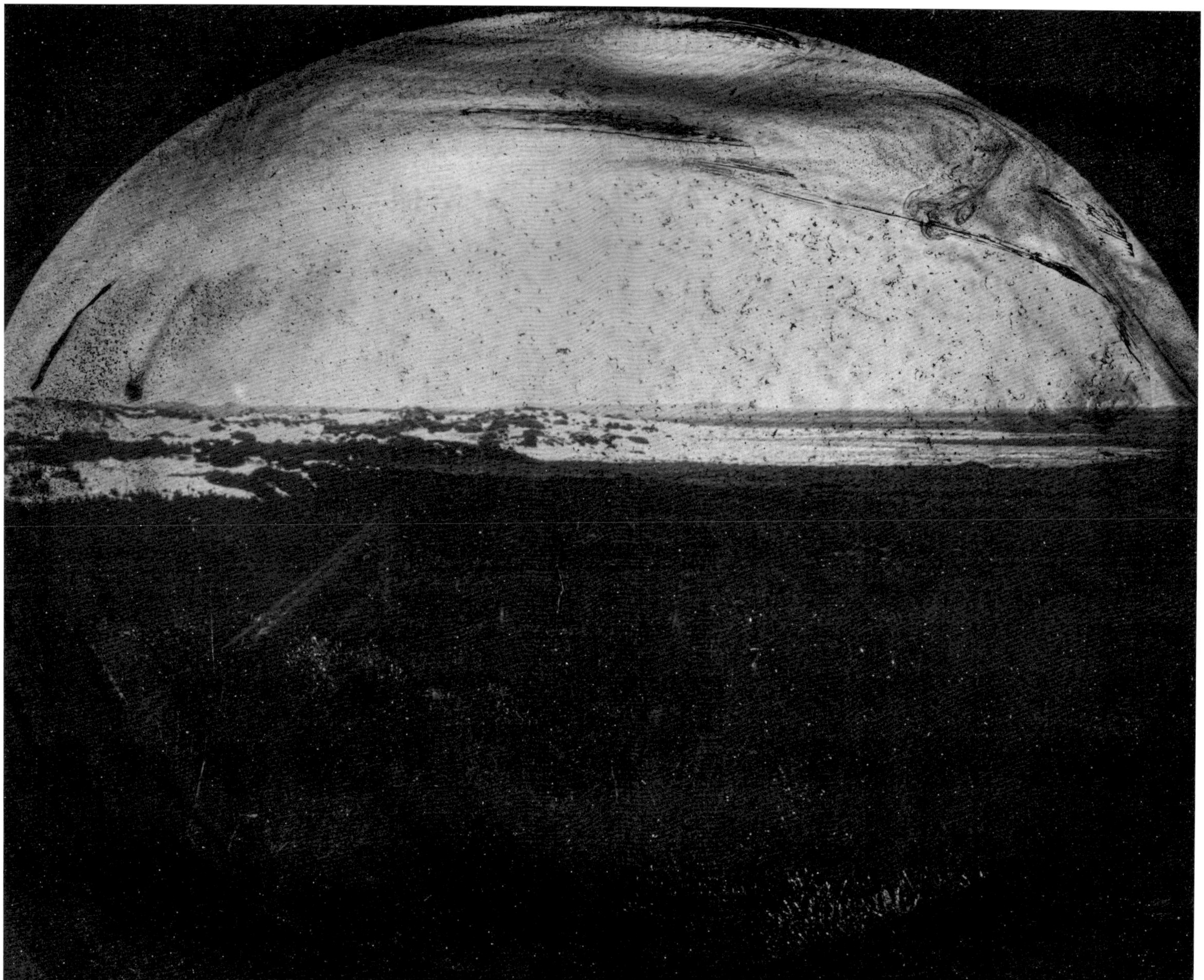

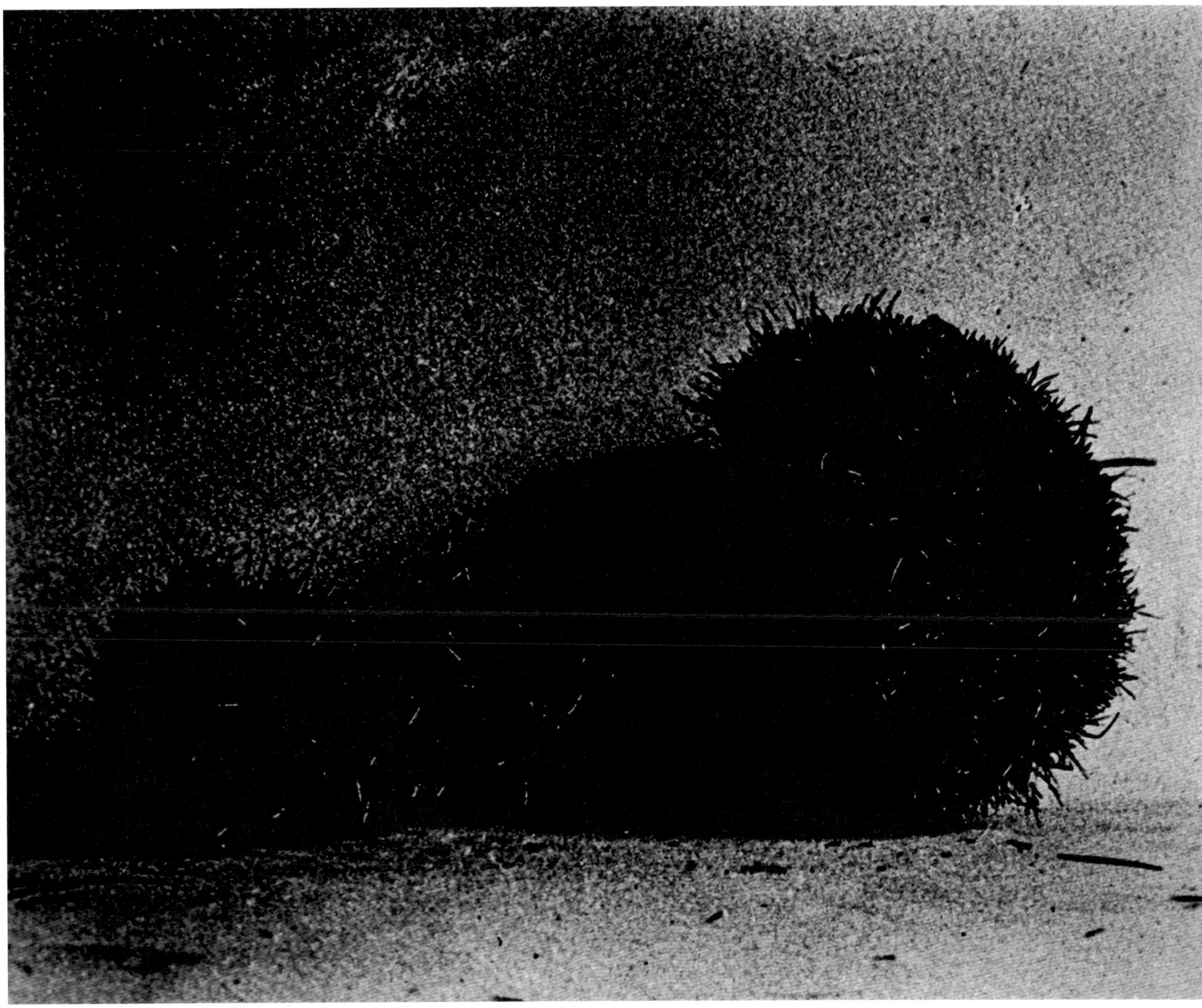

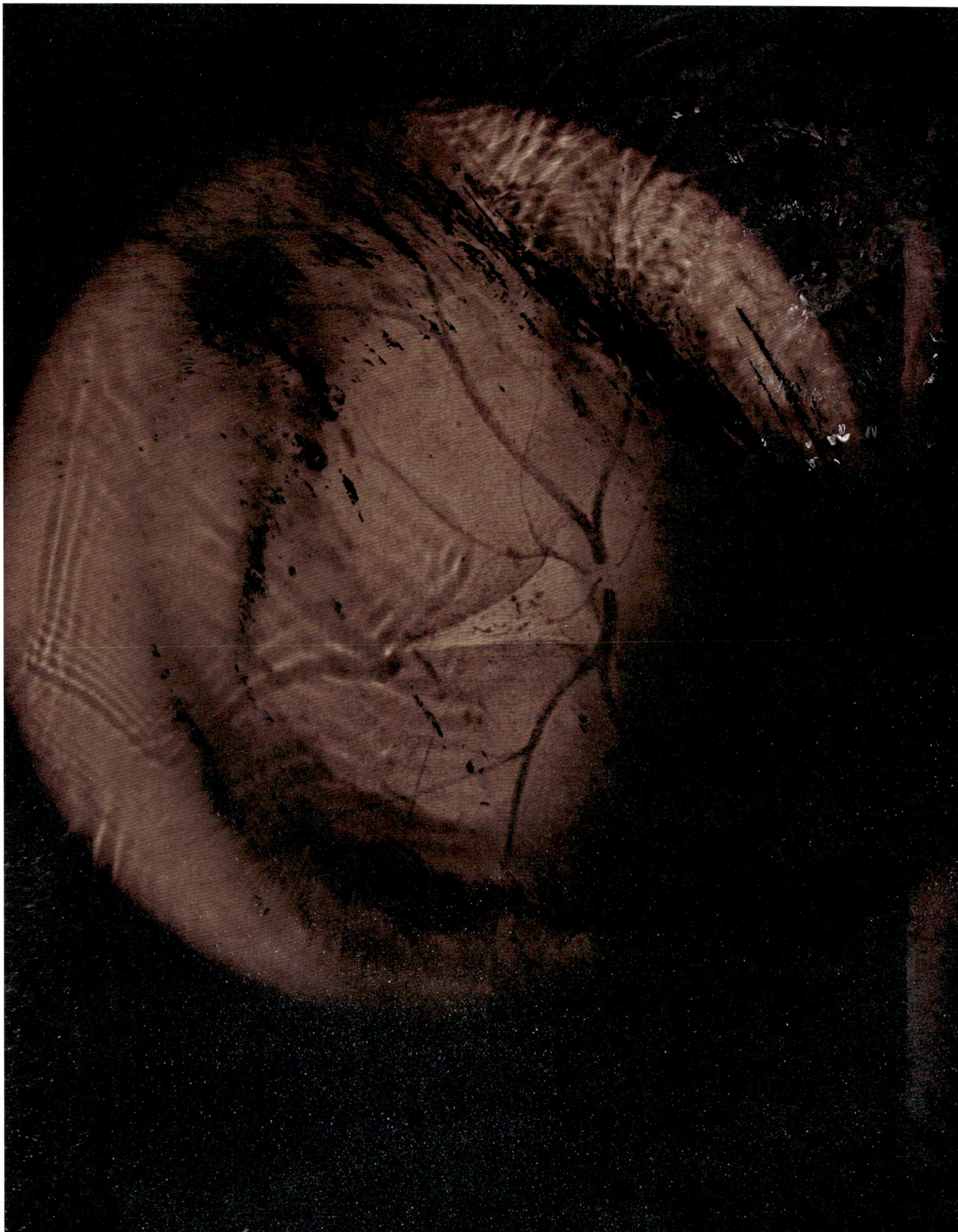

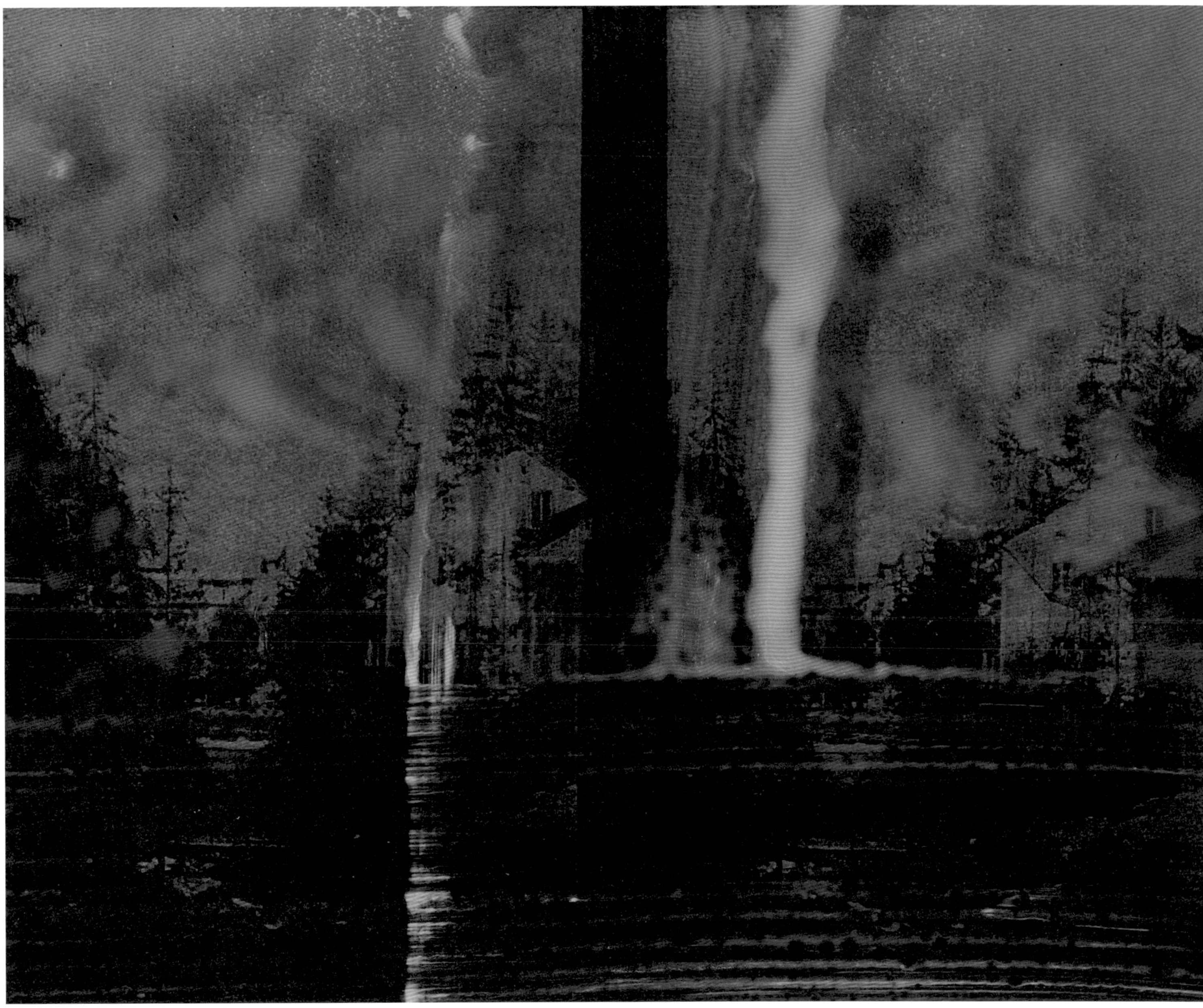

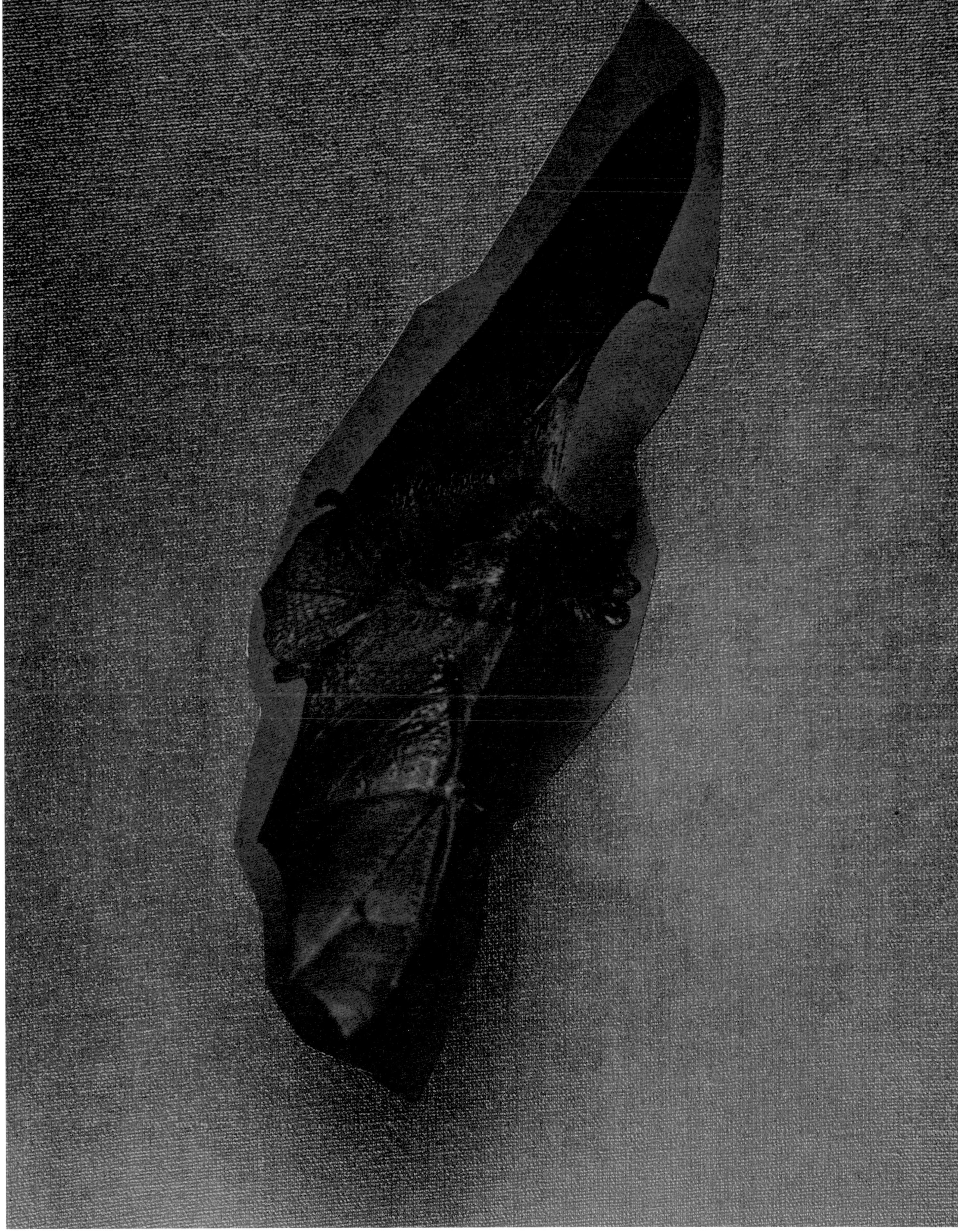

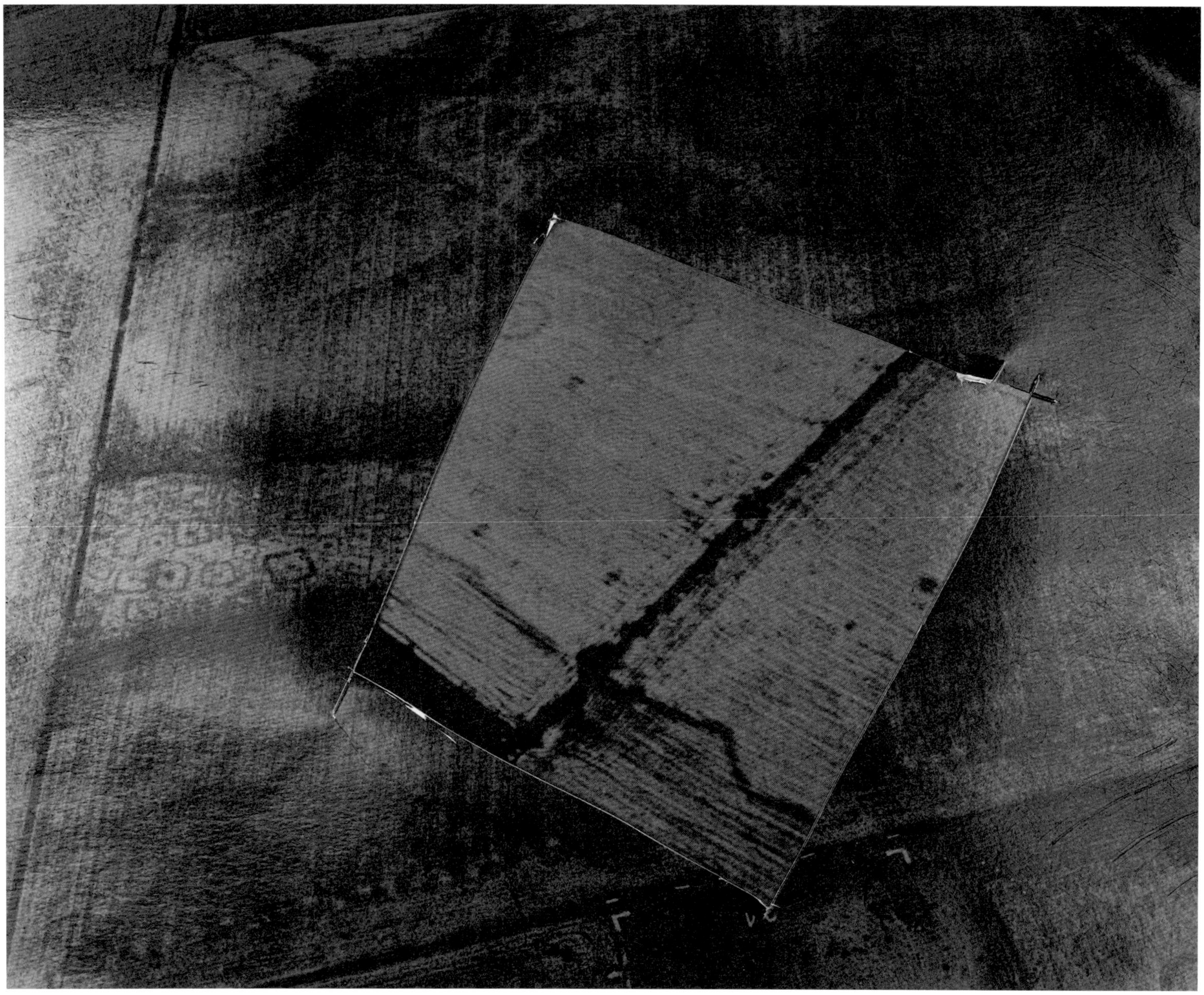

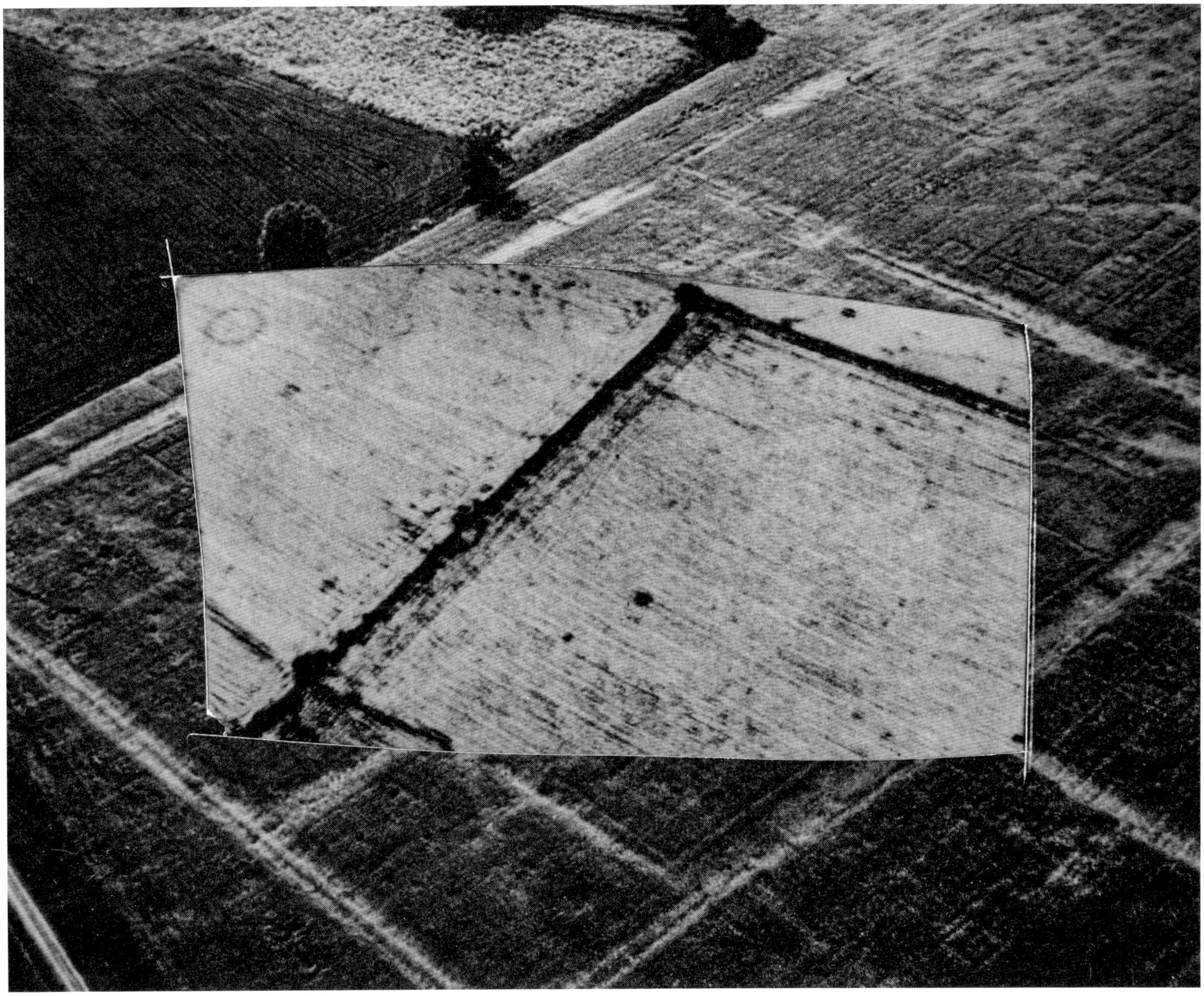

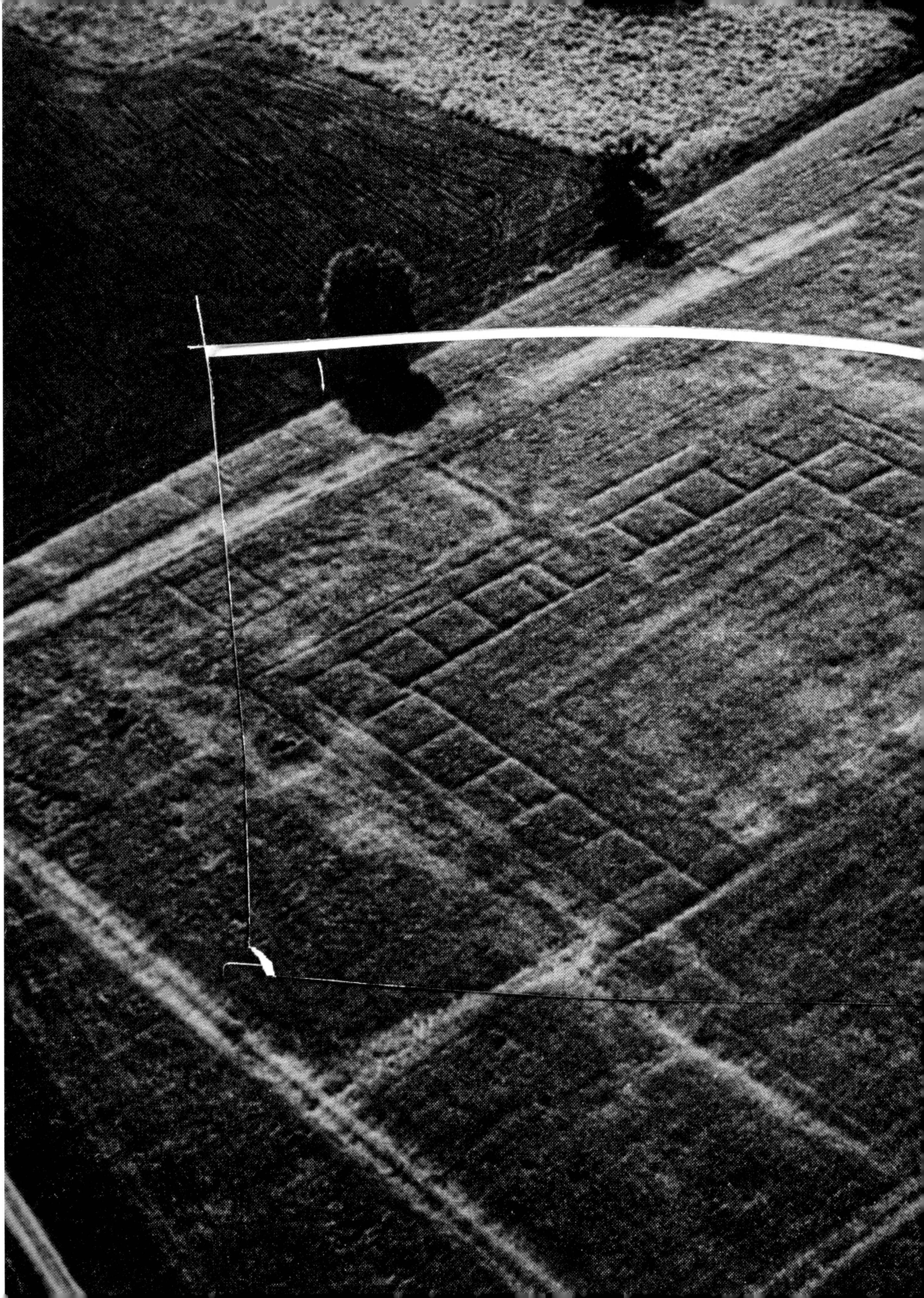

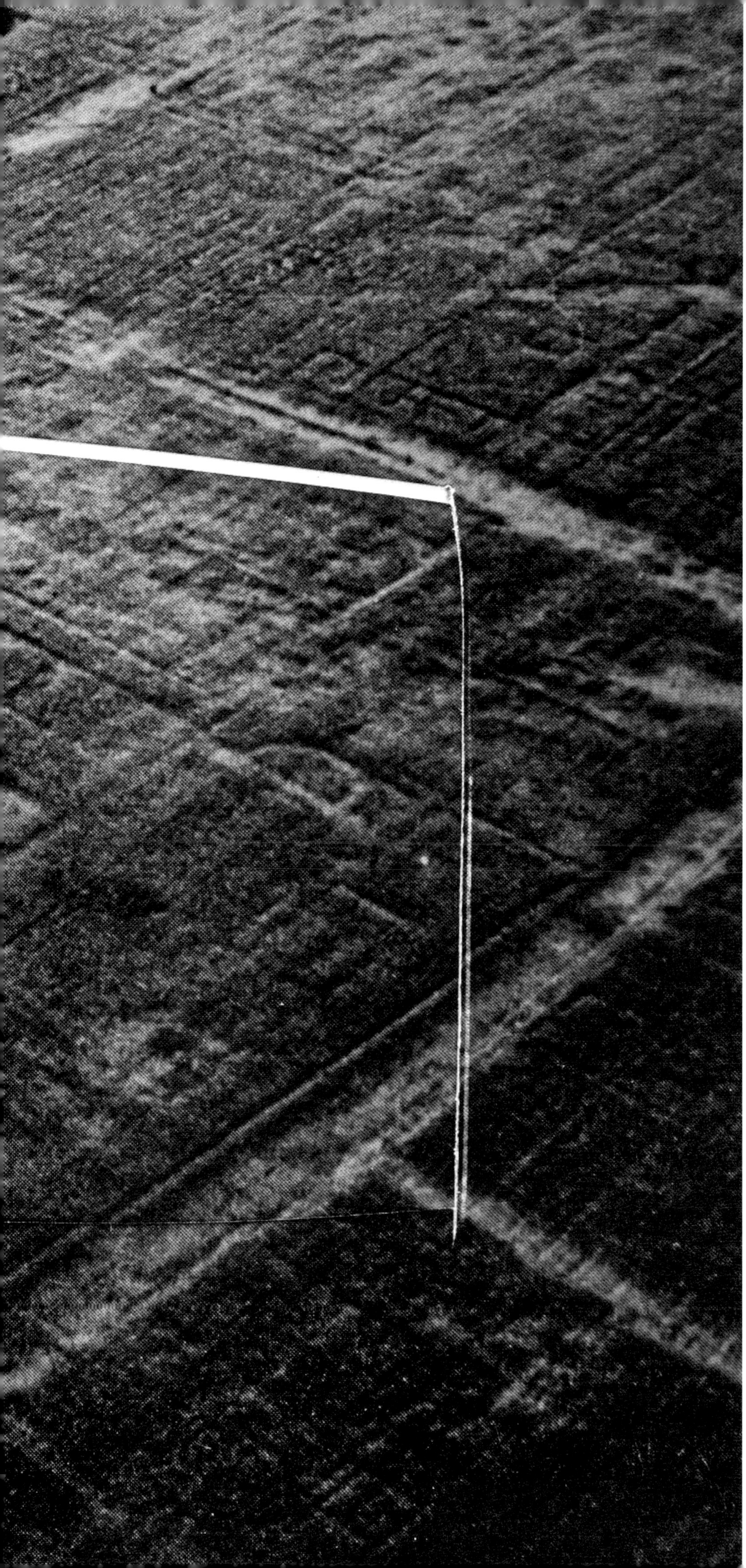

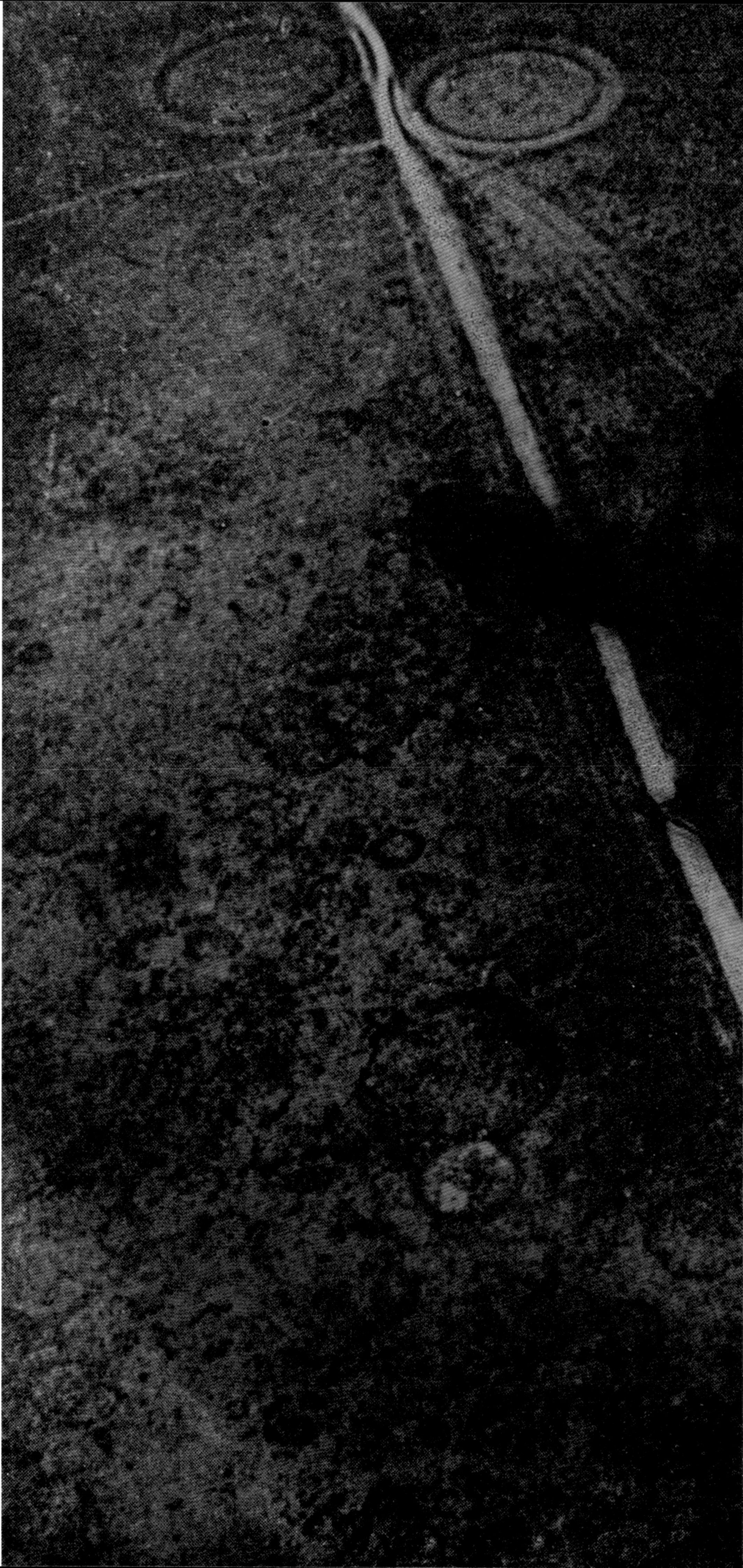

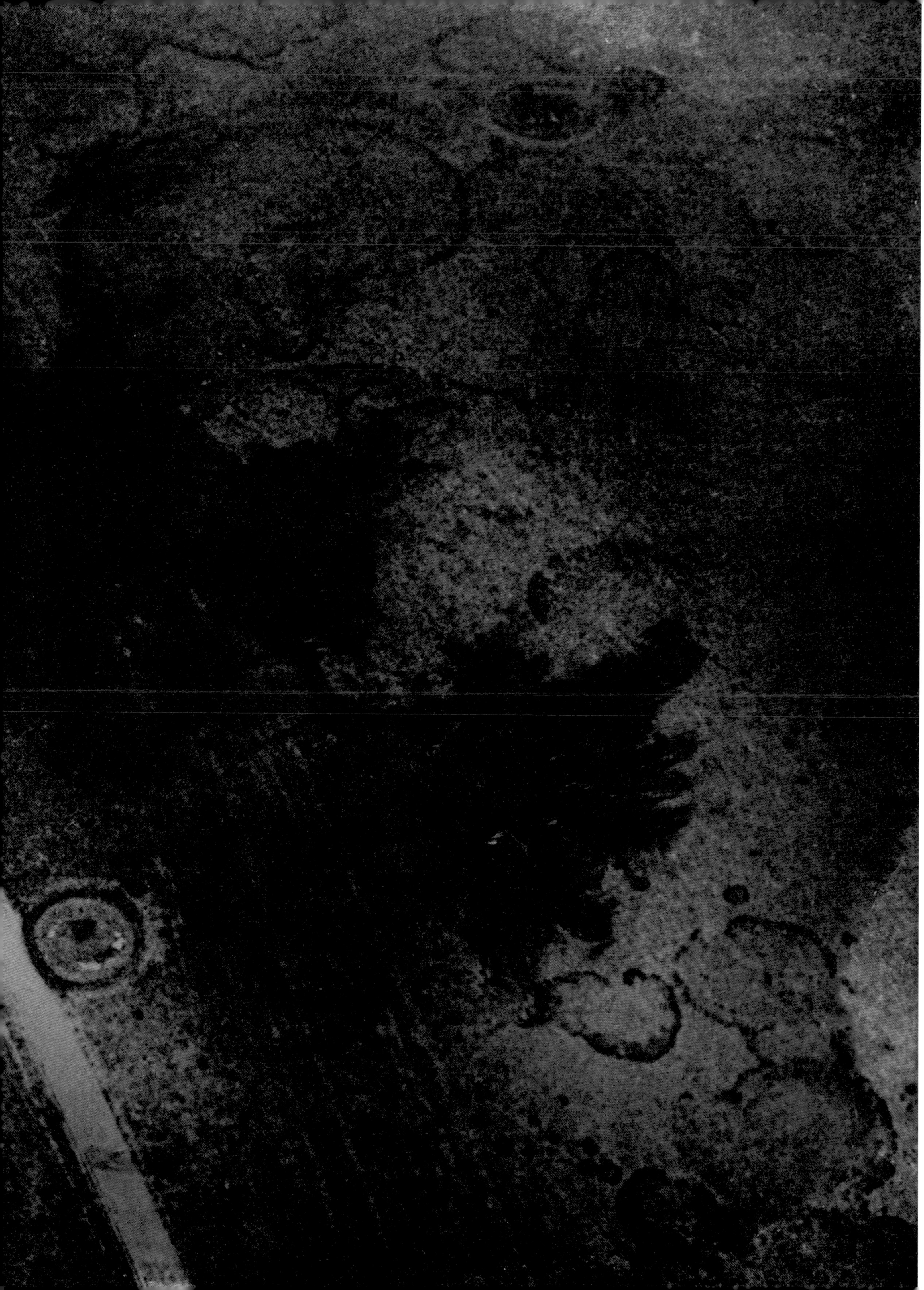

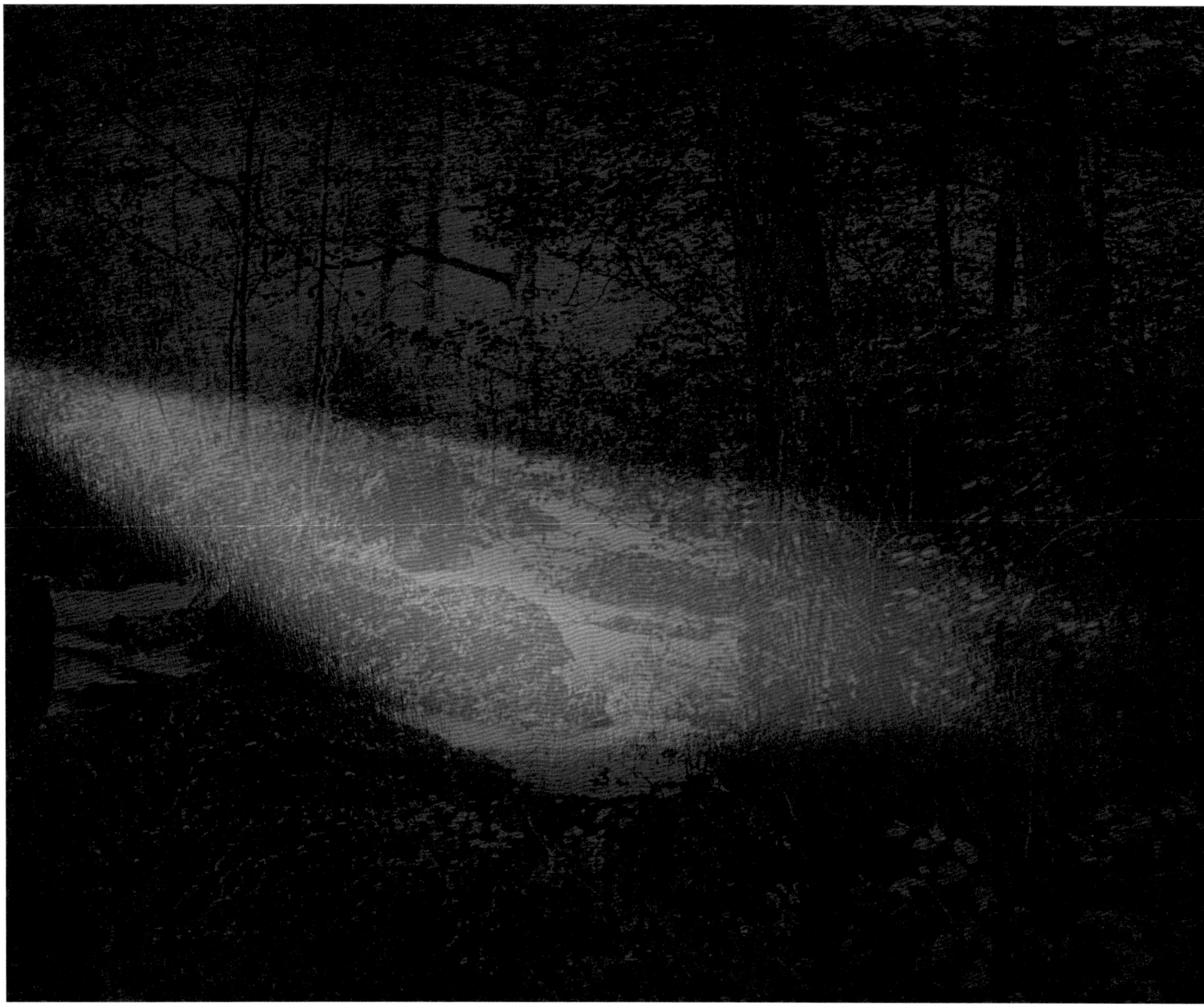

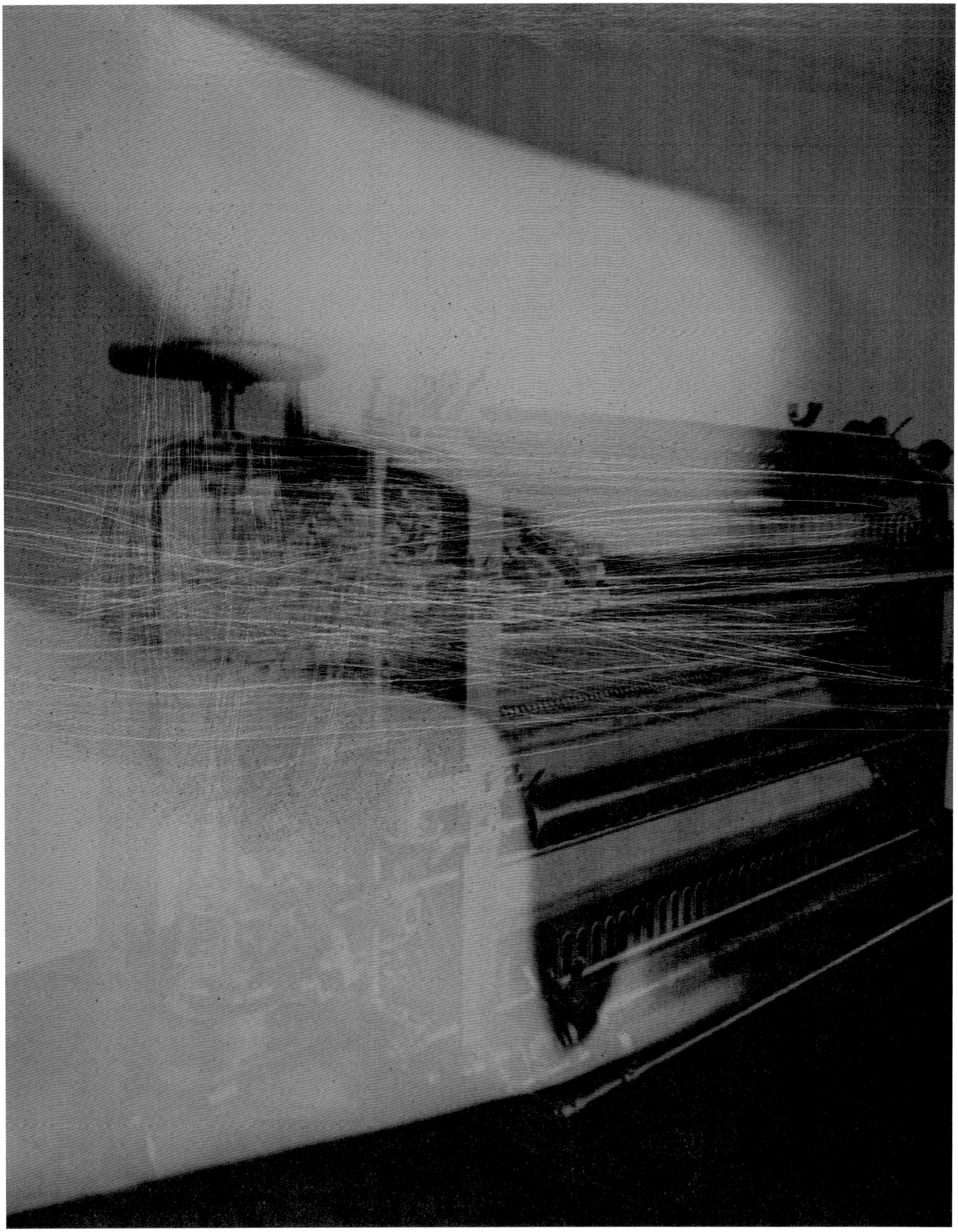

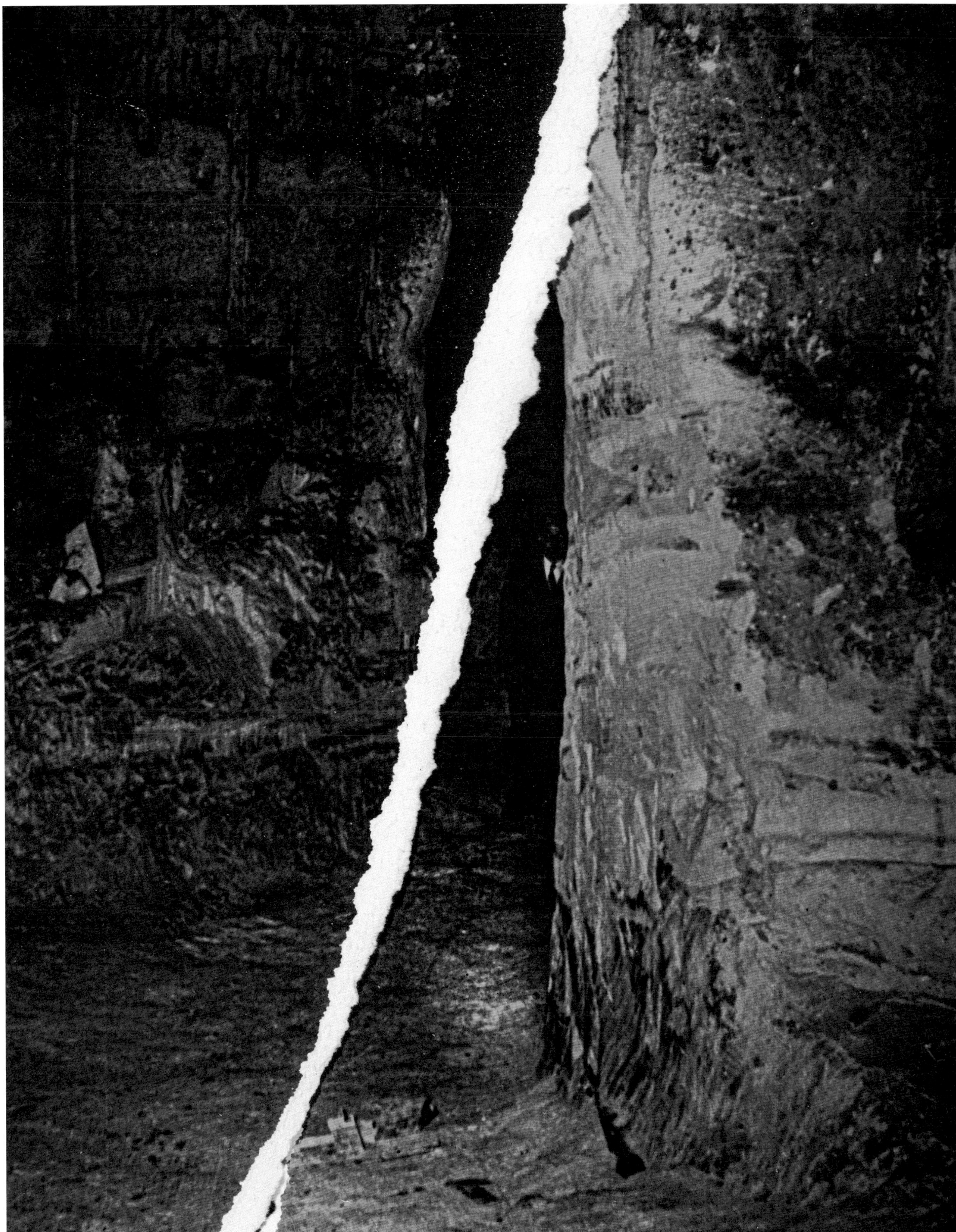

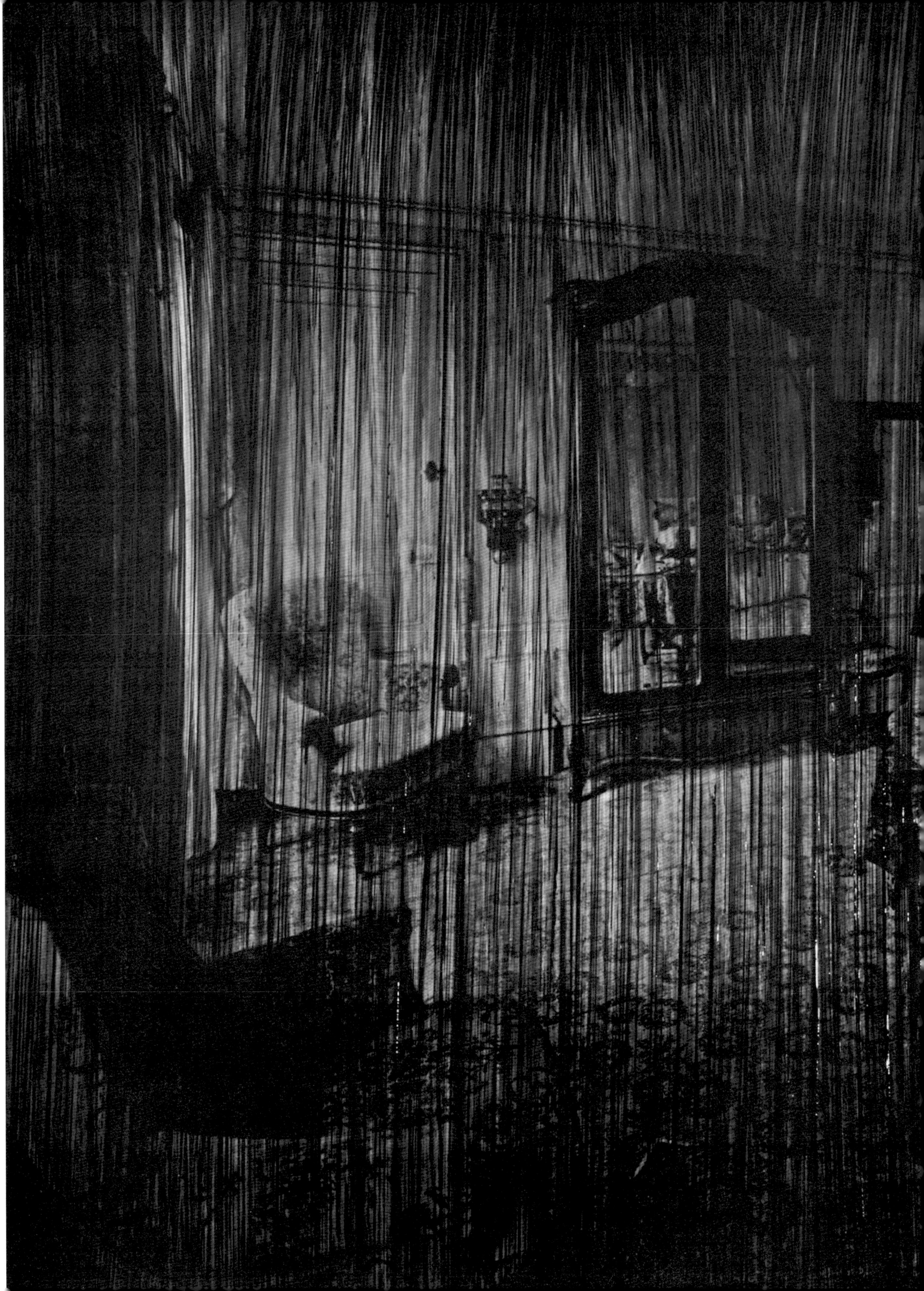

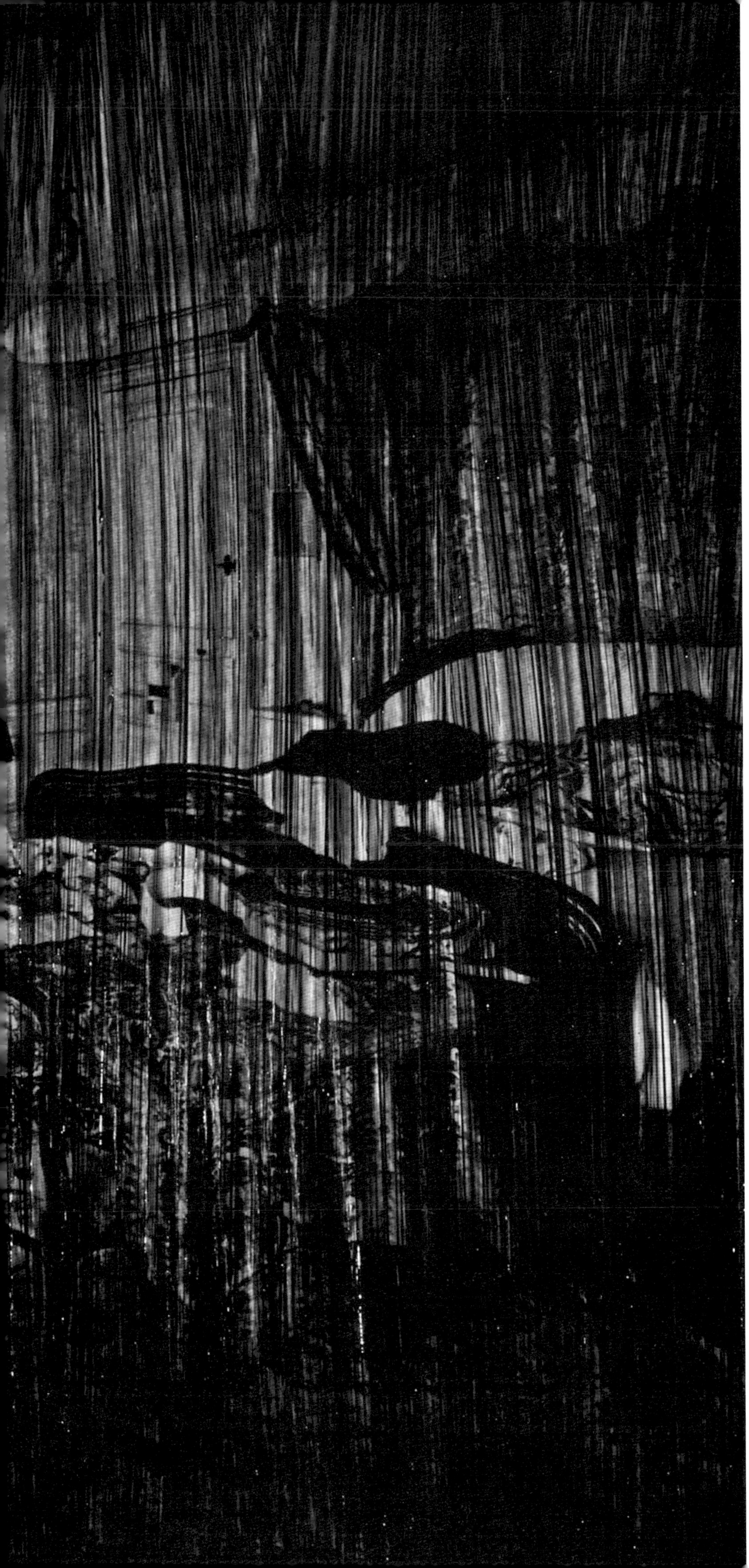

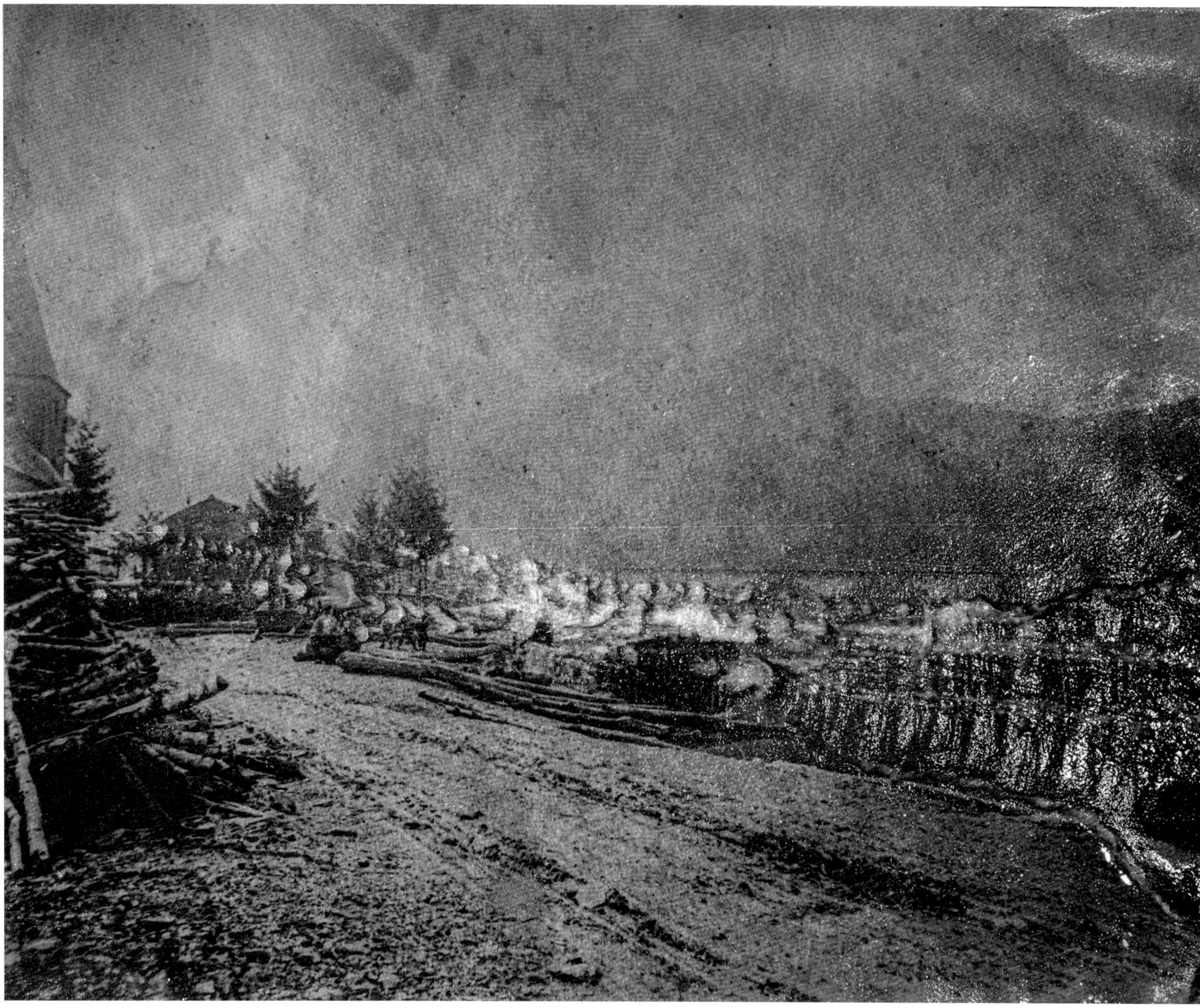

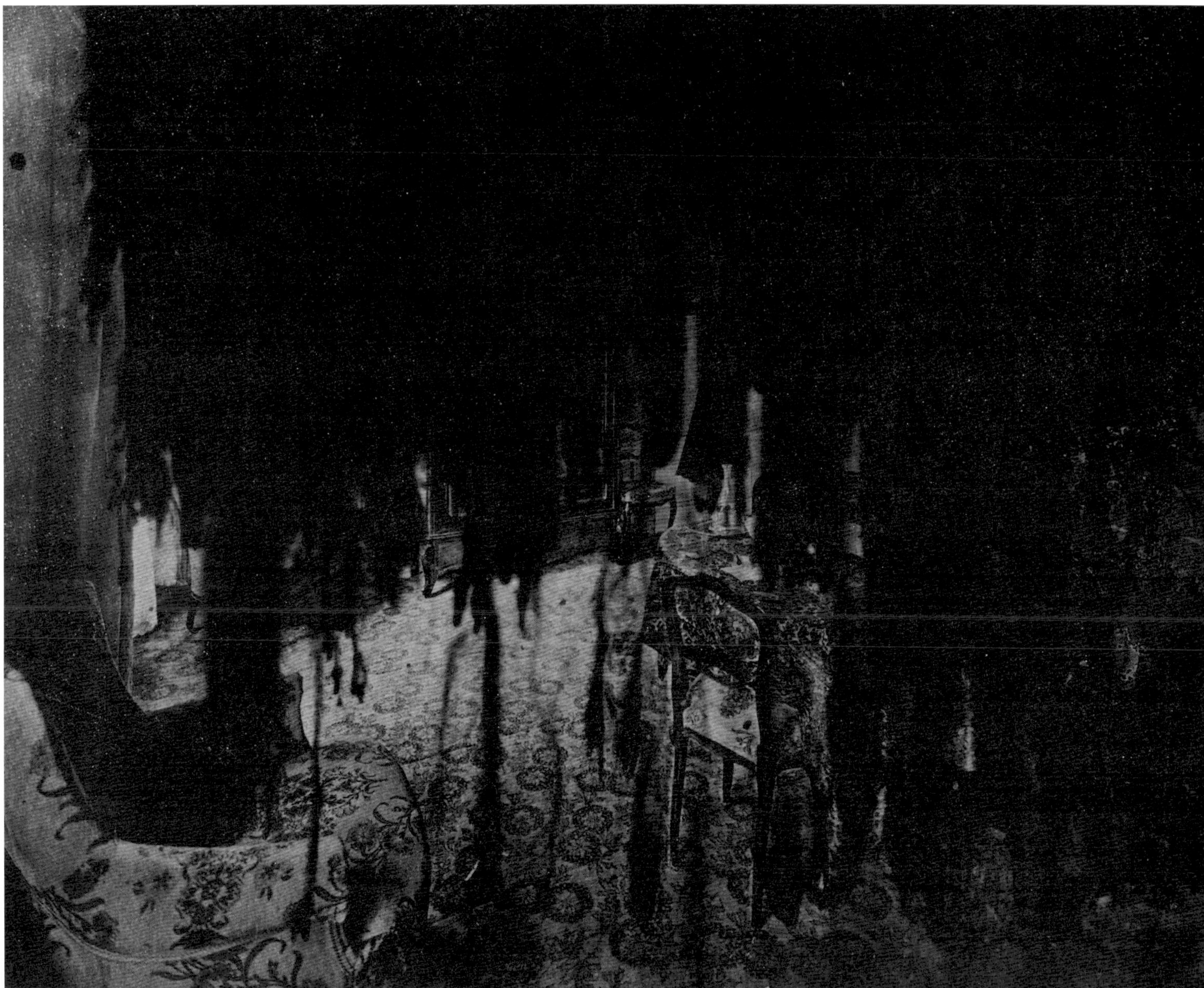

THE ART OF THE FUNCTIONAL

Tamara Berghmans, Curator FOMU

The exhibition *Dirk Braeckman. Echtzeit* (2024) represents a new chapter in showcasing the FOMU collection. It moves away from a chronological or genre-specific display to an open presentation that invites an emotional experience. Following Grace Ndiritu's shamanistic approach in 2023, FOMU is giving its collection to an artist with a very different focus this year. Dirk Braeckman has opted for functional photography and focused his artistic gaze on it. By selecting photographs from the FOMU collection and creating new work, inspired on these existing images, he allows the viewer to discover how much beauty and mystery there is in photographs that were originally made without artistic intent. Function becomes art; anomalies and mistakes become sources of wonder.

MAKING MUSEUM COLLECTIONS RELEVANT

FOMU houses a collection of more than four million photographs, cameras, archives and books. This rich collection, created in 1965, is both international and Belgian, stretching from the beginnings of photography to the present day.
For a long time, FOMU has been looking for ways to display its collection that differ from the classic, chronological or thematic arrangement. In recent decades, the approach to collecting and presenting a collection has changed significantly, as has society. How do you make a collection relevant for a contemporary audience? In what narrative do you place collection pieces? Which objects are put in the spotlight? These are but a few of the issues the museum has been addressing in recent years.
FOMU's new focus on opening up its collection is linked to the museum's broader mission and vision. FOMU aims to sharpen image awareness by making photography accessible from a historical perspective and within a contemporary context. Today's experimentation is tomorrow's heritage. That's why FOMU encourages creation, dynamism and innovation. The museum wants to be a place where people can broaden their horizons through photography. To achieve this, we pay specific attention to photographic projects that are topically relevant and multi-voiced, that reflect critically on the medium and/or history of photography, and that take an ethical position.
The collection exhibition *Re-collect* (2021), in which FOMU presented a selection of recent acquisitions, was a turning point in the way we collect and display collection pieces.[1] Traditionally, a collection exhibition is often a chronological itinerary of objects through which the history of photography is told, compiled from a white art-historical perspective. In practice, you tend to see a reiteration of the same photographs — the so-called canon — in different museums. This was also the case at FOMU. But like other museums, we asked ourselves: is there still a need for a canon, or can we work more intuitively? With *Re-collect*, we opted for an associative stroll through our latest additions to the collection in a non-chronological display.
But we wanted to go one step further and open up the collection to new perspectives and visions. Today, we see the emergence of more and more social paradigms that veer away from rational thinking. Museums are increasingly becoming meeting places where you can enjoy an emotional experience. This inspired the idea of inviting a different artist, whose work we hold, to curate an exhibition with the museum's collection every year. The artists can use their own photographs from our collection as a springboard or create new work inspired by the FOMU collection. This collaboration with guest curators and departure from the beaten track enables us to introduce different perspectives on our collection and illustrate its full breadth and diversity.
In 2023, FOMU asked the British-Kenyan visual artist Grace Ndiritu to act as guest curator. Ndiritu views shamanism as a means to reactivate museum collections. As such, she was the perfect first artist to delve into our collection and shake up entrenched visions.[2] For the second edition, FOMU has chosen a guest curator who takes a very different approach to the photographic image: Dirk Braeckman.[3]

DIRK BRAECKMAN FACE-TO-FACE WITH THE FOMU COLLECTION

FOMU has been following Braeckman since the beginning of his career and is the largest collector of his work in a global museum context. Over the course of more than 40 years, Braeckman has developed an impressive body of work. He explores the photographic medium in understated and obscure images and does not shy away from experimentation. Braeckman's work is highly subjective, evocative and autobiographical. His photographs are not documents that capture reality. He manipulates his images in the darkroom, thereby revealing a multitude of interpretations. FOMU invited him to use this perspective to look at the museum collection. Braeckman's expressed love for photography's historical and technical aspects — which are also extensively present in the FOMU collection — was an important reason for giving him carte blanche.

Braeckman worked on preparations for the exhibition for a whole year. After an initial brainstorming session, we had a list of keywords with which the search in the FOMU collection could begin: functional photography, crime scenes, everyday scenes, imperfections, etc. Braeckman did not want narrative images or portraits in which the person is looking into the lens. He eventually selected some 250 photographs and objects from the FOMU collection, exclusively functional photography. This is also known as *vernacular photography*, in other words, photography that isn't necessarily made with artistic intent. It includes historical, often commissioned images by unknown authors, such as product photography, private photographs, legal and scientific photography. Braeckman was interested in discoveries, atypical images from the collection, and objects usually hidden in depots or drawers. Take the photo album of the Antwerp doctor Paul Sano, which features a combination of his medical photography, collages and photographic experiments, or Georges Filleul's mysterious product photo in which a hand appears out of nowhere. Other examples include a strange scene with a man, a woman and a plaster horse by Belgian sculptor and painter Jacques de Lalaing, an aerial photograph taken by the Belgian Army's photo department, an empty interior of a crime scene and 19th-century images of wheelchairs by François Smeesters.

Braeckman is inspired by photographs that do not pretend to be art but become art nonetheless.[4] Almost all of the collection pieces he selected show commonalities with his own work. They are often suggestive images of empty spaces with barely any people, photographs with imperfections and representations that leave much to the imagination. Braeckman explores the materiality of photos. A crease or a dull spot shows that a photograph is an object you can hold, not just a window into reality. He is interested in accidental compositions and elements that the original photographer may not have intended but which, for Braeckman, are precisely what make the photograph captivating.

An important source of inspiration for Braeckman was the book *Evidence* (1992) by Luc Sante (b. 1954). This contains a series of black-and-white photos of crime scenes taken by the New York police in 1914-1918.

Actually, I've always looked at images this way. A crime scene, that's horrible to look at, but I see the beauty in it. Especially the shots where the body has already been removed, where only the space remains. Those images suggest a lot. If you look at the sharpness, the clutter, but also the beauty of certain interiors with an aesthetic eye, you see images differently.[5]

APPROPRIATION ART

While preparing the exhibition, Braeckman constantly asked himself how he could present the FOMU collection from his personal point of view. He felt that merely showing the selected museum objects was insufficient. Braeckman chose functional photographs without artistic ambition but in which he recognised visual qualities. For him, the challenge was to make visitors look at these images differently. He wanted to accentuate this by doing something with the collection images and transforming them into new works. So Braeckman reinterpreted the museum collection by rephotographing the pictures. He appropriated the photographs: you experience them through his camera, his eyes and his hands.

The term for deliberately altering existing objects to create new works of art is appropriation art. Throughout history, artists have used it to convey new meanings, question authorship, challenge established norms or comment on contemporary issues.

Appropriation art isn't new. We have seen artists quoting the work of others, borrowing from it, appropriating it to create new work since the 19th century. Today, more than ever, we live in a digital society where recycling and re-mixing are part of our culture. With the help of the internet, it's becoming not only effortless but also a widely accepted reality for today's generation of visual artists, DJs, filmmakers, writers, dancers and theatre-makers to refer to and reuse existing concepts and ideas.

Braeckman first came into contact with appropriation art in the early 1980s when he saw an exhibition in New York featuring the work of American artists Sherrie Levine (b. 1947) and Richard Prince (b. 1949). Those images made a strong impression on him.

In that same period, Braeckman made prints of negatives that were not his own for the first time. A friend gave him a wooden box containing around 100 negatives from an unknown photographer depicting scenes from World War I. In one day, Braeckman made 12 large-format prints from the negatives. He then returned the negatives and put the photographs away for more than 25 years because he didn't feel he owned the images. In 2013, with the commemoration of World War I approaching, he finally felt ready to go public with the *Schwarzschild* series.[6]

Today, the practice of 're-photographing' is part of Braeckman's way of working:

I have been working with the concept of appropriation for some time. I often re-photograph my own work. For example, I take out details. Theoretically, that's not appropriation because it's my own work, but the feeling tends towards it. So my way of working is similar to this new series in FOMU but different because here I start with images that don't belong to me.

For Braeckman, appropriation is about how you place an existing image in a different context so that it becomes yours. And that starts in one's own head:

The first step in appropriation is to look at an image with a very different perspective than perhaps intended. That's where it all begins.

Re-photographing is a highly personal process. In Braeckman's case, it has nothing to do with objectively registering or reproducing art objects. He searches for the sheen of the existing photographs and reflects his flash on them, thereby causing the image surface to be pushed in front of the image. Braeckman is not a purist. As an artist, he expresses himself best with photography, but he stretches the possibilities and limits of the medium as far as he can. From shot to print, he adds several layers. He takes many side roads and incorporates all sorts of things. Yet his work has been very recognisable for the last 40 years because of the format and techniques he uses. The only thing that is always different is the path to the final result.

HOW FAR CAN YOU GO?

For FOMU, Braeckman worked with photographs he didn't take himself for the first time. This was a challenge and a learning process for him. He created new work based on functional photos from the museum's collection. Braeckman emphasised visual qualities he recognised in them, thereby accentuating his preferences and fascination for these kinds of images. While photographing the selected images, he employed the same gaze with which he looks at reality, with which he searches for meaningless or banal things that everyone passes by, for other qualities in reality.

Braeckman reinvented himself by using other people's photographs as source material and applying new artistic techniques in his creations. In his experiments with the medium, he continues to surprise and innovate. Braeckman continues to be a versatile artist who works with unprecedented freedom and does not cling frenetically to known ideas and methods.

The collection objects inspired him to such an extent that it became tough to make choices. How does he stay true to himself as an artist with images that are not his own? How far can he go in manipulating someone else's photos? When does something become disrespectful?

Initially, Braeckman underestimated how difficult it was to call himself the author of these images. He resolutely chose functional images rather than autonomous work by contemporary artists. For him, this was also an ethical issue. Although he leaves the future open, he currently doesn't feel free enough to create new work from photographs taken by a fellow artist:

While artists finish their photos like a work of art, functional photographers send their work out into the world like craftsmen. What I am doing here may seem disrespectful, but I have great respect for these photographers.

It's also this respect that initially blocked Braeckman. He dug deep within himself and looked for new ways to deal with this inner conflict without losing himself as an artist in all the possibilities. For him, there were two options to make the photographs his own: to intervene minimally or to destroy the work. There was no middle ground.

Creating collages is an example of such extreme image distortion. To free himself from crippling respect for the museum objects, Braeckman chose a physical action that was new to his artistic process — he attacked the reproductions. Using scissors, he cut holes — very quickly and intuitively — in the photographed collection images and then inserted new images into them. Other interventions included making prints on different textures and surfaces, re-photographing these photographic papers, adding dust, and painting or smearing the images before processing them further in his analogue and digital darkroom. The final result is the disappearance of the original image.

The original small, functional photographs, often straightforward, sharp and clearly legible, are transformed into monumental images that demand a conscious, slow reading and encourage reflection and contemplation. Braeckman added a kind of filter between the image and the viewer. Although he abstracted the collection photos, the new images never

lapse into total abstraction. The link to reality is still there. Braeckman's photographs become gateways to another world, to his world, in which the visitor is left guessing about the state of mind in which these images were created. They hide more than they show.
Braeckman manipulated the collection objects and gave them a new dimension: the context falls away, the format changes, the original meaning shifts, a title is added. The image is transformed from a functional document into a piece of art. Braeckman makes you look beyond the original function of photographs. They become timeless visual poems, raising more questions than they answer.
With the German title *Echtzeit*, Braeckman refers to the bridge he creates between past and present. At the same moment, and in real-time, there is a meeting of three perspectives: the original photographer's vision, Braeckman's interpretation and the viewer's gaze. The richness and complexity of the photographic medium are given a platform here.

AN OPEN DIALOGUE ABOUT THE COLLECTION

During this process, both Braeckman and FOMU were confronted with many ethical questions that are more topical than ever. As an artist, how do you treat other people's work with respect? When is a photograph merely functional and when does it become artistic? Is it at all possible to ascertain the original intention of the photographer? When can you call yourself the author of a work? A seemingly aggressive act, like cutting into images, perhaps makes us think more deeply about whose gaze we are displaying.
At FOMU, we also asked ourselves how far we could let an artist go with someone else's images. After all, as a photography museum, we are responsible for the legitimate and proper use of the photographs we preserve. The distinction between functional and artistic photography is often a blurry line. With this project, we also want to engage in dialogue about these subjects.
This collaboration with Braeckman was a further step for FOMU in renewing and opening up the collection. In a co-creative way, we want to abandon the traditional view of the canon to offer the public various perspectives. Opening up a collection for reinterpretation is an exciting and ongoing process that allows us to remain innovative and relevant as a museum. Dirk Braeckman provided a profound, enriching impetus to continue this process and the dialogue surrounding it.

1 Collection exhibition *Re-collect*. FOMU Antwerp. 7 May 2021 – 7 November 2021.

2 Collection exhibition *Grace Ndiritu Reimagines the FOMU Collection*. FOMU Antwerp. 17 February 2023 – 26 February 2024. For more information, see: Judah, H. (2023, January 27). A Map Through Time: Grace Ndiritu Reimagines the FOMU Collection. *Trigger*. www.fomu.be/trigger/articles/grace-ndiritu.

3 Collection exhibition *Dirk Braeckman. Echtzeit*. FOMU Antwerp. 29 March 2024 – 19 January 2025.

4 Versteeg, W. (2017, May 17). The Loneliness of the Darkroom. *Aperture*. aperture.org/editorial/loneliness-darkroom-braeckman.

5 All quotes by Dirk Braeckman are from a conversation between Tamara Berghmans and Dirk Braeckman, in his studio in Ghent, 26 September 2023.

6 Canonne, X. (2013). Conversation with Dirk Braeckman. In Anonymus & D. Braeckman, *Schwarzschild* (pp. 51-55). Antwerp: Pandora.

THE SPECTRE'S PERSPECTIVE

Clément Chéroux

THE RAPTURE OF IMAGES

There are photographs that make you sit up and take notice. Anyone who has ever found themselves with a box full of pictures in front of them, in the storeroom of a museum or on a flea market stall, and started to look at them carefully, one by one, knows this very well. It's tacit knowledge, implicit knowledge about which no book has ever been written, but which is nevertheless very widely shared. In the end, it doesn't matter whether they're art or not — some photographs *speak* to us, or perhaps we should say *seize* our attention. They attract our gaze like a magnet attracts filings. They seem to be equipped with small telescopic grabbers that instantly harpoon us. Roland Barthes explains this admirably in some of the most poignant pages of *Camera Lucida*: in certain images there is a detail "which rises from the scene, shoots out of it like an arrow, and pierces me."[1] "This *something* has triggered me, has provoked a tiny shock, a *satori* [...]."[2] "A photograph's *punctum*," he adds, "is that accident which pricks me."[3] This intensity that pierces me can just as easily be an element in the picture, an arrangement of shapes, a simple gesture, the position of a body or a singular light, or even a chemical alteration, a crack in the sensitive surface. But, whatever the case, there is a form of visual injunction here that speaks directly to my identity, my subconscious, my memory perhaps, my experience, my knowledge, or my culture; something that is intimately related to *who I am*. The result is usually an irrepressible desire to *possess* the image (or a copy of it). Like the other's body in carnal desire. So that the rapture can be replayed at will.

UNTAMED BRAECKMANS

For several months now, Dirk Braeckman has been immersed in the millions of photographs that make up the collections of the FOMU (Fotomuseum Antwerp). He has opened countless boxes, searched through registers and leafed through albums. He has allowed himself to be *seized* — at the exact point of the 'shock', 'tilt' or 'satori' that Barthes speaks of — by some of the images that make up the raw material of the works in this volume and that are reproduced, unchanged, at the beginning of the volume. Although I wasn't present at the selection, I think I can guess quite precisely what led the artist to choose these images. Firstly, he removed all the photographs taken by artists from an initial selection, which was fairly broad and intuitive, and kept only the *anonymous* shots, i.e. those without an identified author. For his project, he needed images that were neutral, not charged, or to put it another way: devoid of artistic intention. Out of respect for the creative process, he didn't want his own to overlap with someone else's. But beyond the fact that they are devoid of authorship, the common feature of the images selected is that they are *open*, to use a term dear to the Italian philosopher and semiotician Umberto Eco.[4] Their main quality is a kind of irresolution, a capacity to raise questions in those who look at them. What all these pictures chosen by Braeckman have in *common* is, in fact, a *question mark*.[5] Looking at them, even though in most cases they are documentary pictures, I am constantly asking myself what exactly they show or mean. They do not impose a meaning on me, but rather invite me to give one. Need we point out here that this is exactly what Braeckman was looking for in the pictures he took himself? Most of his works have an enigmatic quality. The few photographs he chose from the FOMU collection *naturally* possess the qualities he seeks in his own work. In a way, they are *untamed* Braeckmans. And that's why he selected them. He recognised himself in them.

REOPENING THE IMAGE

Once the image has been chosen, Braeckman photographs it again, often playing with the reflections that form on its gleaming surface. He loves nothing more than the shimmer or halos that enhance the print with an auratic sparkle. Then he reworks the shot on the computer. He deliberately reframes, saturates, solarises and veils. He superimposes several shots. He sometimes uses a form of montage, not by addition but, on the contrary, by subtraction: he incises the image, cuts it out broadly and uses the void he has thus formed as a new frame. When talking about his experiments, Man Ray used to talk about the "rape of materials."[6] Braeckman does as much. Some of the photographs are painted over: he covers them with large dark patches or colours them with a watered-down tint. He then enlarges his photographs to a format that has nothing in common with the original. The artist's work on images is a kind of filtering. His creative process consists of interposing screens between the image and the viewer. This strategy of distancing responds to an imperative: *defunctionalisation*. The photographs taken from the FOMU collection were primarily used for documentary purposes. They were used to promote a new instrument, report on the completion of a project, record a memory, identify a disease, recognise a battleground and so on. When I look at Braeckman's work, I no longer recognise the medical microphotograph, the advertising document or the aerial reconnaissance view. His images have lost their useful value. They don't tell me *where*, *when* or *how*, let alone *why*. They have definitely lost their purpose. They are literally *out of service*. But this makes them even more mysterious. Through his work, Braeckman succeeds in multiplying the enigmatic power of his images, *reopening* them to intensify the imaginative projection of those who contemplate them.

DESTROY, HE SAYS

What is the nature of the transformation that Braeckman puts these images through? It's essentially alchemical. It's a transmutation. It's really turning lead into gold. This is based first and foremost on the principle of reduction. The first step is to take the image out of its merely informative context, thereby destroying its original documentary function. When I meet Braeckman in his studio in Ghent to talk about how he has taken ownership of these images, he keeps using the word 'destroy'. He wants to attack them, bash them, distort them. "I can only respect them or destroy them," he says.[7] The title of Marguerite Duras's book inevitably comes to mind: *Détruire, dit-elle*.[8] This masterful work, published in the year following the social revolution of 1968, features two men and two women in a large house on the edge of a forest. Its main theme is the power of desire. When she talks about the film that follows on from her book, Duras evokes a violent desire that destroys everything it touches: "I'm in favour of [...] starting all over again. That's the deepest part of my book, *Détruire, dit-elle*. Starting from zero. I'm in favour of forgetting History, the History of France, the History of the world. Completely. Let there be no memory of what was experienced — what was intolerable — on all fronts, in every respect. Break everything."[9] This is exactly what Braeckman is trying to do. He begins by reducing the image to its most appropriate share of reality. He knows that he is walking an extremely narrow ridge. He doesn't want to fall into abstraction. Something tangible must enable him to stay standing and keep moving forward. It's his own tightrope. He's keen to preserve a certain substratum of reality from which he can then redeploy the image. André Breton, the leader of Surrealism, understood this well in his day: "All things are called upon to serve purposes other than those generally attributed to them. It is even from the conscious sacrifice of their primary purpose [...] that certain *transcendent properties* are deduced which are attached to them."[10] Freed from their initial purpose and reopened to the potential of enchantment, the photographs Braeckman uses become veritable conduits for the imagination.

OUT OF BODY

Beyond the sense of destruction, death is ubiquitous in this collection of photographs by Dirk Braeckman. The way he perceives the world through these images is reminiscent of an out-of-body journey as described in near-death experiences. Astral travel, psychic excursion, ecsomatic trance, Out of Body Experience (OBE) — whatever the name of the phenomenon, it has given rise to a wealth of testimonies.[11] When you read them, what is perhaps most striking is the repetition of the same narrative patterns, in other words a supposed commonality of experience. When, just after death, the soul leaves its vehicle, it is sucked upwards. Not to the height of an airliner, but rather that of a kite or an ultra-light aircraft. High above the ground, a few metres above its carnal envelope, the soul, newly freed from the body's gravity, is not only endowed with a keen sense of sight, but also with the ability to move gently and smoothly, as if propelled on a cushion of air. The words most commonly used are 'hanging', 'weightlessness' and 'floating'. "The journey was short and we found ourselves about fifteen metres above the street, says someone who returned from the afterlife [...]. We were floating just above the ground and I was looking down [...] We were hovering about a hundred or two hundred metres above the earth. It was dark and every now and then a light would come on in the countryside. Just below us was a shimmering body of water, a pond or small lake. Beyond it was a green building in the shape of a pyramid, inside which a light could be seen shining."[12] This is precisely where Braeckman's gaze lies in *Echtzeit*. Through his images, he places himself in the position of someone haunting the world. He has found the spectre's perspective.

1 Barthes, R. (2010). *Camera Lucida, Reflections on Photography* (R. Howard, Trans.). New York: Hill and Wang, p. 26.

2 Ibid., p. 49.

3 Ibid., p. 27.

4 Eco, U. (1965). *L'Œuvre ouverte*. Paris: Seuil.

5 On this question, see: Chéroux, C. (2010). L'image comme point d'interrogation ou la valeur d'extase du document surréaliste. *Les carnets du bal, L'image-document, entre réalité et fiction*, (1), pp. 26-47.

6 Man Ray (1933). L'Âge de la lumière. *Minotaure*, (3-4), p. 1.

7 Interview conducted by the author with Dirk Braeckman, in his studio in Ghent, 23 November 2023.

8 Duras, M. (1969). *Détruire, dit-elle*. Paris: Minuit.

9 Interview with Marguerite Duras on the set of *Détruire, dit-elle*, broadcast in *Banc d'essai*, a programme produced by Jean-Claude Bergeret, 1969, available on the INA website: www.ina.fr/ina-eclaire-actu/video/i05125289/marguerite-duras-a-propos-de-detruire-dit-elle, retrieved 2 December 2023.

10 Breton, A. (1992). Avis au lecteur pour *La Femme 100 têtes* de Max Ernst. In *Œuvres complètes*, (Vol. 2). Paris: Gallimard, p. 305. Emphasis added.

11 Monroe, R.A. (1996). *Le Voyage hors du corps. Techniques de projection du corps astral*. Monaco: Les éditions du Rocher. (Original work published in 1971)

12 Monroe, R.A. (1990). *Fantastiques expériences de voyage astral*. Paris: Robert Laffont, pp. 293, 342, 357-358. (Original work published in 1985)

QUAND LA FONCTIONNALITÉ DEVIENT ART

Tamara Berghmans, conservatrice du FOMU

L'exposition *Dirk Braeckman. Echtzeit* (2024) s'ouvre un nouveau chapitre de la présentation de la collection FOMU. À mille lieues d'un classement chronologique ou axé sur les genres, il s'agit ici d'une présentation ouverte invitant le visiteur à ressentir et à expérimenter. Après l'approche chamanique de Grace Ndiritu en 2023, le FOMU confie cette année la collection à un artiste visant un tout autre objectif. Dirk Braeckman opte pour une photographie fonctionnelle, qu'il couve de son regard artistique. En sélectionnant des photographies de la collection du FOMU et en créant de nouvelles œuvres inspirées de ces images existantes, il permet au spectateur de découvrir la beauté et le mystère qui se cachent dans des photographies prises initialement sans intention artistique. La fonctionnalité devient art, les anomalies et les erreurs se muent en sources d'émerveillement.

RESTAURER LA PERTINENCE DES COLLECTIONS MUSÉALES

Le FOMU abrite une collection totalisant plus de quatre millions de photographies, d'appareils photo, de fonds d'archives et de livres. Créée en 1965, cette riche collection, à la fois belge et internationale, retrace les débuts de la photographie jusqu'à nos jours.

Depuis un certain temps, le FOMU cherche à innover pour présenter sa collection, en s'écartant d'une présentation chronologique ou par genre. Au cours des dernières décennies, l'approche de la collection et de la présentation a évolué de manière significative, à l'image de la société. Comment rendre une collection pertinente pour le public contemporain ? Dans quel processus narratif placer les pièces de collection ? Quels objets mettre en valeur ? Ce sont là quelques-unes des questions sur lesquelles le musée s'est penché ces dernières années.

La nouvelle direction prise par le FOMU pour présenter sa collection est intimement liée à la mission et à la vision plus larges du musée. Le FOMU vise à aiguiser la conscience de l'image en rendant la photographie accessible sous un angle historique et dans un contexte actuel. Ainsi, l'expérience d'aujourd'hui devient l'héritage de demain. C'est pourquoi le FOMU encourage la création, le dynamisme et l'innovation. Le musée entend incarner un lieu où les visiteurs peuvent élargir leurs horizons au travers de la photographie. Pour y parvenir, nous accordons une attention particulière aux projets photographiques pertinents sur le plan de l'actualité et qui s'expriment à plusieurs voix, qui mènent une réflexion critique sur le médium et/ou l'histoire de la photographie et qui adoptent une position éthique.

L'exposition *Re-collect* (2021), au cours de laquelle le FOMU a présenté une sélection d'acquisitions récentes, a marqué un tournant dans notre manière de collectionner et d'exposer des pièces de collection.[1] Traditionnellement, une exposition de collection s'apparente souvent à un parcours chronologique d'objets racontant l'histoire de « la » photographie, compilé sous une perspective blanche de l'histoire de l'art. Dans différents musées, on note une certaine récurrence des mêmes images, mieux connues sous le nom de « canon ». Le FOMU n'y dérogeait pas. Mais comme d'autres musées, nous nous sommes posé la question suivante : est-il encore nécessaire d'avoir un canon ou est-il possible de travailler de manière plus intuitive ? Avec *Re-collect*, nous avions opté pour un parcours associatif à la découverte des pièces les plus récentes de la collection, présentées dans un ordre non chronologique.

Nous voulions aller encore plus loin et ouvrir la collection à de nouveaux regards et de nouvelles visions. Aujourd'hui, on assiste de plus en plus à l'émergence de cadres de pensée sociaux en marge du rationnel. Les musées s'apparentent de plus en plus à des lieux de rencontre, invitant à ressentir et à expérimenter. C'est ainsi qu'est née l'idée d'inviter chaque année un artiste, dont les œuvres font partie de la collection du FOMU, à organiser une exposition à partir de ce qui est en possession du musée. Cet artiste peut donc utiliser ses propres photos de la collection comme point de départ ou créer des nouvelles œuvres en s'inspirant de la collection du FOMU. En collaborant avec ces commissaires invités et en sortant des sentiers battus, nous introduisons de nouvelles perspectives sur la collection et la présentons dans toute son étendue et sa diversité. En 2023, le FOMU a demandé à l'artiste visuelle britanno-kenyane Grace Ndiritu d'être la commissaire invitée. Elle perçoit le chamanisme comme un moyen de réactiver les collections des musées. Il n'y avait donc pas meilleure artiste pour plonger la première dans notre collection et bousculer des points de vue bien ancrés.[2] Pour cette deuxième édition le FOMU a choisi un commissaire invité dont l'approche de l'image photographique est très différente : Dirk Braeckman.[3]

DIRK BRAECKMAN : LES YEUX DANS LES YEUX AVEC LA COLLECTION DU FOMU

Le FOMU suit Dirk Braeckman depuis le début de sa carrière et représente le plus grand collectionneur de son œuvre dans un contexte muséal mondial. Durant plus de quatre décennies, il a développé une œuvre impressionnante. Au travers d'images sombres et subtiles, il explore le médium photographique, sans jamais reculer devant l'expérimentation. Le travail de Dirk Braeckman est extrêmement subjectif, évocateur et autobiographique. Ses photographies ne sont pas des documents consignant la réalité. Il manipule ses images dans la chambre noire, livrant ainsi une multitude d'interprétations.

C'est sous cet angle que le FOMU l'a invité à considérer la collection du musée. L'amour de Dirk Braeckman pour les aspects historiques et techniques de la photographie — également très présents dans la collection du FOMU — a été un argument majeur pour lui donner carte blanche. Durant un an, Dirk Braeckman s'est donc employé à la préparation de l'exposition. Après une première séance de brainstorming, nous avons établi une liste de mots-clés qui ont permis d'amorcer la recherche dans la vaste collection du FOMU : photographie fonctionnelle, scènes de crime, scènes de la vie quotidienne, imperfections... Dirk Braeckman ne voulait pas d'images narratives ou de portraits dont le sujet fixait l'objectif.

Finalement, son choix s'est porté sur quelque 250 photographies et objets de la collection du FOMU, et exclusivement des photographies fonctionnelles. On parle aussi de *photographie vernaculaire*, soit une photographie qui n'a pas nécessairement d'ambition artistique. Il s'agit d'images historiques, souvent anonymes, commandées, telles que des photographies de produits, des photos privées, des photographies juridiques et scientifiques. Dirk Braeckman s'est intéressé aux découvertes, aux images atypiques de la collection, aux objets qui restent généralement cachés dans les dépôts ou les tiroirs. Prenons l'exemple de l'album photo du médecin anversois Paul Sano, qui présente un mélange de photographies médicales, de collages et d'expérimentations photographiques. Ou encore la mystérieuse photo de produit de Georges Filleul sur laquelle une main apparaît de nulle part. Mais aussi cette scène aliénante représentant un homme, une femme et un cheval en plâtre du peintre et sculpteur belge Jacques de Lalaing, cette photo aérienne prise par le service photographique de l'armée belge, cet intérieur vide d'une scène de crime ou ces images de chaises roulantes de François Smeesters datant du XIXe siècle.

Dirk Braeckman se sent inspiré par les œuvres qui ne prétendent pas être de l'art, mais qui le deviennent malgré elles.[4] Les pièces de collection qu'il a sélectionnées recèlent presque toutes un élément de son propre travail. Il s'agit souvent d'images suggestives d'espaces dépouillés avec peu de sujets, de photographies présentant des imperfections et des représentations laissant une grande place à l'imagination. Dirk Braeckman explore la matérialité des photographies. Un pli ou une zone matte démontre qu'une photographie est un objet dont on peut se saisir et non une simple perspective de la réalité. Ce sont les compositions fortuites qui l'intéressent, les éléments que le photographe original n'a peut-être pas voulus, mais qui, aux yeux de Dirk Braeckman, rendent la photo captivante.

Le livre *Evidence* (1992) de Luc Sante (°1954) a été une source d'inspiration majeure pour Dirk Braeckman. Il s'agit d'une série de clichés de scènes de crime en noir et blanc pris par la police new-yorkaise au cours de la période 1914-18.

J'ai, en définitive, toujours considéré les images de cette manière. Une scène de crime, c'est horrible à regarder, mais je parviens malgré tout à en percevoir la beauté. Surtout sur les photos où le corps a déjà été enlevé et où seul l'espace subsiste. Ces images suggèrent énormément de choses. Lorsque l'on porte un regard esthétique sur la netteté, le désordre et la beauté de certains intérieurs, on perçoit les images d'une tout autre manière. [5]

ART D'APPROPRIATION

Pendant les préparatifs de l'exposition, Dirk Braeckman a mené un questionnement permanent sur la manière dont il pouvait présenter la collection FOMU de son point de vue personnel. Se contenter d'exposer les objets sélectionnés lui semblait insuffisant. Le choix de Dirk Braeckman s'est porté sur des images fonctionnelles sans ambition artistique, mais dont il percevait les qualités visuelles. Pour lui, l'art consiste à faire en sorte que le visiteur porte un regard différent sur ces images. Il a donc cherché à accentuer ce phénomène en faisant lui-même quelque chose des images de la collection et en créant de nouvelles œuvres à partir de celles-ci. Dirk Braeckman a ainsi réinterprété la collection du musée en rephotographiant les photographies. Il s'approprie donc celles-ci : vous les découvrez à travers son objectif, ses yeux et ses mains.

Le terme « l'appropriation » désigne le fait de modifier délibérément des objets existants pour créer de nouvelles œuvres d'art. Tout au long de l'histoire, les artistes y ont eu recours pour transmettre de nouvelles significations, remettre en question la paternité de l'œuvre, contester les normes établies ou commenter des questions contemporaines. L'art d'appropriation n'est donc pas nouveau. Depuis le XIXe siècle, certains artistes citent les œuvres d'autres, les empruntent, se les approprient pour créer de nouvelles œuvres. Aujourd'hui, plus que jamais, nous vivons dans une société numérique où le recyclage et la réinterprétation font partie de notre culture. Grâce à Internet, faire référence à des concepts et des idées existants et les réutiliser devient non seulement très facile, mais est aussi très largement accepté par la génération actuelle d'artistes visuels, de DJ, de cinéastes, d'écrivains, de danseurs et de metteurs en scène. C'est au début des années 1980 que Dirk Braeckman entre en contact avec l'art d'appropriation, alors qu'il visite à New York une exposition présentant les œuvres des artistes américains Sherrie Levine (°1947) et Richard Prince (°1949). Ces images l'ont beaucoup impressionné. À la même époque, Dirk Braeckman réalise pour la première fois des tirages à partir de négatifs qui ne sont pas les siens. Un ami lui a confié un coffret en bois contenant une centaine de négatifs d'un photographe anonyme, représentant des scènes de combat de la Première Guerre mondiale. Sur la base de ceux-ci, il réalise 12 tirages grand format en l'espace d'une seule journée. Ne se sentant malgré tout pas propriétaire de ces images, il restitue les négatifs et mets ces photographies de côté pendant plus de 25 ans. Ce n'est qu'en 2013, à l'approche de la commémoration de la Première Guerre mondiale, qu'il s'est senti prêt à exposer la série *Schwarzschild*.[6]

Aujourd'hui, la « rephotographie » s'inscrit dans la méthode de travail de Dirk Braeckman :

Je m'intéresse au concept d'appropriation depuis un certain temps déjà. Je rephotographie souvent mon propre travail. Cela me permet notamment d'en extraire des détails. En théorie, il ne s'agit pas d'une appropriation à part entière, étant donné qu'il s'agit de mon propre travail, mais on tend vers cela. Ma méthode de travail est donc à la fois similaire et différente de celle adoptée pour la nouvelle série du FOMU. Car je m'éloigne ici d'images qui ne sont pas les miennes.

Pour Dirk Braeckman, l'appropriation consiste à placer une image existante dans un contexte différent pour qu'elle devienne la vôtre. Et cela commence dans sa propre tête :

La première étape de l'appropriation consiste à regarder une image sous une perspective très différente de celle qui était vraisemblablement prévue. Tout part de là.

La rephotographie est un processus très personnel qui, dans le cas de Dirk Braeckman, n'a rien à voir avec l'enregistrement ou la reproduction froide d'objets d'art. Il cherche l'éclat des clichés existants et s'emploie à y faire réfléchir son flash, ce qui a pour effet de décaler la surface de l'image devant l'image.
Dirk Braeckman n'a rien d'un puriste. En tant qu'artiste, c'est au travers de la photographie qu'il s'exprime le mieux, mais il étend les possibilités et les limites du médium au maximum de ses possibilités. De la prise de vue à l'impression, il ajoute plusieurs couches. Il emprunte de nombreux chemins de traverse et est très touche-à-tout. Malgré cela, son travail est très reconnaissable depuis 40 ans, étant donné le format et les techniques qu'il utilise. Seul le chemin menant au résultat final est toujours différent.

JUSQU'OÙ EST-IL POSSIBLE D'ALLER ?

Au FOMU, Dirk Braeckman travaille pour la première fois avec des photographies qu'il n'a pas prises lui-même. Lui voit cela comme un défi et un processus d'apprentissage. Il réalise de nouvelles œuvres à partir de photographies fonctionnelles de la collection du musée. Dirk Braeckman met en évidence les qualités visuelles qu'il a perçues, accentuant ainsi ses préférences et sa fascination pour ce type d'images. En photographiant la sélection, il adopte le même regard que celui qu'il porte sur la réalité : ce regard avec lequel il cherche à transposer des choses insignifiantes ou banales devant lesquelles tout le monde passe, en d'autres qualités dans le monde réel.
L'artiste se réinvente en utilisant des photographies d'autres personnes comme matériel de base et en appliquant de nouvelles techniques artistiques dans ses créations. Tout en expérimentant avec le médium, il continue de surprendre et d'innover. Dirk Braeckman est un artiste polyvalent s'offrant une liberté de travail insoupçonnée, sans se cantonner à des idées et à des méthodes connues.
Les objets de la collection l'inspirent tellement qu'il devient difficile de faire des choix. Mais comment reste-t-il fidèle à lui-même en tant qu'artiste, alors que ces images ne sont pas les siennes ? Jusqu'où peut-il aller dans la manipulation des photos d'un autre ? Quelles sont les limites du respect de l'œuvre d'autrui ?
Dans un premier temps, il sous-estime la difficulté de se dire l'auteur de ces images. Dirk Braeckman a résolument choisi des images fonctionnelles plutôt que des œuvres autonomes d'artistes contemporains. Pour lui, il s'agit également d'une question d'éthique. Même s'il laisse la porte ouverte, il ne se sent pas suffisamment libre

aujourd'hui pour créer de nouvelles œuvres à partir de photographies d'un collègue artiste :

Tandis que l'artiste livre ses photos terminées telles des œuvres d'art, le photographe fonctionnel soumet son travail au monde extérieur tel un artisan. Ce que je fais ici peut sembler irrespectueux. Or j'ai beaucoup de respect pour ces photographes.

D'ailleurs, c'est aussi ce respect qui bloque Dirk Braeckman dans un premier temps. Il creuse au plus profond de lui-même et cherche de nouvelles façons de gérer ce conflit intérieur, sans se perdre en tant qu'artiste parmi toutes les possibilités qui s'offrent à lui. Pour s'approprier les images, l'artiste envisage deux options : soit il intervient de manière minimale, soit il détruit l'œuvre. Il n'y a pas de juste milieu.

La réalisation de collages est un exemple de distorsion extrême de l'image. Pour se libérer d'une éventuelle paralysie imposée par le respect des clichés originaux, Dirk Braeckman a recours à une action physique, ce qui constitue une nouveauté dans son processus artistique. Il s'attaque ainsi aux reproductions : à l'aide de ciseaux, il fait des trous — très rapidement et intuitivement — dans les images de collection photographiées, pour y insérer ensuite de nouvelles images. D'autres interventions consistent à réaliser des tirages sur différentes textures et surfaces, à rephotographier ces papiers photo, à ajouter de la matière, à peindre et à enduire les images avec de la peinture, puis à les retravailler en analogique ou en numérique dans sa chambre noire. L'image originale a alors totalement disparu de l'œuvre finale.

Les photographies originales, petites et fonctionnelles, souvent directes, nettes et clairement lisibles, sont transformées en images monumentales qui exigent une lecture consciente et lente, tout en incitant à la réflexion et à la contemplation. Dirk Braeckman ajoute ainsi une sorte de filtre entre l'image et le spectateur. Bien qu'il abstraie les images de la collection, les nouvelles images ne tombent jamais dans l'abstraction totale. Le lien avec la réalité est toujours présent. Les photographies de Dirk Braeckman s'apparentent ainsi à des portes d'entrée vers un autre monde, son monde, où le visiteur est invité à deviner l'état d'esprit dans lequel ces images ont été créées. Ces images cachent donc bien plus que ce qu'elles montrent.

Dirk Braeckman manipule les objets de la collection et leur donne une nouvelle dimension : le contexte disparaît, le format change, la signification originale évolue, un titre est ajouté. L'image passe du statut de document fonctionnel à celui de photographie artistique. Dirk Braeckman vous pousse à regarder au-delà de la fonction première des photographies. Elles deviennent des poèmes visuels intemporels, soulevant plus de questions que de réponses.

En utilisant le titre allemand *Echtzeit (Temps réel, NDLT.)*, Dirk Braeckman fait référence à ce pont qu'il jette entre le passé et le présent. Différentes perspectives vous sont en effet proposées « en temps réel » : la vision du photographe original, l'interprétation de Dirk Braeckman et le regard du spectateur. La richesse et la complexité du médium photographique sont ici mises en valeur.

UN DIALOGUE OUVERT AUTOUR DE LA COLLECTION

Au fil de ce parcours, Dirk Braeckman et le FOMU ont été confrontés à de nombreuses questions éthiques, plus actuelles que jamais. En tant qu'artiste, comment traiter le travail des autres avec respect ? Où se situe la limite en une photographie purement fonctionnelle et une photo artistique ? Est-il toujours possible de déceler l'intention originale du photographe ? À partir de quel moment peut-on revendiquer être l'auteur d'une œuvre ? Un acte agressif en apparence, tel que le découpage d'images, peut simplement nous inciter à réfléchir davantage sur le regard que nous portons sur l'autre.

Au FOMU, nous nous sommes également posé la question de savoir jusqu'à quel point nous pouvions laisser un artiste interagir avec les images d'un autre. Car en notre qualité de musée de la photographie, nous sommes bien entendu responsables de l'utilisation légale et adéquate des photos que nous conservons. La distinction entre photographie fonctionnelle et artistique est souvent floue. Au travers de ce projet, notre intention est également d'engager un dialogue sur ce thème précis.

Pour le FOMU, cette collaboration avec Dirk Braeckman marque une nouvelle étape dans le renouvellement et l'ouverture de la collection. Dans un esprit de co-création, nous nous détachons de la vision traditionnelle du canon afin d'offrir diverses perspectives au public. Ouvrir une collection à la réinterprétation est un processus passionnant et permanent qui nous permet de rester innovants et pertinents en tant que musée. Dirk Braeckman a donné une impulsion aussi profonde qu'enrichissante à la poursuite de ce processus et du dialogue sur cette thématique.

1 Exposition de collection *Re-collect*. FOMU Anvers. 7 mai 2021 – 7 novembre 2021.

2 Exposition de collection *Grace Ndiritu Reimagines the FOMU Collection*. FOMU Anvers. 17 février 2023 -7 janvier 2024. Pour plus d'informations : Judah, H. (2023, 27 janvier). A Map Through Time: Grace Ndiritu Reimagines the FOMU Collection. *Trigger*, www.fomu.be/trigger/articles/grace-ndiritu.

3 Exposition de collection *Dirk Braeckman. Echtzeit.* FOMU Anvers. 29 mars 2024 – 19 janvier 2025.

4 Versteeg, W. (2017, 17 mai). The Loneliness of the Darkroom. *Aperture.* aperture.org/editorial/loneliness-darkroom-braeckman.

5 Toutes les citations de Dirk Braeckman sont issues d'un entretien entre Tamara Berghmans et Dirk Braeckman, dans son atelier à Gand, 26 septembre 2023.

6 Canonne, X. (2013). Entretien avec Dirk Braeckman. Dans Anonyme, D. Braeckman, *Schwarzschild* (pp. 51-55). Anvers : Pandora.

LE POINT DE VUE DU SPECTRE

Clément Chéroux

LE RAVISSEMENT DES IMAGES

Il y a des photographies qui vous font signes. Quiconque s'est un jour retrouvé devant une boite remplie d'images, dans la réserve d'un musée, ou sur l'étal d'un marché au puce, et a commencé à les regarder attentivement, une à une, le sait très bien. C'est un savoir tacite, une connaissance implicite sur laquelle aucun livre n'a jamais été écrit, mais qui a néanmoins cette particularité d'être très largement partagée. Peu importe, au fond, qu'elles soient d'art ou pas, certaines photographies nous *interpellent*, ou peut-être faudrait-il dire, nous *saisissent*. Elles attirent notre regard comme l'aimant la limaille. Elles semblent munies de petits grapins télescopiques qui instantanément nous harponnent. C'est ce qu'explique admirablement Roland Barthes dans quelques-unes des pages les plus poignantes de *La Chambre claire* : il y a dans certaines images un détail « qui part de la scène, comme une flèche et vient me percer ».[1] « Ce quelque chose a fait *tilt*, il a provoqué en moi un petit ébranlement, un *satori* [...] ».[2] « Le *punctum* d'une photo, ajoute-t-il, c'est ce hasard qui, en elle, *me point* ».[3] Cette intensité qui me transperce, ce peut tout aussi bien être un élément de l'image, un agencement de formes, un simple geste, la position d'un corps ou une lumière singulière, voire une altération chimique, une craquelure dans la surface sensible. Mais, quoiqu'il en soit, il y a là une forme d'injonction visuelle qui s'adresse directement à mon identité, mon inconscient, ma mémoire peut-être, mon expérience, mon savoir, ou ma culture ; quelque chose qui raisonne intimement avec *ce que je suis*. Il s'en suit généralement un désir irrépressible de *posséder* l'image (ou sa reproduction). Comme le corps de l'autre dans le désir charnel. Et ce afin de pouvoir à volonté rejouer le ravissement.

DES BRAECKMANS À L'ÉTAT SAUVAGE

Depuis quelques mois déjà, Dirk Braeckman est plongé dans les millions de photographies qui constituent les collections du FOMU (Musée de la photographie d'Anvers). Il a ouvert un nombre incalculable de boites, compulsé des registres et feuilleté des albums. Il s'est laissé saisir — à ce point exact d'« ébranlement », de « tilt » ou de « satori » dont parle Barthes — par quelques images qui constituent la matière première des œuvres du présent ouvrage et sont reprises, telles quelles, au début de volume. Bien que je n'aie pas été présent lors de la sélection, je crois pouvoir deviner assez précisément ce qui a conduit l'artiste à choisir ces images. Tout d'abord, il a retiré d'une première sélection, assez large et intuitive, toutes les photographies faites par des artistes et n'a gardé que les clichés *anonymes*, c'est-à-dire sans auteur identifié. Pour son projet, il avait besoin d'images neutres, non chargée, ou pour le dire autrement : dénuées d'intentionnalité artistique. Par respect pour le geste créatif, il ne veut pas que le sien vienne recouvrir celui d'un autre. Mais par-delà le fait qu'elles soient privées d'auteur, la particularité commune aux images sélectionnées est qu'elles sont *ouvertes* pour reprendre une qualification chère au philosophe et sémioticien italien Umberto Eco.[4] Elles ont pour qualité principale une sorte d'irrésolution, une capacité à susciter chez ceux qui les regarde un questionnement. Le *point commun* de toutes ces images choisies par Braeckman est, en fait, un *point d'interrogation*.[5] Face à elles, et bien qu'il s'agisse, dans la plupart des cas, d'images documentaires, je suis en permanence en train de me demander ce qu'elles montrent ou ce qu'elles veulent dire exactement. Elles ne m'imposent pas un sens, mais m'invitent plutôt à en donner un. Faut-il préciser ici que c'est exactement ce que cherche Braeckman dans les images pour lesquelles il a lui-même effectué la prise de vue. La plupart de ses œuvres ont une valeur d'énigme. Les quelques clichés qu'il a choisi dans la collection du FOMU possèdent *naturellement* les qualités qu'il recherche dans son propre travail. Ce sont, en quelques sortes, des Braeckmans à l'*état sauvage*. Et c'est bien pour cela qu'il les a élues. Il s'est reconnu en elles.

RÉOUVRIR L'IMAGE

Une fois l'image choisie, Braeckman la rephotographie, en jouant souvent des reflets qui se forment sur sa surface miroitante. Il n'aime rien de plus que les brillances ou les halos qui viennent rehausser le tirage d'un chatoiement auratique. Puis il retravaille le cliché à l'ordinateur. Il recadre, sature, solarise et voile volontairement. Il superpose plusieurs clichés. Il a parfois recours à une forme de montage, non par addition, mais, au contraire, par soustraction : il incise l'image, la découpe largement et utilise le vide qu'il a ainsi formé comme un nouveau cadre. Lorsqu'il évoquait ses expérimentations, Man Ray parlait volontiers du « viol des matériaux ».[6] Braeckman en fait autant. Certains clichés sont badigeonnés : il les recouvre de larges taches sombres ou les colorise à l'aide d'une teinte édulcorée. Puis il agrandit ses photographies à un format qui n'a plus aucune commune mesure avec l'original. Par son travail sur l'image, l'artiste procède à une sorte de filtrage. Son geste créatif consiste à interposer des écrans entre l'image et le regardeur. Cette stratégie de mise à distance répond à un impératif : il s'agit de *défonctionnaliser*. Les photographies prélevées dans la collection du FOMU avait, en effet, une utilité première, le plus souvent documentaire. Elles servaient à faire la promotion d'un nouvel instrument, rendre compte de l'achèvement d'un chantier, enregistrer un souvenir, identifier une maladie, reconnaître un terrain de bataille et ainsi de suite. Devant les œuvres de Braeckman, je ne reconnais plus la microphotographie médicale, le document publicitaire, ou la vue de reconnaissance aérienne. Ses images ont perdu leur valeur d'usage. Elles ne me disent ni *où*, ni *quand*, ni *comment*, et encore moins *pourquoi*. Elles ont définitivement perdu leur utilité. Elles sont littéralement *hors-service*. Mais de ce fait, elles en deviennent encore plus mystérieuses. Par son intervention, Braeckman parvient à démultiplier la puissance énigmatique de ses images, à les *réouvrir* afin d'intensifier la projection imaginative de ceux qui les contemplent.

DÉTRUIRE, DIT-IL

Quelle est la nature de la transformation que Braeckman fait subir à ces images ? Elle est essentiellement d'ordre alchimique. C'est une transmutation. Il s'agit bel et bien de transformer le plomb en or. Cela repose tout d'abord sur un principe de réduction. Il faut commencer par sortir l'image de son contexte simplement informatif et anéantir ainsi sa fonction documentaire originelle. Lorsque je rencontre Braeckman dans son atelier de Gand, pour parler de la manière dont il s'est approprié ces images, il ne cesse d'employer le mot « détruire ». Il veut les attaquer, les cogner, les déformer. « Je ne peux, dit-il, que les respecter ou les détruire ».[7] Le titre du livre de Marguerite Duras me vient immanquablement à l'esprit : *Détruire, dit-elle*.[8] Cette œuvre magistrale, publiée dans l'année qui suit la révolution sociale de 1968, met en scène deux hommes et deux femmes dans une grande demeure en bord de forêt. Elle a pour thème principal la puissance du désir. Lorsqu'elle parle du film qui prolonge son livre Duras évoque ce désir violent qui détruit tout ce qu'il touche : « Je suis pour qu'on [...] recommence tout. C'est le plus profond de *Détruire, dit-elle*, de mon livre. Le départ à zéro. Je suis pour qu'on oublie l'Histoire, l'Histoire de France, l'Histoire du monde. Complètement. Qu'il n'y ait plus aucune mémoire de ce qui a été vécu, c'est-à-dire de l'intolérable, sur tous les fronts, sur tous les points. Tout casser ».[9] C'est bien là ce que cherche aussi Braeckman. Il commence par réduire l'image à sa part de réel la plus congrue. Il sait qu'il marche là sur une ligne de crête extrêmement étroite. Il ne veut pas tomber dans l'abstraction. Quelque chose de tangible doit lui permettre de tenir debout et de continuer à avancer. C'est son fil de funambule à lui. Il tient à conserver un certain substrat de réalité à partir duquel il pourra ensuite redéployer l'image. André Breton, le chef de file du surréalisme, l'avait en son temps bien compris : « Toutes choses sont appelées à d'autres utilités que celles qu'on leur attribue généralement. C'est même du sacrifice conscient de leur utilité première [...] que se déduisent certaines *propriétés transcendantes* qui s'y rattachent ».[10] Libérées de leur utilité initiale, réouvertes aux potentialités de l'enchantement, les photographies dont s'empare Braeckman deviennent ainsi de véritables embrayeurs d'imaginaires.

LE HORS-CORPS

Par-delà le sentiment de destruction, la mort est omniprésente dans cet ensemble de photographies de Dirk Braeckman. La perception du monde qu'il propose à travers ces images fait penser à un voyage hors du corps tel qu'il est notamment décrit dans les récits de mort imminente. Décorporation, voyage astral, excursion psychique, transe ecsomatique, *Out of Body Experience*, ou OBE en anglais, quelle que soit la manière dont ce phénomène est désigné, il a suscité quantité de témoignages.[11] À les lire, ce qui frappe sans doute le plus, c'est la répétition des mêmes schémas narratifs, c'est-à-dire une supposée communauté d'expérience. Lorsque, juste après le trépas, l'âme quitte son véhicule, elle se retrouve aspiré vers le haut. Ce n'est pas la hauteur des avions de ligne, mais plutôt celle d'un cerf-volant, ou d'un ultra léger motorisé. En surplomb, à quelques mètres au-dessus de son enveloppe charnelle, l'âme, nouvellement libérée de la gravité du corps, est non seulement douée d'un sens aigu de la vue, mais aussi de la capacité à se mouvoir doucement et sans heurt, comme propulsée sur un coussin d'air. Les mots les plus couramment employés sont ceux de « suspension », d'« apesanteur » ou de « flottement ». « Le voyage fut bref et nous nous retrouvâmes à environ quinze mètres au-dessus de la rue raconte une personne revenue de l'au-delà [...]. Nous flottions juste au-dessus du sol et je regardais en bas [...] Nous planions à environ cent ou deux cents mètres au-dessus de la terre. Il faisait nuit et, de temps à autre, une lumière s'allumait dans la campagne. Juste en dessous de nous brillait une étendue d'eau, une mare ou un petit étang. Au-delà se dressait un édifice vert en forme de pyramide, à l'intérieur duquel on voyait luire une lumière ».[12] C'est là, précisément, que se situe le regard de Braeckman dans *Echtzeit*. À travers ses images, il se place dans la position de celui qui hante le monde. Il a retrouvé le point de vue du spectre.

1 Barthes, R. (1980). *La Chambre claire, note sur la photographie*. Paris : Éditions de l'étoile, Gallimard, Seuil, p. 49.

2 Ibid., p. 81.

3 Ibid., p. 49.

4 Eco, U. (1965). *L'Œuvre ouverte*. Paris : Seuil.

5 Sur cette question, voir Chéroux, C. (2010). L'image comme point d'interrogation ou la valeur d'extase du document surréaliste. *Les carnets du bal, L'image-document, entre réalité et fiction*, (1), pp. 26-47.

6 Man Ray. (1933). L'Âge de la lumière. *Minotaure*, (3-4), 1933, p. 1.

7 Entretien de l'auteur avec Dirk Braeckman, dans son atelier à Gand, le 23 novembre 2023.

8 Duras, M. (1969). *Détruire, dit-elle*. Paris : Minuit.

9 Interview de Marguerite Duras sur le tournage de *Détruire, dit-elle*, diffusée dans *Banc d'essai*, émission réalisée par Jean-Claude Bergeret, 1969, accessible sur le site de l'INA: www.ina.fr/ina-eclaire-actu/video/i05125289/marguerite-duras-a-propos-de-detruire-dit-elle, consulté le 2 décembre 2023.

10 Breton, A. (1992). Avis au lecteur pour *La Femme 100 têtes* de Max Ernst. Dans Œuvres complètes (t. 2). Paris : Gallimard, p. 305. Je souligne.

11 Monroe, R.A. (1996). *Le Voyage hors du corps. Techniques de projection du corps astral*. Monaco : Les éditions du Rocher. (Œuvre originale publiée en 1971)

12 Monroe, R.A. (1990). *Fantastiques expériences de voyage astral*. Paris : Robert Laffont, pp. 293, 342, 357-358. (Œuvre originale publiée en 1985)

DE KUNST VAN HET FUNCTIONELE

Tamara Berghmans, Curator FOMU

De tentoonstelling *Dirk Braeckman. Echtzeit* (2024) presenteert een nieuw hoofdstuk in het tonen van de FOMU-collectie. Weg van een chronologische of genre-specifieke opstelling, naar een open presentatie die uitnodigt tot voelen en ervaren. Na de sjamanistische benadering van Grace Ndiritu in 2023 geeft FOMU dit jaar de collectie in handen van een kunstenaar met een heel andere focus. Dirk Braeckman kiest voor functionele fotografie en laat daar zijn artistieke blik over gaan. Door foto's uit de FOMU-collectie te selecteren en nieuw werk te creëren, geïnspireerd op deze bestaande beelden, laat hij de kijker ontdekken hoeveel schoonheid en mysterie er schuilt in foto's die aanvankelijk gemaakt zijn zonder artistieke bedoeling. Functie wordt kunst, afwijkingen en fouten worden bronnen van verwondering.

MUSEUMCOLLECTIES RELEVANT MAKEN

FOMU herbergt een verzameling van meer dan vier miljoen foto's, camera's, fondsen en boeken. Deze rijke collectie, die in 1965 ontstond, is zowel internationaal als Belgisch en strekt zich uit van het begin van de fotografie tot nu. FOMU is al een tijd op zoek naar andere manieren om de collectie te tonen dan de klassieke chronologische of thematische opstelling. De laatste decennia is samen met de maatschappij ook de visie op verzamelen en presenteren sterk veranderd. Hoe maak je een collectie relevant voor een hedendaags publiek? In welk narratief plaats je collectiestukken? Welke objecten krijgen een plek in de spotlights? Dat zijn enkele van de vraagstukken waarrond het museum de laatste jaren heeft gewerkt.
De nieuwe richting die FOMU uitgaat om zijn collectie open te stellen hangt samen met de bredere missie en visie van het museum. FOMU wil beeldbewustzijn aanscherpen door fotografie toegankelijk te maken vanuit een historisch perspectief en binnen een actuele context. Het experiment van vandaag is het erfgoed van morgen. Daarom stimuleert FOMU creatie, dynamiek en vernieuwing. Het museum wil een plaats zijn waar mensen via fotografie hun blik kunnen verruimen. Om daartoe te komen hebben we specifieke aandacht voor fotografische projecten die actueel relevant en meerstemmig zijn, kritisch reflecteren op het medium en/of de geschiedenis van fotografie, en een ethische positie innemen.

Een kantelpunt in onze manier van verzamelen en collectiestukken tentoonstellen was de collectietentoonstelling *Re-collect* (2021), waarin FOMU een selectie van recente aanwinsten presenteerde.[1] Traditioneel is een collectietentoonstelling vaak een chronologisch parcours met objecten waarmee de geschiedenis van 'de' fotografie wordt verteld, samengesteld vanuit een wit kunsthistorisch perspectief. In verschillende musea zie je vaak dezelfde foto's — de zogenaamde canon — terugkomen. Ook in FOMU was dat vroeger het geval. Maar net als andere musea stelden we ons de vraag: is er nog nood aan een canon of mag je intuïtiever werken? Met *Re-collect* kozen we voor een associatieve wandeling doorheen de nieuwste collectiestukken, in een niet-chronologische opstelling.
We wilden nog verder gaan en de collectie openstellen voor nieuwe blikken en visies. Vandaag komen er steeds meer maatschappelijke denkkaders op die zich weg van het rationele bewegen. Musea worden alsmaar vaker ontmoetingsplaatsen waar je kan voelen en beleven. Hierdoor ontstond het idee om jaarlijks een kunstenaar van wie FOMU werk in huis heeft uit te nodigen om als curator met de museumcollectie een tentoonstelling te maken. Deze kunstenaar kan eigen foto's in de collectie als startpunt nemen of nieuw werk creëren met de FOMU-collectie als inspiratie. Door samen te werken met gastcuratoren en buiten de gebaande paden te treden, introduceren we nieuwe perspectieven op de collectie en laten we die in al haar omvang en diversiteit aan bod komen.

In 2023 vroeg FOMU de Brits-Keniaanse beeldend kunstenaar Grace Ndiritu als gastcurator. Ndiritu ziet het sjamanisme als een manier om museumcollecties te reactiveren en was dus de uitgelezen kunstenaar om als eerste in onze collectie te duiken en vastgeroeste visies wakker te schudden.[2] Voor de tweede editie kiest FOMU een gastcurator die op een heel andere manier met het fotografisch beeld omgaat: Dirk Braeckman.[3]

DIRK BRAECKMAN OOG IN OOG MET DE FOMU-COLLECTIE

FOMU volgt Braeckman al sinds het begin van zijn carrière en is de grootste verzamelaar van zijn werk in een wereldwijde museale context. Braeckman ontwikkelde in meer dan veertig jaar tijd een indrukwekkend oeuvre. Met donkere, subtiele beelden onderzoekt hij het fotografische medium en schuwt daarbij het experiment niet. Het werk van Braeckman is uiterst subjectief, suggestief en autobiografisch. Zijn foto's zijn geen documenten die de werkelijkheid vastleggen. Hij manipuleert zijn beelden in de donkere kamer en legt zo een veelheid aan interpretaties bloot. FOMU nodigde hem uit om met deze blik naar de museumcollectie te kijken. Braeckmans uitgesproken liefde voor de historische en technische aspecten van de fotografie, die ook uitgebreid aanwezig zijn in de FOMU-collectie, vormden een belangrijke reden om hem carte blanche te geven.

Een jaar lang werkte Braeckman aan de voorbereiding van de tentoonstelling. Na een eerste brainstorm hadden we een lijst trefwoorden waarmee de zoektocht in de FOMU-collectie begon: functionele fotografie, *crime scenes*, alledaagse taferelen, foutjes,... Braeckman wilde geen narratieve beelden en geen portretten waarbij de persoon in de lens kijkt. Uiteindelijk koos hij uit de FOMU-collectie zo'n 250 foto's en objecten, uitsluitend functionele fotografie. Dit wordt ook wel *vernacular photography* genoemd, fotografie die niet per se met artistieke ambities gemaakt is. Het gaat om historische, vaak anonieme beelden die in opdracht gemaakt zijn, zoals productfotografie, privéfoto's, juridische en wetenschappelijke fotografie. Braeckman was geïnteresseerd in ontdekkingen, atypische beelden uit de collectie, objecten die meestal in depots of laden verborgen blijven. Denk maar aan het fotoalbum van de Antwerpse arts Paul Sano, waarin een mix van zijn medische fotografie, collages en fotografische experimenten te zien is. Of de mysterieuze productfoto van Georges Filleul waarop uit het niets een hand verschijnt. Of nog: het bevreemdende tafereel met een man, een vrouw en een gipsen paard van de Belgische beeldhouwer en schilder Jacques de Lalaing, de luchtfoto gemaakt door de fotografische dienst van het Belgisch leger, een leeg interieur van een plaats delict of de 19de-eeuwse foto's van rolstoelen van François Smeesters.

Braeckman voelt zich geïnspireerd door werk dat niet de pretentie heeft om kunst te zijn, maar toch kunst wordt.[4] De collectiestukken die hij heeft geselecteerd, dragen bijna allemaal een element van zijn eigen werk in zich. Vaak zijn het suggestieve beelden van lege ruimtes met amper mensen, foto's met onvolmaaktheden en voorstellingen die veel aan de verbeelding overlaten. Braeckman gaat op zoek naar de materialiteit van de foto's. Een kreuk of een matte plek toont dat een foto een object is dat je kunt vastnemen, niet alleen een doorkijk naar de werkelijkheid. Het zijn de toevallige composities die hem interesseren, de elementen die de originele fotograaf misschien niet zo bedoeld heeft, maar die de foto voor Braeckman net boeiend maken.

Een belangrijke inspiratiebron voor Braeckman was het boek *Evidence* (1992) van Luc Sante (°1954). Dit bevat een reeks zwart-witfoto's van plaatsen delict, gemaakt door de politie van New York in 1914-18.

Ik heb eigenlijk altijd zo naar beelden gekeken. Een crime scene, dat is afschuwelijk om naar te kijken, maar ik zie de schoonheid ervan in. Zeker de foto's waarin het lichaam al verwijderd is, waar enkel de ruimte overblijft. Die beelden suggereren veel. Als je met een esthetische blik kijkt naar de scherpte, de rommel, maar ook de schoonheid van bepaalde interieurs, zie je beelden op een andere manier.[5]

APPROPRIATION ART

Tijdens de voorbereidingen van de tentoonstelling stelde Braeckman zich voortdurend de vraag hoe hij vanuit zijn persoonlijke blik de FOMU-collectie kon presenteren. Enkel de geselecteerde objecten tonen, vond hij onvoldoende. Braeckman koos functionele foto's zonder artistieke ambitie, waarin hij wel visuele kwaliteiten zag. Voor hem bestond de kunst erin de bezoeker anders naar die beelden te laten kijken. Dit wilde hij extra accentueren door ook zelf iets met de collectiebeelden te doen en er nieuwe werken van te maken. Braeckman herinterpreteert de museumcollectie door de foto's opnieuw te fotograferen. Hij eigent zich de foto's toe: je ervaart ze door zijn camera, zijn ogen en zijn handen.

De term voor het opzettelijk veranderen van bestaande objecten om nieuwe kunstwerken te creëren is *appropriation art*. Doorheen de geschiedenis hebben kunstenaars dit toegepast om nieuwe betekenissen over te brengen, vragen te stellen over auteurschap, gevestigde normen uit te dagen of commentaar te geven op hedendaagse kwesties.

Appropriation art is niet nieuw. Sinds de 19de eeuw zien we hoe kunstenaars het werk van anderen citeren, eraan ontlenen, het zich toe-eigenen om nieuw werk te creëren. Vandaag leven we meer dan ooit in een digitale maatschappij waarin recycling en *re-mixing* deel uitmaken van onze cultuur. Met behulp van het internet wordt het voor de huidige generatie beeldend kunstenaars, dj's, filmmakers, schrijvers, dansers en theatermakers niet alleen heel eenvoudig, maar ook een algemeen aanvaarde realiteit om aan bestaande concepten en ideeën te refereren en ze te hergebruiken.

Braeckman kwam voor het eerst in contact met *appropriation art* begin jaren 1980, toen hij in New York een tentoonstelling zag met werk van de Amerikaanse kunstenaars Sherrie Levine (°1947) en Richard Prince (°1949). Die beelden maakten grote indruk op hem.

In dezelfde periode maakte Braeckman voor het eerst afdrukken van negatieven die niet van hem waren. Een vriend stopte hem een houten doosje toe met daarin een honderdtal negatieven van een anonieme fotograaf, met oorlogstaferelen uit de Eerste Wereldoorlog. Op één dag maakte hij twaalf afdrukken op groot formaat. Hij gaf de negatieven terug en stopte de foto's meer dan 25 jaar weg, omdat hij zich niet de eigenaar van deze beelden voelde. Pas in 2013, toen de herdenking van de Eerste Wereldoorlog eraan kwam, voelde hij zich klaar om met de reeks *Schwarzschild* naar buiten te treden.[6]

Vandaag maakt de praktijk van 'herfotograferen' deel uit van Braeckmans manier van werken:

Met het concept van appropriation ben ik al een tijd bezig. Ik herfotografeer dikwijls mijn eigen werk. Zo haal ik er bijvoorbeeld details uit. Theoretisch gezien is dat geen appropriation, omdat het mijn eigen werk is, maar het gevoel neigt er toch naar. Zo is mijn manier van werken dus vergelijkbaar met deze nieuwe reeks in FOMU, maar toch anders. Want hier vertrek ik van beelden die niet van mij zijn.

Voor Braeckman gaat toe-eigening over hoe je een bestaand beeld in een andere context plaatst, zodat het van jou wordt. En dat begint in het eigen hoofd:

De eerste stap in appropriation is dat je naar een beeld kijkt met een heel andere blik dan wellicht de bedoeling is. Daar begint het al.

Herfotograferen is een uiterst persoonlijk proces, dat in Braeckmans geval niets te maken heeft met het koele registreren of reproduceren van kunstobjecten. Hij zoekt de glans van de bestaande foto's op en laat zijn flits erop weerschijnen, waardoor het beeldoppervlak voor het beeld wordt geschoven.
Braeckman is geen purist. Als kunstenaar drukt hij zich het best uit met fotografie, maar hij rekt de mogelijkheden en grenzen van het medium zo ver mogelijk op. Van opname tot afdruk voegt hij verschillende lagen toe. Hij neemt veel zijwegen en neemt van alles in zich op. Toch is zijn werk al veertig jaar erg herkenbaar door het formaat en de technieken die hij gebruikt. Alleen de weg naar het eindresultaat is altijd anders.

HOE VER KUN JE GAAN?

In FOMU werkt Braeckman voor het eerst met foto's die hij niet zelf gemaakt heeft. Voor hem is dat een uitdaging en een leerproces. Hij maakt nieuw werk op basis van functionele foto's uit de museumcollectie. Braeckman benadrukt visuele kwaliteiten die hij erin heeft gezien en accentueert zo ook zijn voorkeuren en fascinatie voor dit soort beelden. Tijdens het fotograferen van de gekozen collectiebeelden hanteert hij dezelfde blik waarmee hij naar de werkelijkheid kijkt, waarmee hij zoekt naar betekenisloze of banale dingen waar iedereen aan voorbijloopt, naar andere kwaliteiten in de werkelijkheid.
Braeckman vindt zichzelf opnieuw uit door foto's van anderen als bronmateriaal te gebruiken en nieuwe artistieke technieken toe te passen in zijn creaties. In zijn experimenten met het medium blijft hij verrassen en vernieuwen. Braeckman is een veelzijdig kunstenaar met een ongekende vrijheid van werken, die niet krampachtig aan gekende ideeen en methoden vasthoudt.

De collectieobjecten inspireren hem in die mate dat het zwaar wordt om keuzes te maken. Hoe blijft hij trouw aan zichzelf als kunstenaar met beelden die de zijne niet zijn? Hoe ver kan hij gaan met het manipuleren van foto's van iemand anders? Wanneer wordt iets respectloos?
Aanvankelijk onderschat hij hoe moeilijk het is om zich auteur van deze beelden te noemen. Braeckman heeft resoluut gekozen voor functionele beelden en niet voor autonoom werk van hedendaagse kunstenaars. Voor hem is dit ook een ethische kwestie. Hoewel hij de toekomst openlaat, voelt hij zich vandaag niet vrij genoeg om nieuw werk te maken van foto's van een collega-kunstenaar:

Terwijl de kunstenaar zijn foto's heeft afgewerkt als een kunstwerk, stuurt de functionele fotograaf zijn werk de wereld in als een vakman. Wat ik hier doe, lijkt misschien respectloos, maar ik heb heel veel respect voor deze fotografen.

Het is ook dit respect dat Braeckman aanvankelijk blokkeert. Hij graaft diep in zichzelf en zoekt naar nieuwe manieren om met dit innerlijke conflict om te gaan, zonder zichzelf als kunstenaar te verliezen in alle mogelijkheden. Voor hem zijn er twee opties om zich de foto's eigen te maken: ofwel grijpt hij minimaal in, ofwel vernielt hij het werk. Er bestaat geen middenweg. Een voorbeeld van zo'n extreme vervorming van het beeld is collages maken. Om zich te bevrijden van het verlammende respect voor de collectieobjecten kiest Braeckman voor een fysieke actie die nieuw is in zijn artistieke proces. Hij valt de reproducties aan: met een schaar knipt hij — heel snel en intuïtief — gaten in de gefotografeerde collectiebeelden, waarin hij dan nieuwe beelden plaatst. Andere ingrepen zijn: afdrukken maken op verschillende structuren en oppervlakken, deze fotopapieren opnieuw fotograferen, stof toevoegen, de beelden met verf beschilderen en bekladden om ze daarna verder te

bewerken in zijn analoge en digitale donkere kamer. Met als finaal resultaat dat het oorspronkelijke beeld verdwijnt.
De originele kleine, functionele foto's, vaak rechttoe-rechtaan, scherp en duidelijk leesbaar, worden getransformeerd tot monumentale beelden die een bewuste, trage lezing vragen en aanzetten tot reflectie en bezinning. Braeckman voegt een soort filter toe tussen het beeld en de kijker. Hoewel hij de collectiefoto's abstraheert, vervallen de nieuwe beelden nooit in de totale abstractie. De link met de realiteit is nog steeds aanwezig. Braeckmans foto's worden poorten naar een andere wereld, naar zijn wereld, waarin je als bezoeker het raden hebt naar de gemoedstoestand waarin deze beelden gecreëerd zijn. Ze verbergen meer dan ze tonen.
Braeckman manipuleert de collectieobjecten en geeft er een nieuwe dimensie aan: de context valt weg, het formaat verandert, de originele betekenis verschuift, er wordt een titel toegevoegd. Het beeld verandert van een functioneel document in een artistieke foto. Braeckman laat je voorbij de oorspronkelijke functie van de foto's kijken. Het worden tijdloze visuele gedichten, die meer vragen oproepen dan antwoorden geven.
Met de Duitse titel *Echtzeit* verwijst Braeckman naar de brug die hij maakt tussen verleden en heden. Op hetzelfde moment — *in real time* — zie je verschillende perspectieven: de visie van de oorspronkelijke fotograaf, de interpretatie van Braeckman en de blik van de toeschouwer. De rijkdom en de complexiteit van het fotografische medium krijgen hier een platform.

EEN OPEN DIALOOG ROND DE COLLECTIE

Zowel Braeckman als FOMU werden tijdens dit traject met vele ethische vragen geconfronteerd, die actueler zijn dan ooit. Hoe ga je als kunstenaar respectvol om met werk van anderen? Wanneer is een foto enkel functioneel en wanneer wordt ze artistiek? Is het überhaupt mogelijk de originele intentie van de fotograaf te achterhalen? Wanneer kun je jezelf auteur van een werk noemen? Een ogenschijnlijk agressieve daad als knippen in beelden is misschien net iets dat ons verder doet nadenken over wiens blik we tonen.
Bij FOMU stelden we ons ook de vraag hoever we een kunstenaar konden laten gaan met de beelden van een ander. Als fotomuseum zijn we immers verantwoordelijk voor het rechtmatige en correcte gebruik van de foto's die we bewaren. Het onderscheid tussen functionele en artistieke fotografie is vaak een vage grens. Met dit project willen we ook de dialoog hierover aangaan.
Deze samenwerking met Dirk Braeckman was voor FOMU een verdere stap in het vernieuwen en openstellen van de collectie. Op een co-creatieve manier laten we de traditionele blik op de canon los om het publiek diverse perspectieven aan te bieden. Een collectie openstellen voor herinterpretatie is een boeiend en doorlopend proces, dat ons toelaat om als museum vernieuwend en relevant te blijven. Dirk Braeckman gaf een diepgaande, verrijkende impuls om dit proces en de dialoog daarover verder te zetten.

1 Collectietentoonstelling *Re-collect*. FOMU Antwerpen. 7 mei 2021 – 7 november 2021.

2 Collectietentoonstelling *Grace Ndiritu Reimagines the FOMU Collection*. FOMU Antwerpen. 17 februari 2023 – 26 februari 2024. Voor meer informatie hierover, zie: Judah, H. (2023, 27 januari). A Map Through Time: Grace Ndiritu Reimagines the FOMU Collection. *Trigger*, www.fomu.be/trigger/articles/grace-ndiritu.

3 Collectietentoonstelling *Dirk Braeckman. Echtzeit*. FOMU Antwerpen. 29 maart 2024 – 19 januari 2025.

4 Versteeg, W. (2017, 17 mei). The Loneliness of the Darkroom. *Aperture*. aperture.org/editorial/loneliness-darkroom-braeckman.

5 Alle citaten van Dirk Braeckman komen uit een gesprek tussen Tamara Berghmans en Dirk Braeckman, in zijn atelier in Gent, 26 september 2023.

6 Canonne, X. (2013). Gesprek met Dirk Braeckman. In Anonymus & D. Braeckman, *Schwarzschild* (pp. 51-55). Antwerpen: Pandora.

DOOR DE OGEN VAN DE SCHIM

Clément Chéroux

DE VERRUKKING VAN FOTO'S

Er zijn van die foto's die tegen je lijken te praten. Iedereen die ooit een doos vol foto's is tegengekomen in het depot van een museum of bij een kraampje op een rommelmarkt, en ze één voor één zorgvuldig heeft bekeken, weet dat maar al te goed. Het is een onuitgesproken kennis, een impliciet weten waarover nog nooit een boek is geschreven, maar dat niettemin door veel mensen wordt gedeeld. Uiteindelijk maakt het niet uit of ze kunst zijn of niet. Sommige foto's spreken ons gewoon aan, of misschien beter gezegd: ze grijpen ons bij ons nekvel. Ze trekken onze aandacht zoals een magneet vijlsel aantrekt. Ze lijken wel kleine uitschuifbare grijpers te hebben die ons in een oogwenk naar zich toe trekken. Roland Barthes beschrijft dit prachtig in enkele van de meest aangrijpende pagina's van *La Chambre Claire*: in bepaalde beelden zit een detail dat zich losmaakt "uit het toneel om mij als een pijl te doorboren".[1] "Dat *iets* heeft in de roos geschoten, het heeft een kleine verschuiving in mij teweeg gebracht, een *satori* [...]."[2] "Het *punctum* van een foto", voegt hij eraan toe, "is het toeval dat mij in die foto *treft*".[3] Die intensiteit die me doorboort kan net zo goed een element van de foto zijn, een rangschikking van vormen, een eenvoudig gebaar, de positie van een lichaam of een bijzondere lichtinval, zelfs een chemische aantasting, een barst in het broze oppervlak. Er is hier hoe dan ook sprake van een zekere visuele aanmaning die rechtstreeks gericht is aan mijn wezen, mijn onbewuste, mijn geheugen misschien, mijn ervaring, mijn kennis of mijn cultuur; iets wat nauw verbonden is met *wie ik ben*. Daarna volgt meestal een onbedwingbaar verlangen om de foto (of de reproductie ervan) te *bezitten*. Zoals het lichaam van de ander bij vleselijk verlangen. En wel met als doel om deze verrukking naar believen opnieuw te kunnen beleven.

BRAECKMANS IN RUWE VORM

Sinds enkele maanden verdiept Dirk Braeckman zich in de miljoenen foto's uit de collecties van FOMU (Fotomuseum Antwerpen). Hij opende ontelbare dozen, doorzocht registers en bladerde door albums. Hij werd *gegrepen* – net zoals de 'schok', 'verschuiving' of 'satori' waar Barthes het over heeft – door enkele van de foto's die de basis vormen van de werken in dit boek en die in hun oorspronkelijke vorm te vinden zijn aan het begin van deze uitgave. Hoewel ik er niet bij was toen de kunstenaar de foto's uitkoos, denk ik een redelijk goed idee te hebben van wat hem ertoe gebracht heeft om net deze beelden te gebruiken. Eerst elimineerde hij alle foto's die door kunstenaars waren genomen uit zijn eerste, relatief grote en intuïtieve selectie en hield hij alleen de *anonieme* beelden over. Foto's waarvan de maker niet bekend is met andere woorden. Voor zijn project had hij foto's nodig die neutraal en niet beladen waren of anders gezegd: beelden zonder artistieke intentie. Uit respect voor de creatieve handeling wil hij niet dat die van hem overlapt met die van iemand anders. Maar afgezien van het feit dat de maker niet bekend is, hebben de geselecteerde foto's ook het gemeenschappelijke kenmerk dat ze *open* zijn, om een term te gebruiken die de Italiaanse filosoof en semioticus Umberto Eco na aan het hart lag.[4] Hun belangrijkste eigenschap is een soort besluiteloosheid, een vermogen om vragen op te roepen bij wie ze bekijkt. Wat al deze door Braeckman gekozen beelden gemeen hebben, is in feite een vraagteken.[5] Hoewel het in de meeste gevallen foto's zijn die gewoon de realiteit afbeelden, vraag ik me voortdurend af wat ze precies tonen of betekenen. Ze leggen me geen betekenis op, maar nodigen me veeleer uit om er zelf een te geven. Dat is trouwens precies wat Braeckman wil bereiken met de foto's die hij zelf maakt. Het merendeel van zijn werken heeft iets raadselachtigs. De paar foto's die hij uit de collectie van FOMU heeft gekozen, beschikken *van nature* over de kwaliteiten die hij nastreeft in zijn eigen werk. Het zijn in zekere zin Braeckmans *in ruwe vorm*. En dat is waarom hij deze beelden heeft gekozen. Hij herkende zichzelf erin.

HET BEELD OPNIEUW OPENEN

Zodra Braeckman een beeld heeft gekozen, fotografeert hij het opnieuw. Daarbij speelt hij vaak met de reflecties op het glanzende oppervlak. Hij is dol op de glinsteringen of halo's die de afdruk de schijn van een aura geven. Vervolgens bewerkt hij de foto op de computer. Hij snijdt bij, verzadigt, solariseert en verduistert met opzet. Hij legt verschillende opnamen boven elkaar. Soms maakt hij gebruik van een soort montage, niet door iets toe te voegen, maar net door iets weg te nemen: hij snijdt het beeld open, knipt een groot stuk weg en gebruikt de leegte die zo ontstaat als een nieuw frame. Man Ray beschreef zijn experimenten vaak als "verkrachting van materialen".[6] Braeckman doet hetzelfde. Sommige foto's worden overschilderd: hij bedekt ze met grote donkere vlekken of kleurt ze in met verwaterde verf. Vervolgens vergroot hij zijn foto's uit tot een formaat dat in geen enkel opzicht nog lijkt op het origineel. Door het beeld te bewerken, filtert de kunstenaar het op een zekere manier. Zijn creatieve handeling bestaat erin filters tussen het beeld en de toeschouwer te plaatsen. Het doel van die distantiëring is om de foto's te *ontdoen van hun functie*. De foto's uit de collectie van FOMU werden in de eerste plaats namelijk gebruikt voor documentaire doeleinden. Ze dienden om een nieuw instrument te promoten, verslag uit te brengen over de voltooiing van een project, een herinnering vast te leggen, een ziekte te identificeren, een slagveld te herkennen enzovoort. Als ik naar Braeckmans werken kijk, zie ik niet langer de medische microfoto, het reclamedocument of de luchtbeelden. Zijn beelden hebben hun gebruikswaarde verloren. Ze vertellen me niet *waar*, *wanneer* of *hoe*, laat staan *waarom*. Ze zijn hun nut voor altijd kwijt. Ze zijn letterlijk *buiten werking*. Maar dat maakt ze des te mysterieuzer. Door zijn tussenkomst slaagt Braeckman erin de raadselachtige kracht van de beelden te vergroten en ze *opnieuw te openen* om de verbeelding te stimuleren van wie ze aanschouwt.

VERNIETIGEN, ZEGT HIJ

Wat voor transformatie laat Braeckman deze beelden ondergaan? Die is voor het grootste stuk alchemistisch. Het gaat om een transmutatie. Hij verandert lood in goud. Dat doet hij eerst en vooral door middel van herleiding. De eerste stap is om het beeld uit zijn louter informatieve context te halen, waardoor de oorspronkelijke documentaire functie tenietgedaan wordt. Wanneer ik Braeckman in zijn atelier in Gent ontmoet om te praten over hoe hij zich deze beelden heeft toegeëigend, gebruikt hij voortdurend het woord 'vernietigen'. Hij wil ze aanvallen, geweld aandoen, vervormen. "Ik kan ze alleen maar respecteren ofwel vernietigen", zo zegt hij.[7] Ik moet meteen denken aan de titel van een boek van Marguerite Duras: *Détruire, dit-elle*.[8] Dit meesterwerk werd gepubliceerd in het jaar na de sociale revolutie van 1968 en gaat over twee mannen en twee vrouwen in een groot huis aan de rand van een bos. Het belangrijkste thema is de kracht van verlangen. Wanneer ze de verfilming van haar boek aanhaalt, heeft Duras het over een intens verlangen dat alles op zijn pad vernietigt: "Ik ben voorstander van [...] een volledig nieuwe start. Dat is de kern van mijn boek *Détruire, dit-elle*. Beginnen met een schone lei. Ik ben er voorstander van om de geschiedenis te vergeten, de geschiedenis van Frankrijk, de geschiedenis van de wereld. Helemaal. Ik zou willen dat er geen enkele herinnering meer overblijft aan wat mensen meegemaakt hebben, met andere woorden aan het ondraaglijke, op alle fronten, op alle vlakken. Alles met de grond gelijkmaken".[9] Dat is precies wat Braeckman ook probeert te doen. Zijn eerste stap is om de realiteit van de foto tot een minimum te herleiden. Hij weet dat hij een erg dunne lijn bewandelt, want hij wil niet in abstractie vervallen. Hij heeft iets tastbaars nodig om zich aan vast te houden en op voort te bouwen. Net als een koorddanser moet hij een evenwicht vinden. Hij vindt het belangrijk om een zekere laag werkelijkheid te bewaren van waaruit hij het beeld opnieuw kan vormgeven. André Breton, de grondlegger van het surrealisme, had dit in zijn tijd al door: "Alle dingen zijn bestemd om andere doeleinden te dienen dan degene die er doorgaans aan worden toegeschreven. Het is zelfs door de bewuste opoffering van hun oorspronkelijke functie [...] dat ze bepaalde *transcendente eigenschappen* krijgen".[10] De foto's die Braeckman gebruikt, worden van hun initiële nut bevrijd en opnieuw opengesteld voor het potentieel van betovering. Zo spreken ze de verbeelding van mensen aan.

BUITENLICHAMELIJKE ERVARING

Naast het gevoel van vernietiging is ook de dood alomtegenwoordig in deze fotoreeks van Dirk Braeckman. De manier waarop hij de wereld door deze beelden waarneemt, doet denken aan een astrale reis zoals mensen die een bijna-doodervaring hebben meegemaakt die beschrijven. Buitenlichamelijke ervaring, astrale projectie, uittreding of *out-of-body experience* (OBE) in het Engels: over dit fenomeen, dat vele namen heeft, bestaan tal van getuigenissen.[11] Wat bij het lezen van die verhalen misschien wel het meest opvalt, is de herhaling van dezelfde narratieve structuren, met andere woorden een vermeende gedeelde ervaring. Wanneer de ziel vlak na de dood het lichaam verlaat, wordt ze omhoog gezogen. Niet zo hoog als een passagiersvliegtuig, maar eerder als een vlieger of een ultralicht motorluchtvaartuig. De ziel hangt een paar meter boven haar vleselijke omhulsel, net bevrijd van de zwaartekracht van het lichaam. Ze is niet alleen begiftigd met een scherp zicht, maar ook met het vermogen om zachtjes en soepel te bewegen, alsof ze op een luchtkussen voortbeweegt. De meest gebruikte woorden zijn 'hangen', 'gewichtloosheid' en 'zweven'. "De reis was kort en we bevonden ons ongeveer vijftien meter boven de straat, vertelt iemand die is teruggekeerd uit het hiernamaals [...]. We hingen net boven de grond en ik keek naar beneden [...]. We zweefden ongeveer honderd of tweehonderd meter boven de aarde. Het was donker en af en toe ging er een lichtje branden op het platteland. Vlak onder ons glinsterde een wateroppervlak, een poel of meertje. Daarachter stond een groen gebouw in de vorm van een piramide, waarin we een licht zagen schijnen."[12] Dat is precies waar Braeckmans perspectief ligt in *Echtzeit*. Via zijn beelden plaatst hij zichzelf in de positie van iemand die in de wereld rondspookt. Hij kijkt door de ogen van de schim.

1 Barthes, R. (1988). *De lichtende kamer, aantekeningen over de fotografie* (M. Luccioni, Trans.). Amsterdam: De Arbeiderspers, p. 35.

2 Ibid., p. 58.

3 Ibid., p. 35.

4 Eco, U. (1965). *L'Œuvre ouverte*. Parijs: Seuil.

5 Voor meer informatie hierover, zie: Chéroux, C. (2010). L'image comme point d'interrogation ou la valeur d'extase du document surréaliste. *Les carnets du bal, L'image-document, entre réalité et fiction*, (1), pp. 26-47.

6 Man Ray. (1933). L'Âge de la lumière. *Minotaure*, (3-4), p. 1.

7 Interview door de auteur met Dirk Braeckman, in zijn atelier in Gent, 23 november 2023.

8 Duras, M. (1969). *Détruire, dit-elle*. Parijs: Minuit.

9 Interview met Marguerite Duras over de opnames van *Détruire, dit-elle*, uitgezonden in *Banc d'essai*, een programma van Jean-Claude Bergeret, 1969, beschikbaar op de website van het INA: www.ina.fr/ina-eclaire-actu/video/i05125289/marguerite-duras-a-propos-de-detruire-dit-elle, geraadpleegd op 2 december 2023.

10 Breton, A. (1992). Avis au lecteur pour *La Femme 100 têtes* de Max Ernst. In *Œuvres complètes* (Vol. 2). Parijs: Gallimard, p. 305. Cursivering door mij.

11 Monroe, R.A. (1996). *Le Voyage hors du corps. Techniques de projection du corps astral*. Monaco: Les éditions du Rocher. (Origineel werk gepubliceerd in 1971)

12 Monroe, R.A. (1990). *Fantastiques expériences de voyage astral*. Parijs: Robert Laffont, pp. 293, 342, 357-358. (Origineel werk gepubliceerd in 1985)

BIOGRAPHY/ BIOGRAPHIE/ BIOGRAFIE

Tamara Berghmans

Tamara Berghmans has worked as Collection Curator at FOMU (Fotomuseum Antwerp) since 2010. She curates the collection exhibitions and is responsible for the acquisition policy. In 2008 she completed her Ph.D. dissertation on the Belgian Subjective Photography. She is the author of *The Making of a Photobook. Sanne Sannes' Maquette for 'Diary of an Erotomaniac'* (Rijksmuseum Studies in Photography 2009); *The Eye of the Photographer* (Lannoo 2011), *Ed van der Elsken. Looking for Love on the Left Bank* (Aman Iman, 2013), *Photography Inc.* (Lannoo 2015), *Suzy Embo* (CFC-Editions 2017) and *Photobook Belge 1854-Now* (Hannibal / FOMU, 2019).

Tamara Berghmans travaille comme conservatrice de collection au FOMU (Fotomuseum Anvers) depuis 2010. Elle organise les expositions de la collection et est responsable de la politique d'acquisition. Elle a terminé sa thèse de doctorat sur la photographie subjective belge en 2008. Elle est l'autrice de *The Making of a Photobook. Sanne Sannes' Maquette for 'Diary of an Erotomaniac'* (Rijksmuseum Studies in Photography 2009) ; *The Eye of the Photographer* (Lannoo 2011), *Ed van der Elsken. Looking for Love on the Left Bank* (Aman Iman, 2013), *Photography Inc.* (Lannoo 2015), *Suzy Embo* (CFC-Editions 2017) *et Photobook Belge 1854-Now* (Hannibal / FOMU, 2019).

Tamara Berghmans is sinds 2010 collectiecurator in FOMU (Fotomuseum Antwerpen). Ze cureert de tentoonstellingen met werken uit de collectie en is verantwoordelijk voor het aankoopbeleid. In 2008 voltooide ze haar doctoraatsthesis over de Belgische subjectieve fotografie. Berghmans schreef *The Making of a Photobook. Sanne Sannes' Maquette for 'Diary of an Erotomaniac'* (Rijksmuseum Studies in Photography, 2009); *The Eye of the Photographer* (Lannoo, 2011); *Ed van der Elsken. Looking for Love on the Left Bank* (Aman Iman, 2013); *Photography Inc.* (Lannoo, 2015); *Suzy Embo* (CFC-Editions, 2017) en *Photobook Belge 1854-Now* (Hannibal / FOMU, 2019).

Clément Chéroux

Clément Chéroux is the director of the Henri Cartier-Bresson Foundation in Paris. Prior to that he has hold positions at MoMA (Chief Curator 2020-22), at SFMOMA (Senior Curator 2017-2020) and Centre Pompidou (Curator and Chief Curator 2007-2016). Chéroux is a photo-historian. He holds a PhD in Art History. He has curated numerous exhibitions and published more than 50 books about photography and its history.

Clément Chéroux est directeur de la Fondation Henri Cartier-Bresson à Paris. Il a auparavant été Chief Curator au MoMA de New York (2020-2022), Senior Curator au San Francisco Museum of Modern Art (2017-2020), Conservateur puis Chef de Service au Centre Pompidou (2007-2016). Chéroux est historien de la photographie et docteur en histoire de l'art. Il a été le commissaire de nombreuses expositions et a publié, comme auteur ou directeur d'ouvrage, plus d'une cinquantaine d'ouvrages sur la photographie et son histoire.

Clément Chéroux is directeur van de Fondation Henri Cartier-Bresson in Parijs. Daarvoor bekleedde hij functies bij MoMA (hoofdconservator 2020-22), SFMOMA (senior conservator 2017-2020) en Centre Pompidou (conservator en hoofdconservator 2007-2016). Chéroux is fotohistoricus. Hij heeft een doctoraat in de kunstgeschiedenis. Hij cureerde talloze tentoonstellingen en publiceerde meer dan 50 boeken over fotografie en haar geschiedenis.

LIST OF WORKS

19 **ECHTZEIT#117-24**
2024, 144 x 180 cm, Ultrachrome inkjet print mounted on aluminium support in stainless steel frame

20 **ECHTZEIT#006-23**
2023, 120 x 96 cm, Ultrachrome inkjet print mounted on aluminium support in stainless steel frame

21 **ECHTZEIT#138-24**
2024, 90 x 72 cm, Ultrachrome inkjet print mounted on aluminium support in stainless steel frame

23 **ECHTZEIT#024-24**
2024, 120 x 96 cm, Ultrachrome inkjet print mounted on aluminium support in stainless steel frame

24 **ECHTZEIT#007-24**
2024, 96 x 120 cm, Ultrachrome inkjet print mounted on aluminium support in stainless steel frame

25 **ECHTZEIT#164-24**
2024, 96 x 120 cm, Ultrachrome inkjet print mounted on aluminium support in stainless steel frame

27 **ECHTZEIT#099-24**
2024, 120 x 96 cm, Ultrachrome inkjet print mounted on aluminium support in stainless steel frame

28 **ECHTZEIT#093-24**
2024, 72 x 90 cm, Ultrachrome inkjet print mounted on aluminium support in stainless steel frame

29 **ECHTZEIT#065-24**
2024, 180 x 144 cm, Ultrachrome inkjet print mounted on aluminium support in stainless steel frame

30 **ECHTZEIT#067-24**
2024, 60 x 48 cm, Ultrachrome inkjet print mounted on aluminium support in stainless steel frame

31 **ECHTZEIT#091-23**
2023, 60 x 48 cm, Ultrachrome inkjet print mounted on aluminium support in stainless steel frame

32 **ECHTZEIT#087-24**
2024, 180 x 144 cm, Ultrachrome inkjet print mounted on aluminium support in stainless steel frame

33 **ECHTZEIT#029-24**
2024, 96 x 120 cm, Ultrachrome inkjet print mounted on aluminium support in stainless steel frame

35 **ECHTZEIT#025-24**
2024, 90 x 72 cm, Ultrachrome inkjet print mounted on aluminium support in stainless steel frame

36 **ECHTZEIT#077-23**
2023, 120 x 96 cm, Ultrachrome inkjet print mounted on aluminium support in stainless steel frame

37 **ECHTZEIT#185-24**
2024, 96 x 120 cm, Ultrachrome inkjet print mounted on aluminium support in stainless steel frame

38 **ECHTZEIT#057-24**
2024, 72 x 90 cm, Ultrachrome inkjet print mounted on aluminium support in stainless steel frame

39 **ECHTZEIT#011-23**
2023, 180 x 144 cm, Ultrachrome inkjet print mounted on aluminium support in stainless steel frame

40 **ECHTZEIT#170-24**
2024, 96 x 120 cm, Ultrachrome inkjet print mounted on aluminium support in stainless steel frame

41 **ECHTZEIT#126-24**
2024, 144 x 180 cm, Ultrachrome inkjet print mounted on aluminium support in stainless steel frame

43 **ECHTZEIT#001-23**
2023, 60 x 48 cm, Ultrachrome inkjet print mounted on aluminium support in stainless steel frame

44 **ECHTZEIT#012-23**
2023, 120 x 96 cm, Ultrachrome inkjet print mounted on aluminium support in stainless steel frame

45 **ECHTZEIT#141-24**
2024, 72 x 90 cm, Ultrachrome inkjet print mounted on aluminium support in stainless steel frame

47 **ECHTZEIT#013-23**
2023, 180 x 144 cm, Ultrachrome inkjet print mounted on aluminium support in stainless steel frame

48 **ECHTZEIT#137-23**
2023, 90 x 72 cm, Ultrachrome inkjet print mounted on aluminium support in stainless steel frame

49 **ECHTZEIT#002-24**
2024, 180 x 144 cm, Ultrachrome inkjet print mounted on aluminium support in stainless steel frame

50 **ECHTZEIT#016-23**
2023, 120 x 96 cm, Ultrachrome inkjet print mounted on aluminium support in stainless steel frame

51 **ECHTZEIT#018-24**
2024, 96 x 120 cm, Ultrachrome inkjet print mounted on aluminium support in stainless steel frame

53 **ECHTZEIT#168-24**
2024, 120 x 96 cm, Ultrachrome inkjet print mounted on aluminium support in stainless steel frame

54 **ECHTZEIT#171-24**
2024, 144 x 180 cm, Ultrachrome inkjet print mounted on aluminium support in stainless steel frame

56 **ECHTZEIT#132-24**
2024, 120 x 96 cm, Ultrachrome inkjet print mounted on aluminium support in stainless steel frame

56 **ECHTZEIT#133-24**
2024, 120 x 96 cm, Ultrachrome inkjet print mounted on aluminium support in stainless steel frame

57 **ECHTZEIT#135-24**
2024, 120 x 96 cm, Ultrachrome inkjet print mounted on aluminium support in stainless steel frame

57 **ECHTZEIT#136-24**
2024, 120 x 96 cm, Ultrachrome inkjet print mounted on aluminium support in stainless steel frame

58 **ECHTZEIT#022-23**
2023, 48 x 60 cm, Ultrachrome inkjet print mounted on aluminium support in stainless steel frame

59 **ECHTZEIT#023-23**
2023, Ultrachrome inkjet print mounted on aluminium support in stainless steel frame

61 **ECHTZEIT#026-23**
2023, 144 x 180 cm, Ultrachrome inkjet print mounted on aluminium support in stainless steel frame

62 **ECHTZEIT#027-24**
2024, 96 x 120 cm, Ultrachrome inkjet print mounted on aluminium support in stainless steel frame

63 **ECHTZEIT#080-24**
2024, 72 x 90 cm, Ultrachrome inkjet print mounted on aluminium support in stainless steel frame

64 **ECHTZEIT#028-24**
2024, 72 x 90 cm, Ultrachrome inkjet print mounted on aluminium support in stainless steel frame

65 **ECHTZEIT#030-23**
2023, 120 x 96 cm, Ultrachrome inkjet print mounted on aluminium support in stainless steel frame

67 **ECHTZEIT#031-24//AP**
2024, 144 x 180 cm, Ultrachrome inkjet print mounted on aluminium support in stainlesss steel frame

68 **ECHTZEIT#032-23**
2023, 180 x 144 cm, Ultrachrome inkjet print mounted on aluminium support in stainless steel frame

69 **ECHTZEIT#033-24**
2024, 96 x 120 cm, Ultrachrome inkjet print mounted on aluminium support in stainless steel frame

70 **ECHTZEIT#169-23**
2023, 72 x 90 cm, Ultrachrome inkjet print mounted on aluminium support in stainless steel frame

71 **ECHTZEIT#172-24**
2024, 96 x 120 cm, Ultrachrome inkjet print mounted on aluminium support in stainless steel frame

72 **ECHTZEIT#010-24**
2024, 72 x 90 cm, Ultrachrome inkjet print mounted on aluminium support in stainless steel frame

73 **ECHTZEIT#051-23**
2023, 96 x 120 cm, Ultrachrome inkjet print mounted on aluminium support in stainless steel frame

75 **ECHTZEIT#058-24**
2024, 96 x 120 cm, Ultrachrome inkjet print mounted on aluminium support in stainless steel frame

76 **ECHTZEIT#060-23**
2023, 60 x 48 cm, Ultrachrome inkjet print mounted on aluminium support in stainless steel frame

77 **ECHTZEIT#150-23**
2023, 50 x 40 cm, Platinum-palladium print

78 **ECHTZEIT#142-24**
2024, 144 x 180 cm, Ultrachrome inkjet print mounted on aluminium support in stainless steel frame

79 **ECHTZEIT#041-23**
2023, 120 x 96 cm, Ultrachrome inkjet print mounted on aluminium support in stainless steel frame

81 **ECHTZEIT#165-24**
2024, 90 x 72 cm, Ultrachrome inkjet print mounted on aluminium support in stainless steel frame

82 **ECHTZEIT#040-23**
2023, 96 x 120 cm, Ultrachrome inkjet print mounted on aluminium support in stainless steel frame

83 **ECHTZEIT#064-23**
2023, 96 x 120 cm, Ultrachrome inkjet print mounted on aluminium support in stainless steel frame

84 **ECHTZEIT#043-23**
2023, 96 x 120 cm, Ultrachrome inkjet print mounted on aluminium support in stainless steel frame

85 **ECHTZEIT#003-24**
2024, 90 x 72 cm, Ultrachrome inkjet print mounted on aluminium support in stainless steel frame

87 **ECHTZEIT#119-23**
2023, 72 x 90 cm, Ultrachrome inkjet print mounted on aluminium support in stainless steel frame

88 **ECHTZEIT#054-23**
2023, 144 x 180 cm, Ultrachrome inkjet print mounted on aluminium support in stainless steel frame

89 **ECHTZEIT#046-24**
2024, 96 x 120 cm, Ultrachrome inkjet print mounted on aluminium support in stainless steel frame

90 **ECHTZEIT#114-24**
2024, 72 x 90 cm, Ultrachrome inkjet print mounted on aluminium support in stainless steel frame

91 **ECHTZEIT#075-23**
2023, 120 x 96 cm, Ultrachrome inkjet print mounted on aluminium support in stainless steel frame

92 **ECHTZEIT#134-24**
2024, 72 x 90 cm, Ultrachrome inkjet print mounted on aluminium support in stainless steel frame

93 **ECHTZEIT#049-23**
2023, 180 x 144 cm, Ultrachrome inkjet print mounted on aluminium support in stainless steel frame

95 **ECHTZEIT#008-23**
2023, 144 x 180 cm, Ultrachrome inkjet print mounted on aluminium support in stainless steel frame

96 **ECHTZEIT#152-24**
2024, 96 x 120 cm, Ultrachrome inkjet print mounted on aluminium support in stainless steel frame

97 **ECHTZEIT#151-24**
2024, 96 x 120 cm, Ultrachrome inkjet print mounted on aluminium support in stainless steel frame

98 **ECHTZEIT#153-24**
2024, 96 x 120 cm, Ultrachrome inkjet print mounted on aluminium support in stainless steel frame

99 **ECHTZEIT#158-24**
2024, 96 x 120 cm, Ultrachrome inkjet print mounted on aluminium support in stainless steel frame

100 **ECHTZEIT#173-23**
2023, 144 x 180 cm, Ultrachrome inkjet print mounted on aluminium support in stainless steel frame

103 **ECHTZEIT#062-24**
2024, 90 x 72 cm, Ultrachrome inkjet print mounted on aluminium support in stainless steel frame

104 **ECHTZEIT#115-24**
2024, 96 x 120 cm, Ultrachrome inkjet print mounted on aluminium support in stainless steel frame

105 **ECHTZEIT#082-23**
2023, 120 x 96 cm, Ultrachrome inkjet print mounted on aluminium support in stainless steel frame

106 **ECHTZEIT#174-24**
2024, 90 x 72 cm, Ultrachrome inkjet print mounted on aluminium support in stainless steel frame

107 **ECHTZEIT#066-23**
2023, 180 x 144 cm, Ultrachrome inkjet print mounted on aluminium support in stainless steel frame

108 **ECHTZEIT#112-24**
2024, 96 x 120 cm, Ultrachrome inkjet print mounted on aluminium support in stainless steel frame

110 **ECHTZEIT#050-23**
2023, 180 x 144 cm, Ultrachrome inkjet print mounted on aluminium support in stainless steel frame

111 **ECHTZEIT#175-24**
2024, 144 x 180 cm, Ultrachrome inkjet print mounted on aluminium support in stainless steel frame

112 **ECHTZEIT#122-24**
2024, 90 x 72 cm, Ultrachrome inkjet print mounted on aluminium support in stainless steel frame

113 **ECHTZEIT#042-23**
2023, 180 x 144 cm, Ultrachrome inkjet print mounted on aluminium support in stainless steel frame

115 **ECHTZEIT#177-24**
2024, 90 x 72 cm, Ultrachrome inkjet print mounted on aluminium support in stainless steel frame

116 **ECHTZEIT#055-23**
2023, 96 x 120 cm, Ultrachrome inkjet print mounted on aluminium support in stainless steel frame

117 **ECHTZEIT#044-23**
2023, 72 x 90 cm, Ultrachrome inkjet print mounted on aluminium support in stainless steel frame

118 **ECHTZEIT#181-24**
2024, 96 x 120 cm, Ultrachrome inkjet print mounted on aluminium support in stainless steel frame

119 **ECHTZEIT#052-23**
2023, 120 x 96 cm, Ultrachrome inkjet print mounted on aluminium support in stainless steel frame

120 **ECHTZEIT#161-24**
2024, 96 x 120 cm, Ultrachrome inkjet print mounted on aluminium support in stainless steel frame

122 **ECHTZEIT#159-24**
2024, 96 x 120 cm, Ultrachrome inkjet print mounted on aluminium support in stainless steel frame

124 **ECHTZEIT#108-24**
2024, 180 x 144 cm, Ultrachrome inkjet print mounted on aluminium support in stainless steel frame

125 **ECHTZEIT#083-23**
2023, 120 x 96 cm, Ultrachrome inkjet print mounted on aluminium support in stainless steel frame

126 **ECHTZEIT#073-24**
2024, 180 x 144 cm, Ultrachrome inkjet print mounted on aluminium support in stainless steel frame

129 **ECHTZEIT#076-23**
2023, 72 x 90 cm, Ultrachrome inkjet print mounted on aluminium support in stainless steel frame

130 **ECHTZEIT#103-24**
2024, 96 x 120 cm, Ultrachrome inkjet print mounted on aluminium support in stainless steel frame

131 **ECHTZEIT#113-24**
2024, 96 x 120 cm, Ultrachrome inkjet print mounted on aluminium support in stainless steel frame

132 **ECHTZEIT#111-24**
2024, 96 x 120 cm, Ultrachrome inkjet print mounted on aluminium support in stainless steel frame

133 **ECHTZEIT#118-24**
2024, 96 x 120 cm, Ultrachrome inkjet print mounted on aluminium support in stainless steel frame

134 **ECHTZEIT#047-23**
2023, 72 x 90 cm, Ultrachrome inkjet print mounted on aluminium support in stainless steel frame

135 **ECHTZEIT#037-24**
2024, 72 x 90 cm, Ultrachrome inkjet print mounted on aluminium support in stainless steel frame

137 **ECHTZEIT#094-24**
2024, 120 x 96 cm, Ultrachrome inkjet print mounted on aluminium support in stainless steel frame

138 **ECHTZEIT#102-24**
2024, 96 x 120 cm, Ultrachrome inkjet print mounted on aluminium support in stainless steel frame

139 **ECHTZEIT#179-24**
2024, 90 x 72 cm, Ultrachrome inkjet print mounted on aluminium support in stainless steel frame

140 **ECHTZEIT#105-24**
2024, 180 x 144 cm, Ultrachrome inkjet print mounted on aluminium support in stainless steel frame

141 **ECHTZEIT#045-24**
2024, 30 x 24 cm, Platinum-palladium print

142 **ECHTZEIT#048-23**
2023, 180 x 144 cm, Ultrachrome inkjet print mounted on aluminium support in stainless steel frame

143 **ECHTZEIT#004-24**
2024, 96 x 120 cm, Ultrachrome inkjet print mounted on aluminium support in stainless steel frame

145 **ECHTZEIT#019-23**
2023, 60 x 48 cm, Ultrachrome inkjet print mounted on aluminium support in stainless steel frame

146 **ECHTZEIT#104-24**
2024, 144 x 180 cm, Ultrachrome inkjet print mounted on aluminium support in stainless steel frame

147 **ECHTZEIT#125-24**
2024, 96 x 120 cm, Ultrachrome inkjet print mounted on aluminium support in stainless steel frame

148 **ECHTZEIT#131-24**
2024, 120 x 96 cm, Ultrachrome inkjet print mounted on aluminium support in stainless steel frame

149 **ECHTZEIT#039-24**
2024, 120 x 96 cm, Ultrachrome inkjet print mounted on aluminium support in stainless steel frame

150 **ECHTZEIT#101-24**
2024, 144 x 180 cm, Ultrachrome inkjet print mounted on aluminium support in stainless steel frame

152 **ECHTZEIT#184-24**
2024, 90 x 72 cm, Ultrachrome inkjet print mounted on aluminium support in stainless steel frame

153 **ECHTZEIT#167-24**
2024, 90 x 72 cm, Ultrachrome inkjet print mounted on aluminium support in stainless steel frame

154 **ECHTZEIT#123-24**
2024, 144 x 180 cm, Ultrachrome inkjet print mounted on aluminium support in stainless steel frame

155 **ECHTZEIT#149-23**
2023, 48 x 60 cm, Ultrachrome inkjet print mounted on aluminium support in stainless steel frame

156 **ECHTZEIT#183-24**
2024, 60 x 48 cm, Ultrachrome inkjet print mounted on aluminium support in stainless steel frame

157 **ECHTZEIT#109-24**
2024, 96 x 120 cm, Ultrachrome inkjet print mounted on aluminium support in stainless steel frame

159 **ECHTZEIT#070-23**
2023, 60 x 48 cm, Ultrachrome inkjet print mounted on aluminium support in stainless steel frame

160 **ECHTZEIT#145-23**
2023, 96 x 120 cm, Ultrachrome inkjet print mounted on aluminium support in stainless steel frame

161 **ECHTZEIT#140-23**
2023, 96 x 120 cm, Ultrachrome inkjet print mounted on aluminium support in stainless steel frame

162 **ECHTZEIT#139-23**
2023, 144 x 180 cm, Ultrachrome inkjet print mounted on aluminium support in stainless steel frame

165 **ECHTZEIT#086-23**
2023, 96 x 120 cm, Ultrachrome inkjet print mounted on aluminium support in stainless steel frame

166 **ECHTZEIT#085-23**
2023, 96 x 120 cm, Ultrachrome inkjet print mounted on aluminium support in stainless steel frame

167 **ECHTZEIT#096-23**
2023, 120 x 96 cm, Ultrachrome inkjet print mounted on aluminium support in stainless steel frame

169 **ECHTZEIT#176-24**
2024, 120 x 96 cm, Ultrachrome inkjet print mounted on aluminium support in stainless steel frame

170 **ECHTZEIT#178-24**
2024, 144 x 180 cm, Ultrachrome inkjet print mounted on aluminium support in stainless steel frame

172 **ECHTZEIT#130-24**
2024, 96 x 120 cm, Ultrachrome inkjet print mounted on aluminium support in stainless steel frame

173 **ECHTZEIT#128-24**
2024, 96 x 120 cm, Ultrachrome inkjet print mounted on aluminium support in stainless steel frame

175 **ECHTZEIT#180-24**
2024, 144 x 180 cm, Ultrachrome inkjet print mounted on aluminium support in stainless steel frame

COLOPHON

AUTHOR
Dirk Braeckman
dirkbraeckman.be

TEXTS
Tamara Berghmans
Clément Chéroux

EDITING & TRANSLATIONS
Joëlle Daems, ElaN Languages,
Mia Verstraete

REPRODUCTIONS FOMU COLLECTION
Guy Voet

IMAGE CORRECTION
Sarah Bruyninckx

WITH SPECIAL THANKS TO
Studio Dirk Braeckman

PUBLISHER
Bruno Devos
HOPPER&FUCHS, Belgium, 2024
in collaboration with FOMU (Fotomuseum Antwerp), Belgium

GRAPHIC DESIGN
Reg Herygers
undercast.com

PRINTING
Stockmans Art Books, Duffel, Belgium

PAPER
Arctic Volume White 150 gsm
& Munken Lynx Rough 1.4 120 gsm

ISBN 9789464002331

First print, March 2024 in an edition of 1.250 copies.

This artist's book accompanies the exhibition 'DIRK BRAECKMAN. ECHTZEIT' at FOMU (Fotomuseum Antwerp) from 29/03/2024-19/01/2025.

HOPPER &FUCHS
ARCTIC PAPER
FOMU

DEDICATED TO

Dirk Braeckman dedicates the book
to Clarisse M (2004-2023)